STUDIES IN THE JUDICIAL METHODOLOGY OF RABBI DAVID IBN ABI ZIMRA

Samuel Morell

Studies in Judaism

University Press of America,® Inc.
Dallas · Lanham · Boulder · New York · Oxford

4501 Forbes Boulevard
Suite 200
Lanham, Maryland 20706

12 Hid's Copse Rd.
Cumnor Hill, Oxford OX2 9JJ

Printed in the United States of America
British Library Cataloging in Publication Information Available

Library of Congress Control Number: 2003114216
ISBN 0-7618-2707-2 (paperback : alk. ppr.)

™ The paper used in this publication meets the minimum requirements of American National Standard for Information Sciences—Permanence of Paper for Printed Library Materials, ANSI Z39.48—1984

Studies in Judaism

To the memory of my late wife

Audrey

Who stood by my side in all my endeavors
For many years
Until her untimely passing.

יהי זכרה ברוך

Contents

Part One

Part Two

Rules of Transliteration

The General Transliteration Rules of the *Encyclopaedia Judaica* are followed, with the following exceptions.

א	’	Used occasionally as necessary, to separate consonants in the middle of a word.
ח	<u>h</u>	
ע	‘	
צ	ts	As with ש – *sh*, this is not doubled with dagesh.
ק	q	

Final ה is ignored in transliteration. Exceptions are Mishnah, Torah, final consonantal הּ, and cases where it represents a word in an acronym.

Prefixes (definite article, conjunction, prefixed prepositions, and relative pronoun –ש) are separated from the word by a hyphen. The resulting spirantization of בגדכפת is ignored under these circumstances, as is any resulting gemination of the following consonant. On rare occasion, where the spirantization has become established by usage as integral to the word, it is represented in the transliteration.

Preface

Halakha, the term used for the body of Jewish law deriving ultimately from the Talmud, is regularly presented by rabbinic jurists as a closed system. Rulings are justified by reference to the Talmud itself, and to the rulings of earlier jurists whose legal authority has been established by rabbinic consensus. The literature which presents the reasoned opinions of these rabbinic authorities is the Responsa Literature, in Hebrew *She'elot u-Teshuvot*, that is, "Questions and Answers." It derives this name from the nature of its origin, answers by rabbinic authorities to legal questions sent to them, most frequently by local courts. The author of a responsum presents his decision as deriving from an objective analysis of the law, and as the only legitimate interpretation of it. In this regard, rabbinic law is not different from most legal systems. Historians of the law are well aware, of course, that this conception of legal decision making is a fiction. Extra-legal considerations, conscious and unconscious, enter into the process. But in rabbinic responsa, at least, the fiction of objectivity is maintained. A reader seeking to uncover the extra-legal motivations at play in the decision must read between the lines, and his conclusions must necessarily remain tentative.

The responsa considered in this study, the work of a sixteenth-century rabbi known by the acronym Radbaz, are atypical in a number of respects. Among these is one that attracted my attention when, in connection with a previous project, I first had occasion to compare Radbaz's responsa on a specific topic to those of his contemporaries. Radbaz is unusually open about the extra-legal considerations that motivate his decisions. I decided to investigate the published corpus of Radbaz's responsa from this perspective. The present work is the result.

Part One is based on material which appeared in an earlier, Hebrew version, in *Atara L'Haim: Studies in the Talmud and Medieval Rabbinic Literature in Honor of Professor Haim Zalman Dimitrovsky* (Magnes Press: Jerusalem, 2000). Professor Dimitrovsky had an important role in sparking my interest in sixteenth-century responsa of Sephardic rabbis in the Ottoman Empire, and I would like to thank him again here.

I have had occasion from time to time to direct questions to a number of scholars, and have profited from their answers. I would like to acknowledge specifically the kind assistance of Dr. Abraham David, who has graciously answered my questions regarding the historical and biographical background of Radbaz. Professor Israel Ta-Shma, Professor Joseph Hacker, Professor Norman Stillman, Dr. Edward Fram, Dr. Jeffrey Woolf and Rabbi Dov Linzer have also shared their knowledge and insights with me. I thank them, and the many others with whom I have discussed aspects of this work over a period of many years.

My thanks extend also to the staff of the Jewish Theological Seminary's Rare Book department, and to that of the New York Public Library's Jewish Division, for their assistance in enabling me to consult first editions of Radbaz's responsa, and those of other works which had a bearing upon my research.

I owe a special debt of gratitude to Professor Jacob Neusner, who has kindly and enthusiastically consented to publish this volume, as he did an earlier volume of mine, in his series. He has in addition granted me permission to reproduce an extended quotation from that earlier study in this work. If I may borrow a frequent phrase used by questioners in turning to a rabbi for a responsum, "*yehi sekharo kaful min ha-shamayim*—May his reward be vouchsafed doubly from Heaven."

Most especially, I acknowledge the invaluable support of my dear wife, Marion, who recognized the importance of this work for me, and made a point of enabling and encouraging me to apply myself to its pursuit.

I dedicate this book to the memory of my late wife, Audrey. It was the desire to dedicate this study to her that spurred me on to its successful completion. *Yehi zikhrah barukh.*

Introduction

Rabbi David ben Solomon ibn Abi Zimra, known by the acronym Radbaz, was one of the most respected and influential rabbinic figures of the sixteenth century.[1] He was also the most long-lived. Radbaz was born in pre-Expulsion Spain, in 1479 or 1480.[2] He left Spain with the Expulsion in 1492, and resettled in Palestine, in Safed. At some point, perhaps soon after his arrival, he relocated to Jerusalem.[3] In 1513,

---

1 For general biographies of Radbaz see: Zimmels, *Rabbi David ibn abi Simra,* and his article in the *Encyclopaedia Judaica*, vol. 5, c. 1356; Ashtor, *Jews in Egypt and Syria*, vol. 2, 458-70; Goldman, *Life and Times*. The most current summary of his biography, incorporating the results of recent scholarship, is David, *To Come to the Land*, 142-144.

2 Radbaz left Spain with the Expulsion in 1492, and was in Safed when he was thirteen years old (Zimmels, 6; Goldman, 4; on the basis of Radbaz, *Responsa*, II, 596). This fixes 1479 as the earliest year of his birth. In one of his responsa, IV, 109 (= 1180), he refers to R. Ovadia of Bartenura, who died at the latest in 1510, and writes: "Not forty years have passed since he was summoned to the Academy on High." Thus, he was writing not later than 1550. Earlier in that responsum, he describes himself as having reached a hoary and elderly age (*gam seiva ve-gam ziqna zarqa bi*). On the basis of Mishnah Avot 5:21, *seiva*, hoary age, is defined as seventy. Thus, if he had reached the age of seventy by 1550 at the latest, then he was not born after 1480. The same Mishnah, though, defines *ziqna* as sixty, so Radbaz's intention to define his age precisely might be questioned. Nevertheless, this implication of *seiva* has been generally accepted.

3 Thus Zimmels and Goldman. Their evidence is that Radbaz is familiar with the fact that there was an overabundance of Torah scrolls in the synagogues

perhaps even a bit earlier, he moved to Egypt. He refers to an action he took in a rabbinic capacity "when I was in Alexandria,"[4] but the length of his stay there is uncertain. By 1514 we find him in Cairo as a member of the Court of the official head of Egyptian Jewry, the Nagid Isaac Shulal, in which capacity he is a signatory to a communal enactment in that year.[5] In 1517 Egypt was conquered by the Ottomans, and the centuries-old office of Nagid came to an abrupt end. Radbaz was accepted by the Egyptian Jewish community as its leading rabbinic/judicial authority, thereby inheriting many of the powers previously invested in the Nagid.[6] Cairene Jewry at the time encompassed a number of different Jewish communities, the indigenous community and various immigrant communities, each with its own traditions. Radbaz's pivotal role in communal leadership is expressed in a number of enactments that he put into effect, and in his arbitration of intercommunal disputes.

Radbaz was independently wealthy, and earned his living as a successful merchant.[7] As a matter of principle, he refused to take a

---

in Jerusalem, but professes ignorance about this detail with regard to Safed; III, 522 (= 957).

4 I, 335.

5 II, 644.

6 David, "Termination," 13: "The place of the Nagid, who had been appointed by the central government, is now filled by the chief judge (i.e., Radbaz—SM), and many of the powers of the Nagid were conferred upon him." Zimmels, 10, n. 47, believes that this position was an official one recognized by the Ottoman authorities, entailing affairs of state. He cites IV, 44 (= 1117). Radbaz tells a questioner that he is happy to occupy himself with Torah by answering his question: "Even though I am occupied with the yoke of the realm (*'ol malkhut*) and with earning a living, occupation with a *mitsva* is dear to me." David steers clear of such a conclusion.

7 Two published documents testify to his far-flung business dealings. (1) Assaf, *Sources and Studies*, 199-202. (2) David, "Business Dealings". The 17th-century chronicler David Conforte, in *Qoreh ha-Dorot*, cites a tradition that Radbaz discovered a hidden fortune (36b). Isaac Aqrish, who lived with him for ten years as a tutor to his grandchildren, writes that Radbaz took him in and showed him "his treasures, his pearls, his beryl gemstones, his sapphires, his books which are too numerous to be counted" (from Aqrish's introduction to his publication of three medieval commentaries to the Song of Songs, cited by Nepi-Gerondi, *Toldot Gedolei Yisra'el be-Italia*, Trieste 1853; rpt. Israel, 1968, p. 190). This has been taken as a reference to his great wealth (Ashtor, *Jews in Egypt and Syria*, 461), but it seems to me that these are metaphors for his books. Aqrish's

salary for his rabbinical position. This included even the minimal salary, which he believed that the law allowed for teaching Torah. In apologizing to a correspondent for not having answered his poetic letters in kind, he writes: "For I have upon me the yoke of such a large public (may God watch over them!), and the yoke of student-colleagues (*haverim*) under my tutelage, who are themselves like giants (in learning—SM), and the yoke of business (*derekh erets*), which is the hardest of all—for I have not allowed myself even that which the Torah allows. For I think that no one in this generation is worthy of that."[8] Radbaz's principled stand in this regard is typical of his attitude, and manifested itself in his opinion regarding the inclusion of scholars among the taxable public, as we shall see.

In 1553, forty years after his arrival in Egypt and in the eighth decade of his life, Radbaz left Cairo and settled in Jerusalem.[9] He was appointed there by the leaders of the Jewish community to serve as their judge, in which capacity he served without incident for several years. However, his functioning as judge was against the law, because judges had to be appointed by the *qadi*, the local judicial representative of the Ottoman authorities. Eventually, his attempts to apply sanctions to delinquents resulted in their informing on him. After being humiliated, fined extortionately and threatened with his life, he was removed from his judicial position. Nevertheless, some time later the *qadi* confirmed his appointment as judge.[10] Radbaz remained in Jerusalem until 1564, about which time he moved to Safed.[11] He died

---

words were in the context of an introduction to a publication that was based on manuscripts from Radbaz's library.

8 IV, 109 (= 1180).

9 Aqrish (see n. 7) writes that Radbaz spent forty years in Egypt. Elsewhere he writes that he himself left Egypt soon after Radbaz did, and traveled to Turkey. On the way he stopped in Crete, then under Venetian rule. His books were confiscated there under the terms of a decree proscribing talmudic writings, a decree that can be dated to 1553 (see Ashtor, 461). For a defense of this dating of Radbaz's departure from Egypt against a later dating, see David, "Economic Position," 86, n. 2.

10 See Cohen, *Jewish Life under Islam*, 44, and David, *To Come to the Land*, 75-77, and the references they cite.

11 For the dating of Radbaz's move from Jerusalem to Safed, see Dimitrovsky, "Controversy," 90, n. 71. Isaac Aqrish, in the passage referred to in n. 7, attributes Radbaz's move to his displeasure with the non-Jewish population of Jerusalem, and to the extortionate tax burden there.

during an epidemic in Safed at the age of ninety-three or ninety-four, in 1573.[12]

Radbaz was a prolific writer, producing works both on Rabbinic law and Talmud, and on Kabbalistic subjects.[13] His crowning literary legacy is a large corpus of responsa, answers to questions, which were referred to him by judges and scholars. Over 2600 of these have been published. The present work is based on a study of these responsa.[14]

This brief outline of Radbaz's lengthy career provides a background for an appreciation of his personality. Radbaz was the head of the rabbinical court in Cairo, and the recognized leader of Egyptian Jewry, for forty years. He was consulted, and his word was respected, by his rabbinic peers throughout the Sephardic diaspora. He was a man of principle, a man with independent means who asked no favors. It is not surprising, therefore, that he spoke with the voice of authority. That sense of authority may perhaps explain an unusual feature of Radbaz's responsa, namely, their remarkable brevity. Brevity was common in the early history of the Responsa literature, in the period from the eighth through the eleventh centuries. These were the responsa of the Babylonian Geonim, who saw themselves as the sole legitimate interpreters of talmudic law. Long before Radbaz's time, authors of responsa felt the need to justify their decisions in the eyes of their critical peers, and responsa evolved into detailed legal briefs. A high percentage of Radbaz's responsa, however, are very short, lacking the detailed argumentation conventional in the responsa of his contemporaries. He apparently had the confidence that a concise statement of his opinion, supported by reference to the primary sources for his ruling, was sufficient, under the aura of his personal authority, to carry the necessary weight. On occasion, a brief responsum of this type is followed by a lengthy and detailed rebuttal of an opposing opinion, a reminder of the type of argumentation of which Radbaz was quite capable, but with which he usually felt he could dispense.[15]

Radbaz's sense of personal authority, and his confidence in his own judgment, may explain another feature of his responsa, the high degree

12 The date and circumstances are confirmed by a document written a generation later, published by Bentov, "Notes of R. Joseph mi-Trani," 215.

13 For a list of Radbaz's known works see Goldman, *Life and Times*, 17-21. For an analysis of a central aspect of his Kabbalistic thinking, see Helener, "Reincarnation," 16-50.

14 I have excluded from this study the responsa of Part V, over 600 in number, which respond to exegetical questions about Maimonides' *Mishneh Torah*.

15 See, e.g., VI, 2219 and 2220.

of judicial independence that they manifest.[16] I noted above Radbaz's involvement in communal affairs, an involvement, which no doubt brought him into contact with ordinary people living in a real world. Perhaps Radbaz's career as a businessman was also a factor in this regard. In any case, one can detect in Radbaz's responsa a sensitivity to real-life situations that affected ordinary people. This awareness sometimes clashed with a simplistic reading of the law. Radbaz exhibited a surprising independence from such simplistic readings. Another aspect of Radbaz's self-assuredness, and the independence which it bred, is linked to his sense of principle, in this case, the principle of honesty in the interpretation of sources and in the determination of who, among conflicting authorities, is in fact correct. Similarly, in a significant number of cases he utilizes his own sense of what the law should be in the given case, rather than arrive at a decision through an analysis of legal sources. Radbaz saw his role as the rendering of a decision that was just, even though it may be at the expense of the conventional understanding of the codified law.

Part One of the present work investigates these features of Radbaz's methodology. It deals with aspects of his decision-making that introduce elements outside the codified law, areas which exemplify personal insight and sensitivity in his approach to people, and independent rationality in his approach to the determination of the law.

A perusal of Radbaz's responsa reveals three phrases, which are frequent in his usage, but rare or unattested in the responsa of his forbears and contemporaries. Two of these phrases are presented as rules, the third as only a directional guideline, for arriving at a judicial decision in the face of controversy. Rules for deciding among differing opinions are in evidence from an early period of rabbinic literature, and were certainly current in Radbaz's time. But rules of this type can be manipulated, most obviously by the tacit decision either to utilize them or to ignore them. They can also be neutralized by the introduction of other considerations. In actual practice, what appears at first as a rule for decision-making may turn out to be merely a rhetorical device. Of course, that is not always the case, and a jurist may consider himself bound by a rule. Judicial discretion can be traced through the way a rabbinic authority handles such a rule.

The unique frequency of these three phrases defines them as integral to Radbaz's judicial personality, and calls for an analysis of their role in

16 Ashtor, *Jews in Egypt and Syria*, 462, expressed the opposite assessment. The body of this study bears testimony to Radbaz's daring and originality.

his responsa. Part Two of the present study is dedicated to this task. To these three, I appended two other rules as subjects for analysis. These are much rarer in Radbaz's usage, but they had already infiltrated legal discourse by his time, and he was forced to deal with them. The way he does so has much to teach us about his independence in decision-making.

To aid the reader in finding his or her way among the many rabbinic authorities who are cited in the course of this work, I have appended a brief account of their essential biographies.

Radbaz's responsa were published long after his death. The earliest volume, which later appeared as Part IV, was published in Livorno in 1652, and other volumes were published in the eighteenth and early nineteenth centuries. The standard edition is the Warsaw 1882 edition, and it is that from which current editions were photocopied. In general, that is the edition that I used for this work, though anything that involved textual matters was checked with the first editions.

The Warsaw edition contains seven "Parts." In the present work, references to Radbaz's responsa are indicated by a Roman numeral, representing the Part, followed by an Arabic numeral, representing the responsum. Parts III, IV and V[17] bear a double numeration of the responsa, one representing the numeration of the individual volume when it first appeared, and the other a cumulative numeration.[18] Both are supplied in the references below, the cumulative number in parentheses.[19] Part VII of the Warsaw edition is not integrated into the cumulative numeration. In recent years another volume of Radbaz's responsa was published from manuscript (Bnei Brak, 1975), and will be referred to here as VIII. In addition, a few responsa of Radbaz have been published individually in scholarly literature, and some have been preserved in the responsa of Radbaz's contemporaries.[20] This study did

---

17 Part V, though, was not utilized in this work; see n. 14.

18 Part V ends with no. 1700 in the cumulative numeration. Part VI begins with 2051, maintaining the numeration in the first edition of that volume, Livorno, 1818. The numeration may have been taken from the manuscript that was used. See J. Lifschitz, "The Responsa of Radbaz," 33, n. 35. I thank Professor Joseph Hacker for referring me to this article.

19 Both are in common use, and different authors may use the one or the other in citing Radbaz's responsa. The numeration used in the Bar Ilan Responsa Project is the original numeration.

20 Both categories are identified, and the latter reproduced, in Lifschitz, "The Responsa of Radbaz."

not encompass those responsa of Radbaz that remain extant only in manuscript.

For the purpose of reference, I have numbered the responsa that come under analysis consecutively throughout the work. The numbers appear in brackets, and I refer to them as "Cases." In a number of instances, two or more responsa are part of the same discussion, and these are grouped as one "case." If the same responsum is used in another context elsewhere in the book, I have provided it with another case number. The List of Cases at the end of the book allows ready reference to the page on which each case appears. The Index of Responsa correlates the responsa with the numbered cases.

Translations are generally mine, except for biblical passages, which are from NJPS, unless otherwise indicated. I have adopted the convention of using the present tense when referring to Radbaz's literary activity. Parentheses in the translations are clarifications that I have added, which I felt were implied by the Hebrew. Clarifications beyond that minimum, which I felt were necessary, are enclosed in parentheses with the addition of my initials. In referring to Maimonides' *Mishneh Torah,* I have cited the name of the Book and the Treatise according to the Yale Judaica Series translation of that work, though the translation is mine.[21]

Throughout the book, the title, "Rabbi," is represented by the abbreviation, "R."

---

21 However, with the following exceptions. I have changed "Laws Concerning ..." to "Laws of ..."; I have changed "Laws Concerning Sehittah" to "Laws of Slaughter."

Part One

Beyond the Codified Law

1. The "Real World" and the Codified Law

Questions, which are referred to rabbinic authorities by local courts or communal rabbis, the answers to which are found in the voluminous responsa literature, are generally the kinds of questions, which are called "hard cases." Not infrequently, what makes these cases "hard" is that they reflect the tension between the abstract codified law, and the concrete, unique case, which stands before the judge, the product of multiple contingencies. Radbaz saw as his task the rendering of justice, that is, decisions which were just. This quest sometimes took him beyond what might appear to lesser lights to be "the letter of the law." Radbaz was not unique in this regard, of course. All great rabbinic authorities sought to arrive at decisions, which they felt to be just. If a cursory reading of the codified law led in another direction, they would strive to show that, on the contrary, a proper reading of the codified law would yield an interpretation leading to the decision they sought. Their decision would be presented as implicit in the codified law. Radbaz does the same. However, on many occasions he does not flinch from identifying the unique characteristics of the case before him, and, bypassing the letter of the law, bringing them directly to bear on his decision.

Radbaz's direct incorporation of unique characteristics into an analysis of a point of law varies from responsum to responsum in the weight, which it is given in the context of the final decision and in the degree of its originality. It may be original with Radbaz, or it may be a recognized approach, which Radbaz goes out of his way to stress. Most frequently, Radbaz first develops his case quite adequately in the traditional manner. He arrives at a decision through an analysis of the codified law, and then, redundantly, adds an argument derived from the actualities of the case. But there are times when this kind of consideration, independent of the codified law, is the main basis of the final decision. In fact, occasionally it leads to a decision, which is the opposite of what would have been expected by a straightforward application of the codified law. In all these instances, whether the utilization of specific characteristics in a given situation is original with Radbaz or part of a judicial tradition, whether it is redundant to the decision or vital to it, it is clear that Radbaz has an affinity to arguments which go beyond the codified law and derive directly from the realities of the case before him. In this chapter I will survey several aspects of this feature of Radbaz's judicial methodology.

(*a*) *Challenging Talmudic Presumptions*

[1] I'll begin with a responsum that can serve to introduce two aspects of the subject. Radbaz addresses a question, which derived from Jerusalem. He begins as follows:

> You asked my opinion regarding a controversy, which broke out in Jerusalem between the householders and the rabbis over the issue of paying the guards of the quarter.[1]

The Talmud rules unequivocally that rabbis are exempt from taxation for the purpose of municipal security: "Rabbi Judah said: Everyone (must contribute toward) the gate of the city wall, even orphans. But rabbis do not need guarding."[2] Maimonides, in his restatement, provides the rationale: "Everything which is needed for the guarding of the city is taken from all the men of the city, even from orphans, save only from the rabbis (*talmidei ha-hakhamim*, literally: the students of the sages). For rabbis do not need guarding; their Torah guards them."[3] The Ashkenazic rabbinic authorities severely restricted the compass of the rabbinical exemption from taxes, either to the point of its total elimination, or, at least, to the exemption only of recognized

---

1 II, 752.

2 BT Bava Batra 8a, parallel in BT Bava Metsi'a 108a.

3 *MT*, Acquisitions, Laws of Neighbors, chap. 6, parag. 6.

heads of rabbinic academies.[4] The Sephardic rabbinic authorities, on the other hand, ruled that it be applied broadly to rabbis.[5] These Jerusalem rabbis were products of the Sephardic school. They had a strongly entrenched legal tradition upon which to rely.[6]

One can learn something of the social history of Jerusalem from this responsum. Radbaz writes:

> In the case at hand, the householders are saying, "We don't need guards, because we are poor." And the rabbis are crying out, "Appoint guards!"

The implications are made explicit in the course of Radbaz's response:

> According to what I see in Jerusalem,[7] the thieves were made greedy because of the rabbis, whose clothes were unlike those of the householders, and appeared to be more elegant than theirs were.

It seems, therefore, that the householders were poor, and had little to lose from thieves. On the other hand, the rabbis, according to Radbaz's description, were better off. But these same rabbis, who were insisting on security for the Jewish quarter, were not willing to pay taxes to fund it. In insisting on an exemption, they were relying on an explicit ruling in the Talmud, and on a firmly established legal tradition.

Radbaz ruled against the rabbis of Jerusalem. He based his ruling on two arguments, both of which are of interest to this book's inquiry. One of them is that it is unfair to compel the objecting householders to subsidize the quarter's security, upon the insistence of the rabbis, who would be its primary beneficiaries. This is an argument based on equity, and I shall return to it in another chapter. The second argument is more formal. It responds directly to the claim put forward by the

---

4 The material is summarized by I. Ta-Shma, "Exemption from Taxes," 233–37. Ta-Shma refers to taxes in general, and when he discusses Ashkenazic practice he does not distinguish between taxes imposed by the host country and those imposed internally by the Jewish community.

5 Ta-Shma shows that the Sephardic rabbinate was not successful in this regard in its struggle with the lay communal leadership. He does not, however, refer specifically to taxes for the purpose of guarding the city. Be that as it may, Radbaz's responsum falls in the category of rabbinic ruling on this issue.

6 See Y. Hacker, "*Djizya*," 74, who writes with regard to this specific exemption, "On this matter no one ever took issue, neither the earlier authorities nor the later ones."

7 Radbaz lived in Jerusalem from 1553 until ca. 1564. This responsum is part of a broader attempt of Radbaz to effect a more equitable distribution of taxes in Jerusalem. See David, *To Come to the Land*, 142–143.

rabbis on the basis of its own premise. Radbaz asserts that the unique characteristics of this case exclude it from the parameters of the talmudic ruling. The latter was based on the premise that "rabbis do not need guarding." But these rabbis, by their insistence on security, have admitted that they themselves, at least, are in fact in need of guarding.

Radbaz asserts, therefore, that the codified law is not automatically applicable in all ages and under all conditions. He proceeds to express this in a more radical and explicit manner. He reveals that in his personal opinion, the entire ruling that exempts rabbis from taxation did not properly apply in his day and age. For, unlike the great Sages of the Talmud, he doubts that there is any rabbi in these lesser generations of whom it could truly be said that he does not need guarding, that his Torah guards him. This stand appears to be unique with Radbaz.[8] He is not anxious to go on record with it: "I am not entering into an investigation of this matter now, because what I have to say will discomfort some rabbis. Silence, therefore, is better than speech." He can afford to forgo pursuing this line of thought, because he has decided the case before him on narrower grounds, and the broader issue has not been brought before him for adjudication. But the implication is clear. The reality today, which is apparent to all, is different from the reality, which the Sages of the Talmud took for granted. That latter reality served as the basis for the ruling which the Talmud, and its subsequent codifiers, formulated in so inclusive a manner: Rabbis are exempt from taxes for the purpose of funding the guarding of the city. In the wake of a change in that reality comes a change in the law.

There are numerous rulings in the Talmud which are based on the presumption of a certain reality. This may take the form of a natural, an economic, a social, a cultural or a psychological reality. Few are the instances in which the later rabbinic authorities questioned the validity of those realities in their own day. The main exceptions are instances in which there was an urgent need for a lenient ruling, and, in the Ashkenazic rabbinic tradition, the desire to adapt the codified law to traditional practice. Otherwise, such a questioning is rare. Radbaz's willingness to adopt such an approach is worthy of note. This approach is especially striking in the responsum I have been discussing, because the conclusion is totally dependent on it, and because of the lack of support for it in precedent rabbinic rulings. Most of the time when this

8 See Y. Hacker's words cited above, n. 6. He states there in a footnote, in reference to this statement of Radbaz: "I have seen only one exception in this matter."

approach is utilized by Radbaz these characteristics are not in evidence in such a dramatic fashion. But there are other responsa of Radbaz in which he takes cognizance of a reality in his day which is different from the one assumed by the Talmud, and takes account of that difference in arriving at a decision.

[2] The following is an example:

> You asked regarding a woman who charges that her husband compels her to have sexual intercourse with him while she is still in a state of menstrual impurity—is she believed regarding him, so that she goes out and collects her *ketubba*, or not?[9]

A menstruant is in a state of ritual impurity, and remains in that state until she undergoes a purification process. Sexual intercourse with a woman who is in a state of menstrual impurity is a serious violation of the law of the Torah for both partners. The husband's behavior, if the charge is accepted, is grounds for divorce on behalf of the wife. The husband is compelled to divorce her, and also to pay her the marriage settlement that becomes due at the termination of the marriage (the *ketubba*). The question here is whether the wife's charges are accepted.

Radbaz begins by citing a ruling from the Talmud on another issue regarding the trustworthiness of women who assert facts concerning their husbands:

> Rabbi Hamnuna said: If a woman said to her husband, "You divorced me," she is believed. There is a presumption that a wife would not be brazen to her husband's face.[10]

As Radbaz points out, this presumption applies to situations in which the husband knows the truth. Under those conditions, she would not look him in the face and lie. This ruling, as Radbaz tells us, was accepted as codified law: "All the authorities who are current among us (i.e., who represent the Sephardic legal tradition—SM) ruled that it is law." Our situation is similar. The husband knows the truth, and she is testifying to his face to religious violations on his part which constitute grounds for divorce. Accordingly, it would seem that the wife's charges are to be accepted by the court.

Radbaz then proceeds to gnaw away at this conclusion by circumscribing the range of situations to which Rabbi Hamnuna's ruling would apply. First he cites Ritba, who excluded from this

9 III, 407 (= 850).

10 BT Yevamot 116a and parallels. The parallel that appears to be the original source of the statement is BT Nedarim 91a, but Radbaz is not quoting directly from there.

presumption cases in which, unlike the case in the original Talmudic source, the wife's testimony besmirches the husband and casts him in the role of a transgressor. He then questions whether the talmudic presumption can be extended automatically to other situations. But finally he casts a wider net, employing a frontal attack on the entire applicability of Rabbi Hamnuna's ruling in the present era:

> Further I say, that in this time, in which the generation is such that the breach (in the moral fence) is greater than that which remains standing, and brazenness is extensive throughout all the members of the generation, even in a case like the original ruling of Rabbi Hamnuna we do not believe her to the point of allowing her to remarry.[11]

Radbaz refers to an opinion of a contemporary of Ritba's, the brother of R. Aaron ha-Levi, the latter's teacher, who had recommended a legal separation in a case like this. That, he felt, would be preferable to compelling the husband to divorce her. Radbaz quotes Ritba's reaction to this suggestion:

> This ruling is certainly correct, and it would be proper to rule this way in view of the serious status of a married woman. (I.e., since there is a possibility that compelling a divorce is improper, and an improperly compelled divorce is invalid, the resulting remarriage might entail adultery—SM). But I see that it is the consensus of the authorities to be lenient (with the woman, and to compel a divorce—SM).

However, Radbaz himself has no such reservation:

> He wrote thus in his generation. But in this evil generation, he (the brother of R. Aaron ha-Levi) is worth relying upon. Even the other authorities would agree (were they living) in this generation. For if you don't say this, there would not be a daughter of Abraham our Father who would remain under her husband's domain.... She would certainly be brazen in order to escape from her husband.

In other words, Radbaz would rule in practice against the ruling of the Talmud as formulated by Rabbi Hamnuna, a ruling that is part of the codified law, and which, according to the consensus of rabbinic authorities, should be applied in practice. He does so on the grounds that the social reality has changed. In this case, unlike the preceding one, Radbaz is not unique in his position. He has a precedent that he does not cite, but of which he was surely aware. It is a responsum of R. Meir of Rothenburg (Germany, 13th century), regarding a wife's

---

11 He admits toward the end of the responsum that if she did in fact remarry, the court would not separate her from her husband after the fact.

charge that her husband is incapable of an erection. R. Meir, after restating the law of the Talmud, adds: "But these days, when there are immoral women (*perutsot*), it is not proper to believe them."[12] Radbaz's Sephardic contemporary, R. Moses Alashqar, takes the same stand, as does Radbaz.[13] But another contemporary, R. Levi ben Habib, testifies, as did Radbaz himself, to the breadth of the consensus to the contrary:

> It doesn't seem right, in my humble view, to rule as a general matter that there is a distinction between the earlier generations and the later generations, as did Maharam (R. Meir of Rothenburg) in his responsa... because there is a large crowd of later rabbis who do not distinguish between them at all.[14]

Radbaz may not be unique in his position, but he is aware that he is going against the consensus.[15]

[3] Radbaz's skepticism regarding the Talmud's presumption of trust is paralleled in his response to a question of ritual law. The issue concerns the requirement of searching one's house for possible remains of leavened grain on the evening before Passover, a laborious process.

> You asked me whether maidservants are trustworthy in our time regarding the search (for leaven).[16]

According to the law of the Talmud, male and female non-Jewish slaves undergo a process of conversion, which would make them subject to a restricted range of religious obligations while they are slaves,[17] and fully Jewish upon manumission.[18] If a slave resisted conversion for a period of twelve months, he must be sold to a non-Jew.[19] But, contrary to this law, it had ceased to be common practice

---

12 *Teshuvot Maimoniot* to Book of Women, no. 7; R. Meir bar Barukh, *Responsa Prague*, no. 947; *Mordekhai* to Qiddushin, no. 542; ed. Roth, no. 86, p. 316, and other parallels cited there.

13 Alashqar, *Responsa*, no. 89. Alashqar cites a responsum of Rabbenu Asher, which he found quoted, he says, in a responsum of R. Elijah Mizrahi. According to this, Rabbenu Asher also took the position, that in light of the present moral degeneration, Rabbi Hamnuna's presupposition is not applicable. However, this contradicts Rabbenu Asher in his published responsa, *Kelal* 43, nos. 5 and 12.

14 R. Levi b. Habib, *Responsa*, no. 33, p. 19c.

15 It is not possible that Radbaz was unaware of R. Meir's responsum.

16 IV, 289 (= 1360).

17 *Tur Yoreh De'ah*, no. 267.

18 BT Yevamot 47b.

19 BT Yevamot 48b.

since early Islamic times to in fact convert slaves, a process, which included circumcision for males. There is a loophole in the Talmud, according to which a stipulation prior to the acquisition of the slave would obviate the need for conversion,[20] and this was utilized to extend the practice of non-conversion generally. Nevertheless, the practice of converting slaves did not disappear entirely.[21] The present responsum attests to it, since it is clear that the maidservants in question had undergone conversion. A few other responsa of Radbaz attest to this as well.[22]

The Talmud, in a passage codified by Maimonides, explicitly includes slaves among those who are reliable regarding the search for leaven.[23] Radbaz begins by affirming that such is indeed the law of the Talmud, accepted by all the codifyers. Furthermore, he adds that nowhere do we find a distinction between male and female slaves. Nevertheless, he is unwilling to apply this ruling in practice. First, because the work involved in conducting a proper search is laborious, and maidservants as a rule are lazy, and have not internalized the severity of this religious obligation. To this he adds:

> And further, I see that all the maidservants in this era do not take upon themselves the observance of commandments (as part of the conversion process—SM) at all of their own will.[24] Even if they answer "yes," they do so only from the lips outward. That is because they are Christians,[25] and do not wish to be sold to Muslims. Know that it is so, for when they feel oppressed they convert to Islam, as happens every day.

Radbaz is conscious of the fact that this is against the codified law, and feels the need to justify himself:

---

20 Ibid.

21 For this and much ancillary material see S. Assaf, "Slavery."

22 Case [14] below is an interesting example. See also the responsum cited in n. 24. On the general subject of Jews as slaveholders in Egypt during this period, see Landau (ed.), *Jews in Ottoman Egypt*, 70–72, 395–97.

23 BT Pesaẖim 4a. *MT*, Seasons, Laws of Leavened and Unleavened Bread, chap. 2, parag. 17.

24 *ainan meqabbelot mitsvot kelal mi-da'atan.* As an example of the attitude referred to by Radbaz, see the wording of the question in IV, 49 (=1122): "If this slavewoman immersed, and at the time of her immersion said that she didn't want to leave her people and her God, is such an immersion effective?"

25 *mi-kat ha-'akum.* Jews living in Islamic countries were not permitted to own Muslim slaves. The acronym *'akum* referred in its original sense to idolators, but there is little doubt that here it refers to Christians.

> Do not wonder at me that I rule against what appears to be the case according to the Talmud. For this is not a ruling of law, but a stringency that I adopt, in accordance with what I see in my time. May blessings come to he who is stringent.

Yet in spite of Radbaz's demurral, he was asked a question and he gave an answer, in accordance with the reality of the situation, which he saw before him.

[4] If this is the case with the rulings of the Talmud, it is certainly so with the rulings of post-talmudic rabbinic authorities.

Radbaz was asked about an exchange of "Reuben's" gold dinar for "Simeon's" copper coins.[26] After the two currencies changed hands, some of the copper coins were found to be worthless, and Simeon was asked to replace them. But in the course of the negotiations between them, copper coins became devalued relative to gold. Simeon, who had given the copper coins, wanted to reckon the replacement on the basis of the number of coins. Reuben, who had received the copper coins, wanted it reckoned on the basis of current value. The question revolves around the finality of the transaction. If it was final at the time of the original exchange, then Reuben must suffer the loss of what is already in his possession.

According to the law of the Talmud, moveable property is acquired not by payment of currency, but by physical acquisition. When the commodity changes hands the transaction is complete, even if the currency is still owed in payment. In a case like the present one, which involves an exchange of two currencies, one is identified as the currency and the other as the commodity. The transfer of the one identified as the commodity completes the transaction. In an exchange of silver and gold, the Talmud identifies gold as the commodity and silver as the currency; in an exchange of silver and copper, copper is the commodity and silver, again, the currency.[27] But the Talmud says nothing about the exchange of gold and copper. Radbaz, however, tells us that "we hold that gold is the commodity in relation to copper, and so have agreed Rashba and the later authorities, even though this is not explicit in the words of Maimonides." In other words, the change in the value of the copper coins occurred after they were already in Reuben's possession, and Simeon must replace the number of worthless copper coins, not their original value.

---

26 IV, 171 (= 1242). The roles of "Reuben" and "Simeon" are inadvertently interchanged in the course of the responsum.

27 Mishnah Bava Metsi'a 4:1, BT Bava Metsi'a 44a.

But after dispensing with possible arguments to the contrary, Radbaz challenges the basic premise of this decision. In his opinion, he tells us, Rashba and the other authorities ruled as they did,

> only in their places of residence, because gold was not so common, and copper coins were in more common use—and it is common use which is determinative (in defining currency), as the Talmud states.[28] But in Egypt, gold is in more common use. Most commerce in this country is transacted with gold, and not with copper coins. Only small items are sold with copper coins. That is because there is a danger of significant loss. If they are invalidated, as is done from time to time, one could lose more than half of one's principal. For this reason copper coins are not common at all in Egypt, and gold is in more common use. Therefore I say that gold is considered currency in relation to copper.... And do not be surprised that the law changes in accordance with the change from place to place.

Radbaz is not original in making this point.[29] But it is in harmony with his penchant for departing from the codified law when he feels that the presumptions, which underlie it, do not reflect the realities which confront him.

(*b*) *Laws Based on Reasons That Don't Apply*

If a law was enacted for a specific reason, and the reason is not presently applicable, we find instances in which Radbaz rejects the applicability of the law to the case at hand.

[5] Divorce is effected by the transfer of a bill of divorce from the husband or his agent to the wife or her agent. Tractate Gittin, which deals with the laws of divorce, begins:

> One who brings a bill of divorce from abroad must declare, "It was written before me and signed before me."[30]

This declaration affirms the authenticity of the document, obviating the need for validating the signatures of the witnesses who signed it, in

---

28 See BT Bava Metsi'a 44a–b.

29 See Tosafot to Bava Metsi'a 45a, s.v. *ve-shani halva'a*, where a contradiction between the Talmud and Hai Gaon with regard to the status of gold as currency for the purpose of redeeming "second tithe" is resolved in the same spirit. I thank Professor David Weiss Halivni for this reference.

30 Mishnah Gittin, 1:1.

the event that its authenticity is later challenged by the husband. The validation of signatures for a document signed abroad is difficult to obtain (in the language of the Talmud: "witnesses are not available to authenticate it"), so a provision which would dispense with that necessity is important.[31] The passage of Mishnah just cited goes on to add that this declaration is applicable also between one province and another outside the Land of Israel. Normally, the declaration would not apply to a divorce delivered by an agent within the same province. There are always enough people around in a stable population who could recognize and authenticate others' signatures. However, in a town with a migrant population, or even a population of travelling merchants, that might not be the case. The talmudic sage Rava, whose opinion is authoritative, and who lived in the major commercial city of Mehoza, ruled that the declaration is required even from one neighborhood to another. Rabbenu Tam (France, 12th century) ruled that this applies to all the places of Jewish settlement in his day.

Radbaz was asked the following question.

> You asked my opinion regarding Reuben, who divorced his wife, and appointed the scribe (who wrote the bill of divorce—SM) an agent to bring the bill of divorce to his wife. The witnesses who were signed on the document went with him to her house. Must the agent declare, "It was written before me and signed before me," in spite of the fact that he was the one who wrote it, and he is divorcing her (as the husband's agent—SM) before the very witnesses themselves? Or, perhaps, one might say that it is an enactment of the Sages, which must not be changed at all?[32]

The Talmud rules regarding a situation in which two agents, rather than one, are appointed by the husband to bring a bill of divorce to the wife:

> Two who bring a bill of divorce from abroad do not have to declare, "It was written before me and signed before me."[33]

It is hard to see a significant difference between this and the situation being adjudicated by Radbaz. In Radbaz's case the husband did not

---

31 This reason for the regulation and an alternative one are the subject of an extended discussion at the beginning of BT Gittin. The one I cited is accepted by the Talmud's codifyers. See *MT*, Women, Laws of Divorce, chap. 3, parag. 8.

32 I, 406.

33 BT Gittin 16a–17a. Codified by Maimonides, *MT*, Women, Laws of Divorce, chap. 7, parag. 14.

appoint the two as agents,[34] but on the other hand, these are the very two who signed the document, and can authenticate their own signatures. Nevertheless, Radbaz takes the question seriously, and he includes in his answer wording which is directly relevant to our concern:

> One should not say, that since they enacted that the agent must declare, "It was written before me and signed before me," we must not annul their enactment even when it is unnecessary. For the enactment was not unspecified (as to its rationale—SM), but was put into effect because witnesses were not available to authenticate it. Since this is its raison d'être, where there is no reason to fear, it (i.e., the declaration) is not necessary.

Radbaz proceeds to quote Naḫmanides to the same effect, except that Naḫmanides used this principle in the direction of stringency. Now that there are no established courts in the Land of Israel, Naḫmanides argued, the declaration is required in the Land of Israel too:

> For in every place, everything is according to the situation.

That is an apt summary of Radbaz's own point of view, which goes beyond the specific question he was asked. The ruling in the case at hand is pretty straightforward. Radbaz uses the questioner's alternative suggestion as a foil. He makes a point of stressing that it is *not* true that "it is an enactment of the Sages which must not be changed at all." On the contrary, "everything is according to the situation." The enactment was put into effect for a reason. If the reason does not apply, the enactment does not apply either.

[6] In the previous case Radbaz followed the lead of the Talmud itself, which dispensed with the declaration, "It was written before me and signed before me," when the husband had appointed two agents. The responsum was nevertheless useful in determining Radbaz's mindset, because of the special emphasis, which he gave to the nexus between the enactment and its rationale.

That nexus is evident in the following responsum too.[35] In this instance, Radbaz's decision is not as patently evident from the Talmud as it appeared in the previous case, but he does build a well-reasoned argument from the talmudic sources. After he does so, though, he goes

---

34 Maimonides makes the importance of this issue explicit, as does Tosafot, Gittin 16b, s.v. *alma*.

35 I, 39.

out of his way to support his decision by appealing to the realities of the case.

The question is whether one of priestly descent who is blind in both eyes may participate in the ritual of blessing the congregation with the threefold priestly benediction. The text of that benediction is found in the Book of Numbers.[36] It is introduced there with God telling Moses to speak to Aaron and his sons, and say to them: "Thus shall you bless the people of Israel. Say to them:..." The text of the blessing follows, and the passage concludes: "And they shall place my Name on the people of Israel, and I shall bless them." This is understood in the Talmud as a threefold affirmative commandment; a priest who does not bless the people this way is triply delinquent in the duty imposed upon him by the Torah.[37] This priestly ritual is called, "the raising of hands."

On the other hand, the Talmud prohibits a priest with an obvious physical blemish from "raising his hands," because it would distract the congregation from the blessing.[38] However, explains the Talmud, if he is an accustomed sight in his town, the prohibition does not apply. In this context the Talmud states:

> One who is blind in one of his eyes should not raise his hands. But if he is an accustomed sight in his town, it is permitted.[39]

In accordance with this Maimonides writes:

> One whose saliva drops onto his beard when he speaks, and likewise one who is blind in one of his eyes, should not raise his hands. But if he is an accustomed sight in his town, and everyone is used to this, then he who is blind in one of his eyes, or whose saliva flows, is permitted to do so, because people don't stare at him.[40]

Radbaz points out that it is possible to deduce from Maimonides' wording: "If he is an accustomed sight in his town... then he who is blind in one of his eyes... is permitted to do so," that only if he is blind in *one* of his eyes is he permitted to "raise his hands" if he is an accustomed sight; however, if he is blind in both eyes, then even if he is an accustomed sight he is not permitted to participate in this public

---

36 Numbers 6:22–27.

37 BT Sota 38b. Triply: "Thus shall you bless," "Say to them," "And they shall place my name on the people of Israel."

38 BT Megilla 25a. Mishnah: "Because the congregation would stare at it." The interpretation that this is because of distraction is in PT Megilla 75c, 4:8.

39 BT Megilla 25a.

40 *MT*, Love, Laws of Prayer and the Raising of Hands, chap. 15, parag. 2.

ritual. The argument draws strength from the fact that if indeed this exception applied to one who was blind in both eyes, Maimonides would have worded his statement to indicate that even the more extreme disability would be permitted if people were accustomed to him. As a matter of fact, Radbaz tells us, that very inference was drawn by Rabbenu Yeru<u>h</u>am in his code.[41]

Radbaz produces a variety of arguments against this position: Rabbenu Yeru<u>h</u>am represents a lone opinion;[42] the inference from Maimonides' wording is not conclusive; the priests have developed the custom of covering their faces during the blessing, so that physical blemishes are not really distracting nowadays anyway; if it is indeed a matter of distraction, it should make no difference whether he is blind in one eye or both. And then, having proven his case, he adds by way of overkill:

> And there is another reason. This disease is very common in this land, and it is not a cause for amazement. Even if they did not cover their faces it would be proper to permit it, because people stare only at something which is a matter of amazement.

And he concludes:

> Therefore there is no basis for apprehension, and the priest should not desist from three affirmative precepts.[43]

Thus Radbaz makes a special point of incorporating into his case an argument drawn from the specific reality in which it is imbedded.[44]

[7] The same technique is evident in another responsum. Radbaz builds a case on the basis of the codified law, and then argues that the codified law does not apply in that instance because of its special circumstances. What makes this example particularly interesting is that

---

41 *Sefer Toledot Adam ve-<u>H</u>ava, <u>H</u>eleq Adam, Netiv* 2, Sec. 6: "A blind man should not raise his hands. A man blind in one of his eyes may raise his hands, but only if he is an accustomed sight in his town...."

42 His ruling is a corollary of his opinion that the blind are generally not obligated by ritual commandments, but this is a lone opinion.

43 See n. 37.

44 However, Radbaz contradicts himself on this issue in VI, 2117. There he rules that if the priests don't cover their faces, then, on the basis of the deduction from Maimonides' wording, only a priest who is blind in one eye may "raise his hands" if people are accustomed to him. It is thus possible that Radbaz's statement in our responsum is merely rhetorical, for in fact, the priests did cover their faces. For the use of questionable legal positions as rhetorical arguments, see Soloveitchik, "Law and Rhetoric."

Radbaz's ultimate ruling in the responsum is based on other considerations entirely, and turns out to be the opposite of where the earlier discussion was leading him. It cannot even be said in this instance that Radbaz's argument from reality comes to strengthen his ultimate conclusion. He just felt the need to go on record with what he believed to be the truth.

The question has to do with an apostate who was refusing to give a divorce to his wife.[45] That left his wife in the unfortunate position of not being able to remarry. He eventually agreed to divorce her when he was promised a payment. So "some of the learned people (*maskilin*) came together with the leader of the community, who was also the scribe," and asked him if they should write a bill of divorce for his wife. The apostate refused until the money was in hand, and then agreed.

There are many details connected with the writing and delivery of a bill of divorce. Since a bill of divorce is an instrument of the husband, it is important that the husband understand precisely what is required of him. Furthermore, the directions he gives regarding who shall actually write the document, who shall be the witnesses, and who shall be his agent for its delivery must be clear and unambiguous. The husband is instructed in the legal manner of indicating his consent and conveying his directions by the authorities who are supervising the process. But since all these instructions are routine, and manifest themselves as technicalities, it is not uncommon to run through the list *pro forma*.

This instance was a particularly egregious instance of *pro forma*, because the instructions were recited in Hebrew, whereas the husband, as was discovered after the fact, did not know Hebrew, and when he gave his assent he did not really understand what it was he was assenting to. It is true that the basic request for permission to write a bill of divorce on his behalf was in his native Judeo-Spanish. But the instruction to appoint a specific person to be the scribe who would write it, and to appoint two specific people to be the witnesses who would sign it, was all in Hebrew. To make the matter worse, one of the two witnesses who signed the bill of divorce asserted that even the initial request to write the bill of divorce was in Hebrew. He was thus contradicting the others, who had testified that it was conveyed in Judeo-Spanish.

When it became known, after the bill of divorce was written, that the husband was not in a position to understand what he had ostensibly

45 III, 459 (= 900).

agreed to, the learned men were in a quandary. A dispute began as to how to proceed, and they decided to tear up the bill of divorce. After having done so, they belatedly decided to write to Radbaz and ask whether what they had done was right.

There was one particular issue, which the questioners saw as the core of the problem. It concerns the procedure to be followed when a husband commissions a group of people to write a bill of divorce and deliver it to his wife. Maimonides writes:

> If he said to ten people, "Write a bill of divorce, sign it, and deliver it to my wife," one of them writes it, two of them sign it, and one of them delivers it to her....
>
> The Sages enacted that one who tells a number of people to write a bill of divorce, or to sign one, or to deliver one to his wife—if with regard to writing, he should say to them: "Any one of you should write a bill of divorce for my wife"; and so with regard to bringing it, he should say: "Any one of you should bring it"; and if with regard to signing it, he should say: "Any two of you should sign the bill of divorce and give it to my wife."[46]

The Talmud mandates this formulation lest a husband, intending to empower the members of a group to write and deliver a bill of divorce, say to them: "All of you...," in which case they would all have to write it or sign it or deliver it together. If one of the group were to die, the bill of divorce would be invalid.[47] But in the case before Radbaz, the husband did not use the required terminology when he spoke to the group. And, since he could not have followed the Hebrew instructions to affirm the specifying of the scribe and the witnesses, it was indeed the group as a whole that he commissioned.

Radbaz argues that the bill of divorce was not invalid for the reason the questioners feared. He proves that the formulation was only mandated *a priori*, but if the bill of divorce was nevertheless written without it, then the document is not invalid, unless the husband actually said, "All of you." Having proven that, Radbaz could have stopped at this point. However, he goes on to assert that in this case, the entire law regarding the wording does not apply. It only applies, he says, when the husband initiates the commissioning of a group. But in this case the group initiated it and formulated the wording, which they suggested to

---

46 *MT*, Women, Laws of Divorce, chap. 9. parags. 27 and 28.

47 Mishnah Gittin 6:7, BT Gittin 66a–b, for the basic law; BT Gittin 67a for the mandated wording.

the husband, who simply assented to whatever they suggested. There is no reason to fear lest he might on his own initiative say, "All of you." Radbaz has no precedent for this ruling. Here again he bypasses the letter of the law in order to respond to the realities of the situation. And, as in the previous example, he does so redundantly, rather than arrive at the same point by ruling on narrower grounds.

The original question was whether they had made a mistake in tearing up the bill of divorce, whether perhaps the bill of divorce had actually been valid. At this point in the responsum the answer would be that they were wrong. It was not invalid because of the husband's failure to use the mandated wording. But that is not how Radbaz ends. They were actually correct in tearing it up, he asserts, but for a different reason. As stated by the questioners, one witness to the event had testified that even the basic request to write and deliver a bill of divorce on his behalf was conveyed in Hebrew. As it happens, that individual was one of the two mandatory signatories on the document. By so testifying, he in effect withdrew his signature, and the bill of divorce became invalid. (Radbaz admits to having great difficulty believing that the general nature of the proceedings was not clear to the husband, but he issues his ruling on the basis of the testimony as presented by the questioners.)

The result is that Radbaz's emphasis on the realities of the situation, which induced him to formulate a point of law which had no precedent, was not only redundant for the argument he was making at the time, but was actually contrary to his conclusion in the case at hand. He goes out of his way to teach us that the codified law should not be followed blindly.[48]

(*c*) *Bypassing Codified Law* Ad Hoc

[8] Case [2] was a responsum "regarding a woman who charges that her husband compels her to have sexual intercourse with him while she is still in a state of menstrual impurity." The law of the Talmud, that a

---

48 See VI, 2216, for another instance of Radbaz's assertion that the realities of his day are different from those assumed by the Talmud, with a consequent change in law. This instance is less significant than the examples cited above. Radbaz rules according to Maimonides, but wants to show that even those who disagree with his ruling (Rashba *et al.*) would agree "in this era," because of current realities. Cf. *MT*, Acquisition, Laws of Sales, chap. 30, parag. 5, and *Maggid Mishneh* ad loc.

wife is considered trustworthy in making such a charge, is explicitly based on the presumption that a wife will not lie to her husband's face in a matter of which he has personal knowledge. Among his other arguments, Radbaz advanced the claim that the Talmud's presumption is not applicable in the present generation of widespread brazenness. Today, said Radbaz, it cannot be presumed that a wife would not lie to her husband's face regarding such a matter in order to obtain a divorce. In its essence, this is the argument that reality has changed since the days of the Talmud, and the change brings in its wake a change in law. It is worthwhile comparing that argument to one in another responsum, which also deals with the issue of the trustworthiness of women.

> You asked my opinion regarding a brazen woman (*perutsa*) who came and said, "My husband has died, so I may remarry." We asked her where he died, and she said, "In such-and-such a place."[49]

The questioners want to know whether she is compelled to wait until messengers are sent to clarify the matter, a process which would delay her remarriage, or whether she is to be permitted to remarry immediately, as she wishes.

The Mishnah appears to speak unambiguously to this issue:

> If a woman went abroad with her husband, and there was peace between them and peace in the world, and she came and said, "My husband has died"—she may remarry.[50]

That is, she is not required to wait for positive confirmation of her testimony, but may remarry on the basis of her own word. The reason for this leniency, as it emerges from the discussion of a related issue, is that the penalties, which accrue to her if her husband turns out to be alive after she remarries, are so severe, that there is a presumption that she is truthful.[51] The questioners are well aware, of course, of this passage in the Mishnah. But they want to know if an element of judicial discretion enters into this. May the Court exercise judicial discretion in assessing the trustworthiness of the particular woman before them? Or did the Talmud intend to make no distinctions in this presumption, so that they are bound to presume the trustworthiness of any woman who

49 III, 542 (= 975).

50 Mishnah Yevamot 15:1, BT Yevamot 114b. "Peace between them," for otherwise she is suspected of lying to get out of the marriage. "Peace in the world," because otherwise he may have disappeared in a war zone, and she may have assumed that he was dead, without positive knowledge.

51 BT Yevamot 88a, on the right of the woman to remarry with just one witness testifying to her husband's death.

comes before them with this claim—even a woman such as this one, of whom the questioners testify that she is brazen?

Radbaz accepts without reservation the basic law, that a woman is trusted to assert that her husband has died, and is permitted on that basis alone to remarry, without further confirmation of his death. This is so even if the death is confirmable, but its confirmation would take time. If the woman were not known to be brazen, there would be no question about this. Furthermore, adds Radbaz, if the death was not subject to confirmation, then even if the woman were brazen, she would be permitted to remarry without further ado. That is because, as Radbaz admits, in laying down this presumption, "the Sages did not draw a distinction between modest women and brazen ones." With this, Radbaz has answered the question put to him. No, there is no judicial discretion, even for a brazen woman such as this one.

But that is not Radbaz's answer to this question. This case is different, says Radbaz, because there are two factors at play here. First, it is possible to confirm her account, though it would take time. And second, she is brazen. Radbaz takes into account the probability that the matter can be clarified within a reasonable period of time. He brings evidence from other areas of talmudic law, that if clarification of the facts is possible, it is to be pursued. Furthermore, Radbaz is suspicious of this woman, because he feels that she could have brought some written testimony with her, and didn't. So he rules that if the matter can be clarified in a reasonable amount of time, the woman must wait.

Nevertheless, though the Talmud insists on clarification where possible in other areas of law, it pointedly does not do so here. So it turns out that Radbaz introduces a distinction in law on the basis of his own assessment of the situation, even though it runs counter to a presumption of the Talmud. For after all, Radbaz himself admits that "the Sages did not draw a distinction between modest women and brazen ones," and with modest women we do not wait even a reasonable amount of time for clarification. In other words, the situation, according to Radbaz, requires an *ad hoc* ruling, which ignores the Talmud's presumption.

It seems to me, that this example, of taking the specific situation into account, is more radical than the examples we have encountered earlier. In the previous instances we have surveyed, the argument was that the Sages of the Talmud themselves had never intended to rule the way they did in the situation which is prevalent today. Given the situation with which we are confronted today, the Sages themselves would have admitted that the law which they formulated does not apply. In the present responsum, there is an admission that the Talmud did not empower the judges of the court to apply judicial discretion in this case ("the Sages did not draw a distinction between modest women and brazen ones"). Nevertheless, in the specific case before us, the situation demands that we circumvent the law of the Talmud, and apply judicial discretion where the Talmud itself did not empower us to do so.

[9] A similar approach, in which the specific nature of the case leads Radbaz to an *ad hoc* decision, appears to underlie the ruling in another responsum, though in this case Radbaz provides the facade of a conventional argument for his ruling. This is the situation:

> It occurred that Reuben divorced his wife, and within three months became ill and near to death. His divorced wife moved in with him while he was ill and his illness intensified. She was secluded with him, as can be testified by witnesses. He died of the same illness three days later. He has no children, and he has a brother.[52]

The question goes on to refer to the fact that after his divorce he became engaged to another woman, who also secluded herself with him.

Our interest is in the original wife. There are two issues involved here. The first is levirate marriage. The law of levirate marriage, as formulated in Deuteronomy, demands that if a man die childless, his brother (the levir) should marry the widow. If he refuses to do so, he must undergo a ceremony by means of which he releases her.[53] Until the levir either marries her or releases her, the widow, called a *yevama*, is said to be "bound to a levir," and may not remarry. However, the woman in this responsum was not the deceased's wife, but his divorcee. This leads to a consideration of the second issue, namely, whether the woman's seclusion with him affects her status as a divorcee.

The Mishnah states:

> If a man divorces his wife and then spends the night with her at an inn, the School of Shammai rules that she does not need another divorce from him; the School of Hillel rules that she does need another divorce from him.[54]

---

52 III, 541 (=974).

53 Deut. 25:5–10. I am restricting myself in the text to the talmudic understanding of this law, which differs in some important respects from the plain sense of the biblical passage.

54 Mishnah Gittin 8:9, BT Gittin 81a. Cited above, 32.

The law follows the School of Hillel, and the Babylonian Talmud analyzes the reason for its ruling. In essence, it has to do with the fact that a man may betroth a woman by the simple act of intercourse, if that was their intention and witnesses were aware of it.[55] Betrothal is similar to marriage, in that it requires a divorce for its severance. In the case discussed by the Mishnah, there was no positive evidence of such intention. However, the Talmud attributes to the School of Hillel a presumption of licit, rather than illicit, sex, i.e., an intention to betroth.

But the Talmud records two traditions regarding the situation to which the controversy refers. According to one version, attested by R. Yohanan, the act of intercourse was observed by witnesses. But according to the second version, the witnesses can testify only to the fact that the two were secluded. This latter version necessitates a second presumption (or at least a recognition of grounds for apprehension) that intercourse in fact took place. Alfasi, Maimonides, and the other major authorities in their wake, rule in accordance with this second version. This is the more stringent position, because it means that mere knowledge of the couple's seclusion necessitates a second divorce. In the case referred to Radbaz, it would mean that the divorcee is suspected of having been betrothed anew by means of intercourse with her former husband during her seclusion with him, and is therefore "bound to a levir." In Radbaz's response there is an allusion to an unwillingness on the part of the levir to release her (perhaps as a means of extortion). The questioners were apparently seeking an end run around an obstinate levir.

Radbaz agrees that if it is at all possible, it would be best that the levir be induced, by force or trickery,[56] to release the widow, in order to forestall later gossip that she remarried improperly. But, he asserts, as a point of law it is not necessary, and even if a release cannot be obtained, the woman is not "bound to a levir" and may remarry at will. In support of this ruling he brings three arguments drawn from rabbinic sources. All three are weak in the extreme.

First, he refers to "several great luminaries" (*kama geonei 'olam*) who rule in accordance with R. Yohanan, that the Schools' dispute refers to a case in which the actual act of intercourse was observed by witnesses. According to this version, all would agree that if the act

---

55 Mishnah Qiddushin 1:1; *MT*, Women, Laws of Marriage, chap. 1, parag. 2; chap. 3, parag. 5.

56 *le-khufo la-halots o le-hat'oto*. "Trickery" means telling him that he may still marry her after the ceremony, which is not true; BT Yevamot 106a.

itself was not witnessed, the woman would not require a second divorce. Radbaz does not cite his source, but it appears to be the commentary of Rabbenu Nissim to Alfasi's compendium *ad loc.* If so, Radbaz has expanded rhetorically on Rabbenu Nissim's words. The latter merely wrote: "There are those who rule (*ve-yesh she-posqin*) like R. Yohanan." In any case, all the recognized authorities, including Rabbenu Nissim himself, rule according to the stricter version, that witnesses to the seclusion alone render the woman subject to the need for a second divorce.

Second, Radbaz cites the *'Ittur*, a work composed in Provence in the 12th century.[57] The *'Ittur* refers to two reasons adduced by the Palestinian Talmud for the ruling of the School of Hillel, that a divorcee who spent a night with her former husband in an inn requires a second divorce. These reasons are different from those suggested in the Babylonian Talmud. One of them is compatible with the general conception of the Babylonian Talmud, but the other is incompatible with it. According to this latter view, the husband in the Mishnah had not actually divorced his wife yet. He had prepared a *get*, the instrument that effects the divorce upon delivery to the wife, but had not as yet delivered it. According to the School of Hillel, if a man has sexual relations with his wife after he has prepared a *get* for her, the *get* is rendered an "antiquated *get*," and should not be used for divorcing her (though it is not invalid after the fact).[58] Therefore, according to this suggestion in the Palestinian Talmud, the "divorcee" in the Mishnah needs a second *get* according to the School of Hillel, because the first one became "antiquated." If the stringency of the School of Hillel is based on this reason, then it does not apply at all to the woman in Radbaz's responsum. She had already been divorced by a proper *get*.

This view, that the *get* involved in the "divorce" of the woman in the Mishnah had not yet been delivered, is introduced by the author of the *'Ittur* with the words, "There are those among the early great ones (*ve-ikka me-ravevata qamma'ei*) who say...."[59] These anonymous "great ones" are cited by Radbaz as a reason for his ruling:

57 *'Ittur*, 29c–d (58–9 in Arabic numeration). Radbaz cites the *'Ittur* from *Mordekhai*.

58 Mishnah Gittin 8:4, BT Gittin 79b. *MT*, Women, Laws of Divorce, chap. 3, parag. 5.

59 *'Ittur*: *de-mefarshei*. Radbaz: *de-amar* ("who says"), apparently a one-letter error for *de-ameru*.

> Here you have it explicitly, that there are those among the early great ones who have no apprehension (that there might have been an act) of betrothal at all.

In other words, according to this view, the Mishnah never referred to a woman who was actually divorced. There is no reason at all to entertain the suspicion of a subsequent betrothal to the former husband.

The weakness of this argument is patent. First of all, it is one of the fundamental premises of rabbinic rulings that the Palestinian Talmud is never followed when it contradicts the Babylonian Talmud. Second, these anonymous "early great ones" have no standing against all of the accepted rabbinic authorities.

Radbaz's third argument in defense of freeing the woman from the levirate bond is a hypothesis that there is a difference, regarding the ruling of the School of Hillel, between a married woman and a woman "bound to a levir." There are different levels of prohibition in Jewish law. A woman whom the law considers married, who unlawfully marries another, is guilty of adultery, the most serious level of prohibition. A widow "bound to a levir" who marries another, though she is living in sin, is only in violation of the most basic level of prohibition; after the fact, her marriage is not even invalid. So, says Radbaz:

> It is understandable with regard to a married woman, which is a stringent matter, that they required a second divorce, out of doubt as to whether he had intercourse with her for the purpose of betrothal. But with regard to a *yevama* who marries out, which is a basic-level prohibition (*de-issur lav hu*), we are not so stringent.

But this hypothesis, that the presumption of betrothal by intercourse pursuant to the seclusion of a formerly married couple does not apply in reference to a *yevama*, is unproven. Radbaz merely asserts it, but makes no attempt to substantiate it.

It is clear, therefore, that arguments such as these do not support the conclusion that ultimately the widow is not "bound to a levir," and may remarry without any release. However, Radbaz immediately follows these three arguments with a string of another three. These are not rooted in the sources, but in a consideration of the specific situation. Radbaz does not formally distinguish between the two sets of arguments. He connects them all in the same continuous series, introducing each one after the first with "Furthermore."

Furthermore, since he was smitten[60] with plague, and his illness immediately intensified, he had no strength for sexual intercourse, for he was already close to being in the process of dying (*qarov le-goses*).

Furthermore, he was already not in his right mind (*kevar nitraf da'ato*), and he did not have the mental capacity for the intention to betroth by intercourse.

Furthermore, since he divorced this woman and became engaged to another, there are grounds for believing that he did not desire her any longer, and did not have intercourse for the purpose of betrothal.

In conclusion, in light of the combination of all these arguments, there is no basis for apprehension at all. If he does not want to release her, or if they cannot trick him into it, she may marry without further ado. (*lekhatehilla*).

There is no question that the first series of arguments was mere window dressing. It was this latter series of considerations, which led Radbaz to bypass the codified law and to free the woman from the levirate bond.

[10] The first of this series of "furthermores" is the improbability of sexual intercourse as a justification for bypassing the codified law, since the latter was based on the probability of intercourse. The same line of argument appears in another responsum.

Sexual intercourse is prohibited with a woman who is in a state of menstrual impurity. In order to avoid circumstances that might lead to it, the law prohibits physical contact between husband and wife when the wife is menstrually impure. Radbaz was asked the following question:

Reuben and his wife were in hiding, with no one there to attend them. She became ill, and she was (during that time) menstrually impure. May her husband touch her, for instance, to lay her down, and to raise her, and to perform all her needs? If he is a doctor, may he feel her pulse? If he is an experienced bloodletter, may he bleed her? And is there a distinction between an illness which is life threatening and one, which is not?[61]

Radbaz begins by citing *Terumat ha-Deshen*, an influential volume of responsa by R. Israel Isserlein of 15th-century Austria. Isserlein had dealt with a similar case:

---

60 Emending *she-hukheha*, by deleting *het*, to yield: *she-hukka*.

61 IV, 2 (= 1076).

> If a woman is sick, and her husband wants to touch her in order to attend her, for instance, to raise her, and to lay her down, and to support her—is it permitted or forbidden?[62]

Isserlein had ruled very stringently: "It is forbidden to touch her even with one's small finger." He cites Rabbenu Asher, who had allowed a wife to touch a sick husband under analogous circumstances.[63] On the tacit premise that it is the man who assumes the active sexual role, Isserlein interprets this to apply only to a wife touching a sick husband, since he is not in a position to impose himself sexually on his healthy wife. The reverse, however, is not true, argues Isserlein. A healthy husband can impose himself on a sick wife, who would not be in a position to ward him off.

Radbaz cannot accept the plain sense of this responsum. After all, Scripture says regarding the Torah: "Its ways are ways of pleasantness."[64] Referring to this, Radbaz says: "Should she be left to die? This is not the ways of pleasantness!" So, ostensibly accepting Isserlein's responsum, he subjects it to a forced interpretation, according to which it would not apply to the case before him. Isserlein, says Radbaz, meant to prohibit a husband's physical contact with his ill, menstrually impure wife, only if it was possible to hire a female aide to attend her instead of his doing so himself. In accordance with Isserlein's reading of Rabbenu Asher, such an aide would have to be hired if the wife was the one who was sick; if the husband was sick, then his menstrually impure wife could attend him herself. Radbaz points to the language of the question in *Terumat ha-Deshen*: "If a woman is sick, and her husband *wants* to touch her," that is, wants to do so himself rather than hire an aide. But, says Radbaz:

> In the case at hand, in which they are in hiding and there is no one to attend her, should she be left to die? This is not the ways of pleasantness!

The same is true, says Radbaz later in the responsum, even if the wife's illness is not life threatening, because if she is not cared for properly then it will ultimately become so.

In other words, any interpretation of the law, which would prevent the ill wife from being properly attended, is not acceptable, because the

---

62 *Terumat ha-Deshen*, 252.

63 Cited from *Tur Yoreh De'a*, 195. See Rabbenu Asher, *Responsa*, *Kelal* 29, no. 3.

64 Proverbs 3:17, in reference to Wisdom, understood by the Rabbis as the Torah. On the uses of this verse in the context of Jewish law, see Kirschenbaum, *Equity*, 159–83.

ways of the Torah are "ways of pleasantness." Radbaz strengthens his case by adducing the "improbability of sexual intercourse" argument:

> It is an improbable fear that he will have intercourse with her, for several reasons.
>
> First, since her illness has reached the point that she needs someone to lay her down and raise her, no one would lust for her....[65]
>
> Second, since she is ill and weak, she will not permit him. And we do not fear that he will have intercourse with her by means of force....[66]

The codified law, of course, made no such distinction. Presuming that a husband's physical contact with his wife might lead to sexual intercourse, it declared a blanket prohibition on such contact when she was in a state of menstrual impurity. Radbaz, however, believes that "the ways of pleasantness" take precedence over the codified law in this instance. He buttresses his ruling by bringing to the fore the realities of the situation, which belie the presumption of the codified law.

[11] We have seen that Radbaz creates *ad hoc* distinctions that have no basis in the codified law, but are drawn from the specific realities of the case as he sees them. The first of the cases surveyed in this section concerned a woman, described as "brazen" by the questioners, who sought to act on the right, entrusted to her by the Talmud, to remarry on the strength of her own word that her husband had died. Radbaz drew a distinction, which he admits that the Talmud did not, between brazen and modest women. This was an innovation in the law, based on Radbaz's own assessment of the woman. There is another very similar example of a distinction drawn by Radbaz, without support in the Talmud, on the basis of a personal assessment of the individuals involved.

"Reuben" owed money to a non-Jew.[67] He asked "Simeon" to pay the creditor on his behalf. Subsequently, the non-Jew claimed that he

---

65 The continuation: "for one does not lust for a dead woman (*ki ain adam mitavveh el ha-meta*)." A similar wording recurs later, see the next note. The idiom seems rather strange, especially since Radbaz applies it "even if the wife's illness is not life-threatening"!

66 Radbaz adds a third reason, but it could not have been meant seriously, rather as a *senif* ("appendage," a makeweight argument) to the main arguments: "Even the non-Jews put the menstruant at a distance, certainly the holy Jews, and certainly one who is 'dead' and ill." This would seem to obviate the entire law, which prohibits physical contact with a menstruant!

was never paid. Simeon claimed that he did indeed advance the money to him.

The basic law in a case such as this is formulated by Maimonides.[68] If the debtor's agent asserts that he paid the creditor, and the creditor asserts that he didn't receive the money, each is seen independently in litigation with the debtor. Each must take an oath to substantiate his version. Even though the two oaths conflict and one of them is lying, neither of them bears the burden of proof in relationship to the debtor. The debtor must pay the creditor, and the agent is not liable. This ruling is based on the rule that an agent is not under obligation to transfer the money to the creditor before witnesses, unless the debtor had specifically instructed him to do so. The agent, therefore, was not negligent in not ensuring witnesses to the transaction.

But this law applies to a case in which the creditor is a Jew. In the case before Radbaz, however, he was not. Reuben can argue that a non-Jew is *ipso facto* not considered trustworthy by Jewish law, and this should have been understood by Simeon. Therefore, Simeon certainly was negligent in this specific instance in not providing witnesses, even without a specific directive from Reuben. There is no question that this approach is justified by the Talmud's attitude toward the lack of trustworthiness of non-Jews. In a discussion in the Talmud in which it is suggested that a non-Jew should be given the presumption of being law-abiding if the circumstances appear to support it, the conclusion rejects the idea, and insists on the presumption that a non-Jew is not trustworthy. In this connection it cites Psalm 144, which refers to "foreigners" as those "whose mouths speak lies."[69]

Radbaz first shows that the law in general is the way it was outlined above. He then raises the possibility that the rabbinic authorities, who ruled that the agent was not negligible in failing to ensure witnesses to the transfer of the money, did not have in mind a case in which the creditor was a non-Jew. Rather, even if the debtor did not specifically instruct the agent to provide witnesses, that should have been self-understood: "His silence is equivalent to his specifying." He suggests that the burden of proof that the authorities meant this rule to include a non-Jew as well, rests upon Simeon, the agent:

> He (Reuben) may say: "Bring proof that the words of the authorities apply even to a non-Jew!" For perhaps (in the case

---

67 I, 405.

68 *MT*, Acquisition, Laws of Agents and Partners, chap. 1, parag. 7.

69 BT Bava Batra 45a. Psalms 144:7–8, 11.

> of a non-Jew) his silence (about witnesses) is equivalent to his specifying, and it is as if he said explicitly, "Give it to him before witnesses." For (after all, these are non-Jews,) "whose mouths speak lies."
>
> Therefore, it seems to me that the judge should adopt a compromise position, and the compromise should be based on his assessment of the non-Jew. If he is assessed as one who is in the habit[70] of consuming the property of others, he should incline the compromise against Simeon, because he was close to being negligent. But if the non-Jew is not assessed as one who consumes the property of others, he should incline the compromise against Reuben, since he didn't say to him explicitly, "Give it to him before witnesses."

"Incline the compromise against" suggests a compromise verdict weighing more strongly in favor of one of the parties. It is not identical with ruling outright in favor of one of the litigants. Nevertheless, the whole concept of a distinction between a non-Jew who is trustworthy in the eyes of Jewish law and one who is not lacks any basis in the codified law,[71] and appears to be imposed on his own initiative by Radbaz. This is parallel to the distinction between a brazen woman and a modest one. It derives from Radbaz's intuitive understanding of the world in which he lived, and is superimposed on the codified law.

(*d*) *Assessing Intentions*

A number of responsa adduced so far are evidence of the tendency of Radbaz to delve into the intentions of the principals, and base himself on what he believes to be their state of mind. A number of other examples demonstrate this penchant.

[12] In the discussion of Case [9], we learned that if a divorced couple spent the night at an inn with the knowledge of ("in the presence of") witnesses, then the law presumes them to have had intercourse ("the witnesses to the seclusion are the witnesses to the act of intercourse"), and to have done so with the intention of betrothal. The woman therefore needs a second divorce in order to marry someone

70 "who is in the habit," emending *ve-ragil* to *she-ragil*.

71 The hypothesis that there is such a distinction is raised in BT Bava Batra 45a and is rejected there. Radbaz's citation of Ps. 144 derives directly from that rejection. Radbaz does not reject the decision deriving from the Talmud, but simply bypasses it.

else. Maimonides construed the latter presumption of intention narrowly, restricting it to a divorced couple, and explicitly rejecting a suggested broad construction, which would include other couples who may have similarly secluded themselves, or even who are known to have had intercourse.[72] Against this background, Radbaz addressed the following question:

> You asked, my friend, my opinion regarding Reuben, who had been secluding himself with his fiancée in the presence of witnesses. Do we say, "The witnesses to the seclusion are the witnesses to the act of intercourse," and he had intercourse with the intention of betrothal, and she needs a divorce," or not? And ... if they (the witnesses) saw the act of intercourse, what is the law?[73]

There are three stages to a marriage. The first is an engagement to be married. The second is a betrothal, after which a divorce is needed to sever the relationship. The betrothal is effected by the groom's transfer of some item of value to the bride, but exceptionally—and improperly—it may be effected by an act of sexual intercourse, if betrothal was its intention. The third is the marriage itself, at which point the couple begins to live together as husband and wife. Over the course of time, in most communities the marriage was merged with the betrothal into a single ceremony containing both elements. But in theory—and, in Radbaz's time and place, sometimes in practice—a betrothal could take place independently of the marriage.

Talmudic law does not attribute any special status to a woman engaged to be married, until she is actually betrothed. She is simply considered an unattached woman. But in the real world of social relationships, of course, there is a big difference between a fiancée and an unattached woman. Radbaz points out that rabbinic opinion was divided on the issue of a man's seclusion with his fiancée with the knowledge of witnesses. Is she to be placed in the category of a divorced woman who secludes herself with her former husband, so that she is considered betrothed? Or is she rather to be placed in the category of an unattached woman, whose status (following Maimonides) would not be affected by the seclusion? Radbaz shows that the school of authorities which is considered decisive by the Sephardic consensus rules according to the second, more lenient opinion, i.e., a fiancée is no different than an unattached woman. The

---

72 *MT*, Women, Laws of Divorce, chap. 10, parag. 19.

73 IV, 216 (= 1287).

position of the codified law in the case before him is that the fiancée in question does not need a divorce to sever the relationship.

Radbaz, however, backs away from this conclusion: "But if you examine it closely, you will find that not all things are equal." Uncertain of the exact circumstances, he suggests, as one of two scenarios, that the groom had been pursuing his fiancée because her family was stalling, having had second thoughts about the match.[74] Radbaz asserts that this situation sheds light on the intentions of the parties. Seclusion under these circumstances must be construed as implying an act of intercourse for the purpose of betrothal. He can adduce a parallel in the Talmud for this reasoning. Normally, when a man betroths a woman by transferring to her an object of value, he must make his intention clear, so that his act cannot be construed as a simple gift. But if he was in the midst of "speaking with her regarding matters of her betrothal," and then presents her with a gift, the Talmud rules that the declaration is unnecessary because his intentions were sufficiently clear.[75] The same is true here, says, Radbaz, even though nothing was made explicit in words. But the comparison is not necessarily compelling. Radbaz himself cites Rashba, on the issue of an engaged couple that secluded itself, to the effect that "an engaged woman does not have the same status as 'speaking with her regarding matters of her betrothal.'"[76] Radbaz asserts that in this specific case Rashba would agree with him, but that is far from certain. It is Radbaz's assessment of the intentions of the couple in the given situation that determines his ruling.[77]

---

74 Note the remarkable state of affairs presupposed here, of a woman who is engaged to be married against the will of her family. We find an even more remarkable example of this situation in IV, 56(= 1128, = VII, 51), ed. Warsaw 10c: "She was engaged (*meshuddekhet*) to him for several years (!)... the father of the girl had warned her not to accept anything from him (which might be construed as a betrothal gift—SM), and they would guard her from him... (ibid., 10d:) and he was seeking to betroth her...." *Meshuddekhet* usually implies a formal arrangement, with the involvement of the family. Was she openly engaged against the wishes of her family? Did the family back out of a former arrangement, without her consent?

75 BT Qiddushin 6a; *MT*, Women, Laws of Marriage, chap. 3, parag. 8. Maimonides makes it explicit that this applies to betrothal by intercourse as well.

76 See Rashba, *Attributed Responsa*, 135.

77 Compare Alashqar, *Responsa*, no. 3, regarding a similar situation. Alashqar, a contemporary of Radbaz, rules in accordance with Rashba, that intercourse (and certainly merely seclusion) with a fiancée is no different

[13] State of mind, as inferred by Radbaz from his reading of the situation, plays a role in an interesting case involving divorce.

Travel was dangerous. If a husband were to disappear on his travels, his wife would not be permitted to remarry unless satisfactory evidence of his death was forthcoming. It was not unusual for a man, about to undertake a journey, to give his wife a conditional divorce which would be activated retroactively by his failure to return in a designated period of time. A typical example of such a condition would be: "You are divorced as of now, if I do not return and appear before you within twelve months' time." In order to obviate any disagreement as to whether or not he in fact returned in the designated time, it was common to empower the wife to establish that he did not return by her unilateral assertion to that effect.

The question addressed to Radbaz was as follows:

> You asked about one who divorced his wife (using the wording): "As of now, if I do not pass before you prior to such-and-such a time." He empowered her with the force of a hundred witnesses (to assert) that he did not come and did not appease her. But the woman went and hid herself, so that when the time arrived, the husband came and sought her, but couldn't find her. After a while, the woman came and demanded the *ketubba* (i.e., the settlement agreed to at the time of the marriage, but which was payable at the time of divorce—SM). And he is protesting, saying, "I was under compulsion!"[78]

In the course of the responsum, we learn that the length of time the husband was away amounted to three years.[79]

Radbaz answers concisely: "This woman is a total divorcee, and she collects her *ketubba*. He is like one who protests about his house which has collapsed or about his ship which has sunk at sea." He presents two reasons for arriving at this decision. First, because this type of "compulsion" is not uncommon, and the husband should have foreseen such a possibility and precluded it in the wording of the condition.

---

than intercourse with an unattached woman, and she does not need a divorce. But his case does not concern an instance in which "the groom had been pursuing his fiancée because her family was stalling."

78 VI, 2219.

79 As a rule, the questions that appear in responsa have been reformulated by the respondent. In Radbaz's case, sometimes significant details are not included, and this is a case in point. See also Case [35] in Chapter 2, n. 3; Case [41] in Chapter 2, n. 45; Case [85] in Chapter 5, n. 77; Case [147] in Chapter 10, n. 38.

Second, because he empowered her to assert on her own cognizance that he did not come. That would have been the end of the matter, had not a contrary responsum come to his attention, to which he felt the need to respond: "And now, another responsum,[80] the author of which I know not, has reached me, and he (the author) persists in saying that the divorce is invalid." Radbaz felt it necessary, therefore, to proceed with a lengthy, point-by-point rebuttal of the anonymous responsum.[81] Though Radbaz did not know it, the author of the responsum was R. Joseph ibn Tsiyah of Damascus. His signed responsum is included in the volume of R. Joseph Caro's responsa. Caro had responded to a question about the same incident that Radbaz was asked about, and, like Radbaz, supported the validity of the divorce. He then presented the entirety of Ibn Tsiyah's responsum invalidating the divorce, which had reached him subsequently, and followed it with his own rejoinder.[82]

In his responsum, Ibn Tsiyah explained why the stipulation did not include wording, which would preclude the activation of the divorce on the wife's initiative. He relates the circumstances in which the divorce was issued:

> The divorce document was written without conditions,[83] but the wife's relatives asked him to deliver it to her with the aforementioned condition. He himself didn't know anything about these matters. I, in my innocence, acted on this, and directed him to give it to her with the aforementioned condition. He, too, did in his innocence as I had directed him, doing so all of a sudden, as he was in a rush to start on his way, and had to begin his travels. He did not pay attention to this.[84]

It turns out, therefore, that Ibn Tsiyah himself was the rabbi who had supervised the divorce, and it was he who had formulated the wording of the condition. He did so on the insistence of the wife's relatives, who, it seems, felt that they were acting in her interests in heading off an outright divorce. She, however, apparently had other ideas.

One of the main points of contention between Radbaz and Ibn Tsiyah is the degree to which the course of events was unpredictable. Ibn Tsiyah maintained that there was no way that the husband could

---

80 *kundres aher*. Perhaps it should be emended to: *kundres ehad*, "a certain responsum."

81 VI, 2220.

82 Caro, *Responsa of Beit Yosef*, Laws of Divorce, no. 9 (Jerusalem, 1960).

83 *be-setam*

84 *Responsa Beit Yosef*, p. 186.

have predicted that his wife would actually want to activate the divorce against his intentions. He did whatever he could to fulfill the condition that would prevent the divorce from taking effect, and his inability to do so was a result of circumstances beyond his control. This argument in itself would not normally be sufficient to nullify the divorce. The Talmud, fearing that the claim of "circumstances beyond my control" may result in divorces of ambiguous status, had ruled that such a plea on the husband's part is not accepted.[85] But Rabbenu Asher had interpreted this to apply only to circumstances that generally could not be anticipated, not to those which were totally unpredictable.[86] Ibn Tsiyah̲ argued that the possibility of the wife's going into hiding in order to activate the divorce fell into the latter category.

Ibn Tsiyah̲ was basing himself on a weak reed in terms of the realities of the situation, when he categorized the wife's actions as totally unpredictable. Radbaz states in this regard:

> These are, after all, daily occurrences, that wives who are being divorced hide themselves from their husbands so that the divorce not be invalidated. This is a common thing. For there are a number of women for whom it is an advantage to extricate themselves from their husbands. He should have considered that she might be one of them, and included it in the stipulation.[87]

Radbaz wrote this toward the very end of the responsum. But he addressed himself to this issue earlier. This is what he wrote:

> From the wording of the condition I have learned that this was a foreseeable occurrence.[88] For he stipulated regarding her, "As long as I do not pass before you for three continuous years." Is there greater quarrel and hatred than this, that he chooses to chain her (to an absent husband) for three years? Surely, she would not forgive him personal suffering! He should have put his mind to the fact that because of this hatred she might hide herself from him because she would no longer desire him. He should have stipulated (regarding this possibility), for it was certainly foreseeable!

---

85 BT Ketubbot 2b.

86 *Pisqei ha-Rosh*, Kettubot, ch. 1, no. 2.

87 VI, ed. Warsaw 29a. There are indeed other such cases in the responsa of the period. See, for example, R. Joseph ibn Lev, *Responsa*, II, 2, cited by me in *Precedent and Judicial Discretion*, 12.

88 *milta de-shakhi'ah̲*, literally: "a common occurrence."

The passage is indicative of Radbaz's penchant for delving into the litigants' state of mind. It exemplifies his readiness to bring a personal insight into human nature to bear on the interpretation of the law.

[14] In another responsum, Radbaz builds his case on a string of arguments, many of which derive from his assessment of the realities of the situation. The first of them draws on his inference of the principal's intention.

The case involves Jewish slave ownership in Egypt.[89] This matter was discussed above, in Case [3]. As explained there, the talmudic law regarding this issue had generally fallen into abeyance in the early Islamic period, but was nevertheless operative in Egypt in Radbaz's time. According to this law, a Jew who acquired a male or female non-Jewish slave, if he wanted to keep the slave, had to have him or her converted, with the slave's consent, to Judaism. That process converted the slave into a Jew with a limited range of religious obligations. Upon manumission, the former slave would be considered a full Jew. Manumission was the unilateral prerogative of the slave owner. It was accomplished by delivery of a document to the slave, parallel to a divorce document. The document of manumission could either be delivered personally to the slave, or given to a third party who would act as the slave's agent.[90]

In sharp contrast to Islamic law, talmudic law did not permit cohabitation between a slave owner and his female slave. Children born of such a union had the status of the mother, that is to say, they were slaves. Jews living in Islamic environments tended to assimilate the cultural mores of the host culture, and the rabbis were generally unsuccessful in instilling Jews with this particular prohibition. On the other hand, if a slave owner wished to do so, he could manumit his slavewoman and marry her, or at least maintain her as a concubine, rather than violate the prohibition of cohabiting with a slavewoman. Maimonides cited a Geonic opinion, that if a Jew has children with his slavewoman, the law presumes that he manumitted her first and betrothed her, and the children are presumed to be legitimate. That is because of the general presumption that people's actions should be interpreted, if at all possible, in a way, which would render them legitimate. In the words of the Talmud, "A man does not make his act

---

89 I, 409.

90 The slave need not be consulted in the appointment of the agent, since the law presumes his consent.

of intercourse an act of fornication." Maimonides himself restricted the application of this talmudic presumption to the two situations in which it is mentioned explicitly in the Talmud, and strongly objected to its broadening to include casual sex between unattached partners.[91]

The question addressed to Radbaz was as follows:

> You asked my opinion regarding Reuben, who purchased a slavewoman, and fathered a son and daughter with her. He now wants to give her (i.e., the daughter[92]—SM) in marriage to Simeon. They said to him, "Manumit her, and give her her document of manumission, so that she will be permitted to marry into the Community of Israel." He said, "I have already benefited her (i.e., the mother—SM) with a manumission document before I had sexual relations with her."

Reuben explained that he manumitted her by giving the manumission document to "So-and-so," who received it on her behalf. When questioned, the named party still had the document, which had been torn, the normal procedure after the document had taken effect. He didn't remember if he was the agent who received it on the woman's behalf or if it was entrusted to him after the fact:

> But he was sure that it was one of those two possibilities, because Reuben wanted to betroth her, and "So-and-so" had said to him, "Betrothal is not effective with regard to a slavewoman." Therefore he wanted to manumit her.

However, there were no witnesses then accessible to confirm the manumission.

Radbaz presents eight arguments in swift succession to prove that the woman's children from Reuben are legitimate, that is to say, that the law presumes a manumission before Reuben's cohabitation with her.[93] A number of these are drawn from Radbaz's reading of the unique circumstances of the specific case. For instance, the last one is that if there were no manumission the daughter would have the status of a slave, and Reuben would not have sought to marry her to Simeon. To do so would be an entrapment of Simeon in sin, without any benefit to Reuben himself. What interests us here, however, is the first in the sequence of arguments:

---

91 *MT*, Women, Laws of Divorce, chap. 10, Parag. 19.

92 The context demands this reading. Furthermore, it is clear from Radbaz's repeated references to the status of the children, that the subject here is the daughter. The wording itself, however, is ambiguous.

93 It is not necessary for the purpose of the child's legitimacy that he betroth her. Children born from a Jewish mother out of wedlock are legitimate in rabbinic law, as long as the union was not incestuous or adulterous.

> Even Maimonides and the later scholars (who follow him), who say that he (the child of such a union) is not legitimate, would agree that in the case at hand the children are legitimate, and that for several reasons. One, since he betrothed her, that shows that he strived for legitimacy, and does not want to "make his act of intercourse an act of fornication." So he certainly manumitted her.

Radbaz learns what Reuben's intentions were from his behavior, and applies those intentions to his legal ruling in the case at hand.

There is another responsum, very similar to this one.[94] In that case there is more positive evidence that the man did indeed manumit the slavewoman first and marry her, but there were some technicalities which led the questioners to ask whether that evidence is sufficient to allow their son to marry within the Jewish community as a free man. There too Radbaz brings a series of proofs for the legitimacy of the son, and one of them is basically the same as the one cited above, that is, that the slaveowner sought to marry the woman legitimately. He writes:

> Furthermore, it can be seen from his actions ... for after all, he betrothed her.

I have been stressing the willingness of Radbaz to arrive at a decision by relying on his own inferences from the specific circumstances. However, in this responsum Radbaz warns us against attributing too great an importance to any single argument:

> It is not that I rely on any one of the reasons (I have adduced) by itself. Rather, I rely only on the combination of all of them together to (arrive at the decision to) say that he (the son) is permitted to marry within the Community.

This is the concept of the combined power of weak arguments (*senifim*).[95] Nevertheless, it is plausible to infer from what we have seen that this argument contributed significantly to Radbaz's ruling.

[15] Just as Radbaz takes into account his assessment of the probable intentions of the principals in the specific case, thus he takes into account the probable intentions of people in general in order to arrive at a just decision. Consider the following question:

> You asked my opinion regarding one who borrowed a cloak from his neighbor. Is he permitted to lie on it? For perhaps (his

94 IV, 149 (= 2220) = VII, 4.

95 For a discussion of *senifim*, see Morell, *Precedent and Judicial Discretion*, Chapter 7.

> neighbor) lent it to him (just) to wear, but not for him to lie on.[96]

Radbaz begins with a discussion in the Talmud about whether priestly garments are permitted for the priest's personal use.[97] An inference could ostensibly be drawn from that discussion to the effect that one may not lie on a borrowed cloak. This inference, which assumes an analogy between priestly garments and a borrowed cloak, had been drawn by Tosafot.[98] But Tosafot then rejected it:

> But it appears that one should distinguish between a cloak, where the whole idea of wearing it is for the purpose of one's personal benefit, and priestly garments, where the idea of wearing it is for the purpose of the Temple worship.

After citing this passage, Radbaz concludes: "One learns from this, that since he lent it to him so that he may derive benefit from it, all (manner of) benefit is meant."

All this is from Radbaz's sources. But then he draws a distinction, which in effect rejects Tosafot:

> It seems to me (*u-mistabbera li*, "it makes sense to me") that one should draw a distinction. Even though he lent it to him without specifying (what it may be used for), if he lent it to him to adorn himself to go to a party, or to a house of mourning, or to a synagogue, or to similar places which require a dignified manner, it is forbidden for him to lie on it, because it can be assumed that he did not lend it to him for that purpose. But if he lent it to him to cover himself because of the cold, or to warm himself by means of it, in which case he would derive personal benefit from it, then it is permitted for one to lie on it, because it can be assumed that he lent it to him for this too, for he (the lender) intended to fulfill a righteous deed.

This is a distinction based on an assessment of people's motives. Radbaz draws this distinction entirely on his own initiative ("it makes sense to me"), and it is this distinction which determines his ruling.

[16] Other responsa also give evidence of employing an assessment of what people would normally have in mind when they enter into an agreement.

---

96 I, 225.

97 BT Yoma 68b–69a. The printed editions of Radbaz's responsa refer erroneously to "the beginning of 'Eruvin."

98 Tosafot to Hullin 110b, s.v. *tallit she'ula*. The quote that follows is from the last line there.

When a man marries, he undertakes a financial obligation toward his wife, which is due at the termination of the marriage. This obligation is called a *ketubba*. Various ancillary stipulations were customarily attached to the *ketubba*. By the time of the Mishnah, these stipulations, called "stipulations of the Court," had become mandatory, and were considered part and parcel of the *ketubba* itself. One of them stipulated that if the husband were to die, his wife's minor daughters would continue to be maintained by the estate until they were either betrothed or reached maturity.

The law of the Talmud was that the *ketubba* is collectable in real estate only, and not from moveable property. The Geonim, faced with a different economic reality, enacted a change in this law, whereby the *ketubba* was collectable from moveable property as well. Maimonides understood this to apply to the mandatory "stipulations of the Court" too.[99] In later periods, it was customary to stipulate specifically that the *ketubba* is collectable from moveable property. Since the right of contract was seen as a law of the Torah, the right to collect the *ketubba* from moveable property thus achieved the status of Torah law.

The Mishnah anticipates a situation in which the estate is too small to support both the claims of the daughters and of the sons, and addresses the issue of precedence:

> One who died and left sons and daughters—when the assets are ample, the sons inherit and the daughters are maintained; when the assets are small, the daughters are maintained and the sons beg at doorsteps. Admon said: Should I lose out because I am a male?[100]

Maimonides ruled according to the first view. According to the law of the Talmud, wrote Maimonides, the *ketubba* and its ancillary obligations are collectable only from real estate. If there is not enough to support both the sons and the daughters, the daughters must be maintained by force of the stipulation, while the sons beg at doorsteps.[101]

However, the law in force today is not the law of the Talmud. Does the precedence of daughters apply under the Geonic enactment, which allowed collection of the *ketubba* and its ancillary obligations from moveable property? In the paragraph that follows the one above, Maimonides ruled that it does not. The Geonim, he explained, did not intend by their enactment to give precedence to daughters over sons. If

---

99 *MT*, Women, Laws of Marriage, chap. 16, parag. 7.

100 Mishnah Bava Batra 9:1; BT Bava Batra 139b.

101 *MT*, Women, Laws of Marriage, chap. 19, parag. 17.

the *ketubba* is being collected from moveable property, and there is not enough to go around, both sons and daughters are equally maintained from the little that there is.[102]

But later practice included a specific stipulation in the *ketubba*, which allowed for the collection from movables while bypassing the Geonic enactment. What is the status of the daughters' claim when faced with an insufficient estate under these conditions? That is the question that Radbaz was asked:

> You asked my opinion regarding one who died and left few moveable assets. Should the daughters be maintained and the sons beg at doorsteps? Or perhaps both these and the others are maintained (from the estate)?[103]

The questioner goes on to explain that essentially he is asking whether the stipulation about collection from movables, which was written into the *ketubba*, applied to all the "stipulations of the *ketubba*," or applied only to the *ketubba* in its narrow sense, that is, the sum collected by the widow herself.

Radbaz answers that here too, as is the case with the Geonic enactment, both sons and daughters are maintained equally from the movables. First he shows that a close analysis of Maimonides can be made to yield that conclusion. Then he offers his own rationale for ruling that way. Observing that the stipulation allowing the collection of the *ketubba* from movables was included for the benefit of the woman, he continues:

> Is it pleasing to her that the daughters take everything and the sons beg at doorsteps? Surely, she intended that stipulation to apply only to herself! But with regard to her children, she left them under the enactment of the Geonim, that both these and the others are maintained. That is what is pleasing to her.

The stipulation is interpreted by Radbaz in light of what he believes to be the intention of women in general, for whose benefit it was formulated.

[17] Another example can be adduced from the area of commercial law. The legal arrangement between the litigants is described in the opening words of the question as follows:

> You asked: Reuben took money from Simeon and gave him merchandise to sell in another place in the manner of a *cammio*, and he entrusted him (with the merchandise to do as

102 Ibid., parag. 18.

103 VI, 2159.

> he sees fit with it). He also wrote (in the contract) that if the merchandise yields less than the sum that he took plus a margin of profit which he allotted him, that he, Reuben, would reimburse him.[104]

The commercial arrangement which is described here ("*cammio,*" a contraction of *cambium,*) was one which was common in the time of Radbaz. It functioned as a means of providing capital for a venture in international trade and at the same time of insuring the cargo against loss at sea and other mishaps.[105] In essence, the money which Reuben "took" from Simeon, the price of the merchandise, was not actually paid at the time of the "sale," but later, after the merchandise was sold and a profit realized. However, if the cargo was lost at sea, or if a profit failed to be realized for other unforeseen or unpreventable reasons, Simeon's debt would be cancelled. In the present instance, it appears that a threshold of profit was built in for Simeon. The "price" for which the merchandise was "sold" to Simeon was much higher than its true price, and the difference represented Reuben's profit for the risk he undertook. The contract was disguised as a sale rather than as an outright loan, in order to avoid the problem of interest, which is forbidden among Jews by Jewish law.

Simeon was "entrusted," that is, he was empowered to act as he saw fit with regard to the sale of the merchandise and the incurring of expenses pursuant to the venture. As it happens, Simeon was subjected to an (allegedly false) criminal charge, and was able to extricate himself from the situation only by a large expenditure. He claimed that the expenditure was within the definition of "pursuant to the venture," and it was Reuben who must bear the expense and reimburse him (by a reduction in what he owed Reuben). Reuben, however, asserted that he had witnesses who would testify to the fact that Simeon's partner engaged in an act of negligence, which triggered the sequence of events.[106]

---

104 I, 7.

105 On the *cambium* as a form of maritime insurance, see Bazak, "Maritime Insurance," 41–60; see especially 51, "Three Main Types of Insurance Transactions." For a concise explanation of the *cambium* in this capacity see S. Passamaneck, *Insurance in Rabbinic Law*, 101. See also Slae, *Insurance in the Halakha*, especially chapters 1 and 4.

106 "I have witnesses that your partner gave a note in his own handwriting to a non-Jew, and that as a result of that note the loss came about."

Radbaz finds in favor of Reuben for several reasons. At the end, he extends his remarks beyond the specific case before him, and formulates a rule regarding the general issue of entrusting a merchant:

> Know that my opinion regarding investment of trust of this type is that it applies to the sale of the merchandise and the customary expenses. If he sold it for less (than expected), or if he spent a little more than is customary, the investment of trust applies. But regarding the matter of incurring expenses which are not customary, he did not entrust him at all, unless he brings proof (to the contrary).

The wording of the documents, in which merchants were entrusted to incur expenses pursuant to the venture, did not make this distinction. Radbaz, relying on his own understanding of what the intentions of the parties must have been, reads into all contracts of this type an implied condition.

[18] The examples adduced in this section have dealt with assessments of intention, that is, of a psychological reality, which lead Radbaz to alter the literal application of the codified law, or at least support his argument for doing so. As a postscript, I will cite a case in which he takes physical reality into account in a similar way.

The issue concerns divorce.[107] Divorce is effected by the transfer of a written instrument, called a *get*, by the husband to the wife. The writing and delivery of the *get* is circumscribed by many technicalities, and one of these is the date, which is written out in words rather than numbers. The year in which the *get* was written in this case was 1551, which in the Hebrew calendar was 5311. But the scribe had inadvertently omitted the "three hundred." The error was not picked up by the others who were present. In the meantime, the husband left town and his whereabouts are unknown. The scribe, who had been the only one appointed by the husband as the agent to write the *get*, had died. The woman has not yet married, and, if the *get* is invalidated, will in all likelihood never be permitted to do so.

A similar question had been addressed a century earlier to the great Ashkenazic rabbinic authority, R. Israel Isserlein.[108] Isserlein's interlocutor had suggested a number of reasons to rule leniently in the case, and allow the woman to remarry. Isserlein, however, had rejected each in turn, and invalidated the *get*, as long as the woman has not yet remarried. He insisted that as long as her remarriage was not a *fait*

---

107 I, 469.

108 *Pesaqim u-Ketavim*, 11.

accompli, the law must take into account the theoretical possibility that the *get* was written for another woman of the same name, two hundred years earlier. Even though we know that is not so, Isserlein was concerned lest others who see the *get* will mistakenly think so, and cast aspersions on the legitimacy of the divorce after she remarries with rabbinic approval.

Radbaz begins by referring to Isserlein's responsum. He expresses his concurrence with Isserlein's interlocutors, without going into a specific justification for each of their views. He cites a number of reasons of his own for legitimating the *get*. Most of them are based on a dismissal of the possibility of future error by third parties. Among those is the following:

> Furthermore, people would never think this. Because paper which is three hundred years old—even if it is not moth-eaten—is in any case changed in its form from new paper. This is plainly visible. Therefore, people will not think that it was written three hundred years ago.

Radbaz has little patience for an insistence on the letter of the law in the face of either physical or psychological realities to the contrary.

(*e*) *Contextual Definitions of Legal Concepts*

In some instances Radbaz rejects the tendency to adopt a literal, fixed definition of a legal concept. Instead, his analysis and his rhetoric indicate a preference for a flexible definition, which takes account of the purpose of the law and the context in which it would be applied. The following are cases in point.

[19] The first is an instance of extortion. It involves a husband's attempt to force his wife to forgo her legal rights as defined in her *ketubba*. These are the obligations of the husband to his wife, which he undertook when they were married, and which are due when the marriage is terminated. The *ketubba* customarily also included stipulations which gave the wife non-fiscal rights, for instance, a veto on the husband's right to marry a second wife. The question begins:

> You asked my opinion regarding Reuben, who married a woman in Cairo,[109] and then went to Safed, leaving his wife (in Cairo). He wrote to her from there that if she does not deduct such-and-such an amount from her *ketubba*, or free him from

109 *mitsrayim*, which could also mean Egypt.

> such-and-such a stipulation which is included in her *ketubba*, he will not return to his home any more.[110]

The wife followed a procedure that was common when one was about to sign a legal document under duress. She first recorded a disclaimer that she was about to sign under duress, and then signed. Radbaz was asked whether the disclaimer was valid in this case.

Radbaz determines that the relevant legal question is whether or not this type of extortion constitutes "duress" under the law governing disclaimers. Duress is defined as a threat to person or property. This was not a threat to her person. Nor was it technically a threat to her property, because she was being asked to cede a future claim, not to relinquish property now in her possession. Radbaz, however, refuses to define "threat to person or property" in narrow, literal terms, and defines the case at hand as in fact involving a threat to both property and person:

> It seems to me that this is total duress.... Since he is threatening her that he will not return to his home any more, it means that she is losing her sustenance, her *ketubba*, and her clothing (which he is obligated to provide for her—SM). Furthermore, there is personal suffering, that is to say, (withholding of) her conjugal rights. Is there greater duress than this, that she should remain a "chained" woman (i.e., chained to an absent husband, without possibility of remarriage—SM)? And it is possible that for the rest of her life he will wander afar!

Radbaz is aware of the objection that she has the option of pursuing him legally in Safed and forcing him to return. She was therefore not under duress, technically speaking, when she signed away her rights. But Radbaz sees these as technical possibilities, removed from the realities of her situation. In reality, this is duress in the extreme:

> You may say: "Let her go to where he is, or let her appoint an agent to go there, so that they force him legally (to return). This is not duress!" One can answer that it is so if he is in the city with her, then if[111] she does not go to court, it is not considered duress. But to go to another place, or to appoint an agent (to go there)—there is no greater duress than this! For she will have to spend one hundred after another to travel to where her husband is. And he may flee, and go elsewhere, and there is no end in sight!

---

110 III, 630 (= 1055).

111 I am emending the abbreviation *alef nun* (usually: *i nami*, "also") to the word *alef mem* (*im*, "if").

And he concludes:

> Therefore I say that this is total duress. It is proper to write a disclaimer for this, more so than for financial duress.

The legal concept of "duress" must be interpreted in broad, contextual terms, and the tendency to define it in literal terms must be resisted.

[20] The Hebrew term *yi<u>h</u>ud* refers to the seclusion of a man and a woman. Because of the possibility, and in some situations probability, of sexual intercourse under such conditions, *yi<u>h</u>ud* is a concept which has a number of important legal ramifications. Radbaz was asked to define the parameters of the seclusion that constitutes *yi<u>h</u>ud*. His questioners refer to a difference of opinion among the rabbis regarding this issue:

> You asked my opinion regarding the *yi<u>h</u>ud* that the Sages mentioned frequently. Is it necessary that the door to the house or the room be closed, or perhaps (it applies) even (if the door is) open? For a controversy has occurred among the rabbis regarding this.[112]

Radbaz leaves no doubt that in his opinion a formal definition of *yi<u>h</u>ud*, that the seclusion must be behind closed doors, without regard to other circumstances, is to be rejected:

> The definition of *yi<u>h</u>ud* is that both of them are in one place, so that if he wishes to engage in sexual intercourse no one would see them.... One need not be concerned about the door of the house, whether it is closed or open.

Later in the responsum, Radbaz has occasion to refer to the custom of secluding the bride and groom as part of the wedding ceremony. The practice was to close the door behind them, even though no one would be allowed to intrude even without the door being physically closed. Since the *yi<u>h</u>ud* was considered as a consummation of the marriage, the insistence on a closed door, even though it was redundant to their total seclusion, seems to argue in favor of a formal definition of *yi<u>h</u>ud*. Rabaz writes:

> In my opinion, if it is a place that is appropriate for sexual intercourse (because of their seclusion—SM), then the closing of the door does not matter at all, as long as others have no permission to enter there. Nevertheless, (in this case) they were apprehensive lest because of the many people who were coming and going someone may unintentionally enter. They therefore adopted the practice of closing the door. It is a custom of modesty.

---

112 I, 121.

"Custom of modesty" means beyond the requirements of the law. The actual legal definition of *yihud* does not require it. That definition is not to be defined by formal criteria, but by the specific circumstances as they relate to the purpose of the law.

[21] In the following example, Radbaz's inclination to stress the contextual definition of a legal concept manifests itself more in rhetoric than in substance. In the case of the latter, he simply fleshes out a ruling of Maimonides.

In the case before Radbaz, a man appointed an agent to betroth a woman in another town.[113] The appointment of the agent was accomplished by means of a document, and two witnesses were signed on it. However, one of them was a relative of the bride. In cases in which witnesses are mandated by the law, familial relationship to any of the principles is in itself a technical disqualification. When the fact of the relationship was pointed out at the time, the rabbi supervising the matter ruled that it didn't matter. Witnesses to the actual betrothal are mandatory for the betrothal's validity, but these were only witnesses to the appointment of the agent. The matter was subsequently appealed to Radbaz.

Radbaz feels strongly that the supervising rabbi was wrong, that the disqualification of the witness as a relative invalidates the document and the appointment of agency. Admittedly, there is a controversy whether witnesses are required on such document at all. Maimonides had ruled that they were not, and Rabad had ruled that they were.[114] Radbaz makes his point for the invalidity of the document without forgoing the general rule of deciding the law according to Maimonides. First, he describes scenarios in which the witnesses on the document become in effect determinative for the betrothal itself.[115] Then he argues that even though witnesses on the document may not be required, once they are there they must be valid. He points out that if the validity of the document were called into question in the future, a document without witnesses would induce the judges to investigate the matter themselves to establish its validity. But if there are witnesses on

---

113 VII, 53. I have emended *be-maqom ehad* (already in the *editio princeps*) to *be-maqom aher*.

114 *MT*, Women, Laws of Marriage, chap. 3. parag. 15; Rabad, *Maggid Mishneh* and *Kesef Mishneh* ad loc.

115 If, after the betrothal effected by the agent, the bride or the groom challenges the fact that the agent was in fact appointed as such, then the testimony of the witness may be determinative.

it, the judges would assume that they are valid witnesses, and not investigate the matter further. Later in the responsum, Radbaz argues that even if we rule like Maimonides, and witnesses are not legally necessary, it is nevertheless proper procedure to require witnesses on such a document.

The issue in this responsum is the disqualification of witnesses for reason of familial relationship, as it applies to the husband's document of agency. That was the basis of the original query, and, as we have seen, it is to that issue that Radbaz addresses himself and arrives conclusively at his decision. However, he redundantly makes an effort to introduce another basis for the disqualification of a witness, one that had already been defined by Maimonides broadly, not by formal characteristics but by context. That is a disqualification by reason of being an interested party. Maimonides left it to the judge to determine if any benefit might accrue to the witness from his testimony, even if it be in "an indirect and far-fetched way (*be-derekh re<u>h</u>oqa ve-nifla'a*)."[116] In the only place in which he strays from the issue of disqualification for reason of relationship, Radbaz refers to this passage of Maimonides. He then concludes:

> In the case at hand, it is neither indirect nor far-fetched. It is desirable for the witnesses who are related to the woman that the agency be valid, so that the woman will thereby be betrothed, because Reuben is great and wealthy. Is there any greater benefit than this?

Radbaz thus converts what is essentially a disqualification by virtue of relationship into a disqualification by virtue of being an interested party. He does this in an aside. It seems to me that he is attracted to this argument because it gives play to his predilection for contextually defined legal concepts.

[22] In this next example, attention to context leads in precisely the opposite direction from that to which one would be lead by formal similarities.

The Mishnah rules that an employer cannot choose unilaterally to pay the wages of his agricultural employee in kind from what he has harvested, rather than in cash.[117] Rabbenu Tam learned from this that in general the employer of a hired laborer does not have the option of paying him in kind (or, "the equivalent of money," in the Talmud's idiom). If the employer does not have the cash, it is his responsibility,

116 *MT*, Judges, Laws of Evidence, chap. 16, parag. 4.

117 Mishnah Bava Metsi'a 10:5, BT Bava Metsi'a 118a.

and not the employee's, to bear the burden of converting goods into cash. This is to be distinguished, Rabbenu Tam explains, from a debt on a loan. In that case, if the debtor does not have cash available, he has the option of paying in kind.[118] Radbaz's questioner wanted to know what the law would be with regard to rental on a house or an appliance. Is such a rental to be seen as analogous to a debt on a loan, so that the lessee can pay in kind, or to a salary payment to an employee, in which case he must pay the rent in cash? The questioner strengthened the latter interpretation with a formal definition of "rental," which in Hebrew is the same word as "hiring" (*sekhirut*). Since both transactions are forms of the same phenomenon, *sekhirut*, perhaps the law is the same.[119]

Radbaz cites a controversy on this matter. "I have seen in *Sefer ha-Tashbets*, that he (the lessee) can give (the lessor) the equivalent of money."[120] However, Radbaz tells us, R. Perets of Corbeil[121] had ruled the contrary way: "If the lessee does not have cash, he cannot acquit himself by giving the equivalent of money. We do not say (as we do in other contexts—SM[122]), "the equivalent of money is like money," with regard to rental. Rather, he (the lessee) should sell (the goods in his possession) and pay."

Radbaz, after an expression of humility, rules against R. Perets and according to *Sefer ha-Tashbets*. He explains his reasoning by referring to Deuteronomy 26:15. The passage teaches that a hired laborer must be paid the same day, "for he is needy and urgently depends on it." The phrase "urgently depends on it" is more literally translated, "lifts up his

118 Tosafot to Bava Qamma 9a, s.v. Rav Huna.

119 III, 458 (= 899).

120 The reference is to the work of that name by R. Samson ben Tsadoq, no. 521 (ed. Lemberg, 1858, no. 524). The passage appears also in *Kol Bo*, no. 124, in the section, "Laws from *Sefer ha-Tashbets*," no. 25. The latter appears almost verbatim in Rashba, *Responsa*, VII, 515. Radbaz's citation is close to the Kol Bo-Rashba version, closest to the latter. However, these versions all refer to *sakhir/sokher*, which would normally mean a hired laborer. None of them indicate that the reference is to a lessee of a house or an appliance.

121 The text of Radbaz, already in the first edition of III (Furth, 1781), reads: "RI'F" (= Riaf), and the text of Rashba: "RIF," both of which normally refer to R. Isaac Alfasi. This is clearly an error for "RF," i.e., R. Perets.

122 See BT Bava Qamma 7a and parallels.

life to it," that is, his life depends on it. Radbaz, citing Rabbenu Tam as his source,[123] explains:

> The reason for (the law regarding) the laborer is that he "lifts up his life to it," and if he (the employer) gives him the equivalent of money, he will die of starvation (by the time he is able to convert it to cash). But this reason does not apply to the same extent to one who leases a house or an appliance to his neighbor. Since he (the lessor) has a house or appliances to lease, he is not wont to die of hunger, and does not "lift up his life" to the rental of his house, as (the laborer does) to the wages of his labor. On the contrary. I would say that if the lessee of the house is poor, and if you encumber him with having to sell and produce cash in excess of the letter of the law, you cause him harm for the benefit of the landlord, which is the opposite of (the law which is meant) for the benefit of the laborer.

In other words, notwithstanding the formal similarity between leasing and hiring (both being forms of *sekhirut*), it is the intent of the law which is determinative.

(*f*) *The Effects of Legal Rulings on Human Lives*

[23] The previous case is an example of how Radbaz's responsa indicate his sensitivity to the way in which his rulings bear upon the lives of the flesh-and-blood human beings who are affected by them.[124] I believe that this sensitivity can be shown to be the motivating factor in his approach to the issue of the *'aguna.*

Rabbinic law does not recognize a presumption of death after a lapse of time, and a wife whose husband is missing cannot remarry

---

123 I have not found this reference. See Tosafot to Bava Qamma 9a, s.v. Rav Huna, for Rabbenu Tam's ruling that a laborer must be paid in cash. That source and its parallels do not explicitly draw the connection between this ruling and the verse in Deuteronomy.

124 See Hartman, "Maimonides' Epistle on Martyrdom," 368: "In Maimonides' opinion, the tangible effects of a specific legal ruling on its target audience must be taken into *halakhic* account when the ruling is being formulated" (emphasis Hartman's). Hartman wrote this in reaction to Soloveitchik, "Law and Rhetoric." See the latter's counter-argument in Soloveitchik, "Criteria for the Designation 'Halakhic Rulings'." Soloveitchik admits the utilization of these types of considerations in arriving at a practical ruling, but contests their definition as "halakhic."

unless there is positive proof of his death. A woman whose missing husband is believed to be dead, but whose death is yet to be legally determined, is known as an *'aguna* (plural: *'agunot*); she is in a state of *'iggun*. The literal meaning of the term *'aguna* is "anchored woman," that is, she is anchored to a husband who is not there.[125]

The approach of Rabbinic law to the *'aguna* is paradoxical. On the one hand, changing the status of a married woman is viewed with the utmost stringency. After all, an error of fact or of law, followed by a remarriage, would result in adultery. The Mishnah applies stringent penalties to a woman who even inadvertently remarries while her husband is alive. It prescribes divorce from both husbands, and the loss of alimony (the *ketubba*) from both.[126] This is in addition to the very serious sin of adultery, which the woman and her new husband would have committed. Unwarranted leniency on the part of the rabbis may enable such a severe transgression, and that would render the rabbis personally culpable. As a result of this attitude, there is an extremely high standard of certainty that is demanded for the legal determination of death. Virtually no circumstantial evidence is accepted. An example of this is the rule of the Talmud regarding one who fell into a body of water. If the water "has an end," that is, if the shores on all sides are visible, and he was not seen to have emerged, then and then only is there a presumption of death. But if, as is virtually always the case in a mishap at sea, the water "has no end," then he is not presumed dead, because he may have emerged beyond view, as improbable as that may be.[127]

On the other hand, unique leniencies are adopted with regard to the laws of evidence. Sources of information are accepted which are otherwise explicitly excluded. These include hearsay testimony, testimony from a single witness, from a relative, a slave, or even from the wife herself.[128] From a practical point of view, the most significant leniency regards a non-Jew as the source of the information. A non-Jew would normally be disqualified as a witness. But in this situation the report of a non-Jew is accepted if he is "speaking in innocence," that is,

---

125 The last two sentences are taken from Morell, "Profile of a Jurist," 173.

126 Mishnah Yevamot 10:1, BT Yevamot 87b.

127 BT Yevamot 121a. One tannaitic opinion does not accept presumption of death in either case.

128 Mishnah Yevamot 16:7. *MT*, Women, Laws of Divorce, chap. 12, parag. 16.

relating what he saw in the course of informal conversation, without any consideration of the legal consequences.[129]

The Talmud reflects upon the reason for this leniency in allowing remarriage, and links it to the severity of the law if it later turns out that the husband is really alive. It is assumed that the woman herself would only remarry if she is personally convinced that he is truly dead:

> Rabbi Zera said: As a result of the stringency that one applies to her at the end, one is lenient with her at the beginning.
>
> So let one not be stringent and one need not be lenient!
>
> Because of *'iggun*, the Rabbis were lenient with regard to her.[130]

Radbaz understands this last phrase as a general directive to rabbis to rule leniently in order to resolve the status of *'agunot* ("to seek out ways of leniency)." He then raises the following question. Is this mandate for leniency, with which the Talmud charges the rabbis in cases of *'iggun*, restricted only to the laws governing the source of the information, or is it to be understood in a broader sense, to encompass the substance of the information itself (in Radbaz's formulation, "the body of the matter"—*gufa de-'uvda*, or "the body of the testimony"—*gufa de-sahaduta*).[131] After all, the operative Talmudic phrase, "Because of *'iggun* the Rabbis were lenient with regard to her," was stated in the context of the relaxation of the laws governing the source of the information. Radbaz raises the question whether there is a mandate for extending it beyond that. In light of the silence of the Talmud and the seriousness of the issue, an affirmative answer is the more daring position.

What does it mean, "to seek out ways of leniency"? One way of "seeking out" would be to resolve uncertainties of fact in favor of leniency. The general rule governing the resolution of uncertainties distinguishes between laws that derive from the Torah and those that derive from rabbinic legislation. The former are resolved by assuming the more stringent possibility, and the latter by assuming the more lenient one.[132] Adultery is a biblical prohibition, and "seeking out ways of leniency" in this sense would be a glaring exception to the rule.

---

129 BT Yevamot 121b. Maimonides, Women, Laws of Divorce, chap. 12, parag. 16; chap. 13, parag. 11.

130 BT Yevamot 88a.

131 VII, 25, ed. Warsaw 10a and b; VII, 26.

132 BT Betsa 3b. This rule does not relate to civil cases, where the burden of proof is always on the plaintiff, and uncertainties always work to the advantage of the defendant.

The authorities were divided on this issue. The lenient position was articulated by Rabbenu Asher. The rule of the Talmud is that identification of the body requires the report of the man's name as well as his city, and in the case before Rabbenu Asher, the city was not included. Rabbenu Asher ruled leniently.[133] After citing various Talmudic rulings bearing on the issue, he concludes:

> You see that the Sages allowed a number of leniencies for the welfare of *'agunot*. They also relied in this matter on (the consideration that) because of the stringency which one applies to her at the end, she investigates carefully and (only then) remarries....[134] And so it is proper for anyone ruling on the law to search from every side in order to rule leniently.[135]

Thus it is Rabbenu Asher whom Radbaz follows in interpreting the Talmud's conclusion, "Because of *'iggun* the Rabbis were lenient with regard to her," as a general directive to incline toward leniency in adjudicating cases of *'iggun*. The phrase that describes this directive, "to seek out ways of leniency (*le-ahadurei a-anpei de-sharyuta*)," appears to be original with Radbaz.[136] Radbaz answers the question he had posed by opting for the more radical alternative, reading the Talmud as a directive to rabbis to deliberately "seek out ways of leniency even in the body of the testimony."[137] In this too he follows Rabbenu Asher, whose case dealt with the substance of the information, not with its source.

The general idea that rabbis must do what they can to find a solution for every *'aguna* whose case comes before them was universally accepted. There are probably more responsa on this issue than on any other in the entire literature. Opinions regarding individual *'agunot* were solicited from the greatest rabbis of even distant communities. They saw it as a personal obligation to devote their time and energy to the resolution of these cases. But there was not a consensus that every possible construction of the evidence that would lead to leniency

---

133 Rabbenu Asher, *Responsa*, *Kelal* 51, nos. 1 and 2.

134 See BT Yevamot 115a–116b. The Talmud leaves unresolved the question whether "she investigates carefully and remarries" is the reason underlying the leniency, or whether the reason is a fear of the possible consequences, since the truth may yet become apparent.

135 Ibid., no. 2.

136 A search of the data base of the Bar Ilan Responsa Project indicates that this wording occurs only with Radbaz. For various formulations of this idea, see Y. Z. Kahana, *Sefer ha-'Agunot*, Introduction, 17f.

137 VII, 25.

should be adopted. Among Radbaz's contemporaries, for instance, R. Joseph ibn Lev, a leading rabbinic authority in Constantinople, addressed the question whether uncertainties in cases of *'iggun* should be resolved stringently or leniently. He summarized the Talmudic evidence on both sides, and declared it indecisive. He therefore announced his unwillingness to go beyond the direct precedent of the Talmud, and came down on the stringent side of this question.[138] In another responsum, he was asked about the lenient responsum of Rabbenu Asher mentioned above, and he rejected it.[139] R. Moses Alashqar, who, like Radbaz, was born in pre-exilic Spain, was asked about a shipwreck in which thirty-one Jews who had been aboard perished and were buried. The identities of the Jews were known in the aggregate. But because they had not been individually identified within an hour of their emergence from the water, as the letter of the law required, he did not see himself able to allow their wives to remarry.[140] There was a range of opinions among Radbaz's contemporaries regarding the weight to be given to circumstantial evidence when the letter of the law was not satisfied. Radbaz stands at the extreme liberal end of this spectrum.[141] I believe this to be reflective of his sensitivity to the effect of his ruling on the people involved.

Incidentally, it is instructive to note an instance in which Radbaz rejects the utilization of reported information about a death. The witness had asked a non-Jew what happened to the ship, and the latter answered with a tale of how the Jews on it were murdered. The rule is that if the information was directly solicited from a non-Jew, it is considered to have not been "spoken in innocence," and the information cannot be used. In this case the non-Jew was asked just about the ship, and proceeded on his own to tell about the Jewish travelers. R. Joseph ibn Lev, responding to the same incident, ruled leniently, allowing the fiction that the non-Jew was "speaking in innocence."[142] Radbaz, in consonance with his general approach to recognizing the realities of the situation, refuses to accept this. When a Jew asks about a ship, it is clear to all, including the non-Jew, that he is

138 R. Joseph ibn Lev, *Responsa*, III, 89.

139 Ibid., III, 90. See my *Precedent and Judicial Discretion*, 174.

140 Alashqar, *Responsa*, no. 25.

141 See Morell, *Precedent and Judicial Discretion*, 177 and 203.

142 R. Joseph ibn Lev, *Responsa*, I, 2.

asking about its Jewish travelers. Here too, though, Radbaz finds a way to release her through other testimony.[143]

[24] The Talmud's phrase, "Because of *'iggun* the Rabbis were lenient with regard to her," came in the context of the classic *'aguna*, a woman whose husband was missing and generally believed to be dead. Radbaz, as we have seen, follows Rabbenu Asher in reading this phrase as a general directive "to seek out ways of leniency," and in applying that directive to all aspects of the law, not just those regarding the source of the testimony. Were we restricted to this alone, it may have been possible to interpret Radbaz's lenient stand as deriving simply from his understanding of the intent of the Talmud. I have suggested, however, that it derives from an underlying sensitivity to the practical effects of his legal decisions. This conclusion is supported by his extension of the principle of deliberate leniency beyond the classic *'aguna*, to whom alone the original formulation in the Talmud explicitly refers.

I will begin with a situation that, from a practical point of view, is equally harsh for the woman, though the underlying legal considerations are totally different. It involves the law of levirate marriage. If a man dies childless, and if he is survived by a brother, his widow, known as a *yevama*, must either marry her brother-in-law, the levir, or, alternatively, be released by him through a ceremony called a *halitsa*. Without a *halitsa*, she is not free to marry anyone else.[144] If the *yevama* is pregnant when he dies and subsequently gives birth, a viable child would release her from the levirate bond. The question referred to Radbaz reads as follows:

> The incident concerns a woman whose husband had died, leaving her pregnant. She gave birth to a son, and those who are knowledgeable (*maggidei emet*) saw that his signs were completed. (Nevertheless), he died within thirty days. His mother wanted to remarry, for she did not know that her husband had a brother. They said to her, "Your husband had an apostate brother, but we do not know if he is dead or alive." ... You asked me if she may marry with our permission or not.[145]

There are two disputed issues at the heart of this question. One concerns the viability of the child. The viability of a baby born before full term was questionable, and it was generally uncertain whether full

143 VII, 25, ed. Warsaw 11d.

144 See Case [9] above.

145 IV, 93 (= 1164). "With our permission"—*le-khatehilla.*

term was reached. According to a rule in the Talmud, survival for thirty days is a sign of viability.[146] The Talmud also records another rule, that developed hair and fingernails at birth is a sign of viability. That is what is meant by "signs."[147] Maimonides had indeed ruled that "signs" are sufficient in themselves to judge the baby viable immediately upon birth.[148] There were those, however, who did not accept "signs" as unequivocal proof of viability, and would insist on *halitsa*, the customary procedure when there was uncertainty of law or fact as to whether or not the widow was bound by the law of levirate marriage.[149]

In this case, the child was born with "signs," but did not survive for thirty days. According to the latter opinion, the child would not be considered to have been unquestionably viable at birth, and a *halitsa* would be necessary for her remarriage, though in fact it would be impossible for the woman to obtain it. Radbaz, who permits the *yevama* to remarry without the need of a *halitsa*, was anxious to establish his ruling in this specific case even according to those who hold the more stringent view. Since, according to them, "signs" are immaterial, and the child did not survive thirty days, Radbaz had to justify his ruling on other grounds. He relied for that on the second disputed issue, to which the bulk of the responsum is consequently dedicated.

That issue concerns the status of an apostate brother. The question whether an apostate brother binds a *yevama* with the levirate bond has a long history, and there were rabbinic voices on both sides. In the conditions of post-Expulsion Spain, in which it was not unusual for conversos to make their way to Ottoman lands leaving their New Christian siblings behind, the issue could not have been an uncommon one. Obtaining a *halitsa* from an apostate levir would often be impossible. (No one would suggest an actual marriage with an apostate levir.) Insistence on a *halitsa* would mean in effect that the woman would be left an *'aguna*, unable to remarry.

The mainstream Sephardic halakhic tradition, to which Radbaz was heir, reflected the position that the apostasy of a levir does not release the *yevama* from the levirate bond. Radbaz begins by referring to this

---

146 BT Shabbat 135b.

147 BT Yevamot 80b.

148 See *MT*, Love, Laws of Circumcision, chap. 1, parag. 13, and *Kesef Mishneh* ad loc. For application of this principle to the case of levirate marriage see Sirkes, *Bayit Hadash* (*BAH*) to *Tur Even ha-'Ezer*, no. 156, s.v. *u-ma she-amar ve-lo mishkahat lah.*

149 See *Tur Even ha-'Ezer*, no. 156, and *Beit Yosef* ad loc., s.v. *u-ma she-amar kegon she-yadua' she-nolad le-ahar tet hodashim.*

tradition, citing as its exponents Sherira Gaon,[150] Maimonides as interpreted in *Maggid Mishneh*,[151] Rashba,[152] Ritba, and the author of the *Turim*.[153] But it is immediately clear from the way he introduces this position ("On the face of it"—*le-khe'ora*) that he intends to reject it.

Radbaz's rejection begins with a reference to a responsum in R. Israel Isserlein's *Terumat ha-Deshen*, in which, ironically, Isserlein ruled stringently in this matter.[154] Isserlein began by citing rulings going back to the Geonic period, to the effect that if the levir was already an apostate at the time of the marriage, then the *yevama* is not bound to him. He also cited a view that it is sufficient for him to have been an apostate at the time of the husband's death for the *yevama* to be released from being bound to the levir.[155] Against these lenient rulings, Isserlein cited Rashi, to the effect that a Jew never loses his Jewish status, in spite of apostasy.[156] He followed this up by citing other authorities who were influenced by Rashi's ruling. Ultimately, Isserlein does not see his way clear to rule leniently in this matter, against Rashi and those who followed in his wake.

Radbaz, however, utilizes the sources marshaled by Isserlein to his own advantage. After laying out the Sephardic tradition that espoused the stringent position, he turns to his rejection of it:

> But if you investigate the matter well, you will discover that in the case at hand one should rely on the lenient school. Look at the responsum of Rabbi Israel (Isserlein), no. 223. You will find several great scholars of the world, early and late, who permit (such a woman to remarry) in a case in which he was an apostate from the time of the marriage. Their arguments are written there, as well as the arguments of those who would forbid (her to remarry without a *haltsa*). From there you will become informed, and there is no reason for length (on my part).

---

150 See *Tur Even ha-'Ezer*, 157; Lewin, *Otsar ha-Geonim*, Yevamot, 36, no. 83, n. 11.

151 To: *MT*, Women, Laws of Levirate Marriage, chap. 1, parag. 6.

152 *Hiddushei ha-Rashba* to Yevamot 22a, s.v. *matnitin mi she-yesh lo ah*.

153 *Tur Even ha-'Ezer*, 157.

154*Terumat ha-Deshen*, no. 223.

155 His sources are *Or Zarua'* (Part 1, no. 605), and *Mordekhai* to Yevamot, chap. 4, no. 28, to which he adds R. Abraham of Regensburg.

156 See the study of this position of Rashi in Katz, "Even though He Sinned."

In other words, Radbaz adopts the position of the lenient school, without taking the trouble to argue the case on its merits, and he does so against the established Sephardic legal stance. Radbaz is aware that this in itself is not enough to sway the doubters. He seeks to show that in the case at hand there are other arguments that, in the aggregate, buttress his position:

> In the case at hand, even those who rule stringently (on the issue in general) would rule leniently, and that for several reasons.

Proving that to be so is particularly important in this instance, in light of the fact that Radbaz had not presented a substantive defense of his preference for the lenient school.

But a perusal of the "several reasons" adduced by Radbaz indicates the weakness of his case on substantive grounds.

First, he refers to the dispute regarding "signs" as unequivocal proof of viability. Though Radbaz himself believes that the baby's birth with developed hair and fingernails is sufficient to define the baby as viable and release the *yevama* from the levirate bond, he seeks to establish his ruling even in accordance with the more stringent opinion. Those who hold that opinion, and would rule that the baby is not considered viable and that the woman needs a *halitsa*, must at least recognize that the issue is in dispute. The requirement of a *halitsa*, therefore, has the status of a matter of uncertainty, a *safeq* (pl.: *sefeqot*). This leads Radbaz to his second point.

Radbaz suggests that those who adopt the stringent view, that an apostate levir binds his sister-in-law, "perhaps" (*dilma*) take that position only when the levirate bond is a matter of certainty, and not when the levirate bond itself is questionable, as it is here because of the dispute about "signs." This suggestion is proposed without any attempt at substantiation, and there is no basis for it, which comes readily to mind.

Radbaz then allows, for the purpose of argument, that the proponents of the stringent opinion maintain their view even when the levirate bond itself is a matter of uncertainty. That does not mean, he says, that their opinion should influence us in our decision when the levirate bond itself has the status of *safeq*, that is, when it is open to question. The obvious problem that comes to mind is that the rule for resolving uncertainties does not lead us to this conclusion. The rule is that uncertainties regarding laws that are of Torah origin are resolved stringently, and those, which are of rabbinic origin, are resolved leniently. The levirate bond, after all, is of Torah origin.[157]

Radbaz next raises another hurdle to his conclusion. Maimonides had ruled:

> One who has a brother of any type—even a bastard or an idol worshipper ...—he (i.e., that brother) binds his (i.e., the deceased's) wife with a levirate bond.[158]

It would seem, therefore, that Maimonides is squarely in the camp of those who do not recognize apostasy as degrading one's legal status as a Jew, and consequently bind his sister-in-law with the levirate bond. The author of the classic commentary to Maimonides' Code, *Maggid Mishneh*, indeed understood this as a deliberate rejection of the Geonic ruling, according to which the levirate bond would not apply if the levir had already been an apostate at the time of the marriage. This ruling of Maimonides is a real obstacle to Radbaz's attempt to free the woman from the levirate bond on this account, because of the tradition in Egypt that the law follows the rulings of Maimonides in "the place of the Master."[159]

In order to extricate himself from the necessity of this conclusion, Radbaz has resource again to the responsum of R. Israel Isserlein with which he started. After summarizing the views of earlier authorities on both sides of the issue, Isserlein continued:

> We have explained the opinions of the illustrious authorities (*ha-geonim*) whose words are available to me in books. Now I will explain the views of the great scholars (*ha-gedolim*) in our days.[160]

These "great scholars" are cited anonymously. Isserlein tells us the source of his information regarding the first of them: "One of them

---

157 Radbaz does not raise this difficulty explicitly, but he responds to it. Expanding on "a rule accepted by most of the authorities we follow, that two (witnesses) against two (witnesses) is (considered) an uncertainty in a law of rabbinic origin," he asserts that the very principle that uncertainties in laws of Torah origin are to be resolved stringently is itself of Rabbinic origin, and given a multiplicity of uncertainties (see below), one should rule leniently. "Two against two" refers to disputed facts, not to disputed law, and the equation of the two types of uncertainty is discussed below. For the definition of "two against two" as a *safeq* of rabbinic origin, see Tosafot to Ketubbot 26b, s.v. *anan ahtinan*. I thank Rabbi Dov Linzer for this reference.

158 *MT*, Women, Laws of Levirate Marriage, chap. 1. parag. 6.

159 This is the subject of Chapter 7.

160 Literally: "who were in our days" – *she-hayu be-yameinu*.

responded to one of the great rabbis (*ravevata*), and a copy was sent to me." The text quoted by Isserlein indicates that the author held the lenient opinion, that a levir who was already an apostate at the time of the marriage does not bind his sister-in-law. In that context, the anonymous writer refers to the passage of Maimonides above, which would appear to contradict his conclusion. He cites "one of the great scholars mentioned above" (an apparent reference to part of the responsum not quoted by Isserlein),[161] who interpreted Maimonides' wording, that a levir who is "an idol worshipper ... binds his (i.e., the deceased's) wife with a levirate bond," as referring to someone who became an idol worshipper only after his brother got married. Radbaz seizes on this late, anonymous, and far-fetched[162] interpretation. Pitting it against the reading of the classic and authoritative *Maggid Mishneh*, who indeed appears to reflect the plain sense of Maimonides' wording, Radbaz frames the issue as an unresolved dispute in the interpretation of Maimonides, which would render the correct interpretation a "matter of uncertainty," a *safeq*.

Radbaz has thus constructed a series of sefeqot: You say that the law is stringent because of A, but A is in dispute, and perhaps the law is really not like A; even if the law is like A, a stringent ruling would also require B, which is also in dispute, and perhaps the law is not like B; and if it is like B, then so with regard to C, which is also in dispute, etc. This successive weakening of probability, built on a sequence of uncertainties, is referred to as a *sefeq sefeqa*, a "double doubt" (literally: "a doubt of a doubt").[163] *Sefeq sefeqa* is known from the Talmud as a factor that would lead to a lenient ruling in cases of uncertainty with regard to ritual matters, even in the instance of a law of Torah origin.

But the instances in the Talmud all dealt with uncertainties of fact. By the sixteenth century, we find the concept applied to uncertainties of

161 Alternatively, perhaps this is Isserlein speaking, citing another one of "the great scholars of our days." But Isserlein concludes, "These are his words and his reasons." It seems most likely that he is indicating the end of the original responsum.

162 It cannot be believed that Maimonides was unaware of this view. If he goes out of his way to include "idol worshiper," the only plausible interpretation is that of *Maggid Mishneh*, that it is a deliberate rebuttal of that view.

163 *Sefeq sefeqa* is the subject of Chapter 9 in Morell, *Precedent and Judicial Discretion*. See there for references to what follows here, and for further detail.

law. This extension betrays a view that earlier disputes are fundamentally unresolvable, because we, in our declined generation, lack the capacity to decide the disputes of our great forbears. This mentality appears to be the product of Ashkenazic (i.e., Central European) Jewry in the fifteenth century, but the legal methodology that it produced had a deep effect on many of the Sephardic rabbis of the sixteenth century.[164] The application of *sefeq sefeqa* to uncertainties of law is not rare among these authorities.[165]

Radbaz, however, was not among those who generally equated uncertainties of law with uncertainties of fact. He expresses himself explicitly on this subject in another responsum:

> We apply the rule, "An uncertainty regarding a law of rabbinic origin is resolved leniently," only in a case in which the uncertainty came into being on its own, that is, we do not know how the fact took place.... But when the uncertainty comes about as a result of our lack of knowledge, that is, we do not know how to decide the law, we do not (necessarily) rule leniently.... (He explains that this is unlike disputes in the Talmud which are explicitly left unresolved, with the notation *tequ*—"let it stand." These are treated as if they were uncertainties of fact. —SM) However, in all other matters in which the Talmud ruled, but where a dispute arose among the authorities and we do not know which of them is in accordance with the intention of the Talmud's authors, we do not (necessarily) rule leniently.[166]

It is clear, therefore, that the arguments produced by Radbaz were not the motivating factor in his decision to allow the woman to remarry. He admits as much, and is forthcoming with regard to his true motivation, at the end of the responsum. He refers to the present situation being a "time of emergency" (*she'at ha-dehaq*), and refers to a statement in the Talmud that the author of a rejected opinion is of sufficient authority to be relied upon in a time of emergency.[167] His statement is worth being quoted in its entirety:

> Furthermore, all the illustrious authorities of the world, early ones and late ones, are of sufficient authority to be relied upon in a time of emergency. And there is no greater time of emergency than this, because memory of the apostate has been

164 For a discussion of this and its legal implications see *Precedent and Judicial Discretion*, chapters 2, 8, and 9.

165 See ibid., Chapter 9.

166 III, 485 (= 923).

167 BT Berakhot 9a.

> lost, his location is unknown and his name has been wiped out. I suggest[168] that even those who forbid (her to remarry) did not forbid it except when the apostate was before us, and *h̲alitsa* was viable, and it was possible to appease him monetarily, or to trick him (i.e., by offering him payment and then refusing it after the fact—SM),[169] for a tricked *h̲alitsa* is valid. But in the case at hand, where the apostate's location is unknown, nor (is it known) whether he is dead or alive—in such a case they did not say (that the *yevama* is bound to him). Moreover, this is not a matter of the stringent status of a married woman, but of the (simple) prohibition of a *yevama* to marry anyone other than the levir. Moreover, this is a case of the "anchoring" (*'igguna*) of a woman, and in a number of things they (i.e., the rabbis of the Talmud—SM) were lenient because of *'igguna.* Even though we should not be lenient with regard to *'igguna* except with what they stated, nevertheless there is an indication of intention that they were sensitive with regard to the *'igguna* of a woman. We too should be sensitive to (the use of) makeweight arguments, as in the case at hand.

Radbaz is aware of the weakness of the technical arguments he marshaled for his cause. "Makeweight arguments" (Hebrew, here and elsewhere with Radbaz: *tsenifin*; usually, and occasionally with Radbaz: *senifin*) are admittedly weak arguments which are pressed into service in order to strengthen a case. They are employed when there is a strong motivation to arrive at a specific conclusion.[170] Here, Radbaz explicitly describes his motivation as sensitivity to the plight of the woman. He relates it by analogy to the leniencies built into the law with regard to the classic *'aguna,* which he understands likewise as intended to ease the plight of the woman. By way of contrast, it may be pointed out that Maimonides understood the leniency of the Talmud's law regarding the release of *'agunot* as restricted to the source of the evidence, and explained it as a result of the fact that the witnesses are presumed to be telling the truth since, if the husband were alive, the truth would sooner or later emerge.[171] This is the polar opposite of Radbaz's approach to the issue. The responsum dramatically bears out the contention that Radbaz's exceptionally lenient attitude to *'agunot*

168 *qarov ani lomar*, literally: I am close to saying.
169 See BT Yevamot 106a.
170 See *Precedent and Judicial Discretion*, Chapter 7.
171 *MT*, Women, Laws of Divorce, chap. 13, parag. 29.

derives from an underlying sensitivity to the practical effects of his legal decisions.[172]

[25] In another situation also Radbaz stretches the limits of plausibility in order to release a woman from a levirate bond which would force her to remain an *'aguna.*

The Mishnah states:

> One who said at the time of his death: "I have sons"—he is trustworthy (to free his wife from the levirate bond—SM); "I have brothers"—he is not trustworthy.[173]

The Talmud understands this to refer to a situation in which there was no prior common knowledge of these facts prior to the husband's remarks. Accordingly, a man is not empowered to bind his wife to a levir, merely on the basis of his own declaration, unsupported by prior common knowledge.

Two of Radbaz's responsa deal with a case in which the husband was the sole source of information that he had brothers. In one of them, the husband had told people prior to the marriage that he had brothers in another land.[174] In the other, he had conveyed similar information during the course of the marriage.[175]

Radbaz rationalizes the Mishnah's second clause as follows:

> The husband is not trustworthy to say: "I have brothers," because (of the fear) lest he intends to bind her.[176]

That is to say, his claim that he has brothers might be a matter of spite. This implies that the husband's untrustworthiness applies only after his marriage. Surely, there is no reason to be concerned about spite toward

---

172 I, 175 is a very similar responsum: "About Reuben, who was married to two wives, and who had an apostate brother. One of his wives apostatized, and married a non-Jew. Reuben died without children. Does his wife require a *halitsa* from his apostate brother, or not?" Radbaz cites *Terumat ha-Deshen*, no. 119, where Isserlein ruled that she does. As he does here, Radbaz builds his case for leniency on the compound strength of two halakhic issues which are subject to dispute, one of them being whether an apostate levir binds his sister-in-law. The other issue, however, is one in which the lenient position is more mainstream, and that is the main force behind Radbaz's argument. That is the question of whether a straying wife (*sota*) frees her rival from the levirate bond.

173 Mishnah Qiddushin 3:8; BT Qiddushin 64a.

174 VI, 2087.

175 VI, 2234.

176 VI, 2234.

a wife he does not yet have! Radbaz tells us that indeed such an interpretation of the law was current:

> There was such an incident in Egypt,[177] and there was a rabbi there who wanted to say this.[178]

But Radbaz rejects this apparently logical conclusion. He continues as follows:

> I was asked about this, and I wrote that since we have not seen that the authorities differed (explicitly) on this point, we should not create a distinction on the basis of our own sense of logic with the result of rendering the woman an *'aguna.* Perhaps his intention was to marry a woman, and he precedes his doing so by saying that he has brothers—in order to bind her.

Here is Radbaz's explanation of the interpretation he relies upon in order to avoid an apparently compelling, but undesirable, conclusion. The husband, prior to his marriage, had decided to spite his future wife by making her an *'aguna*, binding her to a brother who (as Radbaz presumes) doesn't exist. This unbelievable scenario is repeated in the parallel responsum. He draws a distinction there between the husband's conveying the information "at the time of his death," as the Mishnah states it, on the one hand, and his doing so "prior to his marriage," on the other. The period during the marriage is apparently subsumed under the former category. He writes:

> You may say: How can one compare the time of death, in which case (it can be said) that he intends to bind (her), and for this reason is not trustworthy, to (the period) prior to the marriage, in which case (it is presumed) that he does not intend to bind (any future wife)?
>
> This is not a difficulty. There too, one can say that his intention was to marry a woman; and, if death should occur to him, that she should be bound to his brother, that "his name not be blotted out in Israel."[179]

The closing quotation is from Deuteronomy 25:6, from the passage which is the source for the law of levirate marriage. But it makes no

---

177 *mitsrayim*, which may also be understood as Cairo.

178 VI, 2234. The reference might be to VI, 2087, where the husband's statement occurred before he was married. Radbaz argues there too against the apparently logical stringent conclusion. But his description here of what he said in that earlier case (see immediately below) does not accord exactly with VI, 2087. In VI, 2234, he continues: "I have dealt at length with this in another responsum," and this too does not seem to refer to VI, 2087, where he does not deal with the issue "at length."

179 VI, 2087.

sense here, because Radbaz asserts that as far as the law is concerned, the presumption is that in fact he has no brothers.[180] It may have entered here unthinkingly, under the influence of the verse. The only feasible explanation for the husband's action in falsely binding his wife with an unresolvable levirate bond is spite.

We have seen throughout the realism exhibited by Radbaz in his approach to legal rulings. His willingness in this instance to act on the basis of a totally unrealistic presumption can be understood as resulting from a deep sensitivity to the plight of the woman affected by his ruling.

[26] These examples of Radbaz's lenient stand with regard to all types of "anchored women," and not merely the classic *'aguna* of the Talmud, indicate, as I suggested, that Radbaz's leniency derives from an underlying sensitivity to the personal effects of his legal decisions, rather than to his understanding of the textual sources of the law. In the following example, this conclusion is supported not so much by the ruling itself, which can be justified by purely conventional decision-making methodology, but by the rhetoric that Radbaz employs.

A vaginal flow of blood can render a woman unclean, and forbidden sexually to her husband. The rules are complex, and there are many circumstances that affect the woman's status. The Talmud discusses the situation of a woman who repeatedly experiences spotting as a result of sexual intercourse:

> The Rabbis taught: A woman who sees blood as a result of sexual intercourse may have intercourse once, twice, and three times. From then on she may not have intercourse until she is divorced and marries another.... (The same is repeated for the second husband.) If she marries another (i.e., a third), and she sees blood as a result of sexual intercourse, she may have intercourse once, twice, and three times. From then on, she may not have intercourse until she checks herself (to be sure that there is no blood before the intercourse—SM).

The words regarding the first (and second) husband, "From then on she may not have intercourse until she is divorced and marries another," was understood by Maimonides in its apparently plain sense, that intercourse with her present husband is not an option. The implication is that she cannot remain married to him. Maimonides

180 Ed. Warsaw of Radbaz's responsa has a note to VI, 2234, referring to VI, 2087, with the comment that the latter needs clarification (*ve-tsarikh 'iyyun*). The annotator may be referring to this difficulty.

wrote: "If she saw blood this way the third time, she is forbidden to have intercourse with this husband forever."[181] There is a substantial body of opinion, however, which interprets the statement in the Talmud to mean: "She may not have intercourse with him *without first checking herself* until she is divorced and marries another," but she may continue to have intercourse with her first or second husband if she checks herself beforehand each time, as the passage itself indicates with regard to the third husband.[182] Radbaz's responsum is an instance of this situation, and Radbaz has no difficulty in ruling with those many authorities who rule leniently.

The responsum begins with the question:

> You asked my opinion regarding a woman who saw blood as a result of intercourse, and thus a second time and a third time. Does she have a (halakhic) remedy or not? For it is difficult for them to divorce, since they have children, and they love each other.[183]

This phraseology immediately focuses our attention on the tragic personal aspect of the situation. The concisely worded questions that introduce responsa in general, and Radbaz's responsa in particular, are the result of editing by the authors of the responsa. The original questions were no doubt much lengthier, and contained much material that the author of the responsum considered irrelevant.[184] It is likely, therefore, that this is Radbaz's own wording, or at least an emphasis that he deliberately chose to stress.

This probability is strengthened by the introductory remarks of Radbaz's answer to the question. He begins: "Indeed, divorce is hard for a person." He cites proofs that the Talmud recognized the tragedy of divorce, and that the law of the Talmud took it into account. He adds to these Talmudic prooftexts what appears to be his own personal reason for avoiding divorce if at all possible:

> Furthermore, if he divorces her and marries another, his mind will always be on his (first) wife. And she too will marry another, and her mind will always be on her first husband.... For these reasons, we must seek out ways of leniency so that she remain with her husband.

---

181 *MT*, Holiness, Laws of Forbidden Intercourse, chap. 4, parag. 20.

182 See Tosafot to Niddah 66a, s.v. *ve-tivdoq*, and *Maggid Mishneh* ad loc., s.v. *ketsad bodeqet 'atsmah*.

183 I, 410.

184 See n. 79 above, and especially Chap. 2, n. 45, where a crucial fact is omitted in the wording of the question, and appears later in the responsum.

The phrase, "seek out ways of leniency," is telling. As we have seen, Radbaz uses it primarily in connection with the classic *'aguna*. Its extension to this case, where the rhetoric is so clearly focused on the element of personal tragedy affecting the principals, betrays Radbaz's personal sensitivity to that element in the case of the classic *'aguna* as well.

(g) *Trial Judge and Rabbinic Authority*

[27] Consider the following responsum, another example of tailoring the application of the law to the specific conditions of the principals.

The question concerns the procedure for the collection of a note which has become due, and for which the debtor has no funds readily available. Does the court allow the debtor thirty days beyond the due date to raise the funds, or does it proceed immediately to a collection of the debt from the debtor's assets?[185] Radbaz cites three opinions on this issue. One is not to allow any time beyond the due date. A second is to allow a thirty-day extension for the sale of assets, either real estate or movables. The third is to allow thirty days for the sale of real estate only, if no movables are available. This last view is the opinion of Maimonides and Alfasi. It is the intermediate view, the one which "balances" between the extremes. And, declares Radbaz, "the law is like the one who balances (between the extremes)."[186]

So much for the letter of the law. But Radbaz continues:

> It is my practice to compromise between these opinions. When I know that he has funds, I do not allow him any time at all. But if he has movables and he has to sell them, then I allow him an extension of three days to seek to do so, so that he will not have to sell his movables for less (than their value).... And

---

185 I, 21.

186 *halakha ke-divrei ha-makhria'*. Radbaz's source for this array of opinions is *Maggid Mishneh* to *MT*, Civil Laws, Laws of Creditor and Debtor, chap. 22, parag. 1, though there is no attribution. He earlier cites Rabbenu Nissim, who represented the opinions of Alfasi and Maimonides differently. The phrase *halakha ke-divrei ha-makhria'* is also taken from *Maggid Mishneh*. Its source in this sense is Shabbat 39b. Radbaz's own predilection for choosing the intermediate position is explored below, Chap. 6.

when he has to sell real estate, because he has neither funds nor movables, then I allow him an extension of thirty days.

Radbaz appears here in two different roles. One role is that of a *meshiv*, that is, an author of a responsum, a rabbinic authority. The other is that of a judge, who stands before the litigants and decides their case. The judge and the *meshiv* are representative of two different jurisdictions in Jewish law.[187] The *meshiv*, to whom the question is sent by the judges who seek his input, knows only what he has been told, and his answers are always given on the provision that those are indeed the facts of the case. His reasoned answers are based on the authoritative textual sources of Jewish law. The judge, however, faces the litigants directly. He cross-examines them, responds to their non-verbal language, investigates the full range of circumstances, and forms his own impression of the truth. His subsequent ruling, which he is not even under any obligation to justify to the litigants,[188] is informed by his perception of the truth, "in accordance with the way it appears to the judge."[189]

In the responsum under discussion, Radbaz is careful to keep his two roles separate. First he speaks to us as a *meshiv*, then he changes hats and speaks to us as a judge. As a *meshiv*, Radbaz speaks to the letter of the law. He decides that the law is represented by the intermediate position, namely, that only when real estate must be sold should the debtor be allowed an extension, and that it should be for thirty days. As a judge, however, when he himself stands before the litigants, he reserves the right to ignore the letter of the law, and to render justice as it appears to his eyes, in accordance with the facts as he understands them. Another example of a *meshiv's* deference to a judge's flexibility can be found in a responsum by Alfasi himself on this very issue, as paraphrased in the *Turim*:

---

187 See Shochetman, "Reasons for Legal Decisions," where he deals on 339–45 with the distinction between court sentences and rabbinic responsa.

188 See Shochetman, "Reasons for Legal Decisions," for an exhaustive treatment of this issue.

189 There are a number of instances in Radbaz's responsa in which he takes an active role in the proceedings, examining litigants, witnesses and documents himself, at one point tearing up a suspect document. He is acting thereby as a judge, even though he is clearly writing a responsum. This appears not to be in accord with the distinction Shochetman has drawn between the two functions of *meshiv* and judge. See I, 443; I, 471; III, 551 (= 981); IV, 204 (= 1275).

> Rabbi Alfas wrote in a responsum, that the extension is in accordance with the way it appears to the judge. If it appears to him that thirty days will not suffice for him, he may add to it. Or, if it appears to him that he does not need so much time, he may lessen it.[190]

The implication of Alfasi's responsum, and of all such references to the jurisdiction of the courts in the responsa literature, is that the codified law *is* that the judge should make his decision "in accordance with the way it appears" to him. What is interesting about Radbaz's responsum in this case is the allusion to himself in the other role, the role of a judge, and his highlighting of the discrepancy between the two jurisdictions which results from this juxtaposition. The rulings that he customarily applies in the capacity of trial judge are substantively different from the ruling which, as he himself has argued, is required by the codified law.

In Radbaz's responsa, he often relegates the disposition of the case to the local court, "as it appears in the eyes of the judge." He does this after he has analyzed the codified law, and arrived at his conclusions accordingly. In the responsum above, he gave us the two versions of the law *seriatum*. First, as a *meshiv*, he told us what the law is according to the codified law; then, he told us what he himself does as a judge. But when, as part of his responsum, Radbaz specifically relegates the ruling in the case to the judgment of the local judge (which he did not do explicitly in this responsum), he is telling us that such a relegation is itself the codified law. When this follows his own analysis of the codified law, and his resulting conclusions, the implication is that there are two versions of the codified law itself. One is the law in the abstract (*le-halakha*); the other is the law in its practical application (*le-ma'aseh*). In view of the fact that the local judge responds directly to his personal perception of the realities before him, Radbaz's recognition of that response as part of the codified law is another aspect of his integration of the "real world," in theory and not only in practice, into his conception of Jewish law.

[28] Radbaz gives explicit expression to this concept. For instance, one example involves a charge by "Reuben" that "Simeon" collected illegal interest from him and demands its return. Simeon insists that the transaction was done in a legal manner. The question was whether Simeon, the defendant, must be made to take an oath that his account of

---

190 *Tur Hoshen Mishpat*, no. 100.

the events is true. In some situations such an oath is demanded of a defendant, even though the plaintiff lacks proof of his claim. The questioner knows that there is a controversy among the authorities on this matter, and wants to know how the law is decided. Radbaz analyzes the issues, and decides in favor of the position that no oath is required. But he adds a proviso:

> Therefore, in the case at hand, my opinion is that he should not be made to take an oath, because of the reasons that we have written, except if the judge happens to know that it was illegal interest. For a judge rules on the basis of what he knows in truth, and not on the basis of the arguments. This is something that is in agreement with reason and intelligence.[191]

[29] Another responsum, one emanating from Rhodes, involves the same legal issue. "Reuben" asserted that a note of indebtedness to his sister, "Leah," included in its sum an element of illegal interest. As the events unfolded, Leah was abetted by her son-in-law, "Jacob," who withheld his own debt to Leah's brother, as a means of exerting pressure on him to give up the case. Radbaz reviews the same sources as in the responsum discussed above, weighing the alternative positions. Because of the specifics of the case, he tends toward interpreting the law so that it would require an oath of Leah. But he does not let the matter rest on his own interpretation of the law. He ends:

> I have written all this for the purpose of (clarifying) the law in the abstract (*le-halakha*). But for the purpose of the law in its practical application (*le-ma'aseh*), in the case at hand it is my opinion that she be made to take an oath in any case (i.e., even if one rejects my legal argument—SM). For there are grounds, convincing circumstantial reasons,[192] to believe that she did in fact take interest from him, and that there was a conspiracy of the wicked between her and her son-in-law, Jacob. And a judge must rule on the basis of what he sees and knows in truth, even though it is not in accordance with the law.[193]

---

191 IV, 297 (= 1369). Radbaz refers to the responsa of R. Joseph Colon, see there, *Shoresh* 118, Answer to Question 5 (ed. Deutsch and Schlesinger, 240); *Shoresh* 14, end.

192 *raglayim la-davar ve-umdena de-mokhah̲*

193 III, 485 (= 923).

[30] Similar phrasing, that a judge may act "not in accordance with the law" in response to what he understands to be the truth, appears in another responsum involving what amounts to the imposition of an oath.[194] The defendant, "Simeon," had produced a document that would substantiate his claim, but there is strong reason to suspect that the document is forged. The judge sought to compel anyone with information about the suspect document, including the defendant himself, to appear in court and testify. The instrument he used is called a *herem setam*, that is, an unspecified ban of excommunication (*herem*) on anyone who has information and does not come forward in court. A *herem* was believed to carry the sanction of divine punishment, and its violation was equated with violation of an oath. But Simeon was an interested party, and advanced the argument that as such he could not be forced to testify under threat of *herem*. Radbaz shows that there is a dispute among authorities on this point, and, after analysis, rejects Simeon's plea of immunity. He then asserts that in the present instance, even the authority who rejected the imposition of such a *herem* on an interested party would agree with this ruling:

> In the case at hand, where it is clearly apparent that the argument is suspect of being fraudulent (*din merummeh*), the judge has the right to do things which are against the law in order to render a true verdict (*le-hotsi ha-din le-amito*).

This concept, that the judge's perception of the truth takes precedence over the rules of evidence and procedure as they appear in the codified law, is not original with Radbaz. It had already been codified by Maimonides:

> 1. In matters of civil law, a judge should rule on the basis of what he is convinced is true, and what is firmly established in his mind as being so, even though there is no firm evidence.... (He cites several examples in which judicial discretion would be allowed in the rules of evidence and procedure).
>
> For the matter is entrusted exclusively to the mind of the judge, that he rule on the basis of what appears to him to be a true verdict.... (Witnesses are needed for situations in which the judge himself is uncertain.)
>
> 2. All these things are the essence of the law. But when improper courts multiplied, and even those that were proper in their deeds were not (led by judges) who were sufficiently learned and intelligent, most of the courts of Israel agreed to not reverse the obligation of an oath... (referring back to the specific examples of judicial discretion cited above).

---

194 VI, 2228.

> Nevertheless, if a trustworthy person testified regarding one of these matters (which, since he is only one witness, is unacceptable as evidence—SM), and the judge is convinced that he tells the truth, the judge should wait with the verdict, and not reject his testimony. He should discuss the matter with the litigants until they admit to the testimony of the witness, or arrive at a compromise. Otherwise, he should withdraw from the case.[195]

There is a significant difference between Maimonides and Radbaz. According to Maimonides, the broad scope of judicial discretion, as laid out in Paragraph 1, exists only in theory. In practice, as he tells us in Paragraph 2, judges today are bound by the rules of evidence and procedure. The only option a judge ultimately has is a passive one. He can refuse to rule on the basis of evidence he does not believe, and withdraw from the case. He cannot continue with the case and rule otherwise than the codified law. Radbaz, however, does not hesitate to apply the principle of broad judicial discretion in practice.[196]

[31] The examples cited above, of a judge's broad discretion to bypass the codified law and rule on the basis of his personal conviction of the truth, involve the imposition of oaths and the right of subpoena, matters of court procedure. It is not surprising to discover that matters of court procedure occupy an important place among the kinds of issues that Radbaz submits to the judge's discretion. In one case, for instance, Radbaz allows the hearing of testimony in the absence of the defendant, a practice that is not permitted by the codified law, because the witnesses are intimidated by him.[197] These instances differ from those already cited only by the lack of an explicit acknowledgment that the judge is within his rights even though "it is not in accordance with the law." I will cite one more example of this with regard to court procedure.

The Mishnah rules that if a debt is to be collected on the strength of a note by the creditor's children after his death, they must first take an

---

195 *MT*, Judges, Laws of the Sanhedrin, chap. 24, parags. 1–2.

196 I am not making any claim about Radbaz's uniqueness in this regard, which requires further study. Radbaz himself cites R. Joseph Colon who expressed this idea in the context of a practical ruling, see n. 190 above. See, for the time being, also R. Levi ibn Habib, *Responsa*, no. 25: "It is a simple and completely accepted (*pashut u-mushlam*) matter among all of them (i.e., the rabbinic authorities), that the judge must rule according to what he knows of the truth, and not according to the arguments."

197 VI, 2327.

oath "that Father did not leave us instructions, nor did he tell us, nor did we find anything among Father's papers, to the effect that this note is paid."[198] This oath is referred to as the "heirs' oath." The question before Radbaz presents a reverse situation, in which the heirs are the debtors. "Reuben" claims a sum of money from the heirs, which he asserts was loaned to their father without a note. Are the heirs bound to take the heirs' oath in order to defend themselves against Reuben's unsubstantiated claim?[199] No, says Radbaz. The heirs' oath is a requirement of the Rabbis, not of the Torah, and therefore is not extended beyond its original compass.[200] If Reuben cannot prove his case independently, he has no claim on the money. Having ruled on the law, he then proceeds:

> In any case, if the court sees that Reuben's claim has a basis and a plausible reason (*tsad ve-amatla*) to it, they have the authority in their power to make the orphans take an oath—as long as their intention is to render a true verdict (*le-hotsi ha-din le-amito*), to rescue the robbed from the one who would rob him.

In theory, the burden of proof is on the plaintiff, and the judges may not impose the heirs' oath on the defendant as a requirement for dismissing the plaintiff's unsubstantiated claim. But in practice they may do as they see fit, as long as they feel that it is necessary to establish the truth.[201]

[32] I have been dealing until now with rules of evidence and procedure. But there are more radical examples of broad judicial discretion, which relate directly to the judge's disposition of the case.

"Reuben" took a substantial sum of money from "Yokheved," and in return agreed to support her and her daughter throughout Yokheved's life.[202] Since the cost of the support over time was likely to exceed the original sum, the transaction was in effect a form of interest, which is forbidden. However, interest of this type, which is not formally in the form of a loan, is forbidden only by the authority of the Rabbis, not by the authority of the Torah. The law in such a case is that

---

198 Mishnah Shevu'ot 7:7.

199 VI, 2303.

200 Compare I, 455, where, in a similar question, Radbaz explicitly rules the opposite way.

201 For other examples involving court procedure, see IV, 230 (= 1301); VI, 2327.

202 VI, 2245.

once paid, it cannot be recovered in court, unlike the direct interest forbidden by the Torah, which is recoverable.

Reuben, meanwhile, was true to his word. He supported Yokheved and her daughter, though because of difficult circumstances he never saw a profit on the money he took from her. When Yokheved died, the court, acting as guardian of the daughter, sought to reclaim the total sum of the principal from Reuben, and refused to recognize Reuben's claim that all during the intervening years he supported Yokheved and her daughter out of his own pocket.

Radbaz rules in favor of Reuben. Though the original transaction was illegal, it was a type of interest that is not forbidden by the law of the Torah, only by the law of the Rabbis, and is therefore not recoverable in court. Refusal to deduct the money Reuben spent out of pocket from the principal that is to be returned to Yokheved's heir amounts to recovery in court. Radbaz then concludes:

> So it is with regard to the law. But if it appears to the judge that Reuben is a deceiver, and he is able to compel him to do what is right and good, he has the authority (to do so) in his power. There are several precedent cases (*ma'asim*) in the Talmud which indicate this.

Radbaz does not indicate what those precedents are. But in any case, he grants the right to the judge, on the basis of what "appears" to him to be the truth, to compel Reuben to return the entire principal, though it is "against the law," because it would be "in order to render a true verdict."

[33] Another example concerns a man who was impoverished and did not support his wife.[203] We learn from the question that "Reuben married this woman, and hated her, because she had a blemish in her eyes." Consequently, they have been living separately, with their respective parents. On the basis of the husband's refusal to live with his wife, and his refusal to support her, the woman's family seeks to label him a "rebellious husband," a sanctionable offense. Reuben, for his part, claims to be willing to divorce her, but cannot afford the *ketubba*, that is, the financial settlement which divorce would entail, and wishes it waived. The wife's family refuses divorce under these conditions, and insists that he be compelled to hire himself out to an employer, in order to earn money with which to support her. This he refuses to do.

---

203 III, 566 (=996).

Radbaz rules that the husband should divorce his wife without a waiver, and since he cannot pay the *ketubba*, it shall remain a debt for the future, payable if and when that becomes possible. He explains that the husband cannot be labeled "a rebellious husband," since he professes a willingness to divorce her. Further, Radbaz shows from conventional sources of Jewish law that the husband cannot be forced to work against his will.

On this latter issue, Radbaz, after arguing his point from the sources, adds an original argument:

> And I say that there is a great reason for this, and he who differs with it bears the burden of proof. For the verse says: "For it is to Me that the Israelites are servants" (Lev. 25:55)—and not servants to servants!

The midrashic comment on the verse derives from the Talmud, where it is used in two contexts. One of them is to denigrate a Hebrew slave (in Hebrew the same word as that which is translated here "servant"), who refuses the freedom which is due him after seven years of servitude, as described in Exodus 21:2-6.[204] Radbaz goes on to compare the case at hand to a Hebrew slave:

> Assume that he is nothing more than one who is sold as a Hebrew slave. Can his master compel him to hire himself out to others, and to bring (his salary) to his master? Rather, he (the slave) can say to him: "If you have work, I will do it." But to do the work of others, he cannot compel him! How much more so here.

The other context in which this midrash is used in the Talmud is to provide a prooftext for a day laborer's right to quit his work, even in the middle of the day. Without that right he would be a slave, and Jews are not "slaves to slaves."[205] Radbaz has thus gone beyond his sources, and provided an original, ideologically based argument for the position that the husband in our responsum can in no way be compelled by the court to hire himself out against his will.

It comes as some surprise, therefore, when in his closing remark he leaves the disposition of the whole matter to the discretion of the judge:

> If it appears to the judge that he does not want to earn money and hire himself out in order to feed his wife because his intention is to divorce her and put her out without a settlement, then he (the judge) has the ability to penalize him and to compel him to hire himself out in order to earn money to feed her. Everything is according to the kind of person he is—

204 Qiddushin 22b.
205 Bava Metsi'a 10a.

> whether he is upright, and walks in he way of the blameless, or a deceiver, and walks in the way of the wicked. As long as the intention of the judge is for the sake of Heaven, and to build a fence and protective hedge for the (sake of the) Torah and the words of the Rabbis.

The dissonance between the codified law, the law in theory, and the law of the court, the law in practice, stands in bold relief here because of the juxtaposition of Radbaz's passionately argued, principled stand in favor of the former, and his forthright legitimation of the latter.

[34] These features, a deliberate and impassioned arguing for a specific resolution of the codified law, on the one hand, and its practical nullification on the level of implementation by the retreat to broad judicial discretion, on the other, is in evidence even more starkly in another responsum. The question reads:

> You asked my opinion regarding those outlaws who commit transgressions with arrogance and scorn, and when one tries to chastise them, they threaten to apostatize. Should we chastise them and not be concerned, or not?[206]

Radbaz begins the responsum by laying bare his deep angst regarding this issue, thereby involving himself on a personal, subjective level in its resolution:

> All my life I have felt sorrow over this.... I pray every day about this, that I should not be the cause of a misfortune.

He considers a policy of refraining both from chastising them and from abetting them in any way. But he rejects this passive compliance with a battery of arguments:

> This (passive compliance) is certainly not correct. For we are all responsible for each other, and the verse says: "And if the people of the land shall shut their eyes [to that man when he gives of his offspring to Molech... I Myself shall set My face against that man and his kin]."[207]
>
> Furthermore, if we were to be concerned about this, the Torah would be nullified entirely. For it would become widely known that because of this concern we shut our eyes from the wicked ones, the sons of evil. People will continue to sin, and robbery, violence, adultery and the like will increase. The Torah will not exist except among remnants. So we find in every generation, that they chastise the wicked, and are not concerned with this fear.

---

206 I, 187.

207 Leviticus, 20:4. "We are all responsible for each other," see Sanhedrin 27b.

> Furthermore, just as we adopt the rule that we do not pass over (the performance of) religious acts (but perform whatever act chances to come first—SM), and don't examine them as to which is lighter and which is weightier, so we don't pass over transgressions, even though this one is lighter and the other one weightier.[208] Since it is our obligation to chastise one for this transgression that we have encountered, we don't pass over it.
>
> Furthermore, since one has expressed it in words, the end will be that he will put it in action. So have we seen a number of times, that even though we do not chastise him, he goes and sins (i.e., apostatizes—SM) for no cause.
>
> Therefore, it is proper to do that with which we are charged. If he leaves (the fold), let him leave. We will be relieved of our responsibility for him, for we are not responsible for apostates.

We have here a string of arguments, based on principle and expressed with passion. It is clear from Radbaz's opening statement that they emerge from his very soul. Moreover, some of these arguments are founded on practical considerations. Failure to chastise will invite widespread dereliction; a threat to apostatize may very well become fulfilled regardless of what we do, so we need not be concerned about preventing it through forgoing our duty. Given all this, it is particularly significant to note that this, too, is set aside in the end and relegated to broad judicial discretion:

> Even though I wrote all this for the sake of the law in the abstract (*le-halakha*), nevertheless, the leader of the generation should be deliberate with these matters. Because not all people are alike, and not all transgressions are alike. How so? In the case of a person who is habitual in transgression, and sure in himself and his cause, one should not be concerned about him. Come what may, we should establish the (rule of) Torah. But in the case of one who is not habitual (in transgression), and it is probable that he will heed us, we should draw him with words until he repents little by little, and we should not rush to punish him because of (the possibility of) misfortune. And so (should we deal with him) in all similar ways. Everything is in accordance with the way it appears to the judge, the leader (of the generation), as long as all his actions are for the sake of Heaven.

Radbaz sets up two extremes here, the incorrigible, deliberate outlaw, and the weak sinner whose repentance is anticipated. But by the very nature of things, this is not the simple set of alternatives which

---

208 Radbaz's emphasis on the equality of all religious acts may be related to his Kabbalistic beliefs. See Helener, "Reincarnation," 22.

communal leaders faced in reality. Delinquents come in a wide variety, and from the question itself it is clear that we are dealing with those on the incorrigible end of the spectrum. Clearly, it is with regard to these that Radbaz backs down from his powerful stand on principle, and, in spite of it all, relegates the verdict in each case to the discretion of the communal leaders.

Radbaz's recognition that in theory, as well as in practice, "a judge rules on the basis of what he knows in truth, and not on the basis of the arguments," is another aspect of the important role he assigns to the "real world" in his conception of the law.

2. Popular Practice and Legal Interpretation

The realities which a rabbinical judge finds before him include popular religious and legal practices, which may not accord with the provisions of the codified law. There is a spectrum of attitudes which rabbis have taken toward this situation. These range from rejection coupled with an attempt to change common practice, to resignation, to acceptance, and harmonization with the codified law. Radbaz also faces a number of issues of this type, and in this chapter I will explore his stance toward them. Of particular interest are a number of cases, which reflect popular legal interpretation, or what a halakhist would call misinterpretation.

[35] In the responsum with which we have ended the preceding chapter, Radbaz wrestled with the problem posed by recalcitrant Jews who seek to deflect communal sanctions by a threat of apostasy. He drew a distinction between the law in the abstract (*le-halakha*), which was based on the codified law as Radbaz understood it, and the law in its practical application (*le-ma'aseh*), which is to be based on an *ad hoc* assessment of the individual case. The latter was necessitated by an appreciation of the gap between the nuanced realities of the situation and the purist presumptions of the codified law. A parallel to this situation, and to Radbaz's approach to it, can be found in his treatment of a problem deriving from the reality of popular practice. Here is the situation as it is posed in the question:

> You asked me about the practice in Egypt,[1] that women go to work in the home of a non-Jew, and remain there three or four days and nights. And sometimes there are wives of *kohanim* among them. Is there fear of a prohibition (in this practice) or not?[2]

In the body of the responsum we learn that these women are engaged in the embroidery of fabric, working together with male employees, and eking out a living on a subsistence level in a sweatshop environment.[3] The situation is problematic on two levels. One is the general lack of modesty inherent in married women working together with men, over a period of several consecutive days, under the authority and in the domain of a non-Jewish employer. This in itself is not so much a technical halakhic prohibition as it is a violation of the cultural norms of modesty.

The other level does involve a specific halakhic issue, and the mention in the question of *kohanim* speaks to that point. *Kohanim* (singular: *kohen*) are men of priestly lineage, in contrast to Israelites, that is, ordinary Jews. There are certain specific prohibitions in the area of personal law which apply only to *kohanim* and not to Israelites. The one, which concerns us here, prohibits a *kohen* from being married to a woman who has had sexual relations with a male whom she is not able to marry according to the law. A non-Jew fits into that category. It does not matter whether the sexual relations were consensual or not. For example, if a woman is taken captive by non-Jews, and if there is no one to vouch for her purity, there is a strong probability that she was raped. Consequently, she may not marry a *kohen*. A married woman, of course, cannot at the same time marry someone else, so sexual relations with any male will render her prohibited to her husband if he is a *kohen*, even if it was the result of rape.[4] In contrast, the wife of an Israelite is only forbidden to her husband if an adulterous relationship was consensual.

Radbaz's responsum begins with a strong reaction to the former aspect of the case, the cultural norms of modesty:

> There is great immodesty in this, to an immeasurable extent.

---

1 *mitsrayim*, perhaps to be translated: Cairo.

2 III, 481 (= 919).

3 On the omission of significant information in the question, see Chapter 1, n. 79.

4 *MT*, Holiness, Laws of Forbidden Intercourse, chap. 18, parags. 1, 2, 6, 7, 17.

He tells us that the problem was already recognized in the days of the *Negidim*, the pre-Ottoman leaders of Egyptian Jewry. The last of the *Negidim* was removed from office in 1517, shortly after the Ottoman conquest of Egypt, so that Radbaz takes us back to Mamluk Egypt:

> Enactments were already put in place by the *Negidim* with regard to this matter. Some of them (the women) desisted. But some of them weren't able to abide (by the ban on this type of employment), because they were poor, and their husbands were poor, and provided them with neither clothing nor covering in the cold, nor for their children. They had to seek their livelihood, and they went with their husbands' consent.
>
> What we were able to enact was that men and women should not sit at one table to engage in the work of embroidery, like it was originally, but the men by themselves and the women by themselves; and furthermore, that only women forty years of age and up should go.

Radbaz then proceeds to address the specifically halakhic aspect of the case. After easily removing any lingering doubt about the valid status of the wives of Israelites who are engaged in this employment,[5] he focuses on the real issue, the permissibility of the wives of *kohanim* to remain married to their husbands under these conditions. Radbaz shows that there are three schools of opinion regarding the wife of a *kohen* who has secluded herself with another man.[6] He produces a string of well-reasoned arguments, all of which lead to a lenient ruling. Thus he shows conclusively that the given situation is insufficient to disqualify the wife of a *kohen* from maintaining her marriage in good standing.[7]

---

5 After a series of proofs drawn from an analysis of the codified law, Radbaz adds three, which he characterizes as *senifin*, makeweight arguments. All three relate to the popular aspect of the situation, not to the codified law, and serve to remove the fear of a breach of morality: (a) both the men and the women are absorbed in their work; (b) the fact that the women are over forty will lessen the temptation, and lend greater weight to the fear of discovery; (c) the owners are fearful lest they undermine their ability to recruit skilled employees.

6 The middle position is that she is forbidden to her husband if she was secluded for an extended time, but not just for a brief period. This would include at least some of the women under discussion.

7 He arrives at a stringent ruling, however, in one scenario, where the sleeping arrangements are such that the women are put up in the employer's home, in quarters to which only the employer has access.

Having said all this, Radbaz switches gears, as he did in the previous responsum, from what the law tells us to do, to what we should actually do:

> All of this I have written according to the law in the abstract (*le-halakha*). But as for the law in its practical application (*le-ma'aseh*), my view is that everything should go according to the type of woman she is. If she is immodest, and is in the habit of secluding herself with non-Jews, the one giving the ruling should decide the law according to those who rule stringently, and prohibit her to her husband even if he is an Israelite. If she is modest, and not in the habit of doing this, but she (nevertheless) secluded herself (with a non-Jew) on one occasion for some reason, one should not prohibit her to her husband even if he is a *kohen*.

This is an *ad hoc* approach, "as it appears in the eyes of the judge," an approach oblivious to the codified law as Radbaz himself had so skillfully showed it to be. That is most apparent in the stringent side of this ruling, that if the judge deemed her immodest, he should "prohibit her to her husband even if he is an Israelite." This ruling is totally at odds with his earlier reasoned analysis, in which he hardly allowed such a position to be represented at all in the spectrum of opinions. On the level of the law in its practical application, it is the "real world" which wins out.

[36] The accommodation of *halakha* to economic practice is well documented throughout the entire history of Rabbinic law. I will cite two instances of this which give evidence of Radbaz's struggle of conscience in this regard.

In the first example, Radbaz builds a case to justify a common practice, though he admits that he himself does not accept it as valid. The practice was "to give a storekeeper a golden dinar, in order to take back from him copper *perutot* little by little."[8] The problem was that the exchange rate for the copper *perutot* was slightly inflated, so that the storekeeper ended up paying back more than the original value of the dinar. Since, as the questioner points out, this appears to be profit in exchange for advancing the gold dinar, the transaction would fit the definition of illegal interest.

Radbaz sets the record straight regarding his true opinion right from the start:

---

8 III, 452 (= 893). On the coinage in use in Egypt in Radbaz's time see Goldman, *Life and Times*, 149f.

> In my opinion this thing is forbidden, because the value of the gold dinar is known (so that its true value cannot be fudged to allow for the difference—SM).

However, he cannot allow the matter to rest there:

> But since many engage in this practice, and they have become used to it, it is necessary to find a basis for them.

Radbaz builds a case, which he clearly does not accept as legitimate. For instance, he argues that the gold dinar can fluctuate in value (thus contradicting his opening statement, that its value is known), and can therefore be considered a commodity rather than a currency. In this way the transaction can be viewed as a sale of the gold dinar rather than as a loan. In fact, in Case [4] above, he argued the opposite, that in contemporary Egypt, in an exchange of gold and copper, the copper must be seen as the commodity and the gold as the currency. Nevertheless, in spite of his reservations, Radbaz feels it necessary to supply a modicum of legitimacy to a prevailing practice, which he has no power to change.

In his closing remarks, Radbaz places his efforts in perspective:

> "Let Israel be; etc. (= better they be unwitting sinners than deliberate sinners)." This is certainly so in the matter at hand, where they have something on which to rely.

The connotation of the first sentence, a quotation from the Talmud,[9] is that there is no justification for what the people do. Silence on the part of the rabbinic leadership does not imply acquiescence, but rather futility. If there is any mitigation for their actions, it derives from their ignorance, which we, knowing our limitations, should take care to preserve. This stance is in contradiction to the attempt until this point to find some rationalization within the law for their behavior. Nevertheless, such a rationalization, flawed though it is, allows for the fiction that those who engage in this practice mistakenly believe their behavior to be within the law. In other words, Radbaz makes his peace with the reality of popular practice on the level of the law's practical application (*le-ma'aseh*), while maintaining his objection to it on the level of the law's theoretical requirements (*le-halakha*).

[37] The second example is similar, in that Radbaz suggests a legal solution to a problematic practice, while at the same time maintaining his reservations regarding it. In this case, though, the practice was a necessity of commercial life, so that Radbaz felt obligated to bow before the inevitable, and find a way to allow it, in theory as well as in

---

9 BT Betsa 30a.

practice. He takes pains, however, to let us know that he is not happy about it.

The issue is maritime insurance, discussed above in Case [17].[10] An entrepreneur would advance capital to a merchant. A note of indebtedness would be drawn up which exceeded the actual amount of the funds advanced. The merchant would use the funds to finance the purchase of wares and the outfitting of a ship. If the venture was successful, the entrepreneur would collect on his note. If the venture suffered a loss at sea, the debt would be cancelled. Thus the entrepreneur undertook the risk, and was rewarded for it by the profit on his loan.

But profit on a loan is interest, and interest is forbidden by the Torah. So various legal fictions were employed, which defined the transaction differently, as a sale or a partnership, rather than as a loan. Radbaz suggests a specific procedure for conducting the transaction, which would ensure the legal correctness of the fiction. But in spite of this, he is not happy with the matter. Radbaz expresses his dissatisfaction by reference to what the Talmud calls "deceitful evasion of interest" (*ha'aramat ribit*), that is, acting within the letter of the law, but using cunning to obtain the same results. It is best explained by the Talmud's description of it:

> There are things which are permitted (in terms of interest—SM), but are forbidden because it is the deceitful evasion of interest. How so?
>
> > He said to him: "Lend me a *maneh* (i.e., a hundred *zuzim*, which are the equivalent of 25 *sela'im*—SM).
> >
> > He answered him: I don't have a *maneh*, but I have wheat worth a *maneh*, which I will give you.
> >
> > He gave him wheat at (the value of) a *maneh*, and then bought it back from him for 24 *sela'im*.
>
> This is permitted, but it is forbidden to do so because of the deceitful evasion of interest.[11]

"Deceitful evasion of interest" is permitted by the law, but it is forbidden on moral grounds. It is in that category that Radbaz places maritime insurance in the best of circumstances, that is, when the procedure that he himself suggests is followed:

> Even though I know that we haven't acquitted ourselves (by this procedure) of the prohibition of deceitful evasion of

10 See especially Chapter 1, n. 105.

11 BT Bava Metsi'a 62b.

> interest, and that the (present) generation is one in which the breached (extent of the moral) fence is greater than that which is left standing, and people draw analogies from one thing (which may be permitted) to another (which is not) because of greed, and thus come to permit that which is forbidden, nevertheless I have agreed to permit this thing, in order to provide livelihood for the sons of the covenant.[12]

The phrase, "to provide livelihood for the sons of the covenant," which rationalizes the adaptation of the law to the realities of economic life, derives from Rabbenu Tam. Rabbenu Tam designed a legal fiction to permit the use of credit between Jews, which relied on the use of a non-Jewish "straw man," to whom the first Jew "loaned" and from whom the second Jew "borrowed." He justified his legal fiction in these terms:

> It seems to me completely permissible, and in fact a choice religious act (*mitsva min ha-muvhar*), to provide livelihood for the sons of the covenant, (to rule) that it is permissible for the lender and the borrower ... (to conduct loans in the manner which he then prescribes—SM).[13]

Radbaz uses this phrase in another responsum as well in the same context.[14] The phrase was not in common use in the 16th century. As far as I can determine, these two responsa are the only places where it appears in 16th century responsa.[15] Radbaz's use of it thus affirms his sensitivity to "real world" needs. However, he does not share Rabbenu Tam's warm espousal of the resultant legal fiction. Radbaz considers this to be the least onerous of evils, an unavoidable violation of "deceitful evasion of interest."

[38] In the case just discussed, Radbaz's forced accommodation of the law to a popular practice was reluctant. However, there is an example in which he is enthusiastic about a popular practice at odds with the law, and in fact waxes lyrical about it.

---

12 I, 359, a series of four questions of which this is the fourth.

13 *Or Zarua'*, pt. 3, Bava Metsi'a, no. 202; *Mordekhai* to Bava Metsi'a, chap. 5, no. 338. On the use of a straw man to circumvent the prohibition of interest see Soloveitchik, *Pawnbroking*, index under *ish-qash*; on Rabbenu Tam in this matter, 66–72.

14 III, 511 (= 986). There he attributes the introduction of illegal forms of maritime insurance to merchants from Salonica.

15 Based on the database of the Bar Ilan Responsa Project, which is, however, not totally inclusive.

The Mishnah incorporates a list of enactments which the Sages put in place "for the general welfare (*mippenei tiqqun ha-'olam*)." Among them is: "Captives are not redeemed for more than their value, for the general welfare."[16] The discussion in the Talmud raises the question, whether the purpose of the enactment was to protect the public from extortion, since the exorbitant ransom would come out of public funds, or whether its purpose was to eliminate an incentive for the perpetrators to target Jews for capture. The distinction made a difference in whether or not it applied to an individual who chose to provide the ransom himself, without recourse to public funds. Maimonides ruled in accordance with the view that it was meant to eliminate an incentive.[17] Accordingly, even an individual who wished to do so was not permitted to pay an exorbitant ransom for a Jewish captive. However, it is well known that Jews ignored this stricture in practice. Special appeals were customarily held to raise money for this cause, and it was considered especially meritorious to donate charitably.[18]

The question to Radbaz was not phrased with explicit reference to this discrepancy. The questioner asked about the proper interpretation of the Mishnah. What is meant by the phrase, "their value"? Does it mean the price of a slave in the market, or the ransom generally paid for the redemption of a non-Jewish captive?[19]

Radbaz begins by describing the situation as it exists in practice:

> It is the practice of all Israel to redeem captives for more than their value (based on those) who are sold in the marketplace. After all, an old man or a minor is not worth in the market more than twenty dinars, and he (an elderly or minor captive) is ransomed for a hundred dinars or more.

Responding to the question, Radbaz rules that "their value" means the accepted ransom of non-Jewish captives. He argues this, first, on logical grounds. As long as the ransom of Jewish captives is not greater than that of captives in general, there is no reason for pirates to target Jews specifically. Furthermore, he argues on linguistic grounds, basing himself, in a somewhat forced manner, on the wording of the Mishnah: *demeihen*, "their cost," rather than *shovyan*, "their worth." The higher redemption price, of captives in general, rather than the lower price, of slaves in the marketplace, would be sufficient to satisfy the purpose of

---

16 Mishnah Gittin 4:6, BT Gittin 45a.

17 *MT*, Agriculture, Laws of Gifts to the Poor, chap. 8, parag. 12.

18 Bashan, *Captivity*, is a study of this issue.

19 I, 40.

the law, namely, that Jews not be targeted specifically. However, the law does not go beyond that point:

> But to redeem them for more than the value of other captives, those of other peoples—that is not proper. Because, since they ransom them for more than other captives, there is reason to fear lest (the pirates) go out purposely in search of Jews, and exert themselves on their account.[20] In addition there is (the factor of) a burden on the community. This is even more so (a consideration), since it has already become well known that Jews redeem captives though they (the captives) themselves have nothing of their own, (so there is a fear) that they (the pirates) will certainly raise their ransom greatly.

In spite of Radbaz's insistence that the legally correct meaning of "their value" in the Mishnah is the higher of the two alternatives suggested by the questioner, there is some indication that he does not completely believe that to be the original sense of the law. For after the presentation of his argument on logical grounds, the stronger part of his case, he finds it necessary to add what sounds like an apology:

> Let Israel be. For they are bestowers of charitable deeds who are the sons of bestowers of charitable deeds.[21]

And in fact, after now having defined the law to allow Jews to pay more for ransom than the bare price of a slave, Radbaz returns to his enthusiasm for the current charitable practice. He begins by spelling out the real issue, the true discrepancy between law and practice:

> But you may say: We see that that they are redeemed for more than the value of other captives! These are events which occur daily, and whoever occupies himself the more with this religious act (*mitsva*) is (considered) the more praiseworthy!

Radbaz proceeds with a defense of this form of ostensibly "illegal" Jewish charity. There is a long history to this problem, of course, and Radbaz summarizes a number of solutions that have been offered in the past. First, some wealthy non-Jews are indeed ransomed for the exorbitant sums paid by Jews.[22] Second, it has been argued that the law does not refer to scholars of Torah, for whom there is no limit on their

---

20 However, he asserted earlier in the responsum that in fact there is no deliberate attempt to target Jews.

21 *gomelei h̲esed benei gomelei h̲esed*

22 This is probably the real point of Radbaz's extending himself in order to define "their value" the way he does. Radbaz points out that wealthy non-Jews are ransomed with their own money, whereas Jews are ransomed by the community, regardless of their personal wealth. But he dismisses this distinction as irrelevant.

ransom. Third, the same has been said to apply to anyone who has the potential of becoming a scholar of Torah.[23] Fourth, there may be minors among the captives who are being ransomed as a group:

> Perhaps there are minors among them, who would be forced into religious conversion. This means that what we are really redeeming is the religion. And in general they compel them to violate Sabbaths and festivals, and afflict them with afflictions worse than death.

Radbaz admits that a good case can be made by one who wished to take issue with all these reasons. It can be argued that the Mishnah's prohibition of excessive ransom was intended deliberately to include all these circumstances. Nevertheless, there is the alternate possibility, that the prohibition was indeed intended to exclude these cases. Radbaz's terminology in presenting these alternatives seems to imply that he believes that the former is most likely to be factually correct.[24] He has thus presented a pair of alternatives, even though they are of unequal plausibility. Building on this uncertainty, he launches into a passionate defense of this popular expression of compassionate concern, a trait especially associated with the patriarch Abraham:

> Since the matter is uncertain, let Israel be. (Let them continue) and hold fast to (this) attribute. Since they are happy and joyous with it, they have (coming to them) a great reward. Furthermore, since we do not compel them (to do this), but they themselves generously volunteer (*mitnaddevin*), there is no basis for apprehension. It is a great religious act (*mitsva*). They do well to seize the attribute of Abraham our Father, peace be upon him. As is written, "The great (*nedivei*, understood here to mean: the generous volunteers) of the peoples are gathered together, the retinue of Abraham's God."[25]

In full view here is the glaring gap between codified law and popular practice, alongside a glimpse of Radbaz's passion in favor of the "offending" but praiseworthy practice. It is only by forcing the limits of interpretation, and with full awareness of the forced nature of his effort, does Radbaz find a justification for it within the codified law.

---

23 Based on the second interpretation of Tosafot to Gittin 58a, s.v. *kol mamon she-posqin 'alav*.

24 He introduces the first with: *ve-af 'al pi she-yesh le-ba'al ha-din lomar*, and the second with: *mi-kol maqom yesh li-de*<u>*h*</u>*ot de-dilma*. The latter sounds like he knows he's stretching, a tone totally lacking in the former.

25 Psalms 47:10.

[39] There are a number of places in Radbaz's responsa in which he takes serious account of popular misconceptions of the law. These instances shed unusual light on how the general public, interested in observing the law, perceived it in ways that were at variance with the ways the rabbis defined it.[26] Popular perception is another aspect of the "real world" which faced Radbaz. His willingness to recognize its reality is in line with his methodology as we have seen it so far.

The first two cases are examples of the popular understanding of Scripture in accordance with its plain sense, while the interpretation of the Talmud, which determined the law, differed from the plain sense. In both cases Radbaz gives serious consideration to the popular understanding.

The Torah prohibits interest in three places, in Exodus, Leviticus and Deuteronomy.[27] The words in the latter passage, *lo tashikh*, the plain contextual sense of which is, "you shall not lend," were interpreted by the Talmud to mean, "you shall not borrow." Accordingly, both the lender and the borrower are in violation of the prohibition of interest.[28]

The Talmud distinguishes between the biblical prohibition of interest, and the rabbinically legislated extensions thereof. The former encompasses a transaction that assumes the patent form of a loan, for which a defined additional benefit accrues to the lender over time.[29] It is not difficult to avoid the prohibition by defining the transaction in such a way that it does not meet the precise definition of interest. The Rabbis therefore extended the prohibition to cover many transactions, which in effect brought profit to the lender, while technically remaining free of the biblical prohibition of interest. Biblically prohibited interest was called "stipulated interest" (*ribbit qetsutsa*), and, unlike rabbinically prohibited interest, could be recovered in court by the debtor after he had paid it.

Radbaz's question is as follows:

> You asked my opinion regarding "Reuben," who borrowed a *maneh* without a note (i.e., with only witnesses—SM). When the time came to collect it, he said (to the creditor): "You owe

---

26 See Katz, *Shabbes Goy*, for a number of examples of this phenomenon in the area of Sabbath observance.

27 Exod. 22:24, Lev. 25:36–37, Deut. 23:20–21.

28 BT Bava Metsi'a 75b.

29 See *MT*, Civil Laws, Laws of Creditor and Debtor, chap. 6, parag. 1.

> me a *maneh* of stipulated interest that you took from me." Who is to take an oath?[30]

A plaintiff, who lacks evidence to prove his claim, can nevertheless insist that the defendant take an oath that he is telling the truth. In effect, the questioner is asking Radbaz to determine who the defendant is in this case of counter claims. For a reason having to do with the undocumented nature of the loan, Radbaz decides that the borrower's claim, that he paid stipulated interest, is accepted by the court. What remains is the creditor's claim on the borrower, and it is the borrower who is considered the defendant. Accordingly, he is the one who should be taking the oath.

The aspect of the responsum that concerns us here is the propriety of administering an oath to the borrower. After all, the borrower, in admitting that he paid stipulated interest, is admitting to a prohibited act. He should therefore be suspect with regard to monetary matters, and disqualified from taking an oath in his own monetary interest. Furthermore, self-incrimination is not accepted in Jewish law. In the words of the Talmud, "one cannot cast oneself as a guilty one."[31] So how can the court allow him to incriminate himself with an oath?

Radbaz addresses this by relying on the popular understanding of the verse in Deuteronomy:

> Even though he casts himself as a guilty one, he is not suspect with regard to monetary matters. For he did not take interest, but rather gave interest to his neighbor. And people understand the scriptural phrase *lo tashikh* in its plain sense, as a prohibition for the lender. He (the borrower) does not cast himself as a guilty one this way, and he is not disqualified from taking an oath this way.

The fact that the borrower, in common with the general public, mistakenly understood the verse in its plain sense is determinative. Such a stance is not to be taken for granted. For instance, in a responsum on the same subject by Radbaz's contemporary, R. Joseph ibn Lev, we find exactly the opposite tack: "One is not trustworthy to claim that he had paid interest, because one cannot cast oneself as a guilty one."[32] And in fact Radbaz himself contradicts what he says here in another responsum:

> As for the borrower, it is obvious that he is disqualified from testifying. For so it says in (Chapter) "One Chooses" (the

---

30 VIII, 133.

31 BT Sanhedrin 9b. On this subject see Kirschenbaum, *Self-Incrimination.*

32 R. Joseph ibn Lev, Responsa, III, 21.

> third chapter of Tractate Sanhedrin—SM): "Rava says: One who borrows money on interest is disqualified from testifying, for the Torah has said: Do not put a guilty one as a witness."[33]

This merely serves to underline Radbaz's daring and ingenuity in the responsum under discussion. He takes seriously the situation as it is in actual fact.

[40] Radbaz's willingness to deal seriously with popular interpretations of Scripture, based on the plain sense of the text, is in evidence in this next responsum as well. Radbaz builds a case for a lenient ruling. One of his proofs depends on a law in the Talmud, which is based on a midrashic interpretation of a Scriptural passage. The plain-sense understanding of that passage, which he attributes to the broad uninitiated public, would not favor Radbaz's desired conclusion. Rather than ignore the popular understanding of the passage, Radbaz feels it necessary to recognize it and counter it. He explains that it is not feasible to attribute this specific misunderstanding of the law to the principal in the case. In the course of strengthening this point, he has recourse to another popular, but mistaken, perception of the law.

The Mishnah reads:

> If one divorces his wife and (then) spends the night with her at an inn, the School of Shammai says: She does not need a second divorce from him. The School of Hillel says: She does need a second divorce from him.[34]

The reason why she might need a second divorce is that the act of intercourse itself can effect a betrothal, if that was the intention of the act. The School of Hillel presupposes, on the basis of their seclusion, that an act of intercourse has taken place.[35] It further presupposes that such an act of intercourse was perpetrated with a licit intention, that is, with the intention of betrothal, rather than fornication. It is the possibility of this second betrothal that now requires a divorce for her to be free to marry someone else. The law, as usual, follows the School of Hillel.

Radbaz's question is a case in point:

---

33 I, 317. Quoting BT Sanhedrin 27a. "Do not put..." is the conclusion drawn from Rava on the basis of Exod. 23:1. The verse is cited by the Talmud, but omitted here.

34 Mishnah Gittin 8:9. BT Gittin 81a.

35 The Talmud offers two interpretations of the situation presupposed by this controversy; see above, 32. I am following the one adopted by Maimonides, *MT*, Women, Laws of Divorce, chap. 10, parag. 18.

> Concerning a woman, whose husband divorced her because of fornication, and who (later) secluded herself with him with (the knowledge of) witnesses—does she need a second divorce from him, in accordance with the School of Hillel?[36]

Radbaz argues that the basic presumption of the School of Hillel, that intercourse took place, is unlikely here. If he divorced her because he believed that she was adulterous, he would be no less disgusted with her now. He would not, says Radbaz, borrowing a phrase from Proverbs, "return to his vomit like a dog."[37]

This is a psychological argument for the presumption that no intercourse occurred. Radbaz supplements it with a more formal, legally oriented one. The Rabbis generally held the position that secluded couples were suspect of fornication, and accordingly they prohibited such seclusion. But fornication between unattached partners is not forbidden by the Torah, according to most authorities.[38] That is not the case, however, with regard to sexual intercourse with one's adulterous wife. Deuteronomy 24:4 prohibits a husband from remarrying his divorcee if she has in the meantime been married to someone else, "since she has been defiled," and the Talmud interprets that prohibition to include also a wife who had committed adultery.[39] Radbaz suggests that the suspicion of fornication, which stems from the seclusion of unmarried couples generally, does not apply, if the possible act of intercourse constitutes a prohibition of the Torah. Faced with a prohibition deriving from the Torah itself, and not merely from Rabbinic legislation, the presumption is that one would restrain oneself and not sin.

It is at this point that Radbaz takes account of the common, plain-sense understanding of Deuteronomy 24:1–4:

> You may say: People understand that the plain sense of Scripture refers (only) to one who remarries his divorcee (but not to an adulterous wife too—SM)!
>
> (To this I answer:) There is no way that they didn't tell him when he divorced her that she is prohibited to him by the Torah. On the contrary—this prohibition is more stringent for them than (general) fornication.

---

36 IV, 277 (= 1348). A similar question (perhaps the very same one) was asked of R. Moses Alashqar, Responsa, no. 88, and his arguments are similar to those of Radbaz.

37 Pr. 26:11.

38 The main exception is Maimonides, see below.

39 BT Yevamot 11b.

It was not necessary for Radbaz to introduce this popular, plain-sense, but mistaken understanding of the Scriptural law. As the author of a responsum he is responsible to the sources of the law, and need take no cognizance of popular misconceptions. But that would not be true to the "real world" facts of the case. Radbaz recognizes popular perception as a legitimate issue here, and moves to counter the argument.

Radbaz goes on to counter another argument against his position, and in doing so has recourse again to popular misconceptions. Maimonides had in fact ruled that fornication among unattached couples is indeed forbidden by the Torah.[40] Even so, we do entertain a suspicion that it will lead to sex! How is that different, then, from sex with an adulterous divorcee? Radbaz responds by testifying to the lenient popular attitudes toward fornication in general. Even if one holds the position that the law is in accordance with Maimonides, namely, that fornication among unattached couples is forbidden by the Torah, nevertheless:

> Fornication has become for them as if it is licit, and they are of the opinion that it is not forbidden by the Torah.

We rabbis may rule as we please. But our presumptions must be based on what common people actually believe.

[41] Another example of the influence of popular belief on the application of the law occurs in a responsum that was discussed in another connection in Chapter 1. A borrower charged that the note that the creditor, in this case his sister, seeks to collect contains hidden interest.[41] Among the issues Radbaz deals with is a demand by the debtor that the creditor take an oath affirming that the debtor's allegation is not true. Radbaz indicates that there is a controversy among the authorities on this issue. Maimonides ruled that the debtor must first pay, but then he may require the creditor to take such an oath.[42] Rabbenu Asher ruled that the debtor's allegation, without any proof, is dismissed entirely, and he cannot demand an oath at all.[43]

---

40 *MT*, Women, Laws of Marriage, chap. 1. parag. 4. He derives the prohibition from Deuteronomy 23:18.

41 III, 485 (= 923); Case [29].

42 *MT*, Civil Laws, Laws of Creditor and Debtor, chap. 14, parag. 3.

43 I have not located this responsum among Rabbenu Asher's responsa. *Tur Hoshen Mishpat*, no. 82, which cites Maimonides' ruling, makes no mention of Rabbenu Asher's opinion. Radbaz attributes this opinion to the

Radbaz rules in accordance with Maimonides,[44] and he seeks to show that in this instance Rabbenu Asher would also require an oath from the creditor.

Rabbenu Asher's position was based on three considerations. The first two we have seen in Case [39]: first, the rule that "one cannot cast oneself as a guilty one"; second, if the debtor casts suspicion on the creditor with regard to charging him interest, he is casting suspicion on him with regard to perjury as well. The third takes into account the fact that the rabbis have devised ways for the transfer of credit in a licit manner, and there is a presumption that the lender would have made use of them, and avoided outright illegal interest.

All three of these arguments are based on the presumption that the lender, in this case a woman, is aware of the prohibition. But Radbaz points out that this is not true in the present case. The money that was loaned was the property of minor orphans, and there is a common but mistaken belief among the unlearned, that the prohibition of lending on interest does not apply to the capital of widows and minor orphans.[45] This is indeed true for certain types of rabbinically prohibited interest, but certainly not for "stipulated interest" prohibited by the Torah. However:

> Women do not learn the law, and think that with regard to minor orphans and widows, it is permitted to lend them on interest.

Radbaz adds that he had ruled this way in the past, and convinced judges, who sought to rule otherwise, to change their mind:

> A case came before me regarding Reuben, an untutored man, who had in his possession capital belonging to minor orphans, and he loaned them on interest. The borrower claimed, "You took stipulated interest from me," and they (the other judges) wanted to acquit him of an oath, in accordance with what Rabbenu Asher had said, rejecting the ruling of Maimonides. But I (argued for the position that) obligated him to take an oath even according to Rabbenu Asher, for the reasons I have written. Therefore, they ruled properly, and obligated him to take an oath.

---

author of the *Turim* as well, but I have not found it in the aforementioned section.

44 In accordance with the rule that Egypt is "the place of the Master"; see Chapter 7 below.

45 The fact that the money was loaned to minor orphans is another example of a significant detail being omitted by Radbaz in his formulation of the question. See Chap. 1, n. 79.

It is the reality of popular misconception that determines the application of the law.

[42] In the following instance, Radbaz takes account of popular perceptions of the law in order to strengthen his case, though it is solid enough on other grounds.

Rabbinic law prohibits intercourse between a man and his slavewoman.[46] This is in marked contrast to Islamic law, where intercourse with one's own slavewoman is considered licit. Jews living in Islamic lands tended to adopt the cultural norms of the majority in this regard, rabbinic objections notwithstanding. If the slavewoman bore children, the slaveowner's paternity was not recognized by Rabbinic law.

Maimonides reports that some Geonim (that is, early Babylonian authorities) ruled that if a man has children with his slavewoman, there is a presumption that he had manumitted her first and then had relations with her.[47] As explained above in Case [3], a slave who had been converted to the semi-Jewish status of "slavery," as required by the law of the Talmud, became a full Jew upon manumission, with the status of a proselyte. Thus, the slavewoman is considered to have had the status of a proselyte at the time of the sexual act, according to this Geonic opinion, with the result that the father's paternity is recognized, even outside of marriage. Maimonides himself takes strong exception to this Geonic opinion. The child is a slave, and its paternity is not recognized.

The case before Radbaz is interesting in a number of respects. The question begins with the following background:

> Reuben bought an Ishmaelite slavewoman, and immersed her for the purpose of slavery. Subsequently, he had sexual relations with her, and she bore him a daughter. The slavewoman (then) went astray (*yatse'a le-tarbut ra'a*), and he sold her to Ishmaelites. The daughter grew up with Reuben. When she reached maturity, he gave her a dowry and married her to Simeon.... Reuben died, and afterwards the daughter died, without living children.[48]

"Ishmaelite" means Muslim. There was, of course, an Islamic ban on non-Muslim ownership of Muslim slaves, but there were exceptions,

---

46 *MT*, Holiness, Laws of Forbidden Intercourse, chap. 12, parag. 11. See also Case [14] above.

47 *MT*, Women, Laws of Divorce, chap. 10, parag. 19.

48 III, 420 (= 955). The responsum that follows is a continuation of the same case.

especially when the Muslim was not an Arab.[49] After the birth of her daughter, Reuben's slavewoman "went astray," that is, reverted to Muslim religious practice, and was sold to Muslims.

According to the legal arrangements then in force, if a wife died childless, the husband, who normally inherits his deceased wife's dowry, must share it with her father or his heirs. In this case, the dowry was very respectable. Reuben had a son, who claimed his share of the dowry under the provisions of the law. One aspect of this complex case is singled out as a separate question:

> Concerning the son of Reuben, the father of the aforementioned daughter who married Simeon—can he testify with regard to Simeon, that he is the husband of his paternal sister?[50]

The law disqualifies the testimony of witnesses who are closely related to the subject of the testimony. The question is whether Simeon's wife is legally considered to be Reuben's daughter.

The answer to that question depends on whether the daughter's mother was a slavewoman or a proselyte when the daughter was conceived. That is the heart of the controversy between Maimonides and the Geonic opinion he cites. The truth is that the Geonic opinion, known to us only from Maimonides himself and totally rejected by him, was not a legitimate option. Radbaz cites it only in order to argue that even the Geonim, who presume that she was a proselyte at the time, would nevertheless admit that in this case their presumption does not apply. They too would agree that she was a slavewoman at the time of the sexual act.

Radbaz brings two proofs for this, one of which is relevant to us here:[51]

> For Reuben was in the habit of having sexual intercourse with his slavewomen, without manumission. He was mistaken with regard to the law, and was under the impression that it is permissible to have sexual intercourse with his slavewoman,

---

49 I owe this information to Professor Norman Stillman, in a personal communication. He also confirmed that to his knowledge, "Ishmaelite" always means Muslim. He knows of no exception to this. A. David, in "Economic Position," discusses the prohibition on Jewish ownership of Muslim slaves. He cites this case, and comments on 97: "But it seems that this incident was exceptional, and does not reflect the general situation."

50 III, 121 (=996).

51 The other one is the fact that he subsequently sold her, so she could not have been manumitted. This point had already been suggested by the questioner.

> because she was his property. In his mind this was not fornication.[52]

Presumptions, according to Radbaz, must be rooted in empirical reality. The reality here is that Reuben, along with the general public, had internalized the values of the broader Islamic majority in the matter of the licit nature of sex with one's slavewoman.

[43] In the following responsum, the critical consideration in Radbaz's ruling is a misconception of a point of law which was shared by women, and which Radbaz takes into account.

The *ketubba* is the marriage contract, which defines the husband's obligations toward his wife. In addition to the conditions that are mandated by the law, there were others that the law considers optional, but which were routinely incorporated into the *ketubba*. One of these granted the wife the power to deny her husband the right to marry a rival. She could not, however, prevent him from divorcing her unilaterally, though of course he would then be obligated to pay her the sizeable sum of money stipulated in the *ketubba*. A common reason for wanting a second wife was the inability of the first to bear children, and a woman faced with such an alternative might well permit a rival.

"Reuben" had once divorced his wife, and then remarried her. But she now suffers from epilepsy, and Reuben alleges that he cannot have sexual relations with her because he is revolted by her condition.[53] He bemoans the deprivation of a licit sexual outlet. Reuben has become impoverished, and cannot divorce his wife because he cannot afford the *ketubba* payments. This situation has persisted for several years. During all that time, Reuben has been asking his wife for permission to take a second wife, and she has continued to refuse it.

But Reuben has discovered a legal loophole. The optional condition that empowered the wife was included in the *ketubba* at the time of the first marriage. The *ketubba* was then carried over into the second marriage. But Reuben has now learned that according to "one of the great decisors," whatever optional conditions were included in the original *ketubba* lapsed at the time of the divorce, and were not automatically reinstated with the second marriage.[54]

Radbaz responds to two issues. One is Reuben's inability to divorce because of his impoverishment. Radbaz rules that he can divorce her in

---

52 III, 121 (=956).

53 I, 53. "Epilepsy"—*ḫoli ha-kefiyya*.

54 See Case [55] for more on this issue.

any case, and the *ketubba* will simply remain a debt, payable as soon as possible.

The other issue is the lapsing of the optional conditions included in the original *ketubba*. Radbaz has this to say:

> And (about) the second argument which he (Reuben) wrote, that since he divorced her the original conditions were nullified, so I (too) think in terms of the law in the abstract (*le-halakha*), and thus wrote Rashba (identifying "one of the great decisors"—SM).... (Radbaz identifies Rashba's source in the Palestinian Talmud—SM).
>
> But in terms of the law in its practical application (*le-ma'aseh*), it is not proper to rule that way. That is because women are not knowledgeable about this law, and she thinks that when he remarries her, he remarries her with all the conditions of the *ketubba* (intact). And he will deceive her, and nullify all the conditions of her *ketubba*.

Radbaz thus draws a distinction between the codified law and the law in its practical application. Regardless of the former, the latter is governed by the reality of what people actually believe.

3. The Role of Equity

(*a*) *Law and Equity*

[44] Case [1] above concerned the Sages of Jerusalem, who were demanding police protection for the city but were unwilling to contribute toward it.[1] They based themselves on the principle that scholars of Torah are protected by their Torah. They maintained that position in spite of the fact that "the greed of the thieves increased because of the Sages, whose dress was unlike the dress of the laymen, and who appeared of a higher class than they," as Radbaz put it. In other words, they sought police protection for their own benefit, while relying on the presumption, which had its roots in the Talmud, that "rabbis do not need protection." In discussing this case, I dealt with the argument which is central to the structure of that responsum, namely, that the reality of the situation which presents itself is different from the reality presumed by the Talmud, when it formulated the rule exempting scholars of Torah from taxes for police protection. But Radbaz's responsum is invested with a degree of emotion, which is not commonly found in the controlled legal style of the genre. After presenting the demand of the Sages, Radbaz continues in the following vein:

> Is it within the bounds of law or of sense that they should compel the laymen to establish police protection, forcing them to do so without contributing along with them to the expense?

---

1 II, 752.

> No one ever said such a thing! And if one had ever said it he should not be obeyed, because the line of justice would be breached.

Later in the responsum he states:

> Even though I know that there are rabbis who disagree with this, they expound the law for their own benefit, and are not to be followed.

Whatever may be the formal legal considerations of Radbaz, there is little doubt that the emotion evoked in him by this issue derives from his revulsion from the injustice and inequity contained in the position argued by the Sages of Jerusalem.

We have touched here on the role of equity in halakhic decision making. No formulation of law can always be relied upon to yield an equitable result, because, as was observed by Aristotle, law deals with generalities, whereas true justice deals with specific situations.[2] Radbaz's insistence on equity is therefore another aspect of the role that he demands for the unique actualities of the case before him in his judicial methodology.

In addressing the tax status of the scholars of Jerusalem, Radbaz argues for his ruling on conventional legal grounds, and then appends to it a plea based on the demands of equity. There is no conflict in this case, between the letter of the law and the spirit of justice, which would have required a resolution. He could have arrived at his goal without discussing that issue. That being the case, the very fact that Radbaz finds it necessary to bring to the fore arguments based on equity, and to highlight them with some passion, is instructive of his mindset.

[45] We can see this process in other responsa of Radbaz. In the following instance, Radbaz emphasizes the argument based on equity by giving it pride of place at the start of his responsum, and then makes a sharp distinction between equity and law before proceeding to his conventional argument, which would have been quite sufficient to prove his point.

The issue concerns an enactment which was widespread throughout the Jewish communities of the Ottoman Empire, according to which a Jew who occupies a dwelling leased from a non-Jew has a presumptive right (a *ḫazaqa*) to continue living there. No one else may rent the dwelling without his consent for a prescribed period of time, commonly three years, after he has vacated it. The purpose of this legislation was to protect members of the Jewish community from non-Jewish

---

2 Nichomachean Ethics, Bk. 5, Chap. 10.

landlords, who might gouge rent by playing off one Jew against another.[3] In the case at hand, the dwelling had originally been leased by a non-Jew, who then subleased it to a Jew. The original lease of the non-Jewish tenant had lapsed. Now another Jew wants to rent the house from the original non-Jewish owner, displacing the Jewish subleasor, and maintains that the enactment does not apply to such a situation.[4]

Radbaz argues that the formulators of the enactment did most definitely have such a situation in mind, for to assume otherwise would open loopholes in the enactment, which would totally vitiate its original intent. He also argues for the contractual rights of the subletting tenant. But all this he prefaces with an allusion to the talmudic dictum: "If a poor man is examining a cake (with the intention of acquiring it), and another comes and takes it away from him, he is called wicked."[5] Radbaz begins his responsum with the following remarks:

> The law is with the Jew currently living in the house, and he has a <u>h</u>azaqa in it; another Jew cannot evict him without his consent. First of all, because it is clear that there is no greater example than this of a poor man examining a cake, in which case one who takes it from him is called wicked. For this man is dwelling in the house, and he will have to move and find another house. And who can say that he will find another house like this one? Therefore, it is clear that this Reuben is called wicked. But even according to the law I say that it is a complete <u>h</u>azaqa, because ... (he proceeds with the line of argument alluded to above).

The talmudic citation about the poor man examining a cake is not a legal ruling, but a moral injunction. The court can apply no redress other than giving the injured party the right to call the other party "wicked."[6] It is not clear whether Radbaz, had he lacked a legal basis for his ruling, would have adjudicated the matter the same way on this moral basis alone. But it is clear that the moral argument, which he explicitly distinguishes from "according to the law" (*le-gabbei ha-din*), was central to his thinking.

[46] The same emphasis on the moral dimension, this time in a situation in which it clearly adds nothing to the strength of the argument, is apparent in the following responsum:

---

3 See Goodblatt, *Jewish Life in Turkey*, 81-86.

4 IV, 213 (= 1284).

5 BT Qiddushin 59a.

6 See Kirschenbaum, *Equity*, 264.

> You asked of me that I give you my opinion about one who told his friend that he would be his "master of circumcision" (*ba'al berit shelo*), that is to say, that he will sit on the chair to hold the infant when he is being circumcised; and now he (the father) has changed his mind, and wants to give the honor to another.[7]

Radbaz treats the honor in question as a property right, and analyzes the issue as a matter of acquisition of property. He draws a sharp distinction between whether or not the baby had already been born when the honor was originally promised. That distinction reflects the rule that property which has not yet come into existence is not subject to legal acquisition, the classic example being dates which have not yet formed on the tree.[8] Thus, if the promise preceded the birth, the first recipient of the honor has no claim to it. On the other hand, if the baby had already been born when the promise was made, the question is whether the legal formalities of acquisition have been satisfied. The Talmud goes into great detail on the means of acquisition of property, and oral agreement is not among them. But in this case, Radbaz tells us:

> All Israel is already accustomed to transferring the acquisition of this religious rite (*mitsvah*) by mere speech. And you know that custom is a great principle (*'iqqar gadol*) in all matters of this type .... (He cites a proof from the Talmud that the law recognizes popularly accepted forms of acquisition even though they do not adhere to the officially sanctioned forms.) Here too, since this is the custom, he must adhere to it.

In the sequel he limits the power of custom. It applies, he says, to the acceptability of otherwise unacceptable forms of acquisition. It does not, however, supplant the rule that something that has not yet come into existence cannot be acquired.

However, the passage cited immediately above continues as follows:

> Here too, since this is the custom, he must adhere to it. For "the remnant of Israel shall do no wrong and speak no falsehood; a deceitful tongue shall not be in their mouths."

The passage cited by Radbaz is from Zephaniah 3:13. It is used in the Talmud to support the legal presumption that people are true to their word.[9] In the present context it is completely superfluous to the argument, which is based on the legitimacy of custom. Not only that, it

---

7 I, 278.

8 See *MT*, Acquisition, Laws of Sales, 22:1-2.

9 BT Pesahim 91a, BT Qiddushin 45b, BT Bava Metsi'a 106b, each with regard to a different issue.

is somewhat antithetical to his ruling, because a presumption that one fulfills one's word allows for no distinction between whether the baby was born before or after the promise. Radbaz himself recognizes that difficulty with regard to the legitimacy of custom, and he takes pains to forestall such an objection. A claim for the legal validity of a promise based on the verse from Zephaniah would not be given to such distinctions. However, this is not a legal argument that Radbaz is invoking, but a moral one. He finds a need to stress it, even though it is extraneous to his line of argument.

[47] Aaron Kirschenbaum, in his book, *Equity in Jewish Law: Halakhic Perspectives*, touches upon the phenomenon of rules of equity evolving into rigid rules, though they were originally intended to provide an escape hatch from the rigidity of formal law. The subject comes up in his discussion of the "law of the abutter." [10] According to that law, if one sells a field, then the owner of the abutting field has a prior right to purchase it. This is enforced to the extent that a purchaser in violation of the law is construed as an agent acting on behalf of the abutter. The Talmud sees the law of the abutter as an actualization of the biblical injunction, "Do what is right and good in the sight of the Lord."[11] In his discussion of the fate of this law in post-talmudic times, Kirschenbaum writes:

> A major source of dissension among the authorities is the question to what extent does the equitable nature of the original motivation of the law of the abutter persist. Does equity, once crystallized in law, become a legal generalization that of necessity must disregard individual circumstances and thereby vitiate the intent of the lawgiver? Or does the expressed equitable intention of the legislator enter the decision of each individual case?[12]

There is no doubt about where Radbaz stands on this issue. In a responsum on the law of the abutter in which equity appears to be on the side of the purchaser, he repeats over and over again that this law is based on the injunction to do what is right and good, and must always be interpreted in accordance with that injunction.[13] Though he bases

---

10 Kirschenbaum, *Equity*, 259-68.

11 BT Bava Metsi'a 108a, citing Deuteronomy 6:18.

12 Kirschenbaum, *Equity*, 266.

13 IV, 300 (= 1372). There is a concurring opinion on this case by R. Moses Alashqar, *Responsa*, no. 118, and an opposing one by R. Levi ibn Habib, *Responsa*, no. 61.

himself in his argumentation on solid precedent, his determined stressing of the principle speaks for itself.

[48] Another responsum dealing with the law of the abutter concerns "Reuben" and "Simeon," who rented a house as partners, and now Reuben wants to sublet part of his premises to "Levi."[14] Simeon objects, claiming his right under the law of the abutter to rent it himself. The operative law, says Radbaz, is that the law of the abutter does not apply to rentals.[15] He understands this to mean that an abutter has no claim if the owner leases his property rather than sells it.[16] The question, explains Radbaz, is whether we follow this restriction, or whether we heed Simeon, when he says, "I don't want a stranger living with me." His conclusion is that we do heed him, because that is what is "right and good." The exclusion of rentals from the law of the abutter means, he asserts, that the law cannot be exercised in favor of a renter in abutting premises, but it surely can be exercised in favor of a renter living in the very same one. Here too it is the intent of the law, not its formulation, which is determinative.

[49] Radbaz makes use of another rationale, which Kirschenbaum sees as a feature of equity. Proverbs 3:17 declares of Wisdom: "Its ways are ways of pleasantness." The Rabbis, who identified Wisdom with Torah, applied this maxim to judicial interpretation.[17] Kirschenbaum provides a survey of the ways in which the post-talmudic rabbis understood the concept "pleasantness,"[18] and examples of Radbaz's understanding of it will be adduced below. Radbaz puts the matter this way: "And also because it is written, 'Its ways are ways of pleasantness,' and it is necessary that the laws of our Torah be in

---

14 I, 167.

15 See *MT*, Acquisition, Laws of Neighbors, Chap. 12, parag. 8. Actually, though, this point is in dispute; see *Tur Hoshen Mishpat*, no. 175 end. The interpretation of Maimonides' passage itself is also in dispute, see the following note.

16 See *Kesef Mishneh* on Maimonides ad loc., and *Beit Yosef* on *Tur* ad loc., where this interpretation of Maimonides' passage is cited along with a different one.

17 See Kirschenbaum, *Equity*, 159-83. Kirschenbaum refers to four of the five examples below in the text to notes 64, 65, 68 and 78. See also his references to Radbaz in the text to notes 52 and, of less interest, 66.

18 Kirschenbaum, *Equity*, 177-80.

accordance with sense and reason (*ha-sekhel veha-sevara*)."[19] It is axiomatic for Radbaz that "sense and reason" implies "pleasantness."

The specific purposes to which Radbaz applies this principle, along with more conventional arguments, include the following:

(a) A son, who is normally obligated to support his needy father, is nevertheless not obligated to beg door to door in order to do so.[20]

(b) Though normally one is not permitted to stand idly by while another's life is in danger, one nevertheless does not have to submit to the loss of a limb if a tyrant makes it a condition for the saving of another's life.[21]

(c) A husband, who is normally not permitted to have physical contact with his wife while she is in a state of menstrual impurity, may nevertheless have such contact in order to minister to her needs.[22]

(d) Property belonging to a man who left town and never returned, which normally may not be sold until his death is ascertained, may nevertheless be sold to support the basic needs of his wife.[23]

(e) The tenant of a store, who normally may not be evicted without twelve months' notice, may nevertheless be evicted without notice if the landlord has become impoverished, and can only sell the store on condition that it is vacant.[24] In a responsum with nearly identical circumstances, Radbaz does not refer to the phrase "ways of pleasantness." But he points to the equivalent concept by means of its opposite, "it is not within the law":

> If the purchaser does not want to buy except on condition that the tenant vacates the house, then one has to see. If the vendor is poor and pressed for money, for instance, if he has

---

19 III, 627 (= 1052). The equivalence of equity with reason appears in another case. It involves a "Reuben," who sold his property to an Arab, who then sold it to "Simeon." Subsequently, the question arose as to whether Reuben's creditors can collect from Simeon. Radbaz rules in favor of Simeon. Among his reasons is that otherwise a vicious cycle would be set up: Simeon would then sue the Arab, who would reclaim the property from Reuben's creditors in an Islamic court and return it to Simeon, whence it could be recovered by Reuben's creditors, etc. And, says Radbaz, lest one suggest that Simeon be prevented from suing the Arab, "Sense does not allow (*ein ha-da'at sovelet*) that we force him to not sue the Arab and lose his money." I, 500.

20 II, 663.

21 III, 627 (= 1052).

22 IV, 2, Case [10] above.

23 VI, 2184.

24 IV, 143 (= 1214).

> debts to non-Jews, or has nothing to eat, then the tenant is evicted. For it is not within the law (*she-eino ba-din*) that this one (the landlord) should beg door to door, or be turned over to non-Jews who have no compassion for him, and the other one (the tenant) should live in his house.[25]

[50] In all of the responsa adduced so far in this chapter, the argument from equity supplemented a conventional legal argument. There was no conflict between the two approaches. In the following instance that is not so.

In the two cases in subsection (e) above, the tenant's lease was terminated without notice. In both responsa, Radbaz's conventional argument was based on an implied condition of the lease, that in extreme situations (the unexpected impoverishment of the landlord), the tenant could be evicted. The argument that the law must accord with "ways of pleasantness," or, in the parallel case, that "it is not within the law" that the landlord should have to go begging, was supportive of the conclusion arrived at by conventional means. In the following case, too, Radbaz takes cognizance of impoverishment as a special category, but in doing so he arrives at a conclusion which overrides the formal law.

A widow has the right to collect her *ketubba*, the settlement agreed upon at the time of the marriage. According to the law of the Talmud, the *ketubba* was collectible only from real property. The wife had a lien on all her husband's real property, and could reclaim it from any subsequent purchaser. In the eighth century, a Geonic enactment extended the law to include the collection of the *ketubba* from movables as well,[26] though a lien was not extended to movables. However, it was customary to include a clause in the *ketubba*, which would have the effect of placing movables in the same category as real property in the matter of a lien too. Since this was based on the right of contract, it held true even in terms of talmudic law. Rabbenu Asher tells us that it was customary in Spain to include such a clause in all notes of indebtedness, but that, in practice, many jurisdictions did not act upon this clause, and movables were not actually reclaimed from their purchasers, for fear of the effect such action would have on normal commerce. Rabbenu Asher goes on to rule, however, that where such a custom of inaction was not firmly established, the law would

---

25 III, 614 (= 1040).

26 See Tykocinsky, *Gaonic Ordinances*, 30-50.

follow the law of the Talmud in this regard, and the lien would extend to movables also.[27]

In the case before Radbaz, a man distributed his assets on his deathbed, leaving nothing for his wife's *ketubba*. The question was whether she could reclaim the movables on the strength of the lien that was written into her *ketubba*.[28] Radbaz cites Rabbenu Asher, and points out that in his own time and place there was no established custom in effect of not honoring the lien. Furthermore, he argues that the reason for not applying the lien (i.e., a deleterious effect on commerce) would in any case not apply to gifts. For these reasons, he rules unequivocally that she may collect the distributed movables. However, he closes his remarks with a distinction at odds with this conclusion. He writes as follows:

> But in any case I admit that if the recipients of the gift are poor and have already consumed it, a deed of indebtedness is not drawn up against them. Similarly, if they were movables and were lost. If there is something that derives directly from the movables of the gift, it should be returned. But if they were consumed, and there is nothing for which they were exchanged, they are not obligated to pay, as is the case with money that was distributed to the poor. Would it occur to us that we should exact from each and every poor man what he has consumed?

In this case, an equitable solution requires a ruling at odds with the implications of the formal law.

(*b*) *Exploiting the Letter of the Law*

The responsa of Radbaz record a variety of instances in which people try to exploit the letter of the law to their own advantage, in ways which Radbaz sees as subversive of true and equitable justice. He takes a dim view of such attempts, and generally dismisses them out of hand. Where he can he will find a basis in the law for doing so, but there are times when he pays little heed to the formalities of the law.

Quite a few of these situations involve marriage and divorce.

27 Rabbenu Asher, *Responsa*, *Kelal* 79, no. 4.
28 VI, 2137.

[51] Radbaz was asked to clarify the custom in Egypt regarding the collection of the *ketubba*.[29] In the course of this discussion he describes the status of the dowry that the wife brought into the marriage. Because of the security it provides the wife, the Talmud terms this property "iron sheep" property. The items constituting the dowry are appraised at the time of the marriage, and the husband obligates himself or his estate to return her the full value of the appraisal when the *ketubba* is paid, subsequent to his divorcing or predeceasing her. According to the law of the Talmud, the husband's responsibility for the "iron sheep" property extends not only to reimbursing her for items that are lost or stolen, but also for any depreciation that may occur. However, the custom in practice was different. Contrary to talmudic law, the husband was not held responsible for loss due to depreciation. He undertook responsibility for full value only in the case of loss or theft, or if the article had depreciated to such a point that it could no longer function in its original capacity. An example is clothing so worn that it is no longer wearable. In those circumstances, when the *ketubba* was paid, the article was assessed at its original value, regardless of its present condition.[30] Later in the responsum, Radbaz tells us that the value of any gifts and clothing he provided her during the marriage (except for common everyday clothing) is figured as part of her *ketubba* payment.

Radbaz summarizes all this, and then continues as follows:

> Even though this is the custom, I have seen a number of charlatans who, contemplating divorce, upon seeing that a robe or garment has reached the end of its useful life, and afraid lest it tear altogether and can no longer function in its original capacity, put it into a box and buy her others. Then, when such a one divorces her, he gives her the worn clothing that he had stored, assessed at its original value.

---

29 I, 383.

30 This practice went back to the Geonic period. See Alfasi to Yevamot chap. 7 beginning, no. 97; Maimonides, *MT*, Women, Laws of Marriage, chap. 22, parag. 35; and *Maggid Mishneh* ad loc., who asserts that in his time and place (Spain, 14th century) the custom followed the talmudic practice. Radbaz notes that the woman was compensated for this loss in the following manner. It was customary to exaggerate the true value of the items constituting the dowry, and according to talmudic practice, they were adjusted down to their true original value when the ketubba was paid. But this adjustment was not done according to the practice described by Radbaz, and payment was made for missing items on the basis of the exaggerated figures.

> In cases like this I assess them according to what they are worth now, or I arbitrate a compromise, because I am certain that the custom was not meant to apply to something like this. If this had explained to the woman at the time of the marriage, she would never have agreed to it. Every judge should act in like fashion in order to frustrate the schemes of the wicked. This is not a change in the custom at all, but an establishment of truth and justice (*ha-emet veha-mishpat*).

[52] In the preceding case, a deceitful husband relies on recognized customary practice, and Radbaz circumvents his scheme by reverting to the law of the Talmud. In this next case the roles are reversed. The husband attempts to exploit the gap between talmudic law and common practice, by insisting on the implementation of the former. Radbaz is on strong ground here in insisting on the legal primacy of accepted custom.

In general, the Talmud does not contemplate property that belongs to a wife as belonging to her entirely. Property which she brings into the marriage in her own name, not as part of her dowry, and property which she may inherit during her marriage, is called in the Talmud *melog* property. Although the property itself is seen as belonging to her, her husband is entitled to enjoy its usufruct, that is, the income that the property produces. Another right that a husband has with regard to his wife's assets is the right to her earnings.

The question that Radbaz was asked is as follows:

> You asked concerning the custom in Egypt[31] according to which the husband stipulates that the bride's earnings should belong to her, and that her clothing should be his obligation, so much per annum. This woman did a great deal of work, and restricted herself with regard to clothing, so that she has money, which she loans on interest to non-Jews. Her husband says that he wants to enjoy the usufruct, in accordance with the law of *melog* property.[32]

The husband sought to distinguish between his wife's earnings from her work, and the money she earned by lending those earnings on interest. The earnings from her work belong to her, he agreed, as in the prenuptial stipulation. But its status is that of *melog* property, and, as her husband, he is entitled to its usufruct, which, he claimed, includes the interest on her loans.

---

31 *mitsrayim*, which could also mean Cairo.

32 IV, 190 (= 1261).

Radbaz makes short shrift of this argument. First, he proves, on technical legal grounds, that the stipulation, ceding the husband's right to the income produced by his wife's earnings, applies to the usufruct as well. Then he argues that the wife's position would be correct even if there were no stipulation at all written into the marriage contract. After all, the fact is that this stipulation reflects common practice, and for that reason alone the law presumes that she married him on those conditions: "For whoever marries a woman without specifying otherwise, marries her on the basis of the custom of the residents of the city, even if this is against the formal law (*ke-neged ha-halakha*), because it is an established custom."

[53] The Talmud rules that either a husband or a wife can compel his or her spouse to agree to move to the Land of Israel. Failure to comply constitutes grounds for divorce. If a wife refuses, she can be divorced without her *ketubba*; if a husband refuses, he can be forced to divorce her with payment of her ketubba.[33] Maimonides codified this law.[34] Tosafot, though, ruled that this law did not apply in their day, because travel was dangerous.[35] Radbaz's sixteenth-century contemporaries generally rejected that argument in its application to their situation, denying that under ordinary conditions danger prevented travel to Palestine from within the Ottoman Empire.[36] Radbaz accepted the law in theory, but was leery of it being used as a ruse. He explains that the law is not applied today when a husband seeks to utilize it. Between the lines, though, it is clear from Radbaz's wording that it was not unheard of for the law to be applied in practice:

> We do not rule (according to this law) today, because, due to our sins, a means of livelihood is not common there. Only if it

---

33 BT Ketubbot 110b.

34 *MT*, Women, Laws of Marriage, chap. 13, parag. 20.

35 Ad. loc., s.v. *hu omer la'alot.* A second reason is offered there too, that there are various religious stringencies contingent on living in Palestine, "and we aren't able to be careful to abide by them."

36 See, e.g., the following responsa: R. Moses Trani, *Responsa*, Pt. 2, no. 216, who argues that there are indeed times of danger, but most of the time travel is safe within the Ottoman Empire, and the law of the Talmud applies; R. Joseph ibn Lev, *Responsa*, Pt. 3, no. 41, who states that the opinion of Tosafot was ignored, and therefore rejected, by later authorities; R. Samuel de Medina, *Responsa*, *Even Ha-'Ezer*, no. 215, who took cognizance of the Tosafot, but argued that under Ottoman rule the danger of travel was not a real problem.

> is clear to us after extensive investigation that he has a trade through which he can make a living, at least with difficulty, then we rule according to it. For we have seen with our own eyes a number of charlatans who advanced this claim, then divorced their wives who lost their *ketubbot*, and afterwards returned. I obligated one of them to remarry his wife or pay her her *ketubba*.[37]

With regard to a wife advancing this claim, Radbaz's rejection is total. In another responsum, after citing the talmudic passage allowing her the right to divorce her husband with collection of the *ketubba*, he continues:

> But now we do not rule this way. Because every woman would intend divorce[38] and would say: "I am immigrating to the Land of Israel"; and livelihood is not available there, and he wouldn't be able to earn a living. Thus he will be divorcing his wife against his will.[39]

In that particular responsum, it should be noted, Radbaz in the end actually rules in favor of the woman, who was asking for the right to go on her own if her husband wouldn't join her, and to use her own dowry to support herself.

[54] A man, who happened to be learned in the law (*talmid hakham*), had married a woman after having divorced his previous wives. The marriage was conditional on his not remarrying them. Now his wife, with her father acting as her agent, was advancing the claim that he had in fact betrothed them, a status that could only be severed by a divorce. The wife was demanding that he either divorce them, or that he divorce her and pay her *ketubba*, in accord with the condition of the marriage.[40] It is clear from the responsum that in Egypt at this time betrothal was not yet merged with marriage into one ceremony, and a betrothed woman continued to live in her father's home. In fact, Radbaz makes the point that betrothal was clearly distinct from

---

37 III, 410 (= 853). See the somewhat similar attitude in Maimonides, Responsa, no. 365, 639-41.

38 *titten eineha be-gerushin*. This could also be understood: "might intend divorce," rather than "would intend divorce." However, see the next note.

39 III, 409 (= 852). This pessimistic view of women's intentions is consistent with Radbaz's statements elsewhere. See, for instance, Case [2] above.

40 IV, 3 (= 1077).

marriage in the public's perception.[41] From a parallel and much fuller account of this case, in the responsa of R. Levi ibn Habib of Jerusalem, we know many more details.[42] We know the names of the principals; that the wife and her family came from Jerusalem; that the case came to court in 1533; and that R. Jacob Berav had ruled in this case in support of the husband. Berav upheld the validity of the condition, but ruled that betrothal itself, without marriage, did not violate it. He consequently ruled that if the woman refused to return to her husband she would be considered a "rebellious wife," with the result that the condition would be voided and he would be allowed to proceed to marry whomever he wished.[43]

The position that "will not marry" does not include "will not betroth" was one of two arguments advanced by the husband as reported by Radbaz. The other had to do with the fact that there were two versions of the condition, the first when it was originally formulated at the time of the engagement (*shiddukhim*), and the second when it was included in the text of the *ketubba*. Both versions employed the terminology that the groom prohibited to himself the pleasure of any sexual relations with his former wives, but the second version added the words: "like his mother and his sister." Now, the prohibition involved here is that of a vow,[44] and in order to clarify the husband's argument, and Radbaz's response to it, certain issues regarding vows must be understood.

A vow is a prohibition undertaken by an individual with regard to the benefit that derives from something. One of the ways of undertaking a vow is to say, regarding object X: "X is like Y to me," when Y is an object prohibited to one by a former vow. But if Y is prohibited in and of itself by a prohibition of the Torah, without any previous vow being involved, for instance, a piece of non-kosher meat, then the vow is not valid.[45] In our case, sexual relations with one's mother and one's sister are prohibited by a prohibition of the Torah, and a vow, which takes the form of likening something else to them, would

41 See Freimann, *Seder Qiddushin ve-Nissuin*, 105. See Westreich, *Transitions*, 100, on the opposite perception prevalent in Germany, already in the thirteenth century.

42 R. Levi ibn Habib, *Responsa*, nos. 26 and 27.

43 Ibid., no. 26.

44 R. Levi ibn Habib strongly contested the notion that the terminology of the condition implied a vow. But the assumption that it did was taken for granted by Radbaz, and apparently by the husband too.

45 See *MT*, Asseverations, Laws of Vows, chap. 1, parag. 7-9.

not be valid. Therefore, argued the husband, the version of the prohibition included in the *ketubba*—i.e., the version actually controlling the conditions of the marriage—was not binding. In response, the wife's father, acting on her behalf, insisted that as of now the husband prohibit his former wives to himself in an unambiguously valid manner.

Radbaz readily admits the distinction between betrothal and marriage, but he rules against the husband's claim that he is not bound by the vow at all. He cites a few reasons, the first of which is relevant to our discussion. The language of the *ketubba*, he says, must be interpreted in light of the language of the engagement agreement.

> And what they added when they wrote, "like his mother and his sister," must be understood not as a comparison establishing the vow (*ke-matpis*), but as added wording. Or else he intended to deceive them, but it availed him naught.

The first interpretation suggested here is that the vow is valid as it stands, that this is not a case of vowing by comparison with an object forbidden by the Torah. The second interpretation, on the other hand, implies that the vow is actually invalid, and was rendered so intentionally.

The notion that there was an intent to deceive, while not subject to proof, is certainly not improbable. First of all, we are told that the husband was learned in the law. Furthermore, we learn from the account presented by R. Levi ibn Habib that the husband, who came to see him in Jerusalem, bemoaned the fact that he cannot remarry his former older wife, because she knew how to take care of a household, whereas his present younger wife did not. It is not unlikely, therefore, that he indeed intended to remarry his former wife at the time he formulated the *ketubba*, though there is nothing to suggest that this was originally his intention at the time of the engagement. In any case, from the description of the events presented as it appears in Ibn Habib 's account, the wife and her family surely understood the change in wording to be a deliberate deceit:

> ... This is the version of the betrothal document. And he went and altered all this ... and this is what he wrote in the *ketubba*.... And he didn't give her[46] the ketubba until after he had been married to her for five days.

Be that as it may, Radbaz acts as if it were deliberate:

---

46 Emended from: "didn't give me," apparently a mistake, but already so in the first edition (Venice, 1565). Alternatively, if the wife is speaking, "married to her" in the sequel should be emended to: "married to me."

> Therefore, if Reuben wants to keep this wife, he must fulfill his condition, and prohibit his divorcees to himself in a proper manner (*ka-ra'ui*). If he does not wish to do so, he must divorce this wife and give her her ketubba.

In insisting that the husband undertake a new and valid vow, Radbaz is in effect admitting that the former may have indeed been invalid, that is, that the added wording in the *ketubba*'s version of the condition was deliberately deceitful. R. Jacob Berav, in responding to this ruling of Radbaz's, challenges him on this very point: "I have studied the ruling of Rabbi David Abi Zimra and the anonymous judge whose name we do not know, it is unknowable.[47] We have seen that they have ruled as they wished, without reason and without proof, and I have seen their words contradicting each other."[48] For on the one hand, he explains, Radbaz maintains that the imposition of a proper vow prohibiting his divorcees is not a new imposition;[49] but if that is the case, why should he have to undertake another vow at all?

It seems clear, therefore, that this is, or is being treated as, another example of someone seeking to take advantage of the letter of the law in an inequitable manner. In response to Berav's objection, this is not a new imposition that the husband is being asked to take upon himself, because it represents the very same self-imposition that he deceitfully sought to convey to his bride. Though the husband may have the letter of the law on his side, Radbaz is not about to let him get away with it, even though that means acting, as Berav would have it, "without reason and without proof."

[55] The preceding case was an example of a condition written into the marriage contract. In that instance the condition was designed for a rather specific set of circumstances. But marriage conditions that reflected more general situations were commonplace. Perhaps the most common was an agreement of the husband not to take another wife without his wife's permission. A problem, with roots going back to the Talmud, was the status of such conditions if the husband divorced and then remarried his wife, without repeating the conditions at the time of

---

47 Playing on Judges 13:18.

48 R. Levi ibn Habib, *Responsa*, no. 27.

49 The wording cited by Berav is not in our text of Radbaz's responsum. But he did write: "The law is also with Reuben regarding his claim that he does not want to take upon himself more than what is written in the ketubba document."

the second marriage.[50] Did the original condition imply that it was binding at any time she was his wife, or only during this marriage? Radbaz was asked about an apparent contradiction in this regard between the Rashba's commentary on the Talmud and his responsa. Radbaz proceeds to resolve the contradiction.[51] At the end of the responsum, he volunteers his own opinion:

> I was asked in the past about one who had divorced his wife and remarried her, whether the conditions of the ketubba were voided. I concluded that such is indeed my opinion as to the law in the abstract (*le-halakha*), but it is not proper to rule that way in practice (*le-ma'aseh*). Because if these matters become public, men will act deceitfully; and the women do not know the law, so that all the *ketubba* conditions of the daughters of Israel will become null and void. A case (of this type) occurred in which we didn't allow him to take a second wife until his wife gave him permission.[52] This is not only so if he (merely) wrote that "he will not take another wife in addition to her," but even if he wrote, "as long as she is with him," wording which unambiguously refers to the first marriage.

Radbaz here echoes Rashba, who states in his responsum, along with other arguments:

> And another reason: Because this man was deceitful, and the law (*ve-shurat ha-din*) is that the court prosecute and convict him. For our perfect Torah is true, and its laws are true, and it convicts liars and intimidators in a manner not in accordance with the law of other people, as in the case of Mari bar Isaq ...[53]

The talmudic case of Mari bar Isaq is instructive.[54] Mari bar Isaq was a wealthy and powerful man. Someone appeared before Rabbi H̱isda and claimed to be Mari's brother, demanding half of his inherited estate. When the plaintiff was asked to produce witnesses who would prove that he was a brother, he alleged that they were intimidated by Mari. Rabbi H̱isda then transferred the burden of proof to the defendant, and asked Mari to produce witnesses that the man was not a brother. When challenged by Mari on the legalities of this ruling, Rabbi

---

50 See Case [43] above.

51 II, 837. See Rashba, *Responsa*, pt. 1, no. 962; Rabbenu Nissim on Alfasi to Ketubbot, beginning of chap. 12, s.v. *Ha-piqẖin*, who presents Rashba's novellum. (The questioner in Radbaz's responsum, however, refers to the latter source as *Nimmuqei Yosef*.)

52 The reference may well be to Case [43].

53 Rashba, *Responsa*, pt. 1, no. 962.

54 BT Bava Metsi'a 39b.

Hisda appealed to judicial discretion as a means of handling intimidating litigants. Maimonides, who codified the law in accordance with this precedent, added a proviso, that this degree of judicial discretion is not operative today in practice.[55] Yet Rashba here seems to accept its current applicability. We have seen earlier that Radbaz also applies this talmudic precedent and others like it.[56] Here too, in dealing with those who would exploit the law to unjust advantage, he does not hesitate to rule on the basis of what he believes to be right, even though it does not fit the letter of the law.

[56] Instances of attempts to exploit the letter of the law in an inequitable manner occur in areas other than relations between husband and wife. In the following case a man took advantage of the fact that his father was a scholar of Torah deserving of special privileges:

> Reuben and Simeon were fighting, and Reuben cursed Simeon and his father. Simeon then went and cursed Reuben and his father. Reuben declared a ban on Simeon (*nidda et shime'on*) in his father's honor, for he was a *hakham* (scholar of Torah), whereas Simeon's father was not a *hakham*.[57]

Radbaz is quick to frustrate Reuben's intention. If anyone is deserving of being banned here, he says, it is Reuben, who began the cursing. In acquitting Simeon, Radbaz cites the rule in the Talmud, "If one acts wrongly, and another comes and acts wrongly against him, he (the defendant in the subsequent suit) is not liable."[58] The context is the lack of liability of the owner of a dog who bit someone who was inciting it against another party. Radbaz's rather original use of this passage appears to be rhetorical, since Radbaz himself explicitly states elsewhere that the rule does not apply to a human being, "who possesses a mind and intelligence," and is expected to control himself from engaging in uninhibited reactions.[59] Radbaz's use of the rule here,

---

55 *MT*, Judges, Laws of the Sanhedrin, chap. 24, parags. 1-2. Cited in abridged form in Case [30] above. The case of Mari bar Isaq is part of the ellipsis there.

56 See above, Case [30], and the others in that section.

57 I, 492. See *MT*, Knowledge, Laws of Torah Learning, chap. 6, parag. 12. However, Maimonides rules there that only a *hakham* himself, may personally, and without supporting witnesses, declare a ban for violation of his honor.

58 BT Bava Qamma 20a and 24b. The context described in the text is from the latter, which is more relevant to this responsum.

59 III, 480 (= 918), regarding one who began a fight with another, and the other called him a bastard; IV, 220 (= 1291), regarding one who hit another

therefore, may be indicative of his ire at Reuben for exploiting the law this way.

[57] Radbaz responds to the attempt of a litigant to escape payment of a debt by basing himself on the technicalities of talmudic law in a rather bald-faced and cynical manner. The case involved maritime insurance.[60] Maritime insurance took various forms.[61] In the present instance, "Simeon" had loaned "Reuben" capital with which to purchase a cargo. In a separate transaction, but included in the same document, Simeon undertook responsibility for any loss which may be incurred, and Reuben undertook to pay Simeon for that risk. However, the technicalities prescribed by rabbinic law for the undertaking of an obligation were omitted. Subsequently, when the ship arrived safely at its port of call and the cargo was sold, Reuben refused to pay Simeon for assuming the risk, arguing that the lack of the required technicalities meant that he had never been responsible for the risk. Of course, one cannot seriously entertain the thought that this argument would have entered Reuben's mind before the voyage. It is beyond the bounds of credibility that he would have undertaken such a voyage unless he himself believed that the risk was covered, and there is every reason to assume that Simeon indeed did feel that he had undertaken the risk. It is therefore nothing but a cynical attempt on Reuben's part to escape payment after the fact.

Radbaz argues cogently that Reuben is wrong in his understanding of the law, since the transfer of the document itself can function as an alternative technicality in establishing Simeon's undertaking of liability. But Radbaz emphasizes the aspect of equity involved here, which is independent of the technicalities of the law. He asserts that even if one were to accept Reuben's argument, that, according to the letter of the law, Simeon could have avoided assuming the risk if the ship were lost, "Who is to tell us that he would not have fulfilled (the words of Zephaniah): 'The remnant of Israel shall do no wrong and speak no falsehood'"?[62] The presumption is that Simeon would have fulfilled his moral, if not legal, obligations, and Reuben is bound by that.

---

in sport, and the other became angry and blinded him. The quote is from the latter.

60 VI, 2290.

61 See above, Case [17], and the literature cited there in n. 105.

62 Zephaniah 3:13. See above, Case [46].

[58] The last responsum to be cited as an example of improper exploitation of the formal law is one of the sharpest expressions of Radbaz's outrage at this phenomenon.[63] Radbaz's sense of being scandalized is fueled by what he considers to be a deliberate attempt to pull the wool over his eyes.

The questions with which Radbaz introduces his responsa are usually highly condensed by him, presenting us with the barest minimum of necessary information, and sometimes not even that.[64] That is not the case here. The questioner, writing from Rhodes, begins with a lengthy encomium to Radbaz, replete with superlatives of the grandest sort expressed in highly flourishing language. Following this panegyric, we are told the substance of the matter. "Reuben" had sold half of his vineyard to "Simeon" for a hundred florins. The sale was processed by an Islamic court, and not by a Jewish court, which, the questioner maintains, would have been the normal procedure for Jewish sales. Subsequently Reuben died. When Simeon, producing the bill of sale, claimed his half of the vineyard from Reuben's heirs, the heirs agreed to buy it back from him for an additional twenty florins. Now, having paid the one hundred and twenty florins and gained acquisition of the bill of sale, Reuben's heirs claim that the sale was invalid because it was not processed by a Jewish court. Therefore, they argue, the hundred florins must be construed as a loan, and the extra twenty florins as stipulated interest, which is recoverable under Jewish law. The questioner asks whether it is Simeon who is liable, or the judges, who made the error of authorizing the payment of the twenty florins.

Radbaz sees the whole thing as a setup. He begins his response with a reaction to the panegyric, and one can assume that he quoted it for the sole purpose of being able to react to it. He interprets it as an attempt to influence him by flattery:

> As for words of praise, leave me out of it.[65] I will not answer you. For regarding this and its like, I rely on the words of the poet and his speech: "The best of poetry is its falsehood."[66]

The questioner had presented Radbaz with two choices: the twenty florins had to be reimbursed either by Simeon, or by the judge who made an erroneous ruling. Radbaz, however, rules in favor of Simeon, that the original sale was valid, for reasons that we will soon discuss.

---

63 I, 29.

64 See Chap. 1, n. 79.

65 *h̲idlu mimmeni*

66 *meitav ha-shir kozvo.* On this aphorism, translated into Hebrew from Arabic, see D. Pagis, *Shirat ha-H̲ol*, 46-51.

The option presented by the questioner, that perhaps the judges who awarded Simeon the twenty florins are liable, is shown by Radbaz to be totally untenable, and he believes that the questioner is fully aware of that. He sees the questioner's presentation as a ploy to hoodwink him, and his ire is palpable:

> For these reasons I say that they (the petitioners) had no question about this (the possible liability of the judges) at all. Rather, the question is whether the judgment (that the heirs pay the extra twenty florins) should be reversed or not. But the questioner had made up his mind that Simeon is obligated to repay the money. And, in order that the rabbinic authority (*ha-moreh*, i.e., Radbaz himself—SM) be drawn to his opinion, he worded his question as to whether the judges are liable or Simeon, so that the rabbi who was asked[67] will decide between the two options, and as a matter of course it will be understood that the judgment should be reversed. But he didn't pay attention that "I look into the case of the stranger."[68]

Radbaz validates the sale in spite of the fact that the deed was drawn up in "the courts of the gentiles," contrary to talmudic law. He bases this conclusion on the principle enunciated in the Babylonian Talmud, that "the law of the kingdom is the law," that is, that the law of the state is binding according to Jewish law.[69] He summarizes three interpretations of this rule: one, which would include in its purview all civil law; a second, which would restrict it to matters of taxation; and a third, which would restrict it to matters of real property. Radbaz adopts this last view,[70] which would bring the present case under its rubric.

Radbaz is extremely skeptical of the questioner's assertion, that the accepted practice regarding the transfer of real estate was in fact in accordance with the law of the Talmud, which prohibited "gentile

---

67 *ha-nishal.* In the first edition the last letter is replaced by an abbreviation mark, which was mistakenly completed in ed. Warsaw meaninglessly as: *ha-nishar.*

68 Citing Job 29:16.

69 BT Bava Batra 54b and parallels. For an exhaustive study of this principle see Shilo, *Dina de-Malkhuta.*

70 For this view see Shilo, 96. Radbaz invokes a rule he often employs in cases of controversy, of deciding according to the median position, see Chap. 6 below. He also attributes this opinion on "the law of the land" to Maimonides, without citing a reference, but it is very questionable whether that attribution is correct; see Shilo, 96-97. Shilo calls attention to the sudden reemergence of this position in the 16th century, and refers *inter alia* to our responsum, p. 97.

courts." In discussing the implications of that unlikely possibility, Radbaz treats such a situation, were it to exist, as a "custom," which would have to meet various requirements before it could become legally binding. He thus marginalizes the law of the Talmud, upon which the plaintiffs sought to base an unjust case. As in all these cases, he has no patience for scoundrels hiding under the shadow of the Torah.

4. Considerations of Public Policy

On a number of occasions, Radbaz, in deciding between conflicting authorities, makes a special point of stressing the desirability of the result that would ensue from the decision, that is, its public policy aspect.[1] Sometimes he presents this rationale as auxiliary to conventional arguments, occasionally even as overkill. Sometimes, however, he presents it as bearing the whole weight of the decision. At times he rules in one case according to one side of a controversy and in another case according to the opposing side, depending on the desired outcome. It is Radbaz's explicit highlighting of these motivations which is so striking. Both his reliance on this type of rationale, in the one case, and his tendency to express these motivations even when they are peripheral to his technical argument, on the other, are demonstrative of the role of public policy in his judicial personality.

[59] Radbaz's approach to matters of public policy can be demonstrated by a responsum that touches upon a matter of great theoretical and practical importance, a conflict of laws.

The first of the two laws involved is the prohibition of interest. Some of the details of the prohibition of interest were explained in Case [39], and I will briefly review the relevant details. First, the prohibition applies to the borrower as well as to the lender. Second, in addition to

---

1 See the exchange between D. Hartman and H. Soloveitchik on the propriety of defining such issues as halakhic; references in Chapter 1, n. 124.

biblically prohibited interest, which the Talmud defines rather narrowly, there are many types of transactions, which were prohibited by the Rabbis. Unlike biblically prohibited interest, rabbinically prohibited interest is not recoverable once paid, but neither can the lender sue for its payment.

The other law is the biblical injunction to fulfill an oath. Oaths were used as a means of ensuring the fulfillment of a contractual obligation. For instance, in another responsum, Radbaz was asked about "Reuben, who swore to Simeon to repay him his debt by a certain date."[2] The question of our responsum asks about a situation in which one swore to pay a lender rabbinically prohibited interest.[3] Failure to do so would then constitute a violation of the biblical law mandating the fulfillment of vows, whereas payment would violate only a rabbinically mandated injunction. It is obvious that in a commercial society the rabbinic extension of the laws of interest affected economic life in important ways, and what is involved here is an attempt at devising a loophole which would in effect evade its onerous provisions. Even if one were to stand guilty before the Heavenly Court for having undertaken such an oath, at least one would be beyond the reach of enforceability in a human court of law for fulfilling it. Radbaz puts the issue into a broader perspective at the outset, in the way he presents the question: "Included in the question is the issue of all rabbinically mandated prohibitions regarding which one takes an oath." In other words, a procedure of this type has the potential of allowing for the evasion of rabbinically legislated prohibitions in general. And though oaths can ordinarily be nullified, the one who undertook the oath has to initiate such a procedure, and cannot be forced to do so.

Radbaz strips the issue down to its hard core. He begins by recommending the nullification of the oath if at all possible. Certain formulations make nullification difficult, and one could expect such formulations to be included in an oath of this type.[4] Radbaz rules, however, that these limitations on nullification do not apply here, "because there is a prohibition involved in the matter." However, Radbaz recognizes that nullification may nevertheless not be possible.

---

2 I, 289.

3 IV, 278 (= 1349).

4 Normally, an oath undertaken upon the consent of another party would require that party's agreement to the nullification. If the party were a famous rabbi in a distant land, requiring his consent would render nullification beyond practical reach. Also, an oath made for the benefit of another party cannot be nullified without that party's presence.

He then draws a distinction between an oath to refrain from a rabbinically mandated act, such as lighting Hanukkah candles, and an oath to perform a rabbinically prohibited act, such as engaging in the kinds of transactions which are at issue here. In the former case, since the violation of the rabbinic command does not entail a positive act, one is bound by one's oath, and should violate the rabbinic command by inaction. The hard core is the latter situation, an oath to perform an act that the Rabbis of the Talmud have forbidden.

This question had been dealt with by earlier authorities, and there is strong precedent for the position that the law of the Torah, exemplified by the oath, overrides the law legislated by the Rabbis. Both Rashba and Rabbenu Asher had taken that position.[5] Radbaz cites an opposing position by Ritba "in the name of his teacher,"[6] basing himself on the talmudic principle that the Court (that is, the Rabbis of the Talmud in their corporate authority) can enact legislation which has the effect of preventing the performance of an act required by the Torah.[7] Radbaz adopts that position against the imposing authority of Rashba and Rabbenu Asher. He justifies doing so in the following manner:

> Most of the enactments of the Sages are preventive regulations (*seyagim*, literally: fences), lest people transgress the words of the Torah. If you were to say that one who takes an oath to nullify them should fulfill his vow, the result would be that people would breach the fences and the barriers. One who wishes to transgress rabbinic prohibitions would take an oath regarding them, and transgress them with the permission of the court. Thus, the intention for which the enactments were established would be frustrated. Therefore, it is better that his oath be violated by a passive act rather than that the enactments of the Rabbis be violated. This is correct and evident.

Asked in another responsum how he could rule against Rashba, he refers to what he had written here:

---

5 Rashba, *Responsa*, Pt.1, no. 64 and no. 614; *Attributed Responsa*, no. 243. Rabbenu Asher, *Responsa*, *Kelal* 8 no. 16 (duplicated in *Kelal* 43 no. 13). The latter appears to be the same question asked of Rashba in *Attributed Responsa*. (Radbaz, however, who refers to both in IV, 281 (=1352), suggests that they understood their respective questions as referring to somewhat different situations.)

6 Ritba studied under R. Aaron ha-Levi, as well as under the aforementioned Rashba, to whom this obviously does not refer.

7 BT Yevamot 89b–90b.

> It is true that such is the view of Rashba and Rosh (Rabbenu Asher). But my weak opinion inclines toward Ritba, for the reason I wrote in that responsum, that anyone who wishes to transgress rabbinic prohibitions would take an oath regarding them, and transgress them with the permission of the court, and people would come to disrespect the prohibitions of the Rabbis.[8]

Thus it is not the authority of Ritba that determines his ruling against two of the most authoritative decisors of Jewish law, nor the convincing power of Ritba's argument, but the desirability of the result.[9]

[60] Radbaz rules against his own understanding of the sense of a talmudic passage in order to arrive at a desirable result, though he follows his understanding of that same passage in circumstances in which an undesirable result is not at issue.

Radbaz is asked about the right of a man to will his assets to the community for the purchase of a Torah scroll, though he would thereby deprive his widow of the wherewithal to collect her *ketubba*.[10] The

---

8 IV, 195 (= 1266). Radbaz, in IV, 281 (=1352), answers the same question addressed by Rashba (in the *Attributed Responsa*) and Rabbenu Asher (see n. 5). If a man swore to pay a debt by a certain date, and that date occurs on a Sabbath, must he pay on the Sabbath? Radbaz echoes Rabbenu Asher's argument, that there was no intention originally of violating the Sabbath. He was just unaware that the designated date was a Sabbath. Radbaz makes a sharp distinction between this situation and that discussed above, where there was a clear intention to evade the law. In the case in which the conflict with Sabbath law was inadvertent, he rules that if no other way out is found, since the Sabbath violation is rabbinic, he should pay him on the Sabbath. Rabbenu Asher said the same, but without explicitly drawing the distinction between a Torah prohibition and a rabbinic prohibition.

9 Radbaz refers to this responsum by way of an *ad majorem* argument in II, 635. The issue there involves a common practice, an oath of a student by his teacher, that he will learn only from him. (This is also the subject of VI, 2215.) Radbaz is indignant about this practice, which he feels limits the study of Torah, and disqualifies such an oath altogether as being in violation of the biblical requirement to learn Torah. He cites our responsum to show that, in his opinion, even an oath to violate a rabbinic prohibition is invalid.

10 I, 334. The question as originally worded was whether he could will that the assets be dedicated to a Torah scroll for his own estate ("for himself"), thus diverting the funds from his wife's *ketubba*. The answer was so obvious to

issue is governed by the rule enunciated by Rava in the Talmud, that the dedication (i.e., consecration) of assets to the Temple removes them from a creditor's lien on them.[11] The dedication of funds for the poor or for communal religious needs was seen as equivalent to dedicating them to the Temple. There are, however, two types of Temple dedication. One type is the dedication of an animal itself directly for purposes of sacrifice ("consecration of the flesh," *qedushat ha-guf*). The other type is the dedication of assets to the Temple treasury ("consecration of funds," *qedushat damim*). Rashi understands Rava to refer only to dedication of the former kind.[12] The dedication of funds for a Torah scroll is clearly of the latter kind, and accordingly, under this interpretation, the wife's lien on her husband's assets is intact. Rabbenu Tam disputes Rashi's interpretation, and understands Rava to refer to both kinds of dedication.[13] Radbaz himself believes Rabbenu Tam's interpretation to be the correct understanding of Rava's intention, proffering the historical argument that "in Rava's time, there existed only dedication to the poor or to a Torah scroll or to a synagogue." But he is not happy with the result in this case, which would deprive the widow of her *ketubba*.

Radbaz first suggests that perhaps Rava may not have intended to include in his rule cases like this, where there were no other resources from which the creditor could collect. He bases the probability of this unproven assumption on considerations of equity:

> Because if you do not say this, everyone would be able to[14] dedicate his assets at the time of his death, and remove the lien on them for payment of his wife's *ketubba* and other creditors.

Nevertheless, he is aware that this assumption of Rava's intention is not totally compelling. Having explained that Rabbenu Tam's interpretation of the text is convincing, but that Rashi's interpretation leads to the more desirable end, he continues as follows:

> Even if you say that Rava said what he did with regard to all cases, even those in which he owes a debt to a wife and a

---

Radbaz that he suggests that it be construed the way it is presented in the text.

11 BT Gittin 40b and parallels, in the name of Rava.

12 Rashi ad loc.

13 Explicitly in *Sefer ha-Yashar*, no. 113, pp. 79–80. See also Tosafot, Gittin 40b s.v. *heqdesh*.

14 "Would be able to" represents my understanding of the text. It could also be understood as "would," without the words, "be able to." Hebrew simply: *ve-yafqia'*.

> creditor, it makes sense (*mistabbera*) to rule like Rashi in situations in which there is nothing from which to collect: for a wife, because of his love;[15] and for a creditor, so that he not lose his money, (resulting in) a closing of the door to borrowers.[16] But where there is no loss, because there is something from which to collect, it makes sense to rule like Rabbenu Tam, because of the benefit accruing to dedicated funds (*heqdesh*, i.e., funds for support of the poor and for the religious needs of the community). And also, because the wording of Rava implies all (i.e., both) kinds of dedication.

Thus, even though he himself believes that Rabbenu Tam's interpretation is correct, he rules in accordance with Rashi's interpretation in order to ensure that the woman is not deprived of her ketubba.[17]

[61] The same dynamic is in evidence in another responsum, this one apparently an academic question rather than an actual case.

There are cases in rabbinic civil law which require an oath by one of the litigants when there is an absence of evidentiary proof. The Mishnah states that whenever the Torah requires such an oath, it is the defendant who takes the oath, thereby absolving himself of the plaintiff's claim against him. The plaintiff cannot win his case and collect on the basis of his own oath.[18] However, the same passage in the Mishnah goes on to list a number of exceptions to this rule, where for one reason or another the Rabbis transferred the oath to the plaintiff. For example, such would be the case if the defendant were considered untrustworthy regarding an oath because he was a gambler, or a usurer,

---

15 That is, the law takes into account the husband's love for his wife at the time of his marriage in construing the legal obligations that he undertook at the time toward her. This rationale occurs in a number of places in the Talmud. See one example in the next note.

16 Preventing a situation that would make people disinclined to lend money is used as a rationale for a number of laws that benefit creditors. For instance, both this consideration and the one above, of the husband's love for his wife, appear in a discussion of the right to collect a *ketubba* or other debt in the absence of the husband or debtor respectively; BT Ketubbot 88a.

17 Radbaz closes with a reference to Rashba, *Responsa*, no. 618 (of vol. 1 in today's editions), where a similar question is asked, and Rashba rules that the creditor can collect the debt. But Rashba there takes for granted Rashi's understanding of Rava's statement.

18 Mishnah Shevu'ot 7:1; BT Shevu'ot 44b.

or a dealer in fruit of the sabbatical year.[19] The first exception in the Mishnah's list is a hired laborer, who claims that he has not been paid, whereas the employer claims that he has paid him. The laborer takes an oath that he has not been paid and collects his payment. The Talmud explains that the employer is preoccupied with many hired laborers, and therefore may have been mistaken about this particular one, so the oath is transferred to the plaintiff, the laborer.

Maimonides, in presenting this law regarding the transfer of an oath to the plaintiff, rules that it applies only if the plaintiff claims a minimum of "two pieces of silver," that is, two *ma'ot* (singular: *ma'a,* a silver coin of low denomination). Maimonides arrives at this minimum by drawing an analogy to another type of claim where it applies.[20] He rules thus, he says, in opposition to "my masters," who had ruled that the minimum amount of two pieces of silver does not apply here.[21] Maimonides' glossator, Rabad, takes exception to this ruling, and supports the view of Maimonides' masters: "What should the poor hireling do who has hired himself out for a *ma'a or* a *pundyon* (half a *ma'a*)? He would go away in despair!" Later authorities were divided on this issue. Rabbenu Nissim ruled against Maimonides: "If the Rabbis believe him upon his oath for a large sum, that is certainly the case for a small one!"[22] On the other hand, the author of the *Turim*, after citing the differing views of Maimonides and Rabad, states without elaboration: "The words of Maimonides make sense (*mistabbera*)."[23]

The question presented to Radbaz was whether we rule like Maimonides "and most of the later authorities," and if so, what remedy is there for the poor hired laborer who claims less than the minimum of two pieces of silver—should he go away in despair?[24] Radbaz's contemporary, R. Joseph Caro, ruled against Maimonides in this matter.[25] Radbaz, however, ruled in principle like Maimonides, producing an original argument for his position based on the language

19 Mishnah Shevu'ot 7:4.

20 The analogy is to the oath taken by a bailee, that the object entrusted to him was lost under conditions for which he is not responsible. Since the plaintiff has no way of knowing the truth, this is an oath taken to ward off a claim advanced in uncertainty.

21 *MT*, Civil Laws, Laws of Pleading, chap. 3, parag. 7.

22 Rabbenu Nissim on Alfasi to Shevu'ot, chap. 6, ed. Romm 19b.

23 *Tur Hoshen Mishpat*, no. 89.

24 IV, 185 (= 1256).

25 *Beit Yosef*, ad loc.

of the talmudic text. In response to Rabad's objection, which was based on the possible inequity which may result, Radbaz rules that in such a case the defendant, the employer, should take the oath, in order to placate the plaintiff, as is normally the case. And what if the defendant is one who is untrustworthy regarding an oath, and cannot therefore be subjected to one? What recourse does the plaintiff have then? In such a case, Radbaz splits his decision, as he did in the previous case, and rules, with Rabad, like Maimonides' masters:

> To sum up: Where the employer is trustworthy regarding an oath, so that the hired laborer does not go away in despair, we rule like Maimonides, **for his reason makes sense** (*de-mistabber ta'ameih*). And where the employer is one who is untrustworthy regarding an oath, so that the hired laborer would go away completely in despair (i.e., without even the satisfaction of a rabbinic oath on the part of the defendant—SM), we rule like the other great authorities, **for their reason makes sense** (*demistabber ta'amaihu*) (emphasis mine—SM).

That is, Maimonides' position makes sense in terms of the wording of the Talmud; his antagonists' position makes sense in terms of an equitable resolution.

[62] A pair of responsa on another issue reflects a similar alternation between opposing positions, which is conditioned on the desirability of the outcome. This example is not as convincing as the previous one, because Radbaz brings substantive reasons for his change of position. Nevertheless, in the final analysis, he admittedly relies on a precedent ruling which, in a previous responsum, he had explicitly rejected.

The issue is one that had received considerable attention by earlier authorities. It is the problem of a Jew, representing himself to a Jewish lender as acting on behalf of a non-Jewish borrower, asserts that the non-Jew wished to borrow money on interest from the lender. The middleman presents the lender with objects in pledge for the loan, which, he says, belong to the non-Jew. When the payment comes due, the Jewish middleman maintains that he had misrepresented himself to the lender, that in fact he himself was the borrower, and that the pledged objects belong to him. Since interest is forbidden among Jews not only to the lender but to the borrower as well,[26] the borrower, now assuming a position of pious self-interest, refuses to violate the law by paying the interest.

---

26 BT Bava Metsi'a 75b. See Case [39] above.

This problem had been addressed by R. Isaac b. Asher ha-Levi of Speyers (Riva), a scholar of the early twelfth century, who had composed a compendium on the laws of interest.[27] He stated that the lender need not recognize the belated assertion of the other Jew that he is indeed the borrower and the owner of the pledge. The lender may assume that the latter's original assertion was correct, and may keep the pledge until it is redeemed by payment of the principal and interest, or, alternatively, may realize his profit by selling it.[28] Riva presents this as the law, though he himself is not happy with it. He advises the lender to take the pious path and not collect interest, either directly or through sale of the pledge, unless he is sure of its gentile ownership. But he realizes that the lender is within his legal rights to do so.

Haym Soloveitchik, who dealt with this issue in his book on pawnbroking,[29] points out that the German rabbis wrestled with this problem throughout the thirteenth century. Soloveitchik explains the prevalence of such misrepresentation in Germany at that time. He sees it as a result of the rejection in Germany of legal fictions that had been accepted in France, which would allow the payment of interest among Jews, a precondition for commercial credit. Since there was no other way to obtain necessary credit, argues Soloveitchik, misrepresentation became a necessity, and the moral edge to it was lost.[30] Although the legal fictions that made borrowing possible eventually filtered into Germany in the thirteenth century, old habits die hard. German Jews continued to utilize misrepresentation as a means of borrowing money, and the issue remained on the agenda of the rabbinic authorities.[31] On the one hand, on an intuitive and common sense level, there is every

---

27 Riva's compendium is discussed by Soloveitchik, *Pawnbroking*, 60–65. The text is presented there, 129–31, from the version preserved in *Shibbolei ha-Leqet*, vol. 2, 79–80; see 60 n. 3. See that note for a list of the other sources in which Riva's compendium, and an abridgment thereof, are preserved. Riva's discussion of our issue is found in Soloveitchik, 131 (= *Shibbolei ha-Leqet*, 80, ll. 29–48).

28 Soloveitchik, *Pawnbroking*, 29ff., shows that the right of the lender to sell the pledge derived from Germanic law, and was a fact of life for Jewish moneylenders, though it would not have been permitted under talmudic law.

29 See n. 27.

30 Soloveitchik points out that discussion of this phenomenon is absent altogether from the writings of the French rabbis.

31 Op cit., 65, n. 25. The note includes a reference to sources that deal with this problem.

reason to accept the borrower's later assertion that he borrowed the money for himself and that the pledge was his. Riva's gut instinct tells him that such is the case regardless of the legal presupposition to the contrary, and some did indeed rule that way in practice.[32] On the other hand, from the perspective of public policy there was every reason to refuse the borrower the right to profit from misrepresentation. An extreme form of this stance was adopted by Rabbenu Asher. He ruled that even though there are witnesses who testify that the pledged article belonged to the Jewish borrower, and that it was under their constant supervision from the time it came into the borrower's possession until he gave it in pledge to the lender, we do not accept their testimony in the face of the borrower's original assertion, that the article given in pledge belonged to a non-Jew.[33]

It was a case of this type that came before Radbaz.[34] If the stigma of deception was blunted in twelfth-century Germany, as Soloveitchik suggests, that was clearly not the case here. Radbaz's scathing denunciation of the deceiving borrower implies that this was not a usual occurrence:

> This Reuben (the borrower) is a wicked man, not included in the generality of Israel, of whom it is written: "The remnant of Israel shall do no wrong and speak no falsehood; a deceitful tongue shall not be in their mouths."[35] He thought to make a profit, and to render useless another's capital (*le-vattel kiso shel haveiro*). But that is not the case.

Radbaz has ample precedent, of course, for rejecting the borrower's belated assertion that the pledge was his and the loan was for himself. He cites a number of the German rabbis in this regard, including especially Rabbenu Asher. However, he has to deal with a responsum of Rashba, to the following effect: "If one loaned money to a Jew on interest on the basis of a pledged article, and eventually it turned out that it (the pledge) was the Jew's, it is forbidden to take interest from

---

32 See, for instance, R. Meir bar Barukh, *Responsa Prague*, no. 737, in reaction to a ruling that the borrower should pay the interest: "It is not clear to Rabbenu Barukh, for how can he pay interest to a Jew? Rather, he (the borrower) should take an oath that the pledge is his, and be free of the interest."

33 Rabbenu Asher, *Responsa*, *Kelal* 108, no. 3.

34 I, 305.

35 Zephaniah 3:13.

him."[36] Radbaz applies a forced interpretation to Rashba. He understands him to refer to a case in which the borrower was not specific about the ownership of the pledged articles, but allowed the lender to draw his own mistaken conclusion. He admits that his interpretation of Rashba is not conclusive, and counters a possible objection along those lines:

> Know, that even if Rashba were to differ (with Rabbenu Asher and the others of the German school), we should not rely on him in this regard; first, because the generation is very lawless in this matter and those similar to it, and it is necessary to establish a (moral) fence; and furthermore, ... (because Rabbenu Asher and the others disagree with Rashba).

Here again we see Radbaz justifying his conclusion on the basis of the desirability of the result. The need to establish a "moral fence" is a factor in deciding between conflicting authorities. Admittedly, the present responsum is not a strong example of this tendency. Radbaz had presented ample reason for ruling as he did. This is a type of argument called a *senif*, a makeweight argument, weak in its own right, which rabbinic jurists commonly added to the main argument for the purpose of strengthening the case. Radbaz himself had warned against relying on a *senif* incorporated in a responsum as a legitimate representation of the author's view.[37] However, this is not an example of a *senif* of the usual type, constructed of legal argumentation. Use of this particular rationale for ruling against Rashba presents us with an explicit recognition of the role played by the desirability of the result in the legal process. It is Radbaz's open expression of this motivation, which usually remains tacit, which marks his distinct judicial personality.

But this is not the whole story. Radbaz revisits Rashba on this point in another responsum,[38] and there he takes the opposite tack. The case has an unusual twist to it. There are three Jews involved, called in the

36 Radbaz refers to Rashba's Responsum no. 759. Radbaz's references to Rashba's responsa correspond to the Bologna 1539 edition, later to become Pt. I of his responsa. The responsum of that number is missing in ed. Bologna and the subsequent Pt. I. Radbaz earlier addressed another responsum of Rashba's, in which he rules in favor of the borrower (Rashba, I, 653). But in that case there was no pledge, and Radbaz draws a distinction between the two situations. For support of this distinction from the German tradition itself see R. Meir of Rothenburg's responsum, ed. Kahana, vol. 2, no. 79.

37 III, 564 (= 994), in ed. Warsaw, 49d.

38 I, 16.

responsum Reuben, Simeon and Levi. Reuben told Simeon that he wanted to borrow money on behalf of a non-Jew. He presented Simeon with articles of value to be pledged for the loan, which he said belonged to the non-Jew. Simeon agreed to loan him the money at an interest rate of "3%."[39] However, Simeon didn't actually have the funds on hand. So he went to Levi and, using the non-Jew's pledged articles, borrowed the money from Levi at "2%," and loaned them to Reuben. When the time came for repayment, Reuben admitted that he had deceived Simeon, that the articles were his and the loan was for himself. Levi, apparently a God-fearing man, did not want any part of taking interest from a fellow Jew, and ceded his 2% interest. But Simeon insisted on collecting the remaining 1% due him, in accordance with the views we have seen above.

Radbaz rules against Simeon. He points out that the main reason it is generally decided to reject a borrower's plea, that the loan was for himself and the pledge belonged to him, was to prevent one from wrongfully rendering another's capital unproductive. Here, however, Simeon had no capital of his own, and the interest due him was the result of unjust enrichment: "He is doing business with his neighbor's cow." Also, the pledge is not in Simeon's possession, and he cannot prevent Levi from returning it.[40] But Radbaz does not present these considerations as independent arguments. He presents them as reasons for deciding according to the ruling of Rashba, the very ruling that he had rejected in the responsum discussed previously:

> Even though I wrote in that responsum that in my opinion Rashba does not differ (with Rabbenu Asher and the others),[41] nevertheless I admit that in our case Simeon does not get anything, because the pledged articles are in Levi's possession ... (he presents the two arguments summarized above). This is certainly so according to the responsum of Rashba **in its plain sense**, the meaning of which is that he differs (with Rabbenu Asher et al.). **And in this case it is proper to rule like him**. (Emphasis mine—SM)

Radbaz thus tells us quite explicitly that he is deciding between conflicting authorities on the basis of the desired outcome in the specific case.

---

39 Apparently an arbitrary figure used to demonstrate the point.

40 Rejection of the borrower's plea is tied to the creditor's possession of the pledge, see n. 36. Here, however, Levi has the pledge, so as far as Simeon is concerned, it is as if the loan were without a pledge.

41 See above, text at n. 36.

[63] Radbaz takes a similar course in another responsum. There too he chooses his position on moral grounds, but justifies it by relying on a ruling he normally rejects. The case involves a man ("Reuben") who wanted to marry the widow of his father-in-law ("Jacob"), a woman who was not his wife's mother.[42] The Babylonian Talmud cites without comment a baraita to the effect that it is permitted to do so, effectively ruling that way.[43] Alfasi quotes the baraita without comment, implying concurrence. Maimonides omits reference to this law altogether, also implying that no prohibition is involved.[44] The Palestinian Talmud, however, prohibits such a union because of appearances (*mar'it 'ayin*).[45] Rabbenu Tam rules according to the Palestinian Talmud,[46] as does Rabbenu Asher,[47] and R. Jacob b. Asher in the *Turim*.[48] Nahmanides rejects Rabbenu Tam, and rules according to the Babylonian Talmud, that it is permitted.[49] Ritba comments that the Babylonian Talmud's permissive ruling was the accepted practice in all of Spain.[50]

Radbaz rules leniently in principle, following the Babylonian Talmud, Alfasi, Maimonides, and Nahmanides. "Wherever Alfasi and Maimonides agree on one opinion, we follow them." But in this specific case the situation was quite unusual. Jacob had two wives, "Rachel" and "Leah." Reuben (the suitor of the widow Leah) was a brother of the other wife, Rachel, and already married to his niece, the daughter of Jacob and Rachel (a licit marriage in Rabbinic law). He was thus constantly in Jacob's house, and many people (including Radbaz himself) were under the false impression that he was actually Jacob's brother, in which case his marriage to Jacob's widow would have been legally incestuous. The fear of the Palestinian Talmud for "appearances" was thus particularly justified here. Radbaz therefore relies on the Palestinian Talmud, "and on the great ones who rule thus," and prohibits the marriage. Lest such a ruling be obvious, it turns out

---

42 II, 675. "Marrying" his wife's mother would be an unambiguously incestuous relationship.

43 BT Yevamot 21a.

44 *MT*, Women, Laws of Marriage, chap. 1, parag. 6.

45 PT Yevamot 3d, chap. 2 *halakha* 4.

46 Tosafot to Yevamot 21a, s.v. *u-muttar be-eshet hamiv*.

47 *Pisqei ha-Rosh*, Yevamot, chap. 2, no. 1.

48 *Tur Even ha-'Ezer*, no. 15.

49 *Hiddushei ha-Ramban*, Yevamot ad loc.

50 *Hiddushei ha-Ritba*, Yevamot ad loc.: *vekhen 'osin be-khol sefarad*.

that they actually did get married (the soonest the law would allow, three months after Jacob's death!),[51] without Radbaz's knowledge. Radbaz, facing the issue of whether to delegitimize the marriage, decides that he cannot do so:

> But I was not present there, and there is no capability of removing her (from him). Therefore I said, "Better that they be errant sinners rather than willful sinners;"[52] for since they have great authorities (on whom to rely), they will not obey.

And he concludes by referring again to his ruling in principle:

> In any case, regarding the law in general, one should rule according to those who are lenient, for the main reason of the Palestinian Talmud is (only) because of appearances. And this is clear.

[64] Elsewhere also Radbaz makes reference to public policy when he rationalizes his ruling in a case of conflicting opinions. In the following instances Radbaz's attitude is evident more from his rhetoric than from the logic of his argument, since the public policy issue does not in itself determine his conclusion.

The credibility of one who claimed to have returned an object that he was earlier seen to have taken from another's house without the latter's permission was a subject of controversy among earlier authorities. Radbaz refers briefly to this controversy, professing a reluctance to decide the issue in principle. Nevertheless, he has no doubt that as a practical matter the issue should be adjudicated according to the view that such a claim is not accepted:

> For if you do not say so, theft and robbery would multiply. Each man would devour his neighbor.[53] People would rob each other brazenly[54] before the eyes of all, and on the morrow say, "I returned it." We would never be able to force the thief to return the stolen property. Even if the law were not that way, it would be proper to pass an enactment, for the sake of the

---

51 It does not say so explicitly, but that is the implication. They arranged the marriage during the three months, and by the time Radbaz heard about it, it was a *fait accompli*.

52 BT Beitsa 30a and parallels.

53 A citation of Mishnah Avot 3:2.

54 *be-yad rammah*, a play on the acronym of the author of the opinion upholding the claim: "I returned it," R. Meir Abulafia ha-Levi (RaMaH). Naḫmanides had asked R. Meir this question, and cites the latter's answer with approval in his novellae to BT Bava Batra 33b.

> proper order of society,[55] to the effect that he is not to be believed upon the claim: "I returned it."[56]

In the absence of such an enactment, Radbaz would rule in practice according to those who hold the view that would contribute to a more positive outcome, even though he does not commit himself to deciding the law in theory.

[65] The burden of proof in a civil case is always on the plaintiff. However, if one claims as a certainty, but without any proof, that another has stolen from him, one can compel the charged party to take an oath of his innocence. This obligation of an oath was not ordained by the Torah, but enacted by the Rabbis. It is not applicable if the plaintiff admits to only suspecting the defendant; he must claim to be sure of the fact, though he cannot prove it. For instance, he may maintain that he witnessed the theft. Radbaz was asked about a case in which two people were the only ones with access to a store of valuables, and the valuables of one of them were stolen. Because of the strong circumstantial evidence the owner believes that the other stole them, but he does not profess to having actually witnessed the act. Is this a claim of certainty, so that he can subject the suspect to an oath of innocence?[57]

Radbaz cites Rashi's commentary on the relevant talmudic passage, which implies that according to him this would indeed be considered a claim of certainty. He shows that the Tosafists, who disagreed with other aspects of Rashi's interpretation, actually concurred with him on this particular point. Maimonides, however, seems to have ruled that a claim of this type falls short of a claim of certainty, and the oath cannot be administered. It should be pointed out that Radbaz, throughout his responsa, professes to follow Maimonides' rulings as a matter of course, since Egypt was "the place of the Master."[58] Radbaz first

---

55 *mipnei yishuv ha-'olam*

56 I, 108. The issue appears again, with parallel treatment, in I, 282. In the sequel, Radbaz indicates his personal opinion that the law in fact favors the view that such a claim is not accepted, but he brings no argument for that position beyond what has been cited here. Radbaz does, though, refer to the fact that *Maggid Mishneh* understands Maimonides to hold the view that the claim is not accepted, and Radbaz is probably relying on this reading of Maimonides. See *Maggid Mishneh* to *MT*, Torts, Laws of Robbery and Lost Property, chap. 4, parag. 14.

57 I, 437.

58 See Chapter 7 below.

shows that Maimonides' wording can be interpreted in such a way as to bring him into consonance with Rashi's view.[59] But he argues for the administration of the oath even if one reads Maimonides according to our original understanding of the passage, i.e., that he opposes the oath in these circumstances:

> Even if you choose to say that it is a matter of controversy, my opinion inclines to administering the oath to him, so that everyone would not go and steal from his neighbor or his partner, and then say, "He cannot compel me to take an oath on the basis of this claim." Now, since he (the potential thief) knows that he (the victim) is able to compel him to take an oath for this, he will abstain (from stealing) because of the severity of the oath and its (divine) sanction. Money is amenable to being returned, whereas a (false) oath has no means of restitution.[60]

The rhetoric implies that considerations of public policy shift the weight of the decision away from Maimonides.[61]

In many of the examples cited in this chapter, Radbaz tells us quite explicitly that he is sacrificing inner consistency and objective correctness for the sake of arriving at a result which is equitable and moral in the given situation.

---

59 *MT*, Civil Laws, Laws of Pleading, chap. 1, parag. 7: "Such an object was stolen from my house. No one was there but you and I, and it seems to me (*ve-qarov be-'einai*) that you stole it ... he is free of a rabbinic oath." Radbaz argues that "it seems to me" implies that he does not claim to be one hundred percent certain. Radbaz's argument would shift the definition of certainty from the objective nature of the asserted circumstances to the subjective nature of the plaintiff's feeling. Radbaz also argues from the context of Maimonides' other examples of uncertainty in that passage.

60 The Talmud asserts that one who is suspect of theft is not necessarily suspect of swearing falsely; Bava Metsi'a 5b. Fear of divine sanction for the latter was greater.

61 "Rhetoric," because Radbaz is relying heavily on his own reading of Maimonides' passage.

5. Sevara

Menachem Elon, in his monumental work, *Jewish Law*,[1] devotes the second part of his opus to the sources of Jewish law. Along with Scripture and Scriptural interpretation, legislation, custom, and precedent, he includes as a source of law also *sevara*, which Elon defines as "the logic in the thinking of the bearers of Jewish law and its sages."[2] The identifying characteristic of sevara, as evidenced by the examples cited by Elon throughout his chapter on the subject, is a lack of reliance on earlier authority. Sevara derives from the jurist's own sense of what is rational. In the post-talmudic period, the derivation of law solely, or even primarily, by the rational judgment of a legal authority, unsupported by prooftext or precedent, while not unknown, is surely not common. Elon, in his chapter on sevara, includes a brief subsection of two pages entitled, "Sevara in the Post-talmudic Era."[3] The use of sevara, in the sense just defined, is in evidence in Radbaz's responsa in a variety of ways. These will be explored in this chapter.

---

1 Elon, *Ha-Mishpat ha-'Ivri*.

2 *ha-higayon shebe-hashivatam shel nose'ei ha-halakha ve-hakhameha*, *Ha-Mishpat ha-'Ivri*, 805. The English version, *Jewish Law*, sidesteps this definition, and translates *sevara*, in a misleadingly broad way, "legal reasoning." Sevara occupies Chapter 24 of Elon's book. See also Sagi, "A Philosophical Analysis of *S'vara,*" and Sagi, "*S'vara* and the Concept of Torah."

3 *Ha-Mishpat ha-'Ivri*, 820-21; *Jewish Law*, 1004-06.

(a) Sevara as the Source of a Legal Rule

[66] The responsa of Radbaz yield a few instances in which sevara functions as the source of a legal rule. Case [59] above is a case in point. Radbaz addressed a situation in which one took an oath, which was binding by the law of the Torah, to perform a rabbinically prohibited act. He ruled that in such cases the oath must be violated and the prohibition remain intact.[4] In that responsum Radbaz was deciding a controversy between earlier jurists, but the weight of the authority was in favor of fulfilling the oath at the expense of the rabbinic prohibition. By Radbaz's own admission, it was only his own sevara, which, having taken account of the practical implications of allowing such an oath, led him to rule the way he did.

[67] In that case, Radbaz relied on a minority opinion, albeit one that would not have been decisive were it not for special considerations. Elsewhere, Radbaz applies sevara to define the law in an original way. In the matter of wife beating, Radbaz accepts the principle that a husband has the right to "correct" his wife's improper behavior by disciplining her through such means, since she is under his authority.[5] He then adds: "But he does not have the right to beat her for matters that bear upon him, for she is not his servant woman."[6] That limitation, which in fact undermines his right to beat her in the vast majority of cases in which such action is likely to occur, appears to be a rule of his own invention, based on sevara.[7]

[68] Sevara plays a determinative role in Radbaz's answer to the question whether fear of what may occur constitutes duress.[8] Radbaz answers that it does. Interestingly, he bases himself solely on an aggadic source, specifically, the aggada that God suspended Mount Sinai over the people of Israel and threatened to bury them under it unless they accepted the Torah. The Talmud comments that this was an acceptance under compulsion, and that they did not voluntarily accept

---

4 IV, 278.

5 See Maimonides, *MT*, Women, Laws of Marriage, chap. 21, parag. 10; *Terumat ha-Deshen*, no. 218; Goitein, *Mediterranean Society*, v. 3, 184-89.

6 III, 447 (= 888).

7 He also limits his right in this regard to instances in which he can produce witnesses to her misbehavior. Taken together, these limitations virtually nullify any theoretical right he may have to discipline her physically.

8 VI, 2307.

the Torah until the time of Mordecai and Esther.[9] Radbaz then qualifies this, apparently on the basis of sevara. Fear of what may occur can only be considered compulsion, he asserts, if the fear is reasonable, as determined by the local court.[10]

[69] If a man had collected alms from the community under the guise of being poor, and it later turned out that he was not poor, Radbaz tells us that there is an unresolved controversy in the Palestinian Talmud as to whether or not he must return the alms.[11] Since the burden of proof is on the plaintiff, and the plaintiff cannot prove that the law supports his claim, in practice this means that the alms are not recoverable. Radbaz distinguishes on the basis of sevara between a small gift and a large one (such as providing him with a dowry for his daughter). In the latter case, he suggests, there may never have been a controversy, and all may have agreed that the gift must be returned. Furthermore, even if one were to grant that the original controversy did indeed include large gifts as well, Radbaz states that he would rule, on the basis of sevara, that the alms are not recoverable for a small gift, and that they are recoverable for a large gift.

What Radbaz does in this case is to define a specific situation (a large gift given under false pretenses), which was not explicitly referred to in an earlier controversy, though included by inference in its general terms (a gift given under false pretenses). He then suggests, for reasons based on sevara, that the controversy did not intend to include this specific situation, and that all were agreed regarding it. Then, taking account of an objection that the earlier controversy may have really been inclusive (as its general wording seems indeed to imply), he asserts that even if he were to grant that, he would rule as he did anyway, against what would seem to be the law, on the basis of sevara. A similar pattern is found in a number of other responsa.

[70] A note of indebtedness was signed by the usual two witnesses, who now testify themselves that the signature is theirs.[12] There is no other authentication of the signatures, and indeed normally none would be needed. But one of those witnesses now asserts that the note has

---

9 BT Shabbat 88a.

10 See above, Chapter 1, Section (*g*), pp. 72ff, regarding the role of the court's discretion in Radbaz's responsa.

11 IV, 158 (= 1229).

12 III, 432 (= 874).

been paid. Radbaz, in analyzing the situation on the basis of sevara (*mistabbera li*), states that the legitimacy of the debt and the status of its repayment are two separate issues, that there are two witnesses to the debt but only one to the repayment, and that since two witnesses are required, the law is with the creditor. He cites Nah̲manides as saying the same, and as bringing proof for his position from the Talmud. True, he admits, Rabbenu Nissim rejected Nah̲manides' proof.[13] Nevertheless, suggests Radbaz, Rabbenu Nissim may have only rejected the proof, but "it is possible that he agrees with regard to the law." He then continues:

> And even if you choose to say that he differs (with regard to the law too), it is reasonable (*mistabbera*) as I have written, that the repayment is a separate matter, and the note remains in place and in force.

[71] The dowry, which a woman brought into a marriage, typically in the form of durable goods, was returned to her as part of her *ketubba* when she was divorced or widowed. The husband also undertook liability for any loss or theft that may have occurred. If she were to cede her rights to all or part of her dowry during the course of the marriage, she can later reassert her rights, claiming that she did so only in order to prevent marital discord: "I acted to please my husband." However, Maimonides ruled that this applies only to the original articles of the dowry, not to his liability for loss and theft. If she ceded her rights to that, he says, she cannot say that she did so "to please my husband."[14] The author of *Maggid Mishneh*, the classic commentary on Maimonides' code, points out that Maimonides had no talmudic proof for this distinction, but derived it by sevara. One could plausibly make a case either for such a distinction or against it. Maimonides' glossator, Rabad, takes the opposite position, that if she ceded her rights to his liability for loss and theft, she may still claim that she did so only "to please my husband."[15] Radbaz discusses this question.[16] In principle, he adopts Maimonides' ruling, as he usually does.[17] But then, after

13 See Rabbenu Nissim on Alfasi, *Hilkhot ha-Rif* at Ketubbot, 6b-7a (to BT Ketubbot 19b).

14 *MT*, Women, Laws of Marriage, chap. 22, parag. 19.

15 In any case, that is the way Radbaz understands Rabad. The author of *Maggid Mishneh* says that Rabad's comment is not clear to him (*uva-hasagot ba-zeh devarim lo nitbareru li*).

16 II, 612.

17 See below, Chapter 7, "The Place of the Master."

presenting Maimonides' position and the reasoning behind it, he draws his own distinction based on sevara:

> It is reasonable to say (*u-mistabbera*) that if the husband (himself) "consumed" them (through his usage), and she subsequently ceded them (to him), her act is not binding, and she may say: "I did so to please my husband." For what she released him from (when she ceded to him any liability for loss and theft of the dowry) was liability for loss deriving from external factors, not for loss deriving from himself.

As we have seen in the previous examples, Radbaz suggests here too that Maimonides himself would have agreed:

> I believe (*ve-qarov etsli*) that the Master (Maimonides) would also agree with this.

After all, says Radbaz, we need not carry Maimonides' position to extremes, in view of the fact that Rabad and others disagree with him on the entire matter. Then, taking account of the argument that Maimonides would not admit that loss caused by the husband is different from other kinds of loss, Radbaz adds:

> Even if you were to say that our Master maintains the distinction (between the dowry itself and the liability for loss and theft) even with regard to articles of the dowry which the husband consumed, and would insist that her ceding is binding, it is reasonable (*mistabber*) to decide the law according to those who say that her ceding is not binding. For had she not done so, it would have caused enmity. The husband would say, "You too 'consumed' some of them. Why will you not (now) cede (that which I 'consumed')?" Therefore, she can say, "I acted to please my husband."

Here again the same pattern appears: (a) a distinction by Radbaz based on sevara; (b) a suggestion that all would agree with his distinction; (c) an admission that perhaps all would not agree, but a ruling in accordance with his sevara nevertheless, (d) even if this meant overriding the accepted weight of authority.

[72] Radbaz was asked whether a debtor can insist on receiving the note of indebtedness before he pays his debt, or whether the creditor can insist on being paid before delivering the note.[18] He begins by reporting that the early authorities recognized the debtor's priority in this regard, a conclusion they derived by inference from the Talmud. He then says that if the creditor does not trust him to pay after he receives the note, the creditor has the right to give the note to a trusted

---

18 II, 760.

third party, who will hold it until payment is made. The debtor cannot refuse payment until he actually receives the note. Radbaz concludes: "This is clear." It may be that Radbaz, in referring to the creditor's explicit lack of trust, is responding to the situation in the actual case. However, though possible, this detail is not reflected in the wording of the question. Admittedly, Radbaz sometimes omits significant details in the questions,[19] but this is not the case as a rule. It is also possible that Radbaz's modification of the basic law may simply be a reflection of common practice. But the question, which begins: "You asked about the matter of a lender and borrower ...," was referred to him, presumably by a local judge, who would not have asked about a well-established practice. It is probable, therefore, that neither of these two possibilities is the case, and what we have is a law derived by Radbaz from sevara.

(*b*) *Common Sense*

In the examples cited until now, Radbaz applied sevara to establish rules that can be utilized in similar cases. The use of sevara in the application of the law to individual cases is of course intrinsic to adjudication in any system of law. However, we find among Radbaz's responsa some, which dispense with the citation of legal sources altogether, and rely instead on sevara of a type which can be characterized as "common sense." Two examples will be cited to demonstrate this phenomenon.

[73] The first concerns "Reuben," who bought fresh fruit from "Simeon" for purpose of resale.[20] He noticed before he bought it that forty percent of them were spoiled. With that in mind he agreed on a price for the lot and took possession of them, with agreement to pay later. After Reuben had sold the fruit, when payment came due, he claimed that many more were spoiled than he had originally estimated, and wanted an accommodation for the excess above forty percent that was spoiled.

Radbaz's very brief responsum cites no sources whatsoever. He rules against Reuben for the following reasons: (a) Since fruit can spoil, perhaps the spoilage took place after Reuben took possession. (b)

19 See Chap. 1, n. 79.
20 I, 147.

Reuben didn't bring the spoilage to the attention of the court immediately, so it may be presumed that he reconciled himself to absorbing the loss. He cannot now retract that reconciliation. (c) Granting that spoilage were a reason for canceling the sale, he should return the spoiled fruit to the vendor. However, he cannot do so, having already sold them. He now wants to profit twice. (d) Even if some could be returned now, the vendor could argue that had they been returned immediately, before spoilage became so extensive, he could have then found another purchaser. These are all arguments based on "common sense." Radbaz concludes: "The matter was not worthy of being asked about."

[74] The second example concerns the rule in the Talmud, that a nursing mother may not remarry until she has nursed for twenty-four months, the usual time before weaning. This is phrased in the Talmud as an absolute rule: "Excluding the day on which it was born and excluding the day on which she became betrothed."[21] Rashi explains: "Lest she become pregnant, and will have to wean her child (prematurely). And her present husband is not its father, who would buy it eggs and milk (as a supplement)."[22] Radbaz was asked about a woman who had nursed the required twenty-four months, and now wanted to remarry. But "the child is sickly and weak, and if she weans him he will be in danger; and the child does not want to nurse from another. Do we force her to nurse him because of the danger, or can she say, 'I want to marry'"?[23]

The hard core of Radbaz's answer is that ultimately the woman does have the right to remarry. But this answer is imbedded in a chain of decisions based on sevara. Radbaz anticipates various contingencies: if there is a father, he is forced to pay his former wife so that she be induced to continue nursing and put off marriage until the child is weaned; if there is no father, or if he is too poor to pay, the community must undertake the expense; if she refuses to agree, she is permitted to remarry, but should still continue nursing; if she refuses to nurse, she should be forced to do so, for she alone can fulfill this obligation, and she should be paid for her labor; all this, according to the judgment of the doctors, who assert that the child would be in danger if he is weaned at this point. In all of this not a single source is cited.

21 BT Ketubbot 60b.

22 Rashi, ibid., top of column, s.v. *'ad 'esrim ve-arba' ḥodesh.*

23 I, 349.

In Section (g) of Chapter 1, pages 72–74, I referred to the distinction between a *meshiv*, the author of a responsum, whose role it is to compose a legal opinion on a subject referred to him for that purpose, and a judge, whose role it is to adjudicate a specific case before him, in a manner which will produce a just result. These two "common sense" rulings of Radbaz, both of which begin: "You asked me," are definitely responsa, apparently referred to him by a local judge. But the nature of the responses is suitable for a trial judge. Their incorporation among Radbaz's responsa reinforces the impression, developed in that section, of Radbaz's tendency to blur the distinction between *meshiv* and judge.[24]

(*c*) *Deciding between Conflicting Opinions*

At times, Radbaz, using his own judgment of the merits of the respective arguments, decides between conflicting opinions of earlier authorities. Radbaz's contemporaries were generally not anxious to assume the authority for deciding such conflicts on their merits, an act, which would place them in the same league with their great forbears. Instead, they relied on rules, which had evolved for deciding controversies, such as following the majority opinion, or giving greater weight to certain authorities over others.[25] Radbaz's willingness to do so on occasion is a testament to his self-assuredness.

[75] The Talmud provides for the collection of a debt by a creditor's heirs, despite the unsubstantiated claim of the debtor that he already satisfied the debt. The heirs need only swear that their father, the creditor, never informed them that the debt was paid, and that they never found any note among his effects affirming that to be the case.[26] Radbaz was asked about a situation in which the original heirs died, and their heirs, many years later, sought to collect the debt.[27] He shows that this is a controversy between the early authorities: on the one hand, Alfasi, R. Judah al-Bargeloni and Rabad, who would deny the right of

24 It is possible that the presence of responsa like these merely testify to the unedited nature of Radbaz's literary legacy. Nevertheless, these are clearly responsa, and the use of sevara is blatantly at work here.

25 See my discussion of R. Joseph ibn Lev's stance on this issue in Morell, *Precedent and Judicial Discretion*, 9-14.

26 Mishnah Shevu'ot 7:7; BT Shevu'ot 45a.

27 I, 443.

the heirs' heirs to take such an oath, thereby denying them the right to collect; and on the other hand, Rabbenu Asher and the author of the *'Ittur*, who would allow them the right to take the oath and collect. Radbaz decides according to the Alfasi camp: "Even though Rosh (i.e., Rabbenu Asher) and the author of the *'Ittur* disagree, we heed the former ones, because they spoke correctly, for several reasons." He proceeds to argue the matter on substantive grounds.

[76] Radbaz argues on substantive grounds in rejecting Rabbenu Asher in another controversy.[28] The situation under discussion is that of a debtor who owed two debts to the same creditor, one for which there was a note, and one for which there were only witnesses but no note. He paid one of the debts, but there is disagreement between the debtor and the creditor regarding which one was paid. The difference matters, even if the amounts are equal. That is because, in case of a subsequent dispute regarding whether the debt was paid or not, the law accepts the claim of the creditor if he possesses a note, but it accepts the claim of the debtor, when accompanied by an oath, if there was no note.[29] Since a debt for which there was a note constituted the creditor's stronger claim, Rabbenu Asher had maintained that there is a presumption that the borrower would liquidate that debt before liquidating the oral debt.[30] R. Aaron ha-Levi, cited in approval by his disciple, Ritba, held the opposite opinion, that the creditor has the right to interpret the nature of the payment.[31] Rashba, in a responsum apparently unknown to Radbaz,[32] also ruled that the creditor can define the nature of the payment, and brought independent proof for that position from the Talmud. His view is echoed by Rabbenu Nissim,[33] whom Radbaz does cite.

The actual question before Radbaz was a bit simpler, because the oral debt was not yet due, whereas the written debt was due. Radbaz disposes of this with the presumption that the borrower would not prepay the oral debt under these circumstances. But he then turns his

28 IV, 181 (= 1252). Radbaz refers to this responsum in I, 249.

29 *MT*, Civil Laws, Laws of Creditor and Debtor, chap. 11, parag. 1.

30 Rabbenu Asher, *Responsa*, *Kelal* 86, no. 15, p. 373.

31 *Hiddushei ha-Ritba* to Shevu'ot 42a.

32 Rashba, *Responsa*, Pt. 2, no. 37. Radbaz cites Rabbenu Nissim, who echoed Rashba, as the author of Rashba's opinion. Radbaz always cites Rashba's responsa from our vol. 1. *Beit Yosef*, however, does refer to Rashba's responsum; *Hoshen Mishpat*, no. 58, s.v. *katav ha-ran*.

33 Commentary on Alfasi at Ketubbot 85a, s.v. *avimei bereih derabbi abbahu*.

attention to the more complex question described above, about an oral and a written debt which are both due. He sides with R. Aaron ha-Levi, whom he cites through Ritba. Radbaz brings a totally independent proof for this position, arguing, in direct opposition to Rabbenu Asher, for a presumption that it is in the borrower's interest to pay off the weaker oral debt first. The reason, says Radbaz, is that the creditor, safe in his reliance on the note, will not dun him, whereas he is likely to do so with regard to the oral debt. Radbaz assumes that we are dealing with honest people, and it can be presumed that the debtor will not swear falsely. He cites Rabbenu Asher, adding, "In any case, what I wrote is more reasonable (*mistabber tefei*)."

[77] Witnesses and judges are disqualified if they are related to the principals or to each other.[34] Radbaz was asked about a case in which the judges, who had verified the authenticity of the witnesses' signatures on a note of indebtedness, were relatives of the judges who, subsequently, were judging the creditor's claim based on that note.[35] He refers to a controversy between R. Aaron ha-Levi, who had ruled that in such a situation the judges deciding the creditor's claim were not disqualified, and Rabbenu Nissim, who had ruled that they were.[36] Radbaz writes: "As for me, I find it reasonable (*va-ani mistabbera li*) according to R. Aaron ha-Levi." He paraphrases R. Aaron ha-Levi's argument, and adds some considerations of his own. He then concludes: "Therefore I find it reasonable according to R. Aaron ha-Levi, even though I am unworthy of deciding (between them)." Thus, Radbaz pays lip service to his (and, by implication, his generation's) inadequacy to decide between earlier authorities on the basis of the merits of their arguments, but in fact does precisely that.

[78] Following the engagement of a couple, it was customary for the groom to send gifts, called *sivlonot*, to his fiancée. The Talmud raises the question of whether the sending of these gifts gives rise to an apprehension that a betrothal had already taken place, in which case a

34 *MT*, Judges, Laws of Evidence, all of chap. 13; Laws of Sanhedrin, chap. 11, parag. 9.
35 III, 632 (= 1057).
36 Rabbenu Nissim to Alfasi, at Ketubbot, ed. Romm 12b bottom–13a top, end of chap. 2.

divorce would be necessary for the termination of her status.[37] The Talmud resolves the issue by distinguishing between localities with different customs. In places where it was customary to send *sivlonot* after betrothal, the *sivlonot* would suggest that betrothal had already taken place, and a divorce would be required. In places where it was customary to send *sivlonot* before betrothal, there was no reason for such apprehension, and no need for a divorce. Subsequently, communities differed regarding how they identified themselves with regard to this criterion. When one of the parties in the marriage was from a place where "they give *sivlonot* first and then betroth," and the other was from a place where "they betroth first and then give *sivlonot*," the status of the woman after receiving *sivlonot* was a subject of considerable discussion. A sense of the unsettled nature of this discussion in the sixteenth century can be gleaned from the wording of a question dealing with this issue which was addressed to Radbaz: "I find it necessary to ask this of His Eminence (*kevod torato*), because a great controversy has taken place regarding this matter among the rabbis of this generation. And you (says Radbaz) wanted to know my opinion as to which way light dwells."[38]

Radbaz, in his response, cites R. Meir of Rothenburg, who adopted a particularly stringent stance on this matter.[39] In this connection Radbaz refers to R. Joseph Colon, who had sought to justify the practice of leniency with regard to *sivlonot*.[40] R. Meir of Rothenburg was a primary authority for Colon. Colon mitigated the impact of R. Meir's ruling by minimizing the range of its application, and rendering it inapplicable to the situation in fifteenth-century Italy, which confronted Colon. Radbaz shows that the same is certainly true for his situation, that of sixteenth-century Egypt. However, instead of stopping there, Radbaz goes on to reject R. Meir of Rothenburg's ruling outright: "But the Master's (i.e., R. Meir's) ruling is not clear to me for several reasons." After listing his objections, Radbaz suggests that R. Meir's ruling regarding *sivlonot* was not meant by him to be taken seriously, but that it was merely a makeweight argument, a *senif*,[41] used to

---

37 BT Qiddushin 50b. The discussion here follows Tosafot's understanding. Rashi understands that the *sivlonot* themselves may have been intended as a means of betrothal.

38 III, 539 (= 972).

39 R. Meir's responsum is cited in *Mordekhai*, Qiddushin, no. 521, to which Radbaz refers.

40 Colon, *Responsa*, no. 170.

41 Regarding *senif*, see Chap. 1, text at n. 170.

buttress the primary argument for his conclusion, but bearing no independent weight of its own. Indeed, the question before R. Meir of Rothenburg was not directly about *sivlonot*, but about a token of betrothal being given without a specific expression of intent. It was R. Meir who introduced the issue of *sivlonot.*[42] Be that as it may, Radbaz could have achieved his immediate aim of removing any apprehension of betrothal resulting from *sivlonot* with regard to Egypt as Colon had done with regard to Italy, without a direct rejection of R. Meir of Rothenburg's opinion. But without any need to do so to arrive at his conclusion, Radbaz asserts his own authority in rejecting R. Meir on the substance of the matter.

(*d*) *Ruling against "the Master" on the Basis of Sevara*

R. Meir of Rothenburg was not a primary authority for Radbaz as he was for Colon, but Maimonides certainly was. Radbaz makes frequent reference to the rule that in Egypt Jews are bound by the rulings of Maimonides, because Egypt is "the place of the Master." This is the subject of Chapter 7 below. As will be shown in Chapter 7, there are cases in which Radbaz departs from a Maimonidean ruling in favor of the opinion of another authority. There are also instances in which he differs with Maimonides as well as with others, and offers an independent ruling on the basis of his own sevara. I will adduce two instances here of the latter phenomenon.

[79] The Talmud states that in a situation of barter, the transaction is completed when one of the parties takes possession of his merchandise.[43] Maimonides addresses the issue of whether the prohibition of overcharging applies in the case of barter. He writes as follows:

> If one exchanges utensils for utensils or cattle for cattle, even if it is a needle for a suit of armor[44] or a lamb for a horse, the aggrieved party has no claim on grounds of overcharging,

42 He argues that the gift given to the woman, if not an act of betrothal, must at the very least be considered as *sivlonot*, and then proceeds to rule stringently with regard to *sivlonot.*

43 BT Bava Metsi'a 28a–b.

44 This is the way Radbaz read it: *shiryon*. The Yale Judaica Series translation of the *Mishneh Torah* translates: "silk garments," reading the same letters: *shirayyin*.

> because though it is of less value, the recipient of the needle wants it more than the armor.[45]

Radbaz had been asked whether a barter of merchandise intended for commercial resale was bound by the prohibition of overcharging.[46] The question was asked in the context of the passage of Maimonides cited above. On the one hand, his ruling was stated inclusively, making no distinction between barter for private use and for commercial purposes. On the other hand, the rationale adduced by Maimonides, that the recipient wants the cheaper item and has no need for the more expensive one which he is giving in exchange, does not seem to apply when the bartered items are intended for resale.

Radbaz adduces a number of reasons, including the one suggested by the questioner, why Maimonides' ruling should be interpreted as not referring to barter for commercial purposes. But before he does so, he discusses in some detail the more general issue of barter for personal use. He shows that Maimonides' opinion is one of three that have been offered on this subject. Whereas Maimonides exempts the barter of articles from the prohibition of overcharging, Rabad had the opposite view, that overcharging does apply to barter. A third view was proffered by Naẖmanides. Naẖmanides ruled that overcharging applies when the aggrieved party had indicated an interest in the value of the article he was receiving in return, and does not apply if he did not indicate such an interest. But Naẖmanides supplied an exceedingly broad definition of "indication of interest." Even the mere viewing of the object that one was receiving would be, for Naẖmanides, an indication of interest in its value. Only if there was a total indifference to what one would be receiving, or an explicit statement of indifference, would Naẖmanides allow that the prohibition of overcharging did not apply.

After presenting this analysis of the controversy regarding barter, and before applying it to the specific question he was asked about the barter of merchandise, Radbaz finds it necessary to issue his own ruling on the general issue of barter for personal use. It turns out that his ruling is not only a rejection of Maimonides, but in fact does not accord with any of the views of the classic authorities he had cited. While he is closest to Naẖmanides, Radbaz defines "indication of interest" in a

45 *MT*, Acquisitions, Laws of Sales, chap. 13, parag. 1. Yale Judaica Series translation, with minor changes.

46 IV, 269 (= 1340).

much narrower way than Nahmanides did, thus including many more situations to which the prohibition of overcharging does not apply.

It should be pointed out that Radbaz's summary of positions was necessary for his argument, because he utilizes the results in his subsequent discussion of the barter of merchandise. But his own ruling on the general case of barter for personal use is irrelevant to the question he was asked, because he argues that according to all views, commercial barter is indeed subject to the law of overcharging. He goes out of his way to rule on a question he was not asked, expressing a view conflicting with Maimonides as well as with the other classical opinions that he had cited.

[80] A similar pattern is found in another responsum.[47] There too Radbaz expands the focus of the question to deal with an issue about which he was not asked. There too he ends up departing from all of the views he had presented earlier, including that of Maimonides, though in this case he suggests that Maimonides can be interpreted in a way which would have him concurring with Radbaz's own conclusion.

Radbaz's responsum deals with the right of a litigant to change his testimony. The issue concerns an alleged loan, for which no deed was drawn up. In such a case, the defendant does not have to prove that he repaid the loan. If he claims to have repaid it, and takes an oath to that effect, then the plaintiff has no recourse. Radbaz's questioner was asked whether the defendant in such a case, who had originally pleaded, "The whole thing never happened!" can now, when contradicted by witnesses, change his testimony and plead, "I already repaid the loan." Perhaps, one may argue in his favor, he is allowed the plea that he had forgotten the facts, since in any case he doesn't owe the plaintiff any money. After all, the burden of proof is on the plaintiff.

Radbaz quickly shows that such a change of plea is not accepted after his original testimony has been proven false. He then goes on to deal with an issue about which he was not asked. May he change his plea on his own accord, when no witnesses had contradicted his original account? Radbaz tells us that there are two schools of thought about this. Most authorities would allow him, in the absence of witnesses, to change a plea of, "It never happened!" to a plea of, "I

47 IV, 137 (= 1207).

have already repaid it." Some authorities would not allow such a plea even then.[48]

Radbaz then presents his own opinion on this question. Beginning with the phrase, "It makes sense (*u-mistabber*)," he draws a distinction between whether or not the defendant had already left the courtroom. If he had, Radbaz would disallow any change in his plea, because of the apprehension that he may have been coached. This distinction was not drawn by either of the two schools he had cited. Admittedly, though, the category of having left the courtroom is not original. Maimonides had ruled that as long as the defendant had not been contradicted by witnesses, he may "withdraw his original plea, and plead a different plea, which contradicts his original plea .... Even if he left the courtroom he may, upon his return thereto, retract and change all his pleas at will, until the witnesses have come and testified."[49] However, whereas Maimonides explicitly rejects any distinction between having left the courtroom or not, Radbaz does not accept him on this point.

But Radbaz does not reject Maimonides entirely. Radbaz's fear is that the litigant may have been coached, and as a result is now lying. As is his wont elsewhere, Radbaz leaves it up to the judges trying the case to form an opinion as to whether the litigant has been coached to lie.[50] He suggests that Maimonides would agree to this, though the latter's comprehensive wording seems to preclude such a distinction. If the judges feel that the litigant has not been coached, Radbaz would agree to follow Maimonides, since Egypt is "the place of the Master." This, in spite of Radbaz's personal inclination to disallow any change of testimony once the litigant has left the courtroom. If, however, the judges suspect that he had in fact been coached, then even if Maimonides would not have agreed with Radbaz's distinction, Radbaz would rule against Maimonides and disallow a change of plea.

---

48 A claim that he never borrowed the money is tantamount to an admission that he never repaid it. Now that he admits having borrowed it, his claim, "I repaid it," must be viewed, according to this opinion, as a retraction of an admission that it was not repaid. Rashba, in a responsum, rules that such a retraction is not allowed. See Rashba, *Responsa*, II, 335, cited in *Kesef Mishneh* to *MT*, Civil Laws, Laws of Pleading, chap. 7, parag. 3.

49 *MT*, Civil Laws, Laws of Pleading, chap. 7, parag. 8; YJS translation.

50 See Chapter 1, Section (*g*), pp. 72ff.

(*e*) *Compromising between Sides in a Controversy*

In the preceding case, Radbaz forges a compromise, which yields a ruling different from those of all the earlier authorities. In justifying his departure from Maimonides' ruling, Radbaz writes:

> This is what seems to me to be the most correct ruling. If it appears to the Court that he was taught to lie, then he is not heeded when he changes his plea. It is possible that Maimonides would agree with this too. But even if he would not agree, it is better to seize the middle way (*minqat milta metsi'ata 'adif tefei*).

Radbaz's frequent reference to the principle of "seizing the middle way" when faced with a number of conflicting opinions is the subject of Chapter 6 below. In the present example, choice of the "middle way" manifests itself not merely in a choice among earlier opinions, but in the forging of a compromise between them, yielding a ruling that differs from all of them. In doing so, Radbaz argues his decision on the basis of sevara. Two further instances of this are offered here. A third will be cited in Chapter 6.

[81] The Mishnah deals with the question of whether a guardian of minors must take an oath when his wards come of age, to the effect that he is returning their property intact.[51] The Mishnah draws a distinction between a court-appointed guardian and one appointed by the minors' father. It records a controversy regarding which of these two types of guardians is required to take such an oath. According to the opinion of Abba Saul, whose ruling is accepted, a guardian appointed by the father need not take the oath. The reasoning is as follows. There was a widespread reluctance to take an oath, even one that was true. Though an oath in this case is in order, the rabbis feared that people would be unwilling to become guardians if they knew that they would eventually have to take an oath. However, if one is appointed by the court, the esteem, which one acquires from the trust that the court has placed in the guardian, outweighs any reluctance deriving from the imposition of an oath.[52]

There was a controversy among the authorities regarding the extent of the immunity that the law affords a guardian in its attempt to overcome his reluctance to accept that responsibility. There is a school that would exempt a guardian from any lawsuits by his wards regarding

---

51 Mishnah Gittin 5:4, BT Gittin 52a.
52 BT Gittin 52b.

negligent management of their assets. This immunity would extend even to cases in which negligence can be proven, and applies even to a court-appointed guardian. It goes without saying, that in the absence of proof the proponents of this view would exempt both kinds of guardian from any oath regarding negligence. Accordingly, the debate in the Talmud about what kind of guardian must take an oath refers only to an oath that the guardian has not withheld any extant assets.[53] Another school holds that a guardian is accountable for negligent management. If negligence can be proven, the guardian is liable; if the heirs lack proof, but claim to have definite knowledge of specific acts of negligence (*ta'anat bari*), the guardian must take an oath denying their charge. Unlike an oath that he has not withheld assets, this oath would apply to both types of guardians.[54]

Radbaz, in response to a question about the liability of a guardian for negligence, refers to the fact that there are many opinions on the issue, and proceeds to stake out what he calls "the middle position" (*ha-davar ha-memutsa'*).[55] Every guardian, he says, is liable for negligence, if it can be proven by witnesses or by an admission of guilt. Thus, so far he rules according to the second school. But if the negligence cannot be proven, even though the heirs claim to have definite knowledge of specific acts of negligence, a guardian appointed by the father is exempt from an oath. A guardian appointed by the court, however, must take an oath exonerating himself under these conditions. Unlike the positions surveyed above, Radbaz's position takes Abba Saul's ruling at full face value: a guardian appointed by the father is exempt from both kinds of oath, that he has not withheld assets and that he was not guilty of negligence; a guardian appointed by the court is obligated to take both kinds of oath.

Radbaz describes his ruling as deriving from sevara: "This is a proper opinion (*sevara nekhona*), which imposes a compromise (*le-*

---

53 Tosafot to Gittin 52b, s.v. *halakha ke-abba sha'ul*, in the name of Rabbenu H̲ayyim. The wording there implies that according to Rabbenu H̲ayyim, immunity from damages for negligence applies even to court-appointed guardians. Nah̲manides, however, in his novellae ad loc., while citing Rabbenu H̲ayyim as concurring with his position of exempting guardians from damages for negligence, restricts his discussion of this point to a guardian appointed by the father.

54 Alfasi at Gittin ad loc., chap. 5, end of no. 487; ed. Romm, 26b; Rabbenu Asher, Gittin, chap. 5, no. 7.

55 II, 661.

hattil peshara) between the authorities." He concludes his responsum as follows:

> Do not think that I have come to decide (*le-hakhria'*, i.e., to decide in principle—SM) between the authorities. Rather, I am saying that in the one matter this one's reason makes sense (*mistabber*), and in the other matter the other's reason makes sense (*mistabber*).

It is of interest that Radbaz appears to be defensive about deciding between earlier authorities on the merits of the case. We have seen that on other occasions he is not at all reluctant to do so. In this instance, too, in spite of his assertion that he has not "come to decide between the authorities," that is precisely what he has done. In fact, he has gone further, and has staked out an independent position, based on his own understanding (sevara) of the talmudic source, which "imposes a compromise between the authorities."

[82] Another responsum parallels this approach, introducing it with a nearly identical phrase, "This is a proper compromise between the two positions (*ve-zo peshara nekhona bein shtei ha-shittot*).[56] At issue is the status of a sale in which the vendor has collected payment, but does not yet own the merchandise that he has contracted to sell. Is the vendor obligated to acquire the merchandise and make good on the transaction, or does he have the option of reneging on the sale and returning the money? Radbaz answers that if the purchaser was aware of the facts, then the purchaser has no claim on the vendor to complete the sale. He therefore narrows the focus of the question to a situation in which the purchaser was under the impression that the vendor did own the merchandise. Radbaz explains that the answer to this question is problematic, because it was a subject of controversy among early authorities. R. Nissim b. Jacob had ruled that the vendor is indeed obligated to purchase the merchandise and supply it to the vendor; Alfasi had ruled to the contrary, that he is under no obligation to make good on the sale.[57] Radbaz clearly supports Alfasi's position.[58] In line

---

56 I, 86.

57 Radbaz cites Alfasi's opinion as deriving from what "is written in one of his versions." The reference is to Alfasi at Bava Batra 69b, chap. 4, no. 773, ed. Romm, 36b. There is, however, a version of Alfasi which attributes the opposite view to him, and is recorded by *Hagahot ha-Baẖ* to Alfasi ad loc. See the extended discussion of these versions by Lieberman, *Tosefta Ki-Fshuta*, Bava Metsi'a, 189–91 (to Tosefta Bava Metsi'a 4:1). Radbaz cites

with this, he deals with one of the main sources of R. Nissim b. Jacob's ruling, a passage in the Tosefta: "If one sells produce to his neighbor upon the presumption that he possesses it, and he does not possess it, it is not his prerogative to nullify the other's right."[59] Radbaz declares that this is not binding, because the Tosefta is not part of the Talmud proper, and the passage is not cited in the Babylonian Talmud.[60]

But Radbaz then proceeds with an alternative ruling, which represents his final word. This ruling is not in agreement with either of the two authorities he had cited. Radbaz suggests that the Tosefta passage refers to a case in which the vendor showed the buyer the merchandise, implying that it was his, and then sold it to the buyer. Accordingly, he would rule that in such a case the vendor would indeed have to make good on the sale. Radbaz presents this as a compromise between the two views based on sevara:

> This is a proper compromise between the two positions. In a case in which he showed it to him, the reason of (R. Nissim as cited by) the *'Ittur* makes sense (*mistabber*); and in a case in which he did not show it to him, the reason of Alfasi makes sense (*mistabber*).

Radbaz thus chooses between the various elements of the two positions on the basis of his own sevara.

Rabbenu Nissim's opinion as recorded in the *'Ittur*; see Lieberman, ibid., for other references to it.

58 In addition to what follows, consider these points. After presenting the opinion of R. Nissim, he proceeds: "But it appears that Alfasi differs with this, for it is written in one of his (work's) versions...." In addition to this manner of presentation, which presents Alfasi as a reason to reject R. Nissim, it should be pointed out that Radbaz ignores the contradictory version of Alfasi, which was obviously known to him, since he refers to "one of his versions." Later, he cites Rashbam to BT Bava Metsi'a 69b, s.v. *ar'a ve-diqlei*, as being in concurrence with Alfasi. The passage he cites, though, is absent from the printed editions of the Talmud.

59 Tosefta Bava Metsi'a 4:1.

60 Though Radbaz presents this argument without attribution, it actually derives from a responsum of R. Joseph ibn Migash, cited in *Shitta Mequbbetset* to Bava Metsi'a 47b, referred to by Lieberman (n. 57 above). Ibn Migash, who follows Alfasi in interpreting the Talmud in a way that would disqualify the sale, says that Tosefta passages, which the Babylonian Talmud does not cite, are not binding when they are contradicted by the Babylonian Talmud. Radbaz does not include this latter condition. Nevertheless, it would seem that Ibn Migash is Radbaz's source.

(*f*) *Rejecting Sevara*

In spite of Radbaz's independence and self-assuredness in his decision making, there are instances, not many to be sure, in which he backs away from his own sevara under the weight of contrary precedent opinion.

[83] The Talmud discusses the case of a debtor who, when the debt becomes due, proposes to the creditor that the money he had borrowed be redefined as payment for a sale of merchandise at its current value which he will deliver to him. The law is: "If he possesses it (the merchandise) it is permitted; if not, it is forbidden."[61] Maimonides had ruled that the permission applies only if the debtor/vendor has in his possession the full stock of merchandise that is being sold.[62] Rashba concurred.[63] Radbaz, however, believes that it is not necessary that he have the full stock in possession. He introduces his argument for that position in the following manner: "If it were not men as great as these that had said it, I would have said...." And he concludes: "But we do not have the prerogative to depart (*ein lanu la-zuz*) from their words."[64]

[84] Radbaz's occasional reluctance to act on his own understanding of the law is exemplified by two responsa which involve, in different ways, the same legal issue.

According to talmudic law, all of a debtor's real property is under lien to the creditor if he holds a note of indebtedness. If such property were sold, and if the debtor had no assets in his possession when the debt became due, then the creditor can collect the value of his debt in real property from its purchasers. The same does not apply to movables, and once they are no longer in the possession of the debtor, the creditor has no claim on them.[65] The Talmud, however, alludes to a legal mechanism by which a lien can indeed be attached to movables. It consists in writing explicitly in the note of indebtedness that the borrower "mortgages movables along with real property (*mittaltelei*

---

61 BT Bava Metsi'a 63a.

62 *MT*, Civil laws, Laws of Creditor and Debtor, chap. 10, parag. 6.

63 *Hiddushei ha-Rashba 'al Massekhet Bava Metsi'a*, to Bava Metsi'a 63a, s.v. *shema' minnah mide-rabbi osha'ya*, cited by Radbaz.

64 I, 525. See also I, 527, where he repeats this, referring to the responsum cited here.

65 See *MT*, Laws of Creditor and Debtor, chap. 18, parags. 1–2.

agav meqarqa'ei)."[66] Subsequently, the inclusion of a clause to this effect in notes of indebtedness became routine among the Jews of Spain. Radbaz was asked a question, which involved, *inter alia*, the status of such a lien on movables that subsequently had been given as a gift to "Simeon." Twenty years later, after the death of the benefactor and the subsequent loss of the inheritance by his heirs, Simeon's movables were being claimed by the benefactor's creditor for satisfaction of the debt.[67] Maimonides had ruled that the inclusion of a clause mortgaging movables along with real property effects a lien on the movables, and from that perspective it would seem that Simeon has no case.[68]

Radbaz, however, suggests a line of defense for Simeon. Rabbenu Asher tells us that when he came to Spain from Germany (1304), he was surprised to find that the clause establishing a lien on the debtor's movables was routinely included in notes of indebtedness, and he wondered how it could not but have a disruptive effect on daily commerce. He was informed, however, that it was general practice not to enforce the lien, precisely because of its disruptive effect.[69] There is, indeed, precedent in the Talmud for a deliberate lack of enforcement of a plaintiff's rights "for the benefit of the market place (*taqqanat ha-shuq*)."[70] The same practice, of including the clause but not enforcing it, was current in Egypt in Radbaz's days. Thus, the plaintiff would seem to have no claim against Simeon.

The case, however, did not involve a sale, but a gift. Radbaz is of the opinion that the enforcement of a lien against a gift would not interfere with commerce, and there is thus no reason to suspend enforcement of the law of the Talmud "for the benefit of the market place." His considered opinion, therefore, is that the movables, which

---

66 BT Bava Batra 44b. The discussion there deals with the assumption of responsibility which a seller of real property extends to the buyer, guaranteeing him reimbursement if its ownership is successfully challenged. The same principle is extended to a borrower's responsibility for repayment.

67 II, 677.

68 According to the question, Simeon had presented a defense, which Radbaz shows to be invalid, if indeed the heirs lost the inheritance through no culpability of their own.

69 Rabbenu Asher, *Responsa*, *Kelal* 79, no. 4.

70 BT Bava Qamma 115a, with reference to the reclaiming of stolen movables after they had been sold to an unsuspecting purchaser.

Simeon had received twenty years earlier, are indeed subject to the lien that his benefactor's creditor seeks to exercise upon them.

But ultimately, Radbaz backs off from ruling on the basis of his own sevara:

> This is what I had thought (*hakhi hava mistabbera li*). But I saw that Rabbenu Asher wrote in a responsum, *Kelal* 79, thus: "But the custom in this land, **and similarly in other places**, is that, because of the benefit of the marketplace, the creditor does not collect from movables that he sold **or that he gave** to another, even though he placed a lien upon them, 'movables along with real property.'" And I hereby withdraw my opinion (*mevattel da'ati*), because of his testimony that such is the practice in other places. (Emphasis mine—SM)[71]

Radbaz admits that in Egypt, too, he has never seen a case in which a creditor seized movables that had been given as a gift by the debtor. That by itself, however, would not have been a precedent for him against his own understanding of the law, because in such instances, which are relatively uncommon, the movables could have been concealed from the creditor, so that cases of this type do not often come to court. But Radbaz considers Rabbenu Asher's seemingly incidental inclusion of gifts in his description of the law in practice to be binding. He suggests that perhaps the inclusion of gifts should be viewed in a broader context than "benefit of the marketplace," namely, "benefit of society in general" (*taqqanat ha-'olam*)."[72] Since a gift is assumed to be reciprocation for an earlier favor that the recipient had bestowed upon his benefactor,[73] non-enforcement of the lien would encourage such favors between people, to the ultimate benefit of society. Radbaz introduces this line of argument as a possible rationalization for Rabbenu Asher's ruling, not as one to which he would personally subscribe. In any case, he submits to Rabbenu Asher's authority: "In sum (*kelala de-milta*), I rely on Rabbenu Asher with regard to this law..., who wrote that this is the practice in all places."[74]

---

71 The phrase, "and similarly in other places," which is emphasized specifically by Radbaz, and appears to be central to his thinking, is absent in the printed edition of Rabbenu Asher's responsum, *Kelal* 79, no. 4.

72 For *taqqanat ha-'olam* see Mishnah Gittin 4:2 and following.

73 See BT Gittin 50b; Alfasi ad loc., Gittin chap. 5, no. 483, ed. Romm, 24b; *MT*, Civil Laws, Laws of Creditor and Debtor, chap. 19, parag. 2.

74 See n. 71. Radbaz writes here: "in all places (*be-khol ha-meqomot*)," but cited Rabbenu Asher as having written: "in other places (*be-sh'ar meqomot*)."

[85] The clause, "movables along with real property," which permits a lien to be placed on the debtor's moveable property, figures in another instance in which Radbaz refrains from applying in practice his own understanding of the law. Radbaz was asked whether the personal clothing of a debtor's wife and children is subject to seizure by the creditor.[75] He begins by referring to Maimonides, who, following Alfasi, had ruled that they are not subject to seizure.[76] Maimonides and Alfasi had made no distinction in this regard as to whether or not the clause placing a lien on movables was included in the note of indebtedness, and Radbaz takes their silence to mean that in all cases the creditor cannot seize these assets.[77] However, Radbaz cites Rabbenu Nissim, who, on the basis of an inference drawn from the Talmud, ruled otherwise. According to Rabbenu Nissim, a lien on the debtor's movables would make the clothing of the debtor's wife and children subject to seizure.[78]

Radbaz is disturbed by this ruling of Rabbenu Nissim: "As for me, it is difficult for me to accept this law." After all, it is customary to include the clause placing a lien on movables in all notes of indebtedness, but it was clearly not the practice to act on it. Furthermore, it was common knowledge (*margela be-pumaihu de-inshei*) that the clothing of one's wife and children was not subject to seizure, yet the clause was always included. Radbaz therefore assumes that a special enactment must have been passed to protect the wife and children of a debtor, just as one must attribute the general non-enforcement of the clause when the movables have been sold to an enactment "for the benefit of the marketplace."

---

75 I, 11.

76 *MT*, Civil Laws, Laws of Creditor and Debtor, chap. 1, parag. 5; Alfasi at Bava Metsi'a 114b, chap. 9, no. 584, ed. Romm, 69b.

77 It seems clear from the responsum that the question was asked with specific regard to this clause. Otherwise, the law, as formulated by Maimonides, would have been obvious. This is another example of Radbaz's tendency to abbreviate the questions, omitting relevant information, which is taken account of in the body of the responsum; see Chap. 1 n. 79. The same thing can be demonstrated in another way with this responsum. At the end of the responsum, Radbaz answers a related question which was clearly part of the original query, though there is no allusion to it in the text of the question.

78 Radbaz cites Rabbenu Nissim from a citation of him in *Nimmuqei Yosef* to Alfasi, ibid. The citation derives from Rabbenu Nissim, *H̲iddushei ha-Ran 'al Bava Metsi'a*, to Bava Metsi'a 114b, p. 361.

But even though Radbaz is sure of his ground, he is hesitant to rule accordingly in practice. For Rabbenu Nissim is not the only one to have ruled that way. Rabbenu Nissim's ruling, along with the argument for it, goes back to Na<u>h</u>manides. And Na<u>h</u>manides, Radbaz tells us, is cited by the author of the *Turim*, who did not cite any contrary opinion.[79] Since it was customary for the author of the *Turim* to cite differing opinions, his failure to do so indicates his concurrence with Na<u>h</u>manides' position. "Therefore," writes Radbaz, "I put aside my weak intellect in favor of the broad intellect of the early authorities (*hilkakh hareini mevattel da'ati ha-qalush mipnei ro<u>h</u>av da'at ha-rishonim*)." Radbaz would thus rule that the clothing of a debtor's wife and children can be seized by a creditor if the debt could not otherwise be satisfied. In practice, this would apply to all creditors holding notes of indebtedness, since they all routinely included the clause. And he would rule this way both against his own better judgment, and against the common assumption of the lay public.

Examples like these are not common among Radbaz's numerous responsa. They are far outweighed by examples of his independent decision making, in which he does not hesitate to put the results of his own sevara into practice.

---

79 *Tur <u>H</u>oshen Mishpat*, no. 97, toward the end. The original source, not cited by Radbaz, is Samuel ha-Sardi's *Sefer ha-Terumot*, *Sha'ar* 1, *<u>H</u>eleq* 1, parag. 5. Sardi, a contemporary of Na<u>h</u>manides, introduces it as a responsum by the latter to himself personally.

Conclusions from Part One

The responsa of Radbaz manifest a great deal of judicial independence. Independence is not usually a valued quality in jurisprudence, which prides itself in upholding the legal status quo. That is more so the case in rabbinic jurisprudence, where the law is seen as having divine sanction. Certainly in rabbinic circles of the sixteenth century, authors of responsa attempted to present their conclusions as the result of an objective analysis of the accepted and codified law. Departure from that law because of extraneous considerations, though surely more frequent than appears at first sight, was not generally acknowledged. A striking aspect of many of Radbaz's responsa is his remarkable openness in acknowledging a departure from the codified law. It is that openness which has made it feasible to track his judicial independence.

Part One of this study traced the effect of considerations external to a straightforward reading of the codified law. Radbaz began with the fundamental worldview that the purpose of judicial decisions was to produce decisions that were just. Justice in this sense is not defined by the law, but by an innate sense of what is right, fair and rational. This approach brought Radbaz into direct consideration of the objective world around him as he perceived it, rather than the world as it was construed by the codified law. In the world as construed by the Talmud, students of Torah are protected from mishap by their Torah, and therefore need not contribute financially to the security of the city. Radbaz, however, perceived that in the objective world of his living contemporaries that is not the case, and issued his ruling accordingly.[1] In the world as construed by the Talmud, a married woman would not dare to make an unprovable allegation regarding her husband in his presence, which the husband knew was not true. Such an allegation should therefore be accepted by the court. In Radbaz's world as he understood it, married women were not so modest, and would indeed be so daring. Such an uprovable allegation should therefore not be accepted automatically at face value.[2] The Talmud presumed that physical contact between a man and his wife may well lead to sexual intercourse, and therefore prohibited physical contact when intercourse was forbidden because of menstrual uncleanness. The prohibition was general, and appeared to allow no exceptions. In the case before Radbaz, the wife was ill and needed her husband's ministrations, no one else being available to help her. Radbaz emphasized the improbability that physical contact of that type would lead to intercourse, and permitted it.[3] The Talmud does not recognize the juridical trustworthiness of non-Jews. Radbaz, from his reading of the world around him, accepted the possibility of an honest non-Jew, and carried through the implications of that recognition to a juridical setting.[4]

In the same spirit of bringing the law into accord with empirical social reality, Radbaz rejected literal interpretations of the law which were not in accord with the requirements of true justice. A husband's attempt to extort from his wife a waiving of her legal rights might have succeeded through a literal interpretation of the concept "duress," but Radbaz interpreted duress in a broad sense, which reflected the wife's situation as she lived it.[5] A literal interpretation of the Hebrew term *sekhirut* (hiring / leasing) would have yielded a result which was inconsistent with the true intent of the law. Radbaz integrated the law's intent into its interpretation, and distinguished between *sekhirut* as "hiring" and *sekhirut* as "leasing."[6]

Radbaz's responsa reveal a sensitivity to the way his rulings affect the lives of people. This is most blatantly apparent in his responsa regarding *'agunot*, women whose missing husbands are believed to be

---

1 Case [1].
2 Case [2].
3 Case [10].
4 Case [11].
5 Case [19].
6 Case [22].

dead, and are awaiting legal recognition of their status as widows so that they can remarry. Radbaz stretched the limits of leniency in his interpretation of the law in these cases. It is instructive that in a case in which he rejected a construction of the facts that would have allowed a lenient ruling, he did so because such a construction was highly implausible in the practical world. Here too, though, he found his way to a lenient ruling on the basis of other testimony.[7]

Consistent with his conception of justice, Radbaz entrusted a great deal of discretion to trial judges, "for a judge rules on the basis of what he knows to be the truth, and not on the basis of the arguments."[8] Although this is attested primarily in rules of evidence and procedure, it is found also with regard to the substantive ruling itself. In one case, the law supported "Reuben," the defendant; "but if it appears to the judge that Reuben is a deceiver, and he is able to compel him to do what is right and good, he has the authority in his power (to do so)," that is, by finding in favor of the plaintiff.[9]

One aspect of the objective world that Radbaz confronted, and integrated into his interpretation of the law, consisted of widespread popular practice, which apparently did not accord with the law. In some cases, Radbaz, recognizing that the questionable practice satisfied an economic necessity, or was an entrenched practice that would not be uprooted by rabbinical objections, found a forced legal basis for it, though he expressed deep reservations about the legitimacy of the practice. Maritime insurance was questionable because it was, in essence, a form of loan on interest, which is forbidden. Radbaz suggested a method in which the transaction could be defined as a sale rather than a loan. Radbaz gave vent to his unease about permitting interest by means of a technicality, but accepted the necessity for doing so.[10] In addressing another entrenched practice, which was questionable because of the prohibition of interest, Radbaz himself clearly believed it to be forbidden. Nevertheless, he presented a case for accepting its legitimacy, a case that he personally felt to be invalid, so that the general public could be construed as following another opinion, and would not be considered sinners.[11] A popular practice, which provided a crucial means of employment for impoverished women, was subject

7 Case [23].
8 Case [28].
9 Case [32].
10 Case [37].
11 Case [36].

to both legal and moral objections. Radbaz removed the legal objections, but maintained that in certain specific situations, where the moral objections were more blatant, the practice should not be allowed, even though there were technical legal grounds for permitting it.[12] His attitude was different, however, with regard to the entrenched practice of redeeming Jewish captives for an exorbitant ransom, which is forbidden by the codified law. After reviewing the rationalizations for this practice, which had been offered by earlier authorities, Radbaz gave it his strong moral backing, waxing enthusiastic about the generosity exhibited by Jews in this matter.[13]

In line with Radbaz's general predilection to interpret the law in light of the empirical world, he takes serious cognizance of widespread popular understandings, or more properly, misunderstandings, of the law. There are instances in which Radbaz allows a popular misconception of the law to have a substantive effect on his ruling.[14] Elsewhere, he takes pains to demonstrate that in the given situation the popular misconception would have been clarified to the litigants, so that there would not have been a misunderstanding on their part in the case at hand.[15]

Radbaz's basic attitude, that law should work to produce justice, and that justice is defined by what is right and equitable, led to a special emphasis on the moral aspects of his decisions. Most frequently this emphasis is rhetorical, reinforcing a decision which is argued on strictly legal grounds.[16] The very redundancy of this emphasis, and the passion with which it is argued, testifies to Radbaz's deep feelings on the importance of equity and its integration into the law itself.[17] In one instance discussed above, considerations of equity led to a decision at variance with the law in its narrow sense.[18] Radbaz has particular scorn for those who would exploit the law inequitably to their own advantage.[19]

---

12 Case [35].
13 Case [38].
14 Cases [39], [41], [43].
15 Case [40].
16 Cases [44], [45], [46].
17 The conception of equity as not supplementary to the legal system, but as an integral part of it, is a central thesis of Kirschenbaum, *Halakhic Perspectives*. See, for instance, the statement of his thesis on p. 37.
18 Case [50].
19 Case [51] through Case [58].

Another factor utilized by Radbaz in arriving at his decisions is public policy. In a number of cases, Radbaz openly admits that his ruling is in accordance with an opinion he would normally reject, and he rules as he does only in the specific case before him, because of the desirable result it would yield.[20]

Rationality is an integral element in Radbaz's conception of justice, and an important ingredient in the way his judicial independence manifests itself. On a number of occasions Radbaz draws distinctions which define the scope of a law, thereby excluding from its purview situations to which it seems, in his opinion, the law should not apply. For instance, he follows Maimonides in the latter's ruling that a husband may discipline his wife for moral infractions by beating her, but then, on the basis of his own rational judgment, excludes him from doing so if it is a matter which concerns him personally.[21] The law is that if a man collects alms on the pretext that he is poor, and turns out to have not been poor, he cannot be compelled to return the alms. Radbaz distinguishes between a large gift and a small one, and rules that a large gift does have to be returned.[22] Radbaz's rationality expresses itself also in his willingness on occasion to decide between conflicting earlier authorities on the basis of his own judgment of the substance of the debate, rather than by relying on rules for resolving such controversies.[23] Radbaz is also known to stake out an independent position in opposition to an earlier authority, even to Maimonides himself.[24] On several occasions, when faced with conflicting opinions, Radbaz forges an independent middle position, which agrees with none of them.[25] In contrast to this trend, there are occasional cases in which Radbaz does back away from his own reasoned opinion because of earlier authorities who had ruled otherwise.[26] These, however, are few in number, and do not change the overall picture of Radbaz's judicial independence.

---

20 Case [60], [61], [62], [63]; Case [59] as well, though it is somewhat less explicit.

21 Case [67].

22 Case [69].

23 Cases [75], [76], [77]. In Case [78] he rejects an earlier authority (R. Meir of Rothenburg) on the basis of his own judgment without the benefit of a differing opinion.

24 Cases [78], [79], [80].

25 Cases [81], [82], [100].

26 Cases [83], [84], [85].

Part Two

Rules and Rhetoric

6. The Middle Way

[86] Radbaz refers frequently to the principle that "it is better to seize the middle way." That is, given three schools of opinion, one should rule according to the middle view. As far as I can determine, he is virtually the only author of responsa until his time to use this phrase.[1] Its most explicit formulation as a general rule is found in a responsum dealing with the laws of kosher foods.

A slaughtered animal is prohibited if it is discovered to have certain internal injuries, which were considered to be ultimately fatal. One of these is a perforation in the lung. There is considerable discussion among the authorities on the extent to which an adhesion in the lung is

---

1 The Bar Ilan Responsa Project lists 66 occurrences of *milta metsi'ata* ("the middle way") in Radbaz's responsa. It lists no usages of the term in this sense by earlier respondents. In the sixteenth century a parallel can be found in a responsum of R. Joseph ibn Lev. In reference to the definition of perishable goods (*davar ha-aved*), with regard to permission to do work on the intermediate days of the festival, Ibn Lev outlines a variety of opinions. He then continues: "It appears to me (*u-mistabbera li*) that the straight path which one should choose is the middle way (*ha-derekh ha-memutsa'*) – not to be entirely stringent, but also not to be lenient, for those who are stringent are also the great ones of the world, great in wisdom and in numbers" (Responsa, Pt. 3, no. 61). For the term *milta metsi'ata* in the sixteenth century exclusive of Radbaz, the Responsa Project lists only R. Joel Sirkes, who suggests that R. Moses Isserles arrived at a certain legal decision by using this method. See *She'elot u-Teshuvot ha-Bah (ha-Yeshanot)*, no. 85.

taken as evidence of a perforation. Radbaz was asked the following question:

> You asked me to tell you what the slaughterers of this city rely on in permitting an adhesion to the bone and the flesh (together), since there are several great earlier and later authorities who declare it to be forbidden.[2]

If the lung adheres to flesh, it was understood that the flesh would seal any perforation in the lung. That is not necessarily true of an adhesion to bone. The question here refers to an adhesion of the lung to ribs that are covered with flesh.[3] Radbaz answers quite simply that the authority they rely on is Maimonides.[4] He then brings two reasons for following Maimonides' ruling:

> They rely on Maimonides, who permits it. This (place, i.e., Egypt—SM) is the place of the Master, and all their affairs they conduct according to him....
>
> Furthermore, the ruling of the Rabbi (i.e., Maimonides) is the middle way. For there are those who prohibit it, and there are those who permit even an adhesion to the bone itself.... Hence the ruling of Maimonides is found to be in the middle; an adhesion to the bone itself renders the animal unfit, but to the bone and the flesh (together) renders it fit. **And everywhere we should seize the middle way**. (Emphasis mine—SM)

The first of these reasons for following Maimonides is that such is the custom in general in Egypt. We will meet this theme again, and it will be explored on its own terms in Chapter 7. The second reason is that "everywhere we should seize the middle way." In spite of this comprehensive formulation, it is rare to find Radbaz relying exclusively on the principle of the "middle way" to arrive at a decision.

(*a*) *The "Middle Way" Presented as a Determinative Factor*

[87] An example of what appears to indeed be an exclusive reliance on the "middle way" is found in a responsum dealing with the cancellation of debts by the sabbatical year.[5] The Mishnah tells us that

---

2 I, 328.

3 The second part of the question asks him to define what is meant by "the bone and the flesh," a term already in use by the authorities who discuss the issue. Radbaz defines it as I have presented it.

4 *MT*, Holiness, Laws of Slaughter, chap. 11, parag. 10. *Kesef Mishneh* ad loc. discusses the various views on this issue.

5 See Deut. 15:1–11.

Hillel the Elder (c. the beginning of the Common Era), seeing that people were reluctant to lend money because of the fear that the debt would be cancelled, enacted a legal fiction in which the debts were transferred to the court. The sabbatical year's cancellation of debts did not apply to debts owed to the court. The instrument effecting this transfer was known as a *prosbul.*[6] There is a dispute in the Talmud as to whether the court should recognize the plea of a creditor, that he originally had a *prosbul* in his possession, but had lost the document.[7] In the case that came before Radbaz, the plaintiff put forth that claim among others.[8]

The plaintiff had presented a series of arguments. Radbaz recognized the validity of each of the arguments (save the first) on its merits, but he felt that taken together they contradict each other, so that the plaintiff's credibility was undermined. He therefore insisted that the plaintiff take an oath affirming that he possessed a *prosbul.* Radbaz then goes on to explain his general position on this issue. He shows that there are three positions among the authorities.[9] (a) The creditor is to be taken at his word. This is the view of Maimonides,[10] Rabbenu Asher[11] and others. (b) The creditor can never collect without the presentation of a prosbul.[12] (c) The creditor is to be believed, but only if he first takes an oath affirming the truth of his claim. This is the view of R. Meir ha-Levi Abulafia (Ramah). After explaining that the plaintiff's lack of credibility demands an oath, Radbaz states:

> So much more so is this the case, since in general I rule according to the opinion of Ramah and some other authorities, that he is believed if he takes an oath, because it is the middle way... (He proceeds to lay out the three-way controversy described above).

Radbaz tells us that he would have insisted on an oath in any case, because he rules in accordance with R. Meir Abulafia. There doesn't seem to be any reason for Radbaz to adopt the position of R. Meir Abulafia, against Maimonides and Rabbenu Asher, two leading authorities, except for it being the "middle way." It should be

---

6 Mishnah Shevi'it 10:3–4.
7 BT Gittin 37b.
8 IV, 170 (= 1241).
9 All of them are reported in *Tur Hoshen Mishpat,* 67.
10 *MT*, Agriculture, Laws of Sabbatical Year, chap. 9, parag. 24.
11 *Pisqei ha-Rosh*, Gittin, chap. 4, parag. 20.
12 *'Ittur*, Part 1, 76b. This view is attributed to Alfasi by Rabbenu Asher (*Pisqei ha-Rosh*, ibid.) and by Rabbenu Nissim (to Alfasi ad loc.).

remembered, though, that this is a ruling in theory only. In the specific case before him, Radbaz has other reasons that lead him to decide the way he does. This consideration mitigates the strength of this case as an example of Radbaz's reliance on the "middle way" in arriving at a decision.

[88] I have identified only a few other cases where the "middle way" is presented as the sole rationale for deciding the law among differing authorities.

One of these is in answer to the question whether it is permitted to tell a non-Jew to bring food to a Jew who is incarcerated in prison on the Sabbath.[13] If not, then he would go hungry until Sunday morning, since there would be no access to him at night. Furthermore, he would be forced to forgo the religious obligation of "enjoying the Sabbath," which is actualized through the enjoyment of satisfying and tasty meals.

Sabbath prohibitions are divided, as are all areas of Jewish law, between those that derive from the authority of the Torah and those which derive from the authority of the Rabbis, and certain leniencies are allowed in the latter case. Telling a non-Jew to do work on the Sabbath is classified as a rabbinic prohibition.[14] Radbaz identifies three views on the subject of whether this prohibition is relaxed in order to relieve a discomfit short of actual illness.[15] One view, that of Nahmanides, would limit relaxation of the prohibition to situations in which it may be necessary for the performance of a circumcision on the Sabbath, thus excluding the present case.[16] The second view is that of Maimonides, who does not limit this to circumcision, but extends the permission to tell a non-Jew to perform a rabbinically prohibited act on the Sabbath to all cases in which "there is some illness, or a great need for the matter, or for the sake of performing a religious obligation."[17] Radbaz attributes this view also to Alfasi, though this attribution is

---

13 III, 577 (= 1005).

14 For this entire subject see Katz, *Shabbes Goy.*

15 All three are discussed by Rabbenu Nissim on Alfasi to Shabbat, Chap. 19, no. 504.

16 Nahmanides is cited by Rabbenu Nissim, ibid. Radbaz suggests that R. Isaac of Dampierre held a similar opinion.

17 *MT*, Seasons, Laws of the Sabbath, Chap. 6, parag. 9.

open to question.[18] The third view is that of the author of the *'Ittur*, who extends this permission even to activities which are biblically prohibited to a Jew on the Sabbath, as long as they can be construed as related to the performance of a religious obligation in some way.[19] Against this background Radbaz states:

> In any case, the most correct among the rulings[20] is the opinion of Alfasi and Maimonides, because it is the "middle way." ... Even though in other rulings I am wont to be stringent, this case is different. Because here, if you are stringent, there is a leniency in its wake, for the Jew would be imprisoned in a state of distress all day and all night.
>
> I am inclined to say[21] that even those who differ would accede in the case under discussion. They did not prohibit (the telling of a non-Jew to perform an act prohibited on the Sabbath) except for (the performance of) an ordinary religious obligation, such as the transporting of a Torah scroll. But in this case, which involves the prohibition of fasting on the Sabbath, and the pain of hunger, and the probability of his becoming ill because of it since he is imprisoned, as well as his being deprived of (fulfilling the obligation of) enjoying the Sabbath, all would agree that the prohibition of telling a non-Jew to do work is permitted on his account when the activity is rabbinically prohibited.

Radbaz's position can be summed up this way. In theory he rules in accordance with the "middle way," which permits one to tell a non-Jew to perform a prohibited act on the Sabbath if there is a justified need for it, and if the act itself is only prohibited by the authority of the Rabbis. In practice he tends to rule stringently, probably in order to discourage abuses. In this specific instance, the need is so justified that he reverts to his basic position, which follows the "middle way."

Of interest to us here is Radbaz's basic general position on the issue of "telling a non-Jew," which, he informs us, was determined by the rule of the "middle way." However, the rationale of the "middle way" might be masking a more conventional reason for Radbaz to rule the

---

18 See Alfasi, op. cit. Alfasi does not explicitly extend this rule beyond the case of circumcision. See Rabbenu Nissim ad loc., who clearly makes this distinction between Alfasi and Maimonides.

19 *'Ittur*, Part 2, 49a. *'Ittur* cites the example of the need for light by which to eat the Sabbath meal.

20 *ha-nakhon she-ba-posqim*, an apparent error for: *ha-nakhon she-ba-pesaqim*.

21 *ve-qarov ani lomar*

way he does. After all, the authority of Maimonides and Alfasi might be sufficient to override that of the other opinions here. In any case, he surely gives no hint here of anything other than the "middle way" being his reason for ruling the way he does on this issue.

[89] The "middle way" is presented as the sole operative principle in a responsum dealing with kosher slaughter.[22] In this case, though, the identification of a specific opinion as being the "middle way" is subject to manipulation, a fact which gives rise to the question of whether other, unstated, factors were at work here in Radbaz's arriving at his decision.

Slaughter is unfit if the knife "slides," that is, if it cuts through an area beyond the prescribed limits of the throat. Radbaz discusses a situation in which part of the slaughter was proper, and part slid. He identifies four views. The most stringent, that of Rashi, is that any amount of sliding renders the slaughter unfit. The most lenient is that of Maimonides, that if only the middle third was slaughtered properly, even though the first and last third of the slaughter slid, the slaughter is still fit. The other two views are in agreement that a contiguous two thirds of a proper slaughter renders the slaughter fit. However, the more stringent of the two views (Rashba) insists that the proper slaughter of two thirds take place first, while the more lenient one (Naẖmanides and R. Zeraẖia ha-Levi) allows the fitness of the slaughter even if the sliding took place in the first third, and the latter two thirds were slaughtered properly. Radbaz follows a well-established procedure, which takes into account the monetary loss that would accrue to a Jew as a factor in deciding such laws leniently. Thus, in the case of an animal belonging to a Jew, he would rule according to the most lenient position, that is, Maimonides, "for it is the place of the Master."[23] Otherwise, he would rule according to Naẖmanides and R. Zeraẖia ha-Levi, "for it is the middle way." He adds, though, that it would not hurt for one to voluntarily adopt the more stringent position of Rashba. However, Rashi's view, which is the most stringent, is ignored in this weighing of alternatives. Taking it into account would perhaps have allowed Rashba's view to be considered as a "middle way," a path not taken by Radbaz.

---

22 I, 253.
23 See Chapter 7.

[90] The "middle way" appears as the sole argument for Radbaz's ruling in a responsum, which involves the requirement of a quorum of ten Jews for group prayer.[24] Radbaz was asked whether an eleven-year-old, a minor by every standard, travelling on a ship with a group of nine adults, can be added to the others to form the required quorum.

Radbaz distinguishes between the general case and the specific question before him. The latter is a special case, since in these circumstances there would be no way to form a quorum without allowing the minor to join. Such a situation was not unknown in earlier times in the small communities of Germany and France, and Radbaz cites precedents for this allowance in such instances. As regards the general case, Radbaz shows that there are three opinions on the requirements for a prayer quorum. Two of them maintain that generally all ten must be adults, but they differ on the definition of adulthood. The more stringent position maintains the ancient definition of male adulthood as defined by physical puberty, specifically, the appearance of two pubic hairs after the age of thirteen. The other position defines adulthood for the purpose of a prayer quorum by age alone; a boy reaching the age of thirteen is automatically considered an adult.[25] There is a third view, however, identified with Rabbenu Tam, that "even a baby lying in a cradle" can be counted as the tenth for a prayer quorum.[26] Radbaz rules according to the opinion that all must be adults, as defined by age alone, "which is the middle way." That is the only rationale he cites. However, it may be that Radbaz's ruling reflects accepted practice, and it is that which primarily guides his decision, rather than the principle of the "middle way." It must be pointed out, though, that in the environment in which Radbaz functioned, there was broad participation in public prayer, and a situation like this would arise only in very unusual circumstances.[27] This makes it less likely that the ruling is based on accepted practice.

---

24 VIII, 11.

25 On the history of the definition of the age of majority for religious obligation and other legal purposes, see Gilat, "Thirteen Years Old."

26 All these views are discussed in *Beit Yosef* to *Tur Orah Hayyim,* no. 55.

27 I thank Professor Norman Stillman for confirmation of this point.

(*b*) *The "Middle Way" as a Supplementary Factor*

[91] There is another responsum dealing with a prayer quorum in which Radbaz casts his ruling as a "middle way." In this case, there is no question that his ruling is an affirmation of general practice.

Radbaz was asked to explain the reason for the opinion of those who insist that the quorum of ten must contain at least seven who have not yet fulfilled their prayer obligation, rather than a minimum of six, a simple majority.[28] In actual practice, a minimum of only six was required, as Radbaz himself tells us, and that is how he himself rules. Radbaz explains the more stringent view, as he was asked to do. (He suggests that seven among ten results in an audibly recognizable majority.) But in affirming the common practice, he presents a "middle way" argument. To do so he presents an idiosyncratic view, attributed to "the students of Rashi," which allows a quorum if only one of the ten has not yet prayed.[29] That opinion serves here only to establish common practice as a "middle way."

[92] The effort to represent a desired legal ruling as the "middle way," even when there are other motivations, sufficient in themselves, that actually govern the decision, as appears to be the case in the former instance, underscores the importance that the concept of the "middle way" occupied in Radbaz's mind. In the following example this is even more evident. In this case he has ample means of arriving at his goal. The "middle way" is used rather casually, and adds very little to the conclusion.

The question that he addresses is of more than common interest.[30] It comes from Candia, in Crete, then under Venetian rule. "Reuben" had donated a large sum for a major refurbishing of the synagogue, and insisted on placing his coat of arms over the ark which houses the Torah scrolls. The coat of arms consisted of a gilded bold relief of a lion with a crown on its head. Reuben had obtained backing from some rabbis, probably local, and surely not of the first rank.[31] R. Elijah

---

28 IV, 240 (= 1311).

29 See *Teshuvot Rashi*, ed. Elfenbein, no. 92, p. 118. The sources Elfenbein draws from attribute this responsum to Rashi himself.

30 IV, 107 (= 1178).

31 Radbaz makes reference to them at the beginning of his responsum: "My wrath burns against the 'shepherds' who uphold the hand of Reuben." R.

Capsali, the rabbi of Candia, had come out strongly against this, and had sought the support of rabbis outside the community. He had obtained such supportive rulings from R. Meir Katzenellenbogen, the Rabbi of Padua with whom he had studied, and from R. Joseph Caro and R. Moses Trani of Safed.[32] The question was sent to Radbaz as well.

Radbaz's response, unlike those previously discussed, is long and thorough, and laced throughout with a high degree of passion. He marshals a whole arsenal of arguments for prohibiting the placement of the coat of arms above the ark. It is clear that Radbaz was going to arrive at his ruling with whatever arguments work. The "middle way" makes its appearance in connection with the most central argument in his arsenal.

The issue involves the prohibition of producing images in bold relief. The rabbis who had supported Reuben had based themselves on the explicit ruling of Maimonides, that images of all living beings except those of humans were permitted even in bold relief.[33] Radbaz, earlier in the responsum, had dismissed Maimonides' lenient ruling because a host of later authorities had ruled against him.[34] He is then left with the following: (1) An Ashkenazic ruling, attributed to R. Elyaqim (12th century), forbade the making of any images of living beings.[35] R. Elyaqim's view had already been cited by R. Elijah Capsali in his original responsum.[36] (2) Nahmanides had ruled that the prohibition applies only to the manufacture and maintenance of reliefs, which are of a type that are worshipped. (Earlier in the responsum Radbaz had asserted that in Christian countries, an image of this type is

---

Meir Katzenellenbogen (see n. 33) cites an argument from a responsum supporting Reuben's position: "That man (*hahu gavra*) wrote that...."

32 Trani, Responsa, Part 1, no. 30; R. Meir Katzenellenbogen, *Avqat Rokhel*, no. 65; Cairo, ibid., no. 63.

33 *MT*, Knowledge, Laws of Idolatrous Worship, chap. 3, parag. 11. It is clear from R. Meir Katzenellenbogen's citation of Reuben's rabbinic supporter that Maimonides' ruling was a crucial element in the argument permitting the coat of arms.

34 "You see with your eyes that according to all these great ones, who are late authorities (*de-batra'ei ninhu*), one who makes an image like this certainly transgresses a negative command" (ed. Warsaw, top of 30a). Radbaz's use of the principle, that the law follows the later authorities (*hilkheta ke-batra'ei*), will be discussed in Chapter 10.

35 Cited in *Mordekhai* to 'Avoda Zara chap. 3, no. 840.

36 This is attested by R. Meir Katzenellenbogen.

certainly suspect in this regard.)[37] (3) Rabbenu Nissim had adopted this view as well. But Radbaz, from a close reading of Rabbenu Nissim, concludes that he differed from Nahmanides in cases in which it is uncertain whether or not the image is one that is worshipped. According to Radbaz, Nahmanides had prohibited images in this category, whereas Rabbenu Nissim had permitted them. Radbaz expresses reservations about the severity of R. Elyaqim's position, and falls back on Nahmanides as the "middle way":

> But it is a great stringency in my eyes that it be forbidden to make any bold relief. Rather it is better to seize the middle way, which is the view of Nahmanides and his disciples.[38]

Radbaz then proceeds to an alternative way of reaching the equivalent result. This sequel, and his providing of another reason for rejecting R. Elyaqim, are indications of the supplementary character of the "middle way" principle. Nevertheless, the very fact that Radbaz feels the need to refer to it even when it is redundant for his purposes, is a testament to its centrality in his mindset.

(c) *Deliberate Efforts to Structure a "Middle Way" Argument*

This procedure, the introduction of the "middle way" as a supplement to what appears, by dint of the rhetoric and structure of the responsum, to be the main rationale for his conclusion, is exemplified in other instances.

[93] In Case [76], we saw Radbaz reject an opinion of Rabbenu Asher, in favor of others who would normally be less authoritative, on the basis of his own sevara.[39] To appreciate the role of the "middle way" in this responsum, it is necessary, at the expense of redundancy, to review the case.

A debtor owed two debts to the same creditor, one for which there was a note, and one for which there were only witnesses, but no note. He repaid one of the debts, but there was disagreement between the debtor and the creditor as to which one was repaid. An oral debt was a less certain asset for a creditor, because the law recognizes the right of the debtor to plead that the debt has already been repaid. That is not the

37 P. 29d.
38 P. 30d.
39 IV, 181 (= 1252).

case when the creditor holds a note. Thus, the creditor asserted that the payment represented the oral debt. The debtor asserted that it represented the debt that bore the note. Rabbenu Asher, in ruling on a situation of this type, approached the issue from the point of view of the debtor's intention in making the payment. He ruled in favor of the debtor, on the basis of the presumption that the debtor would not liquidate an oral debt, in which he was in a stronger position, and remain in debt for a loan that bore a note.

Radbaz begins his discussion by citing the view of R. Aaron ha-Levi, in favor of the creditor.[40] He then adds an original reason for this conclusion. Adopting Rabbenu Asher's perspective of the intention of the debtor, Radbaz asserts a presumption opposite to that of Rabbenu Asher. He presumes that the debtor, in his own interest, would repay the oral loan first. The debtor is presumed to be honest, argues Radbaz, and would not deny a debt that he really owed. Thus, the deniability of the oral debt is not an asset for him. By liquidating the oral debt first, he is protecting himself from dunning by a creditor who is concerned over the lack of a note. Radbaz then refers to Rabbenu Asher's opposite conclusion, that the debtor's interest would lead to a presumption that he intended to liquidate the debt that bore the note. Radbaz comments, "In any case, what I wrote is more reasonable."

Radbaz does not end at that point, but continues with a postscript, supplementing his position with a "middle way" argument. In order to do so, he produces an extreme view in favor of the creditor:

> And furthermore, it is the middle way. For Rabbenu Nissim wrote that even if the debtor said, "I am repaying the one bearing the note," and the creditor accepted payment in silence, he (the creditor) may say afterwards, "I was repaid the oral debt."[41] What I have written is the median opinion (*ha-sevara ha-memutsa'at*): if he paid without specifying, then he relied on the intention of the creditor, allowing that he could take it for whatever (loan) he wanted; but if he specified that it was for the debt bearing the note, then the creditor does not have the right to take it on behalf of the oral note.

The rhetorical structure of this responsum suggests that it is Radbaz's original insight, namely, that it is to the benefit of the debtor to liquidate the oral debt first, which leads him to reject Rabbenu Asher's ruling in favor of R. Aaron ha-Levi. The "middle way" is

---

40 See Chapter 5, text at n. 31.

41 Rabbenu Nissim on Alfasi to Ketubbot, no. 332 (at Ketubbot 85a), s.v. *sitra'i ninhu.*

presented as an afterthought. The extreme position on the opposite side of Rabbenu Asher, the opinion of Rabbenu Nissim, is presented suddenly, deus ex machina, for the sole purpose of establishing Radbaz's own position as a "middle way." In contrast to Rabbenu Asher, whom Radbaz takes seriously by structuring a counter argument, and by explicitly defending his own position against Rabbenu Asher ("what I wrote is more reasonable"), Radbaz does not give the appearance (I am talking only of appearances!) of taking Rabbenu Nissim's position seriously. He relegates it to nothing more than an element in a "middle way" argument. At least (and no more is claimed here) this is what emerges from the responsum's rhetorical structure. Radbaz seems to go out of his way to establish his ruling as the "middle way."

[94] A similar pattern occurs in a responsum dealing with the procedure to be followed when an error is made in the blowing of the *shofar*, the ram's horn, on Rosh Hashana.[42] In dealing with this issue, Radbaz raises the question of where in the sequence of *shofar* blasts must the blower return to. The smallest unit in the sequence, beyond the individual blast itself, is a unit of three blasts—an unbroken blast, followed by a broken one, followed again by an unbroken one. This is repeated three times, forming a larger unit of nine blasts. Radbaz, after announcing that the answer to the question is a matter of dispute, tells us that the proper procedure is to return to the beginning of the smaller, three-blast unit; not, he says, to the beginning of the larger, nine-blast unit; nor, he continues, to just pick up at the point of the erroneous blast. He cites two reasons for his ruling: "This is the middle way, and the opinion of most of the authorities, even though it is not the opinion of Rabbenu Asher." Rabbenu Asher's opinion, not spelled out by Radbaz, is that the blower continues from the erroneous blast.[43]

The argument that the ruling is in accord with "most of the authorities" is, one can assume, tantamount in this type of ritual matter to what must have been the general practice. After all, those are the authorities who would be consulted when this question arose, and there is no vested interest here which would lead us to suspect that their ruling would be ignored in practice. That in itself is sufficient to explain Radbaz's adoption of it against the ruling of Rabbenu Asher.

---

42 IV, 28 (= 1103).
43 *Pisqei ha-Rosh*, Rosh ha-Shana, chap. 4, no. 11.

Nevertheless, Radbaz finds it necessary to append an argument based on the principle of the "middle way."

The "middle way" argument in this case, though technically defensible, is somewhat forced. It rests on the existence of an opinion on the opposite extreme from that of Rabbenu Asher, namely, that the blower should return to the beginning of the larger nine-blast sequence. The earliest record of this opinion derives not from a recognized rabbinic authority, but from an incident in 12th century Mainz (referred to in subsequent literature as "the incident at Mainz"), in which an error was made in blowing, and one faction present in the congregation insisted that the blower repeat the whole nine-blast sequence. The story is found in a contemporary source, *Sefer Ra'avan*, by R. Eliezer ben Nathan. R. Eliezer's father-in-law, R. Elyaqim, was angered by the decision, and R. Eliezer presented a detailed rebuttal of the decision that was made.[44] The same opinion, that the nine-blast sequence be repeated, is recorded in the *Turim*, attributed anonymously to "there are those who say."[45] In any case, this opinion is weak. Its author is, at best, unidentified, and at worst (if the source for the *Turim* is in fact none other than the "incident at Mainz"), the lay populace in Mainz whom R. Eliezer ben Nathan had refuted.

(*d*) *Questionable Efforts to Structure a "Middle Way" Argument*

The fact that Radbaz relies on such a source to establish a "middle way" argues for the importance he attaches to the "middle way" principle, not as a real means for arriving at a decision, but as a rhetorical device. This impression is reinforced by cases in which there is no real question regarding the law, and yet a "middle way" argument is constructed.

[95] An example of this phenomenon is found in a responsum dealing with the requirement of martyrdom, a concept subsumed under the rubric, "the sanctification of God's Name."[46] The calm tone in which the responsum is written affirms the academic nature of the question.

---

44 *Sefer Ra'avan*, Part 1, no. 61. A more accessible account of this story, and R. Eliezer's discussion, is found in *Pisqei ha-Rosh*, ibid.

45 *Tur Orah Hayyim*, no. 590, at the end of the section.

46 VIII, 127.

The Talmud discusses this issue in terms of whether, if one is compelled to transgress a commandment under threat of death, one should "be killed and not transgress," or "transgress and not be killed."[47] There are four distinctions that are drawn in the course of the talmudic discussion. Their precise definitions and the ways in which they relate to each other constitute much of the discussion on the subject.

First, three prohibitions are singled out as cardinal sins and treated with special stringency:

> They voted and ruled in the upper chamber of Beit Nitza in Lod: Regarding all the transgressions in the Torah, if they said to one, "Transgress and be not killed," he should transgress, and not be killed, except for idolatrous worship, uncovering of nakedness (i.e., adultery and incest—SM), and the spilling of blood.[48]

Second, a distinction is drawn between transgression in private and transgression in public:

> Does this apply (i.e., that one should transgress and not be killed—SM) even in public? One learns from the text: "You shall not profane My holy name, that I may be sanctified in the midst of the people of Israel."[49]

"That I may be sanctified" is understood as referring to martyrdom. "In the midst of the people of Israel" is understood as implying a public act.

Third, a special stringency is applied if the imposed transgression is an aspect of a deliberate religious persecution:

> They did not teach this (that only for the three cardinal sins must one be killed rather than transgress—SM) save when it is not a time of royal decree (of religious persecution—SM). But in a time of royal decree, even for a light precept one must be killed and not transgress.[50]

The Talmud provides an enigmatic example of "light precept," and Rashi understands the Talmud to mean: an insignificant custom, which is commonly, identified as Jewish practice.

Fourth, another distinction appears in the course of the talmudic discussion. If the prohibition of Jewish religious practice ("royal decree") is not imposed for religious motives, but for the oppressor's

---

47 The *locus classicus* is Sanhedrin 74a–75a.

48 BT Sanhedrin 74a.

49 BT Sanhedrin 74a, citing Leviticus 22:32.

50 BT Sanhedrin 74a.

own benefit, then one should transgress and not be killed, even if the transgression takes place in public.[51]

Radbaz was asked whether one would be obliged to "be killed and not transgress" if one is faced with this choice in a time of religious persecution which, however, was intended not for the uprooting of Jewish religious practice *per se*, but for the king's own benefit. The term "religious persecution" is defined here in terms of its results, not its motivation. The example given is a law forcing Jews to build a palace for the king on the Sabbath.

Radbaz answers in terms of a "middle way" argument:

> Answer. Know, that in this matter there are three differing opinions, and it is better to seize the middle way.

The position which Radbaz espouses, and which he characterizes as the "middle way," is as follows. For the three cardinal sins (idolatrous worship, adultery and incest, and spilling of blood), one should indeed "be killed and not transgress"; but for other transgressions, such as the example in the question of Sabbath violation, one should "transgress and not be killed." Radbaz attributes this view to Na<u>h</u>manides; he interprets Maimonides as being in concurrence with it; and he brings proof from the Talmud in support of it.

But the extremes, which Radbaz cites to establish this as the "middle way", are not legitimate options.

On the one side is the opinion of R. Zera<u>h</u>ia ha-Levi, an important rabbinic authority in 12th century Provence. He had written that as long as the motivation for the decree was the king's own benefit, then even the three cardinal sins do not require martyrdom, and one should "transgress and not be killed."[52] Radbaz dismisses this view out of hand: "This is a great leniency. It is not proper to rely on it at all."

On the other side is an opinion that as long as there is a religious persecution (again, defined in terms of its result, not its motivation) one must suffer martyrdom even for "light precepts," even if the purpose of the decree was for the king's own benefit. This opinion is attributed to Maimonides by Rabbenu Nissim, who interprets Maimonides' wording on the subject to mean that.[53] But Radbaz disagrees with Rabbenu Nissim's interpretation of Maimonides, and interprets him in accordance with his own opinion of the law. Radbaz, therefore, uses as

---

51 BT Sanhedrin 74b.

52 *Ha-Maor ha-Gadol* to Alfasi at Sanhedrin 74b, s.v. *amar abaye.*

53 *<u>H</u>iddushei ha-Ran* to Sanhedrin 74a, s.v. *aval be-she'at ha-gezera*, in interpreting *MT*, Knowledge, Laws of the Foundations of the Torah, chap. 5, parag. 3.

one extreme of his "middle way" construction an opinion, which he himself considers to be non-existent, namely, the opinion of Maimonides according to the mistaken understanding of Rabbenu Nissim. One cannot even attribute this view to Rabbenu Nissim himself, because he himself did not subscribe to this opinion, nor does Radbaz cite anyone who does.[54]

[96] Radbaz goes to this length in order to frame his ruling as a middle way, even though it represents a virtually unchallenged consensus. Elsewhere, he creates a "middle way" by producing a very dubious extreme opinion, which he cites without specific attribution. The question is the status of a dish of broth into which had fallen a mouse.[55] The Talmud discusses the extent to which the flavor of a prohibited food renders an entire dish unfit. It distinguishes between a flavor that enhances the dish in question, and one that detracts from it. Only in the former instance is the dish prohibited. The Talmud assumes that if the dish in question contained sixty times the quantity of the prohibited food that fell into it, then the flavor of the prohibited food is neutralized, and the dish is fit for consumption. In a discussion related specifically to a mouse, a question about the status of its flavor is raised with regard to beer and with regard to vinegar. The Talmud concludes: "The law is: Both in this and in that (it is neutralized) in sixty (times its quantity)."[56] "This and that" refer to beer and vinegar. This is a stringent ruling. It is in contrast neutralization of "one measure by two," which would render most dishes fit. As is clear from the discussion in the Talmud, the reason for the singling out of beer and vinegar for stringency is that the flavor of the mouse enhances these two foods, whereas it detracts from other foods. The implication, which is drawn by most, but not all, interpreters is that with other types of foods, such as the broth in the question at hand, a mixture of two measures to one of the forbidden mouse would be sufficient for the dish to be permitted.

Radbaz rules in accordance with most interpreters. In the case at issue, the dish is permitted; had the mouse fallen into beer or vinegar, in which case (according to the Talmud) the prohibited flavor enhances the food, the beer or vinegar would be prohibited. This is clearly a

---

54 This view is espoused by R. Joel Sirkes in *Bah̲* to *Tur Orah̲ H̲ayyim*, 157, s.v. *u-ma she-amar be-she'at ha-shemad*. But this postdates Radbaz.

55 II, 717.

56 BT 'Avoda Zara 69a.

consensus view. Radbaz mentions specifically Alfasi, Maimonides, Rashba, Rabbenu Nissim, and "our French Masters (or: Rabbis)" who rule this way.

But Radbaz finds the need to set this up as a "middle way."

One extreme is straightforward. Rabad, a first rank Provencal authority of the 12th century, had written that a mouse only detracts from the flavor because of its fur, but without the fur it actually enhances the flavor of other foods.[57] But, Radbaz tells us, Rabad "is the only one of this opinion, and the other authorities did not agree with him."

The other extreme is presented by Radbaz as follows:

> There are those who are lenient, ruling that even (if it fell) into vinegar and beer it does not enhance it, and sixty times the quantity is not necessary.

This is highly dubious. It appears to fly in the face of the unambiguous ruling in the Talmud, that beer and vinegar require a quantity of sixty times more than the mouse to neutralize its flavor. The source of the opinion is not identified. Radbaz has picked an extremely idiosyncratic and, as far as I can see, untenable opinion in order to cast his ruling, which is after all the undisputed consensus, as the "middle way."

[97] The examples that have been cited above seek to demonstrate the extent to which Radbaz goes in framing his desired opinion as the "middle way." An even more extreme example of this procedure is the representation of an opinion as the "middle way" when in fact that is not the case.

The Talmud tells us: "Resh Laqish stated in the name of Abba Kohen Bardela: A person's four cubits acquire [moveable property] for him."[58] Rashi explains: "If there is ownerless property about him, another is not permitted to seize it." The Talmud goes on to explain: "The Rabbis enacted this so that people wouldn't come to blows." In the subsequent discussion, this rule of acquisition by proximity is challenged by a passage of the Mishnah regarding the obligation of a farmer to leave the edge of his field for the poor. The Mishnah states that if a poor man collecting grain threw himself on a sheaf at the edge of the field, he did not thereby acquire it. Why, it is asked, does he not

57 See Rabad's commentary on 'Avoda Zara at 69a, s.v. *imartutei imartat*, ed. Sofer (New York 1961), 206. Cited by Rabbenu Nissim to Alfasi ad loc.

58 BT Bava Metsi'a 10a.

acquire it by his very proximity, if this rule is correct? There are two answers given to this question, both of which limit the rule, and thereby exclude the case of the edge of the field from its purview. The first is given anonymously. Since he threw himself upon it, his act indicated that he intended to acquire it by that means, rather than by proximity; but unfortunately, the means he chose is not legally effective. The second answer is given by Rabbi Papa. He states that the rule only applies to areas of public access, not to a private field.

Radbaz addresses the question whether one may refuse to accept acquisition of an object by proximity, by indicating, by word or deed, that he does not choose to acquire it by that means.[59] Radbaz identifies three opinions on this subject.

The first, cited anonymously as "there are those who say," distinguishes between methods of acquisition such as this, which derive from a rabbinic enactment, and methods of acquisition which derive from the law of the Torah. According to this opinion, refusal to accept acquisition is recognized in the former situation, but not in the latter.

The second view is that of Rashba. Rashba ruled that in either case one could refuse acquisition; one cannot be forced to take possession of an object against one's will.[60]

Both of these opinions would conclude that one could effectively refuse acquisition by proximity, by indicating refusal by word or by deed. This is in accord with the anonymous answer to the question in the Talmud, that the poor man did not acquire the sheaf from the field's edge by proximity when he threw himself upon it because he indicated his desire not to acquire it in that manner.

The third opinion is that in no case, even with methods of acquisition which derive from rabbinic enactment, can one refuse acquisition if a legally valid method of acquisition is performed. This opinion bases itself on the implications of Rabbi Papa's answer to the Talmud's question. In rejecting the anonymous answer to the question, Rabbi Papa is understood to be rejecting its legal basis, the right to

---

59 I, 431. The original question was broader, asking about the general parameters of this rule. It appears to be an academic question. Radbaz himself, in the course of his answer, poses the specific question described in the text.

60 See the next note for Radbaz's source for Rashba's opinion. Rashba, in his novellae, says quite the opposite. He adopts the first position described here. See Rashba, *Hiddushei ha-Rashba 'al Massekhet Bava Metsi'a*, to Bava Metsi'a 10b, p. 31, s.v. *ha de-amar kevan de-nafal.* I thank Professor Israel Ta-Shma for this reference.

refuse acquisition. Radbaz cites this view anonymously, but Rabbenu Nissim, who is clearly Radbaz's source, attributed it to R. Aaron ha-Levi.[61]

Rabbenu Nissim ruled in accordance with the first view above, that of "those who say," which distinguishes between methods of acquisition deriving from the Torah and those deriving from rabbinic enactment.[62] R. Joseph Caro, in his discussion of this subject in the *Beit Yosef,* interpreted Alfasi, Maimonides and Rabbenu Asher as all ruling in accordance with the third view, that of R. Aaron ha-Levi. According to that view, one can never opt out of a valid means of acquisition.[63]

Radbaz, however, rules in accordance with Rashba, the second position above. He presents Rashba as the "middle way": "The view of Rashba is reasonable to me (*mistabbera li*), because (*lefi she-*) it is a 'middle way.'" He proceeds to present the third view, which he had not mentioned before. But it is difficult to see how Rashba's ruling can be represented as the middle way. He in fact represents one of the extremes, namely, that one can never—regardless of whether the method of acquisition derived from the Torah or from rabbinic enactment—be forced to take possession of an object against one's will. The other extreme is the third position above, that of R. Aaron ha-Levi, that one can always be forced to take possession if the method of acquisition was valid, if only by rabbinic enactment. The median position appears to be the first position above, which draws a distinction in this regard between the law of the Torah and rabbinic enactment. It is hard to escape the conclusion that the key motivation behind Radbaz's ruling is his own opinion in favor of Rashba's position (*mistabbera li*—"it is reasonable to me"). Having seen the extent of Radbaz's reliance on sevara, it is not surprising that he bases his ruling on it in this case. The "middle way" argument, which in fact is based on a misrepresentation, was probably never meant to bear the weight of his conclusion—in spite of the introduction, "because" (*lefi she-*)— but rather to buttress it rhetorically.[64]

---

61 Radbaz's presentation is taken, almost verbatim, from Rabbenu Nissim, *Hiddushei ha-Ran 'al Bava Metsi'a*, ad loc. Radbaz does not indicate his source, but he frequently does not do so.

62 He takes the anonymous voice of the Talmud to be more authoritative than Rabbi Papa.

63 *Beit Yosef, Hoshen Mishpat,* 268. His understanding of their views is based on an argument from silence.

64 For a parallel to this type of rhetorical usage in a halakhic context see Soloveitchik, "Law and Rhetoric."

(*e*) *An Unattested Opinion as One of the Extremes*

The examples cited in the previous section attest to Radbaz's use of the "middle way" in a purely rhetorical manner, in situations in which the "middle way" argument does not really contribute to the substance of his case. This procedure is even more strikingly in evidence when the opinion that forms one of the extremes is unattested, a merely hypothetical opinion.

[98] Radbaz addresses the question of whether, in a case of civil suit, the plaintiff can compel the defendant to submit to a trial in another jurisdiction, where the rabbinical judges are admittedly superior in knowledge and wisdom to the local judges.[65] Radbaz rules that he can, but then qualifies his ruling as follows:

> This is so in a situation where there are no scholars expert in the law in his locality, but only students. However, if there are expert scholars there, even if there are greater experts in another locality, he cannot be compelled to go, but goes to trial in his own town.

Radbaz tells us that he deduced this ruling from a close reading of Maimonides on the subject. Maimonides, following the law as it emerges in the Talmud, had ruled that the plaintiff could compel the defendant to submit to a trial before the Great Court.[66] That was an institution that existed only in talmudic times. Maimonides then applies the same law to the present day, to a situation in which there are "great scholars, recognized by the public as experienced,"[67] in another locality, but in the defendant's locality there are only "students, who are not like them."[68] In that case the plaintiff can indeed compel the defendant to be tried in the other venue. But the jump from "great scholars, recognized by the public as experienced," to "students," is problematic. It skips over the grade of those who are adequate judges though they are not great scholars. Radbaz zeros in on this point:

---

65 III, 578 (= 1007). The issue is introduced in the middle of the responsum, 54b, five lines up from the bottom.

66 *MT*, Judges, Laws of the Sanhedrin, chap. 6, parag. 7. Maimonides follows the Talmud (BT Sanhedrin 31a) which restricts this privilege to the plaintiff, citing Proverbs 22:7: "The borrower is a slave to the lender."

67 *mumhin la-rabbim*

68 *MT*, Judges, Laws of the Sanhedrin, chap. 6, parag. 9.

> This implies that if in that locality there are well-versed scholars, though they are not "great, recognized by the public as experienced" like those in the other place, he (the defendant) is not compelled to go there. And this is proper. Since there is in his locality one who knows how to apply the law truthfully, why should we place the burden on this person (the defendant) to go elsewhere?

Radbaz thus reads this meaning into Maimonides. It is not explicit in Maimonides' words, and it is not the only possible construction of his intention.[69] The impression is that here, too, it is sevara, as expressed in the last sentence of the citation above, which determines Radbaz's conclusion.

As we have seen him do above, Radbaz then cites a "middle way" argument in support of his position. One extreme in his construction of a "middle way" is straightforward. It is the position expressed by Rashba, that a plaintiff could compel a defendant to travel to another region even if there are adequate judges in his home locality, if there are scholars elsewhere who are greater than the local ones.[70] The position on the other extreme is not spelled out explicitly by Radbaz. However, there can be little doubt about what it is, because only one possibility presents itself. Radbaz had set up the dichotomy between "scholars expert in the law" and "students," and had himself ruled that "scholars expert in the law," even though they are less renowned than scholars elsewhere, are sufficient to prevent the plaintiff from imposing a change of venue. He defined this as the "middle way." Rashba had ruled, on one side of this, that the plaintiff can insist on a change of venue if there are greater scholars elsewhere. The other extreme could only be that the plaintiff cannot insist on a change in venue even if there are only "students," and no "scholars expert in the law," available locally. But this is an untenable and entirely hypothetical position. Radbaz does not attribute it to anyone, and it is hard to believe that any rabbinic authority ever advocated such a position. Radbaz uses the term

---

69 See for instance R. Joseph Caro in *Kesef Mishneh* ad loc. Caro interprets Maimonides to mean that if there are only students in the defendant's locality, then the defendant, and not just the plaintiff (see n. 66), can insist on a change in venue.

70 Rashba, Responsa, vol. 1, no. 724. The defendant was from Provence, and the plaintiff wanted him to travel to France. Rashba ruled that in fact there were great scholars in Provence; but were that not the case, the relative greatness of the scholars elsewhere would have allowed the plaintiff to enforce this procedure on the defendant.

"middle way" here to mean "the middle among conceivable positions," not as in the examples cited heretofore, "the middle among stated positions."

[99] The same understanding of the term "middle way" is explicit in another responsum.[71] The question was whether a scholar could be subpoenaed to appear before a judge who is inferior to him in learning. Radbaz rules that he cannot. He cites anonymously a position to the effect that he may not even testify voluntarily under those conditions, for to do so would be degrading to the Torah which he possesses. After explaining the basis of this ruling on technical grounds, Radbaz rejects it on moral grounds:

> But I am not pleased (*ein da'ati no*<u>*h*</u>*a*) with this. First of all, it is a religious obligation (*mitsva*) to testify if he knows information that would help him. And furthermore, he would be causing a monetary loss to another.

He adds a few other objections, and then continues:

> Therefore, it is better to seize the middle way. If he chooses to forgo his honor and to go and testify, or to undergo litigation before a judge who is lesser than he or untutored, then he has the right to do so. But to compel him to appear—no one ever said such a thing!

The position that a scholar may be compelled to appear before a lesser judge is one of the extremes forming Radbaz's "middle way." Yet it is only a conceivable position; in actuality, "no one ever said such a thing."

(*f*) *The "Middle Way" as an Original Compromise*

In Chapter 5, a number of examples were adduced which demonstrated how Radbaz forged a compromise between conflicting opinions on the basis of his personal sevara. The result was an original ruling, which stood in contradiction to all of the authorities he had cited earlier.[72] In some of those instances, Radbaz referred to such a compromise as the "middle way."[73] This use of the term differs from

---

71 IV, 119 (= 1189).

72 Chapter 5, Section (*e*), pp. 189ff.

73 Case [80] and Case [81] (IV, 137 (= 1207) and II, 661 respectively). The structure of IV, 137 is paralleled in IV, 125 (= 1195). Radbaz responds to the question whether the Talmud's requirement of a special benediction for

the way it had been used in the previous examples in this chapter, in which the "middle way" referred to some earlier opinion, actual or putative. But the use of "middle way" to refer to a compromise position is a natural use of the term, since the expression itself, in the halakhic context in which we find it, bespeaks a deliberate tendency toward compromise.

[100] Radbaz's identification of the "middle way" with an original compromise, which draws on both sides of a controversy but agrees with neither, and is the product of his own sevara, is particularly explicit in the following instance.

The questioner had asked about the extent of responsibility borne by heirs who, upon their father's death, having come into possession of his belongings, found among them a borrowed article.[74]

The Mishnah defines three levels of responsibility borne by those who are in possession of another's property.[75]

Least responsibility is borne by a gratuitous bailee, one who has undertaken the safekeeping of another's property as a favor. He is culpable only for loss due to negligence.

The second level is borne by a paid bailee, as well as by one who has rented an object for his own use. These guardians are culpable also for the loss or theft of the object, even if they were not negligent in guarding it.

The highest culpability is borne by one who borrows an object for his own use. He is culpable for any loss of the object, even if it was due to an unpreventable circumstance totally beyond his control.

The Talmud discusses the issue of heirs who come into possession of a borrowed article. The passage refers specifically to a cow, a beast commonly used for agricultural work.

---

better quality wine served in the middle of a meal applies, even if it was served because the wine used until then ran out. Rabad had ruled not. Radbaz rules on the basis of sevara, that if more of the original wine is in storage, but the better wine had been served instead, then the benediction is recited. But if the better wine is produced because no more of the original wine is available, then it is not recited. He suggests that Rabad may have meant that as well; but even if that isn't the case, "what I wrote is the middle way, and is (based on) a reason that makes sense (*ve-ta'ama de-mistabber*).

74 I, 588.

75 The passage occurs twice: Mishnah Bava Metsi'a, 7:8; Mishnah Shevu'ot, 8:1.

> Rava said: If their father left them a borrowed cow, they may use it for the entire period of the loan. If it died, they are not liable for an unpreventable circumstance, which befell it.[76]

The Talmud does not explain why they are not liable for a loss due to an unpreventable circumstance, a liability normally assumed by a borrower. Rashi, however, suggests a reason: "For they are not borrowers regarding it." The implication seems to be that the higher responsibility assumed by a borrower derives from his personal relationship to the lender, and does not devolve upon the heirs.

The question posed to Radbaz was this:

> You asked me to give you my opinion regarding one who borrowed an article from his neighbor, and died, and the heirs acted negligently with it. Are they obligated to pay (for its loss) or not.

Radbaz tells us that this is a matter of controversy among the early authorities in their interpretation of the Talmud's statement in the name of Rava, cited above.

According to one view, proposed by Tosafot and adopted also by Rashba,[77] the Talmud's words, "they are not liable for an unpreventable circumstance," should be construed narrowly. They are not liable only for an unpreventable circumstance, but they are liable for loss and theft (i.e., the second level of responsibility defined above). This position assumes that the heir has the category of a paid bailee. He is, after all, being "paid" by the use of the animal. And if he has not in fact used the animal, the very potential of using it is to be construed as a form of payment, which would confer upon the heir the status of a paid bailee, and obligate him to assume responsibility in case of loss or theft. Thus, this position makes no distinction as to whether the heir actually used the animal or not.

The other view is that of Nahmanides.[78] According to Nahmanides, the Talmud's words, "they are not liable for an unpreventable circumstance," should be construed broadly, to include any liability deriving from guardianship, even the liability for negligence that is assumed by a gratuitous bailee. The term, "unpreventable circumstance," was used only because the statement was cast with reference to a borrower. Nahmanides ' assumption is that the responsibilities of all

76 BT Ketubbot 34a.

77 Tosafot to Ketubbot 34a, s.v. *meta ain hayyavin be-onsin*; Tosafot to Bava Metsi'a 96b, s.v. *ella loke'ah havei*. Rashba, cited in *Shitta Mequbbetset* to Ketubbot 34b, s.v. *mishtamshin bah kol yemei she'elatah.*

78 *Hiddushei ha-Ramban* to Bava Metsi'a 96b, s.v. *ha de-masqinan.*

guardians are personal, and they were never assumed by the heir. This position also makes no distinction as to whether the heir actually used the animal or not.

Radbaz, however, after surveying these different positions, does make such a distinction:

> It is better to seize[79] the middle way:
>
> If they used it and it died, they are not liable; if it was stolen or lost, they are liable—for this is the plain sense of the statement. Furthermore, once they used it, they became paid bailees with respect to it.
>
> If they did not use it and it was stolen or lost, they are not liable. But if they were negligent with it they are liable.

After justifying his conclusion that they should be guilty for negligence in any case, Radbaz concludes:

> What I have come up with is a sort of compromise (*ke-'ein peshara*), a bit according to the words of one and a bit according to the words of the other, and it is what makes the most sense (*u-mistabber tefei*).

Here, "a sort of compromise," which does not accord completely with either view but which accords with sevara, is explicitly identified with the "middle way."

[101] In at least one case, Radbaz's "middle way" compromise is not based as much on sevara, as on an unwillingness to carry the logic of his position through to its ultimate conclusion. His hesitation seems to derive from a sense that to do so would result in an inappropriate leniency.

Radbaz responds to a question about the permissibility of unmarried priests to bestow the priestly benediction.[80] After dealing with that issue, he turns his attention to the status of a priest who has taken human life. He begins with a homily from the Palestinian Talmud, which relates to this issue. Basing itself on the verse which immediately follows the text of the priestly benediction, "So shall they put My name upon the children of Israel, and I will bless them,"[81] the Palestinian Talmud teaches that even a priest who has shed blood may bless the people, because it is God and not the priest who blesses them.[82]

---

79 First edition: *minqat*. Ed. Warsaw mistakenly with an extra letter: *mdnqt*.

80 IV, 128 (= 1198).

81 Numbers 6:27.

82 PT Gittin 5:9, 47b.

Radbaz does not identify other sources that bear on this issue, but in fact his discussion responds to two identifiable sources. One of these is an unambiguous ruling by Maimonides, that a priest who shed blood, even accidentally, may not bestow the priestly blessing.[83] Maimonides' ruling reflects a statement in the Babylonian Talmud: "Rabbi Yohanan said: Any priest who has killed a person shall not raise his hands (to bestow the priestly blessing)."[84] The other source is a view attributed to Rabiah (Germany, 12th–13th century).[85] Rabiah harmonized the apparently conflicting statements in the two Talmuds by construing Rabbi Yohanan 's statement narrowly. He explained that the prohibition of priests with blood on their hands applies only to one who is "widely known to kill, who stands forewarned regarding this."

Radbaz begins his discussion by anonymously presenting Rabiah's ruling, and the passage from the Palestinian Talmud upon which it is based. Rabiah's criterion for disallowing a priest from bestowing the priestly benediction would make it permissible for one who had murdered intentionally, as long as he does not have a history of doing so. Radbaz admits this implicitly.[86] After all, that is the logic of the Palestinian Talmud. It is God, and not the priest, who blesses the people. The disqualification of a regular murderer was a means of harmonizing this approach with the Babylonian Talmud, which

83 *MT*, Love, Laws of Prayer, chap. 15, parag. 3. The words "even accidentally" are absent in the current printed editions of the *Mishneh Torah*. They are present, however, in the Rome 1480 edition (reprinted Jerusalem, 1955) and in the edition of J. Qafih, as well as in the citation in *Beit Yosef* to *Tur Orah Hayyim*, no. 128, s.v. *kohen she-harag*. Radbaz refers also to accidental homicide, and certainly had this reading before him.

84 BT Berakhot 32b.

85 His opinion is cited in *Mordekhai* to Megilla, Chap. 3, no. 818, apparently Radbaz's source. It is reported also in *Hagahot Maimoniot* to Maimonides, op cit., but the latter cites also Rabbenu Simha with a similar though not identical view, and there is no echo of that in Radbaz's wording here. Rabiah's reported ruling is not present in Aptowitzer's edition of Rabiah, no. 151 (vol. 1, 154f.).

86 "How much more so if he killed a person unintentionally." This implies that even if he killed someone intentionally he would be permitted to participate. Radbaz continues: "How much more so if he (killed while he) was occupied in the performance of a religious act, for instance, if he was circumcising a baby and killed him." It is plausible that this was the main concern all along. The continuation of the passage in *Mordekhai* refers to this issue, and this is further proof that *Mordekhai* was Radbaz's source.

restricted murderers from participating in this function. The harmonization is accomplished by reducing that restriction to its absolute minimum.

However, Radbaz is not happy with this conclusion:

> In any case, it is better to seize the middle way. If he killed a person defiantly and with complete intention, he may not raise his hands (to bestow the priestly benediction), even if he underwent penitence. For "his (the victim's) blood and the blood of his (potential) seed are dependent on him."[87] And (this is so) even if he does not stand forewarned regarding this; for a person always stands forewarned,[88] and in a moment of anger he will kill (again).

The position that it is God, and not the priest, who blesses the people, implies that even if a priest had murdered deliberately, he is allowed to bestow the priestly benediction. But Radbaz is not willing to go that far. Rather than following the argument to its logical conclusion, "it is better to seize the middle way."[89]

(g) *Two Exceptional Uses of the Term "Middle Way": (1) Radbaz's Own Opinion as One of the Extremes*

[102] In all of the cases discussed in this chapter, the position that Radbaz characterizes as the "middle way" is the one that he himself adopts. In fact, we have seen instances in which he extends himself to

---

87 Mishnah Sanhedrin 4:5.

88 Mishnah Bava Qamma 2:6.

89 Somewhat similar to this is I, 373, about an attacked animal (*derusa*) which mingles with the herd. Rabbenu Tam had ruled that the members of the herd can be permitted for consumption by forcing them to separate singly (*kol de-parish me-rubba parish*). The anonymous Tosafot disagreed, fearing that they might be taken while still part of the herd. (Tosafot to Sanhedrin 79b–80a, s.v. *be-shor she-lo nigmar dino*, and Tosafot to Zevahim 70b–71a, s.v. *afilu*.) Radbaz is unwilling to go all the way with Rabbenu Tam, and apply his position even to a case in which it is certain that an attacked animal mingled with the herd: "This is a great leniency in my eyes." He is unwilling to go all the way with the anonymous Tosafot, and apply its position to a case in which there is only a suspicion that an attacked animal intermingled with the rest: "This is a great stringency." So he applies Rabbenu Tam's suggested procedure to a case of a suspected intermingling and its rejection by the anonymous Tosafot to the case of a certain intermingling, commenting: "It is better to seize the middle way."

describe a position as a "middle way" in order to strengthen, if only rhetorically, the opinion which he personally supports. However, in one case he espouses an original position, which he then characterizes as one of the extremes which define a different opinion as the middle way, and proceeds to set aside his own ruling in its favor. This concession is mitigated, though, by the fact that in the case at hand this does not affect the outcome.

The case concerns a matter of inheritance.[90] A man had made a deathbed bequest to his granddaughter for the purpose of her dowry. He died, and then the granddaughter died before the bequest was acted upon. The legacy was being contested three ways: by the testator's heirs, who argued that the bequest lapsed with the death of the beneficiary; by the son-in-law, the granddaughter's father, since a father inherits his children if they have no children of their own; and by the deceased granddaughter's sister, who argued that the money should go for her dowry in lieu of her sister's.

Radbaz offers a detailed analysis of the various views relating to the issue. The Talmud states, "The words of one lying grievously ill (who subsequently dies of his illness) are as binding as if they were written and sealed."[91] Radbaz presents two interpretations of this law. According to one, the mere declaration by one lying grievously ill, that he gives his property to John Doe, is sufficient to effect the transfer of ownership upon his death, retroactive to the time of the declaration. This is the view of R. Isaac of Dampierre (Ri), recorded in Tosafot.[92] The claim of the father, who stood to inherit his daughter's property, was based on this reading of the law. According to the other interpretation, the declaration must be accompanied by the entrusting of the property to a third party for the purpose of conveyance to the recipient. This is the view of Rashba.[93] Since in the case at hand the money was not entrusted to a third party, the granddaughter never came into its possession, and her father has no claim to it.

Radbaz offers a third interpretation, his own. According to both opinions above, the transfer of ownership takes place contingent upon the death of the one lying grievously ill, retroactive either to the time of declaration (Tosafot), or the time of conveyance to a third party

---

90 III, 551 (=981).

91 BT Bava Batra 151a.

92 Tosafot to Gittin 14b, s.v. *ha be-shekhiv mera'*.

93 *Hiddushei ha-Rashba* to Gittin 14b, s.v. *holekh maneh le-peloni ve-halakh u-biqsho*.

(Rashba). If, subsequent to the declaration or conveyance, the beneficiary predeceases the testator, that would still be true. Upon the death of the testator the transfer is seen as having taken place while the beneficiary was still alive, and the beneficiary's heirs would inherit him or her. Radbaz disagrees with this.

Radbaz asserts that the law of gifts reflects our assessment of the wishes of the testator, and the testator intended to grant his gift to the beneficiary, and not to his or her heirs. The intention of the testator is particularly relevant in this situation. We are told that the Rabbis enacted the law of the "one grievously ill" because of their fear "lest his mind become confused."[94] That is, the law is an attempt to relieve a dying person of concern that his wishes will not be fulfilled because of the incompletion of legal formalities, a concern that may hasten his decline.[95] Radbaz notes that if the ill testator were to be told that the beneficiary may die before he or she receives the gift, and that it would then fall to the beneficiary's heirs, that information would agitate him even more. In this case in particular, he says, we can be sure that the testator did not intend to grant a gift to his son-in-law, "because they hated each other, (which I know) because I examined them." Therefore, says Radbaz, in his opinion the heirs never inherit a bequest made under the law of the "one grievously ill" when the beneficiary dies before the testator.

Radbaz rules against the father of the deceased granddaughter. However, he doesn't pose this conclusion as being based on his own reading of the law, but rather on Rashba's reading as opposed to that of the Tosafot. After arguing the case for his own view, Radbaz continues:

> Even though I wrote this for the practical application of the law (*le-halakha le- ma'aseh*), I wouldn't rely on myself to do a deed against the fathers of the world (i.e., the great authorities—SM), even in a matter which entails engaging in a passive act of not taking money from the orphans.[96] For I know regarding myself, that I am not worthy of understanding their words, even more so (am I unworthy) of differing with them. But at least my opinion can be of use as a mere makeweight argument (*le-senifin be-'alma*) for the case at hand.

Radbaz's opinion supports the testator's heirs (i.e., "the orphans"). Since the inheritance succeeded automatically to the heirs, they are the defendants. Ruling according to his own opinion against the Tosafot

94 BT Bava Batra 147b.

95 Thus Rashbam to Bava Batra 147b, s.v. *matnat shekhiv mera'*.

96 *ve-afilu be-shev ve-al totsi mamon min ha-yetomim*

would entail a passive stance in favor of the defendants. These defendants are, it is implied, minors, and it is the duty of the court to protect their interests in any case. Thus, in following his own opinion, Radbaz would be "engaging in a passive act of not taking money from the orphans." But Rashba's opinion, with which Radbaz does not wholly agree, would lead to the same conclusion in this instance, since the money was not conveyed to a third party. So Radbaz follows Rashba instead of himself. He summarizes his actual ruling in the case at hand thus:

> Therefore, if Reuben (the grandfather testator) said that they should give his (grand)daughter a sum of money while she was alive, she did not acquire it at all, since he didn't give the sum to a third party.... And even though Ri (R. Isaac of Dampierre) and Rosh (Rabbenu Asher, who agreed with R. Isaac, that a mere oral declaration is sufficient to pass title) disagree (with the need for conveyance to a third party), ... nevertheless I rely on Rashba. First, because it is the middle way....

The "middle way" here is Rashba's position. Radbaz's personal position, which he describes as being "for the practical application of the law (*le-halakha le- ma'aseh*)," is one of the extremes which places it in the middle.

(*h*) *Two Exceptional Uses of the Term "Middle Way": (2) The "Middle Way" among Situations*

[103] On one occasion, Radbaz uses the term "middle way" to refer to the middle way among situations, rather than the middle way among opinions. He does so, as he always does, in a context, which implies that it represents added support to his argument, though in this case it clearly does not. This irregular and misleading use of the term attests to the hold that the concept of "middle way" had on Radbaz's thinking.

Radbaz answers the following question:[97]

> You asked me about the forced converts among the Arabs, to whom were born children and children's children while they were converts. They are now returning to the religion of Israel (already) circumcised.[98] Do they need ritual immersion or not?

97 III, 415 (= 858).

98 The text reads: *vmlyn* (= *u-malin*), which would normally be translated: "and are circumcising." This reading is difficult for two reasons. (1) Having been raised as Muslims, they would have already been circumcised. (2) If not, then it is hard to imagine a hesitation about immersion on the part of

> And if they do, does (the lack of) it impede (their acceptance into the fold) or not?

Radbaz begins by citing a ruling attributed to Rabbenu Simha, that penitent sinners must undergo ritual immersion, but only by rabbinic decree, as an act of penitence. The immersion is not required by the law of the Torah, and therefore failure to immerse would not impede their status as full-fledged Jews. Radbaz adopts Rabbenu Simha's ruling. He offers a reasoned rebuttal of an argument in support of the more stringent position, that failure to immerse would impede their full acceptance as Jews. That argument is based in part on a ruling in the Talmud, that an uncircumcised Jew—one to whom circumcision was deemed life-threatening—may eat the Paschal lamb, but only after he immersed. In rejecting the stringent opinion, Radbaz cites an alternative interpretation of that talmudic ruling. According to this interpretation, immersion is a necessary prerequisite for eating the Paschal lamb only if the uncircumcised Jew happened to be ritually unclean, as would be the case for any Jew. Radbaz sums up the results of his discussion thus:

> It follows, according to this interpretation, that an uncircumcised Jew does not require immersion, even by enactment of the Rabbis. An uncircumcised non-Jew requires immersion (if he would convert) by the law of the Torah. And the children of the apostates require immersion by the enactment of the Rabbis, but it does not impede them—which is (*de-havei*) the middle way.

The middle way, that is, between an uncircumcised Jew, who does not require immersion at all to be a full member of the Jewish fold, and an uncircumcised non-Jew, who requires immersion to become Jewish by the law of the Torah.[99] The term *de-havei* is ambiguous. The translation above represents the more neutral rendering: "which is." But it could also be translated: "for it is," introducing a reason for deciding the law in this particular fashion. That doesn't make sense in this context, but the very use of the term provides a subtext that elicits the reader's support for the ruling.

---

someone who had willingly undergone circumcision. A metathesis yields: *mulin*, "(already) circumcised."

99 A possible alternative understanding, which I do not think is correct, would take "middle way" as referring to the more stringent position cited earlier and rejected, as one extreme, and an assumed position according to which they do not need immersion at all, on the other. But no such lenient position is alluded to in the responsum. Furthermore, the context in which the phrase is used argues in favor of the interpretation I have given it.

(*i*) *Conclusions*

The message of the "middle way" is that there is no substantive preference for one opinion over another. Since all are theoretically valid, it is best to choose the "middle way." Perhaps there is also an implication that the extremes can be harmonized through adoption of the "middle way," so that all the views can somehow be represented. We will yet see examples in another context of Radbaz's tendency to harmonize conflicting opinions.[100]

However, with rare exception (if any), Radbaz does not use the principle of the "middle way" as a real method for arriving at a decision, but rather as a rhetorical device. He goes out of his way to do so, sometimes using means, which do not permit an attempt to view, it as designed to bear the burden of proof. Alongside reference to the "middle way," Radbaz brings substantive arguments, and sometimes these belie the conception that all opinions are equal. Throughout Radbaz's responsa we find him expressing definite preferences for the views of some of his predecessors over others. There seem to be contrary conceptions coexisting here. One is the conception that some opinions are more convincing than others, and that it is the task of the jurist to decide between them. It is this conception which plays a real role in deciding the law. The other is the conception underlying the rhetoric of the "middle way," that all opinions are theoretically equal, and in practice the median position should prevail. It is this conception which has emotional appeal, and Radbaz utilizes it to support the conclusions he has reached by the previous approach.

But what is the attraction of the "middle way" for Radbaz, one that he assumes has a resonance with his audience, and which conveys an emotional appeal that far exceeds its force in substantive argumentation? In view of Radbaz's great interest in Maimonides, it is tempting to suggest that he was influenced by the concept of the "golden mean." It has been pointed out to me that the two notions are not really parallel. Unlike extremes of temperament, which are extremes on the same continuum, halakhic differences are each based on a different rationalization.[101] But Radbaz, in his references to the "middle way," does not relate to the different rationalizations and their relative merits, just to the actual decisions themselves, unlike his

---

100 See Chapter 8, Section (*c*), pp. 249ff.

101 By Professor I. Ta-Shma, in a personal communication (January 16, 1999).

treatment of other arguments often presented in the very same responsa. For all intents and purposes, he treats the different opinions as if they are on the same continuum.

There is one section of this chapter, which presents a very different picture of the "middle way." In general, the rhetoric of the "middle way" conveys a sense of dependence on the views of predecessors. The "middle way" purports to provide an artificial mechanism for ruling in the face of controversy, without having to assume personal responsibility for ruling against one of the earlier opinions. Section (*f*), pp. 191ff, presents us with examples in which the "middle way" supports Radbaz's own view of the law, a compromise position which stands in contrast to the opinions which he cites. The "middle way" here exemplifies the independence of the jurist. Though this conflicts with the implications of the "middle way" as used elsewhere by Radbaz, it accords with Radbaz's actual practice in those other instances. For as we have seen, in spite of his rhetoric, Radbaz never (at most, almost never) rules mechanically, without substantive argumentation.

7. The Place of the Master

Radbaz refers frequently to the practice of deciding law in Egypt in accordance with the rulings of Maimonides.

Such a practice was well known in earlier centuries in Spain. In the wake of the religious persecution of Jews in Spain in 1391, and subsequently during the fifteenth century, there was a migration of Jews from Spain to North Africa, and we find that the practice of ruling in accordance with Maimonides was well entrenched in North Africa in the fifteenth century and later.[1]

When referring to this principle of judicial decision in Egypt, Radbaz frequently uses the expression, "the place of the Master" (*atreih de-mar*). The Bar Ilan Responsa Project data base lists 95 occurrences, representing 73 different responsa of Radbaz, in which this phrase is used. It lists no occurrence of it in this sense before the time of Radbaz, though the Hebrew equivalent, *meqomo shel ha-rav*, is used by Rashba in reference to Alfasi.[2] Among Radbaz's contemporaries, the parallel expressions, "the place of our Master," "the place of our Master Maimonides" (*atreih de-maran, atreih de-maran ha-rambam*), is found several times in the responsa of R. Moses Alashqar, who, like Radbaz, was born in Spain and settled for some

---

1 The material is thoroughly documented in Kahana, "Controversy."

2 Rashba, *Responsa*, I, 1190, referred to by S. Z. Havlin, *Dissertation*, 69, n. 172.

years in Egypt. It is found once in the responsa of his younger contemporary, R. Samuel de-Medina, of Salonica.[3]

A similar expression, used by Radbaz's rabbinic contemporaries to acknowledge the legal authority of Maimonides' rulings, but used only rarely by Radbaz, is the reference to him as "the Master of the place" (*mareih de-atra*). The precise expression, "the place of the Master," appears to be unique to Radbaz and Alashqar among earlier and contemporary rabbinic authors. The phrase itself derives from the Talmud, but there the "Master" refers to a rabbi who is resident in a certain locality, and is recognized by the local inhabitants as their rabbinic authority.[4]

The wording, "the place of the Master," by taking "the place" as the subject of the phrase, appears to refer literally to Egypt as the place of Maimonides' residence, and to base his authority on those specific grounds. This would be distinguished from the general practice of ruling in accordance with him. That seems less to be the case with the phrase, "the Master of the place." Here "the Master" is the subject, and "the place" of which he is Master could be any place which accepts his rulings. The meaning of "the place of the Master" proposed here is strengthened by its use in a different, non-technical context:

> I have searched in all the old books (of Maimonides' Code) which are found here in Cairo (or alternatively: Egypt), which is the place of the Master ... and in all of them it is written: ...[5]

Here the phrase clearly denotes Egypt itself.[6]

(*a*) *Origins*

In spite of the fact that prior to Radbaz and Alashqar the expression, "the place of the Master," does not occur with reference to Maimonides, nor in fact to any rabbinic authority of previous generations,

---

3 Alashqar, *Responsa*, nos. 14, 16 (which deal with the same case), 18, 67. R. Samuel de Medina, *Responsa*, *Even ha-'Ezer*, no. 175.

4 BT Betsa 15a and BT Bava Metsi'a 40a. For the one possible exception, where the reference may be to a master no longer alive, see Case [107] below.

5 IV, 225 (= 1296), duplicated as VII, 33.

6 In the course of the chapter, I will bring further support for this understanding of the phrase. This is *contra* a possible interpretation, that any region which accepted Maimonides' rulings could be called "the place of the Master."

anywhere in the responsa literature, there is evidence in Radbaz's responsa which seems to indicate that the phrase was in wider use.

[104] On one occasion, Radbaz appears to take it for granted that his questioners are familiar with it.[7] A band of armed robbers had attacked a residential compound and had intimidated the residents by beating one person and breaking into a few homes. Most of the valuables that had attracted the robbers were stored in one building, protected by a very strong door. At the time of the attack there was only one woman in the building. The robbers succeeded in intimidating her into opening the door. The questioners raised the issue of the woman's liability, since in all probability the robbers would not have been successful in breaking it down. There is a controversy in the Talmud as to whether strong circumstantial evidence is sufficient, in the lack of eyewitness testimony, to find someone guilty of a tort.[8] Maimonides had ruled according to the view that it does not.[9] Radbaz refers to this ruling, and then adds:

> And you are well aware (*u-kevar yada'ta*) that it is the place of the Master. Therefore, even if you choose to say that there is strong circumstantial evidence (*umdena de-mokhe<u>h</u>a*) that they would not have broken down the door, the woman is not liable for anything.

The implication is that Radbaz's correspondents were well aware of the principle that Egypt is "the place of the Master." However, the specific phrase, "the place of the Master," may reflect Radbaz's own wording, rather than that of his correspondents.

[105] Elsewhere, the expression is attributed directly to the questioner. Thus, for instance, in a question involving the issue of non-kosher wine.[10] Wine, which had been used by idolators for libation, is prohibited as part of an idolatrous rite. But "libation wine" is unlike ordinary non-kosher food in some respects. One of these concerns the mingling of permissible and non-permissible foods. Ordinary non-kosher food that becomes mingled with kosher food of a like kind is neutralized if there is sixty times more kosher food in the mixture. However, even a miniscule amount of libation wine is sufficient to render the entire mixture prohibited.

---

7 VI, 2181.

8 BT Bava Batra 93a.

9 *MT*, Torts, Laws of Damage by Chattels, chap. 8, parag. 13.

10 II, 729.

The ancient Rabbis extended the prohibition of "libation wine" to cover all wine to which non-Jews had free access. This was referred to as "their unspecified wine" (*setam yeinam*). It was a matter of controversy, however, whether the rule, which prohibited a mixture because of miniscule contamination, applies to "unspecified wine" as well.

In the case that came before Radbaz, some Jews were preparing grape syrup (*dibs*), and there were Muslims doing the same in close proximity. After the heated grape juice used in the preparation had just been removed from the fire by the Jews, a small amount of grape juice being prepared by the Muslims fell into it. The question was whether the syrup that had been contaminated was permissible for Jewish use. The question is phrased this way:

> I was in doubt, because the Master (may his memory be for a blessing!) wrote that a miniscule amount of "unspecified wine" contaminates. And even though there are those who permit it, because (they hold the opinion that) it does not render the mixture forbidden except by (more than one in) sixty, as is the case with other prohibitions (of food), and the (talmudic) reference to "a miniscule amount" applies only to wine that was (actually) used for libation—in any case, we are in need of your opinion, because it is the place of the Master.

This question, then, was sent by a local rabbi, familiar with the different aspects of the issue. On the one hand, he knew that there are authorities who permit a mixture that contains "unspecified wine" if the contamination is less than one sixtieth, as was the situation in this case. On the other hand, Maimonides ruled stringently on this issue, making no distinction in this regard between "libation wine" and "unspecified wine."[11] There is an implication that the rabbi would have had no hesitation in ruling leniently, were he not inhibited from doing so because Maimonides' rulings have a special hold in Egypt.[12] After all, Egypt is "the place of the Master."

In this case too, however, even though the wording appears to have been formulated by the questioner, it may nevertheless have been formulated by Radbaz himself.[13]

---

11 *MT*, Holiness, Laws of Forbidden Foods, chap. 16, parag. 29.

12 Radbaz rules leniently. He points out that *dibs* contains other ingredients, so that it is not truly considered wine. The prohibition on its use, he says, derives from pious stringency, and can be waived in this case.

13 See Chapter 1, n. 79.

[106] There is, however, one responsum in which the phrase, "the place of the Master," appears to indeed reflect the words of one party to the dispute. Its context clearly reflects the concept that the source of Maimonides' authority is that Egypt was, quite literally, the place of Maimonides' residence.

The question is one that is of great interest to the history of liturgical practice.[14] The core of the rabbinic liturgy is the *'amida* (standing) prayer. The ancient practice was that the members of the congregation who know how to pray recite the prayer silently, and then the prayer is repeated aloud in its entirety by the precentor, thus allowing those who do not know how to pray to participate through hearing it aloud. Maimonides had instituted a change in that practice in Egypt. Disturbed by the fact that the congregants who had already recited the *'amida* used the repetition as an opportunity for socializing and paid little heed to the prayer, he eliminated the silent *'amida*. Instead, it was to be recited only once, aloud by the precentor, and those who knew how to pray would fulfill their prayer obligation by reciting it silently along with him.[15] In Radbaz's day this practice was still in force in the *musta'rib* community, the indigenous Arabic-speaking community, in Cairo.[16]

Radbaz's responsum concerns an incident which took place, he tells us, in 1539. It was an attempt by the Sephardic Jews, who now constituted the majority of the Jews in Cairo, to impose the historic practice of the silent *'amida* on the *musta'rib* community. Radbaz summarizes a somewhat lengthy string of arguments which were put forth by the *musta'rib* Jews in defense of their centuries-old custom. The last of these is as follows:

> They argued further, that if they were to change their custom, it would be like a student who opposes his teacher (in a halakhic ruling); and (after all) this is the place of the Master.[17]

---

14 IV, 94 (= 1165).

15 See Maimonides, *Responsa*, at the end of Responsum no. 256, pp. 474–76. Maimonides instituted this only for the Sabbath and Festival prayers, but there is no reference to this in Radbaz's responsum.

16 *mitsrayim*. This is ambiguous, since it may mean either Egypt as a whole or Cairo specifically.

17 Radbaz argues against this that Maimonides never intended his innovation to be permanent; if he were to have witnessed how ineffective his innovation was in maintaining proper decorum, he himself would have repealed it.

The Talmud states, "Whoever opposes his teacher—it is as if he opposes the Divine presence."[18] When Maimonides formulated this in his Code, he explicitly stated that the prohibition of opposing the rulings of one's teacher applies only as long as the teacher is alive.[19] This might also well be the case (though not unequivocally so) in almost all of those places where the phrase, "the place of the Master" (or, "of Rabbi So-and-so"), is found in the Talmud.[20] In the impassioned plea of the *musta'rib* Jews, these two concepts are conflated. This identification of "the place of the Master" with fealty to one's teacher leaves no doubt that the phrase was understood to refer to the actual residence of Maimonides. Furthermore, both concepts, now identified with each other, are applied to the 12th-century Maimonides.

It is plausible, therefore, to conclude that the idea, that the source of Maimonides' authority in Egypt derives from his earlier residence there, and the signifying of that idea by the phrase, "the place of the Master," originated with the *musta'rib* Jews.[21]

(*b*) "The *Place of the Master" and the General Practice of Ruling like Maimonides*

[107] Radbaz adopted the notion that the Jews living in Egypt, the place of Maimonides' residence three and a half centuries earlier, were bound by a special fealty to his rulings. For instance, there is a question of whether a wife's fine clothing belongs to her outright, as does her daily ware, so that its value cannot be incorporated as part of the *ketubba*, which her husband has to pay her from his own assets upon divorce. Radbaz interprets Maimonides' position to be that it belongs to the husband, and its value can therefore be counted toward the *ketubba* payment. He writes:

---

18 BT Sanhedrin 110a.

19 *MT*, Knowledge, Laws of Learning Torah, chap. 5, parag. 3.

20 One possible exception will be discussed below.

21 R. Moses b. Joseph Trani, Radbaz's contemporary in Safed, attributes the practice of ruling in accordance with Maimonides, then prevalent in Palestine among the Sephardim, to the influence of the indigenous *musta'rib* Jews; Trani, *Responsa*, III, 56, noted by Kahana, "Controversy," 54.

> Who would dare to exact money from the husband against his will in the place of Maimonides? This would surely be an astounding thing![22]

Asked whether a stipulation to a divorce, included in the husband's oral instructions for the writing of the divorce document, rendered the divorce void, as Maimonides had ruled,[23] in spite of the fact that a number of authorities validated such a divorce, Radbaz replies indignantly, citing, from the Book of Esther, Ahasuerus' exclamation in reference to Haman:

> "Does he mean to ravish the queen in my own palace?"[24] For this is the place of Maimonides, and he is stringent in this matter! How can we be lenient?[25]

Radbaz proceeds to cite a precedent in the Talmud for this attitude that is particularly apt. It is a case where the principle of "the place of the Master" does indeed appear to be used for a Master who is no longer alive. Rabbi Hamnuna, a student of the *amora* Rav, ruled in a specific case of Sabbath law against the accepted opinion and according to Rav's opinion. The Talmud explains Rabbi Hamnuna's action: "It was the place of Rav."[26] However, the town in which the incident occurred was not the residence of Rav, so the word "place" must be understood to refer to a wide territory which was, or had been, under Rav's judicial authority. One cannot therefore assume Rav's death from the fact that he was not involved personally in the case, and it is possible that he was still alive at the time.[27] Radbaz, though, may well have understood that Rav was no longer alive, and that even after his death his rulings were still binding in the locality which had been under his jurisdiction. Nevertheless, it is still a leap from a Master who had passed away within living memory of his constituents, to a Master who had passed away three and a half centuries earlier.

[108] As indicated above, there was a widespread tradition earlier in Spain, and in all of North Africa from the end of the 14th century on, of

---

22 IV, 68 (= 1140).

23 *MT*, Women, Laws of Divorce, chap. 8, parag. 4.

24 Esther 7:8.

25 IV, 105 (= 1176). Compare this to his more lenient position in VI, 2232. Most likely the contradiction is illusory, and the difference results from the extremity of the situation in the latter responsum.

26 BT Shabbat 19b.

27 More accurately, this is not a question of the historical facts, but a question of how to construe the meaning of the anonymous voice in the Talmud.

deciding law in accordance with Maimonides' rulings.[28] In Radbaz's generation we find a well-established tradition to this effect throughout all of Syria and Palestine.[29] With a single exception to be discussed below, Radbaz does not use the phrase, "the place of the Master," with reference to anywhere outside of Egypt,[30] though the general rule of deciding law in accordance with Maimonides is often expressed as applying to "Egypt and all these provinces."

Radbaz clearly distinguishes between the general practice of ruling in accordance with Maimonides, which is not limited to Maimonides' historic residence, and "the place of the Master," which applies only to Egypt. He does so even while he presents both rationales as reinforcing each other. For instance:

> We judge all matters of civil law in accordance with Maimonides; so much more so (*kol she-ken*) since it is the place of the Master.[31]

Alashqar presents the matter in a similar vein:

> Here you see, according to the opinion of Maimonides, according to whom we rule in all these lands, and it is the place of our Master, ...[32]

These are two separate reasons for ruling like Maimonides in Egypt.

Many times Radbaz reflects the tradition of ruling in accordance with Maimonides without recourse to the concept of "the place of the Master." He writes, for instance:

> You know, of course, that the words of the Luminaries (*ha-ge'onim*, referring here to Alfasi and Maimonides—SM) are words of reliable tradition (*divrei qabbala*), so much more so (*ve-kol she-ken*) since in all these provinces they act in accordance with Alfasi and Maimonides.[33]

No mention is made here of "the place of the Master," which in any case could not refer to Alfasi. The geographical origin of the question is

---

28 See Kahana, "Controversy," 14–25; Leon Feldman, in his edition of R. Nissim's *Responsa*, 279 (no. 62), n. 2; Rashba, *Responsa*, I, 253, cited by Havlin, *Dissertation*, 68, n. 167. In the 14th and 15th centuries, however, Rabbenu Asher began to rival Maimonides as the main authority in Spain; see Kahana, "Controversy," 25–27.

29 See Kahana, "Controversy," 39–75.

30 Radbaz does associate "the place of the Master" with "*mitsrayim* and all this kingdom," III, 469 (= 908). But there *mitsrayim* means Cairo, and "all this kingdom" is Egypt in its entirety.

31 IV, 68 (= 1140).

32 Alashqar, *Responsa*, no. 67, p. 219.

33 I, 274.

not indicated, but it may be presumed that in emanated locally, in Egypt. For whatever reason, Radbaz did not choose to employ the concept of "the place of the Master."

[109] I have found only one locality outside of Egypt that is mentioned by name and referred to as "the place of the Master," and that is Rhodes.[34] We have had recourse to this responsum before.[35] A debtor had pleaded that the money he owed his sister included hidden illegal interest, and the question concerned the correctness of the court's decision to subject her to an oath that such was not the case. The matter was the subject of controversy, Maimonides having ruled that an oath was in order, and Rabbenu Asher having ruled that it could not be imposed. Radbaz writes:

> And now, since they have the custom of ruling in all these provinces according to the opinion of Maimonides, it is the place of the Master, and the judges did well in obligating her to take an oath.

The wording of Radbaz implies that Rhodes is considered "the place of the Master" *because* they have the custom of ruling (*kevan she-nahagu*) in accordance with Maimonides, and not that they rule that way because Maimonides had been the rabbinic authority there.

But this sequence of cause and effect is the very opposite of Radbaz's wording elsewhere:

> In any case, we learn from his (Rabbenu Asher's) words the intention of Maimonides, according to whom it is our custom to decide the law because it is the place of the Master.[36]

The wording of another passage is particularly poignant:

> He (the defendant) cannot say that he holds the opinion of these great later authorities (a plea which is normally afforded him, see Section (*e*) below, and Chapter 9—SM). For since it is the place of the Master, it is as if they accepted him upon themselves.[37]

---

34 III, 485.

35 Case [29] and Case [41].

36 I, 369.

37 I, 547. See also the identical phrasing in I, 281. The defendant cannot base his case on opinions which would support his position, "since Maimonides is of the opinion that the creditor can seize them (the debtor's wife's jewelry); and it is "the place of the Master"—it is as if they accepted it upon themselves."

"It is as if"—even if they didn't do so explicitly, even against their will![38] In a similar vein, consider the implication of Radbaz's impassioned outcry, cited above, when faced with the suggestion that Maimonides' ruling be set aside in favor of a more lenient opinion:

> "Does he mean to ravish the queen in my own palace?" For this is the place of Maimonides, and he is stringent in this matter! How can we be lenient?[39]

Egypt is Maimonides' "own palace."

I suggest that there was indeed a difference between Rhodes, on the one hand, and Egypt, on the other. When Radbaz uses the phrase, "the place of the Master," regarding Rhodes, he is using it as a figure of speech, borrowing the wording of the phrase but not the substance. In Rhodes, the custom of ruling like Maimonides came first, and as a result, it is *as if* it is "the place of the Master"—a mirror reflection of the situation in Egypt, where primarily it is "the place of the Master," and as a result "it is as if they accepted him upon themselves."

In fact, the very same responsum to Rhodes bears witness to this difference between Rhodes and Egypt. In the course of the responsum, Radbaz refers to a similar case that had come before him. It can be safely assumed that the case originated in some locality in Egypt. The local court had sent its decision to Radbaz for his confirmation.

> A case came before me concerning Reuben, an unlearned man, who had in his possession funds belonging to orphans, which he loaned on interest. The borrower pleaded, "You took stipulated interest from me!" They (the court) wanted to free him (the lender) from an oath, as Rabbenu Asher had said, rejecting the opinion of Maimonides, as I stated (it) above. But I obligated him to take an oath....

The Talmud distinguishes between "stipulated interest," that is, interest expressly defined as such, and commercial arrangements of various types which guarantee a return on loaned funds, but which fall short of the definition of "stipulated interest." Only "stipulated interest" is prohibited by the authority of the Torah; other transactions, which are in fact loans on interest but are not clearly defined as such, are prohibited only by the authority of the Rabbis. The rabbinic prohibition

---

38 Elsewhere, as a simple declaration of fact: "Even though there are those who differ with the Rabbi on this, in any case it is "the place of the Master," and they have already accepted him upon themselves"; I, 192. Similarly: "In any case Maimonides is 'the Master of the place,' and all these provinces have already accepted his legal decision"; II, 604.

39 IV, 105 (= 1176), quoting Esther 7:8. Cited above, Case [107].

of certain transactions of this type was relaxed for a trustee who was engaged in investing the capital of orphans.[40] Reuben was apparently such a trustee, lending money on interest in a permissible fashion. The borrower, however, claimed that in fact Reuben had loaned him money on "stipulated interest," and brought suit for reimbursement of the interest he had paid. Such a claim by a plaintiff, seeking recovery for money paid, is not accepted without proof. But there was a controversy regarding whether the defendant had to clear himself with an oath. The local court was aware of Maimonides' opinion, but knowingly rejected it, and ruled, following Rabbenu Asher, that he did not have to take an oath. Radbaz, following Maimonides, ruled that he did. He did not base this opinion on the fact that Egypt was "the place of the Master," but on substantive grounds. However, what is of interest to us is that the local court felt no compunction to rule like Maimonides! If Egypt is "the place of the Master," it apparently is not because there was, independently, a grass-roots tradition in the local courts of always ruling in accordance with his opinions. The concept of Egypt as "the place of the Master" came first, and sought its realization in the incorporation of Maimonides' rulings as binding: "Since it is the place of the Master, it is as if they accepted him upon themselves."[41] But the concept was not always successfully realized, as we have just seen.

[110] Another responsum points in a similar direction.[42] As we saw above in Case [107], the every-day clothing of a debtor's wife is considered to belong to the wife, and not to the husband. It is therefore excluded from the assets that the husband's creditor may seize. Her jewelry, however, belongs to the husband, and may be seized by the husband's creditor. There was a question, however, about the status of the wife's fine clothing. Radbaz testifies to the practice of the courts in Egypt to view the fine clothing in her actual possession as hers, and to exclude them from the assets of her husband, which are subject to seizure. They are thus placed in the same category as her every-day clothing. Radbaz himself supports and rationalizes this practice. Maimonides, however, had ruled otherwise, placing her fine clothing in the same category as her jewelry, that is, as belonging to her husband, and therefore subject to seizure. Radbaz concludes his responsum:

---

40 BT Bava Metsi'a 70a; *MT*, Civil Laws, Laws of Creditor and Debtor, chap. 4, parag. 14.

41 Above, at n. 37.

42 I, 281.

> So, since this practice is not completely established (*eino qavua' le-gamrei*), the judge should say to the creditor, by way of compromise, that he should seize the gold and silver jewelry but not the fine clothing. However, if the creditor insists on the letter of the law (*ya'amid 'atsmo 'al ha-din*), he should rule according to the opinion of Maimonides, because it is his place.

Radbaz, after presenting Maimonides' view, tells us: "In any case, they (the courts) have the practice of not seizing them (the fine clothing)." The phrase in Radbaz's conclusion, "this practice is not completely established," apparently means "established in law," rather than "established in practice." There is no allusion to any variance in court practice elsewhere in the responsum. As in the previous example, the courts in Egypt did not follow the ruling of Maimonides. Contrary to the previous example, they had the full support of Radbaz in this matter. He treats this apparently established tradition, though, as a matter of compromise, outside the letter of the law. The role of "the place of the Master" asserts itself in Radbaz's recognition of the right of the creditor to insist on his full legal rights. There is no indication that this was regular procedure in the courts. As we saw above, there was a general, broadly based concept of "the place of the Master," but it did not manifest itself consistently. It preceded, rather than followed, the practice of actually ruling like Maimonides.

(*c*) *"The Place of the Master" and Radbaz's Own Opinion*

The idea, that rabbinic law in Egypt should follow the rulings of Maimonides, is especially striking in Radbaz's responsa on those occasions where he clearly feels that the proper decision lies elsewhere, and yet bows to Maimonides because it is "the place of the Master."

[111] The performance of a ritual obligation is preceded by a benediction, blessing God "Who has commanded us to do" this act. Unnecessary benedictions are frowned upon as being a misuse of God's name, and doubts regarding the propriety of a benediction are resolved by omitting the benediction. However, it is not uncommon that there is a dispute among the rabbinic authorities regarding the proper way of fulfilling a ritual obligation, so that each side in the dispute disqualifies the other's opinion, and considers those who act in accordance with it as having failed to fulfill their religious obligation. Radbaz rules that those who adopt either opinion are regarded as having fulfilled the

obligation properly.[43] Since they acted in the way they understood God to have commanded, they may recite the formula, "Who has commanded us to do" this act. There are, however, two exceptions. One is a case in which one of the views in the dispute has been widely accepted in practice. The other is if the location was "the place of the Master," and the act was being performed contrary to Maimonides' opinion. In both cases the opposing opinion is delegitimized, contrary to Radbaz's strongly expressed personal view on this point in general. In these instances one should not say, "Who has commanded us," with reference to the performance of the ritual act in such a manner. Note that these two exceptions to the rule are independent of each other. Maimonides' ruling is binding in "the place of the Master" even though it does not represent general practice.

[112] The same point is made elsewhere. The question concerns a procedure discussed in the Talmud, in which a borrower formally entrusted the lender with the credibility to assert any time in the future that he had not been paid. The debtor thus accepts upon himself the burden of proof, which would normally rest on the creditor, were the debtor to assert that he had already paid the debt. The Talmud concludes that such a waiver on the debtor's part does not include entrusting the creditor with credibility against the testimony of witnesses that he had indeed been paid.[44] The question asked Radbaz was whether the same applied to a case of only one witness.[45] Radbaz analyzes both sides of this issue, and tends toward the view that the credibility entrusted to the creditor does not extend to his contradiction of even one witness. Following normal procedure when a single witness testifies against a defendant in a civil suit, the defendant may acquit himself by taking an oath attesting to the truth of his plea. Radbaz then adds:

> Even if the matter were subject to a dispute among the legal authorities, we do not exact money from him unless a majority of those (legal authorities) according to whom it is our practice to rule were to say that he entrusted greater credibility to (the creditor) than to a single witness. Or if it was the place of the Master (and Maimonides had ruled that way)—in such a situation it is my practice to issue a verdict in accordance with him, even if it means exacting money. But in this case it is

43 I, 229.
44 BT Shevu'ot 42a.
45 IV, 182 (= 1253).

> clear that he did not entrust him with greater credibility than one witness, as I have made clear.

Note here too the same parallel tracks to the delegitimization of other opinions, including the opinion of Radbaz himself, as viable options in practice: rabbinic consensus, and "the place of the Master."

[113] The starkness of the contrast between Radbaz's personal conviction of what the law is, based on his own analysis of the sources, and his willingness to forgo acting on that conviction in "the place of the Master" because Maimonides had ruled otherwise, is brought home in a responsum dealing with the relationship between co-wives.[46] There are several parts to the question. The first, which concerns us here, asks whether the husband has the right to insist that his new second wife occupy the same dwelling as the first, even though she did not stipulate an independent dwelling as a condition of the marriage. The other parts of the question deal with whether each wife can withhold her personal property from the other's use. There is a passage in the Talmud that deals with the latter issue.[47] Though it does not deal with the first, Radbaz deduces from it by means of an original analysis that in fact the husband can compel his second wife to share quarters with the first if she did not specify otherwise at the time of the marriage. He reinforces this conclusion with several lines of argument, and cites an earlier authority who ruled likewise. Nevertheless, he concludes:

> But Maimonides wrote in Chapter 14 of the Laws of Marriage:[48] "And he cannot compel them to dwell in one courtyard, but each one by herself." And this is the place of the Master.

It seems clear where Radbaz's sympathies lie, and how he would rule if he were living elsewhere. But in "the place of the Master" he forgoes his own opinion in the matter.

In some responsa in which Radbaz refers to "the place of the Master" in support of his ruling, that is the sole criterion that he explicitly cites for arriving at a decision between conflicting opinions.

---

46 III, 561 (= 991).

47 BT Ketubbot 80b: "A certain woman brought in to her husband two maidservants. The husband went and married another woman. He gave her (the new wife) one of them...."

48 Parag. 3: "A man may marry several wives... and his wife cannot prevent him. That is, if he can provide food, clothing, and periodic sexual intercourse as is proper for each one of them. And he cannot compel them" etc.

More commonly, "the place of the Master" is adduced in conjunction with another reason (sometimes more than one), as a supplementary supporting argument for his decision. Among these other reasons are: one rules according to the majority of legal authorities;[49] one rules leniently in a situation of doubt when the prohibition in question derives from the authority of the Rabbis (*sefeiqa de-rabbanan le-qulla*);[50] it is the established practice to rule that way in this case, or to rule according to a specific authority;[51] the law is in accordance with the later authorities;[52] the "middle way."[53]

The principle that great monetary loss for Jews is a reason for leniency can also be added to this list. There are examples where Radbaz rejects Maimonides' opinion as the correct ruling, but relies on it as a "fall-back" position in instances when the application of his own opinion (justified as the "correct" one in the course of the responsum!) would result in a great loss of Jewish money. Radbaz reinforces this rejection of his own opinion in such cases with the principle of "the place of the Master."[54]

[114] "The place of the Master" is also used as an adjunct to a decision reached by Radbaz by means of his own personal understanding (*sevara*). In a question about disembarking from a ship on the Sabbath, Radbaz first cites a considerable body of opinion, which is lenient in this matter.[55] He then adds:

> But I never took it upon myself (*lo samakhti 'al 'atsmi*) to rule that way in practice. First, because there are those who differ, as you (the questioner) wrote. And furthermore, I hold an opinion like that of Maimonides (*ani sover ke-da'at ha-rambam*), who is stringent, as I wrote above. And it is the place of the Master.

---

49 I, 186; I, 510; III, 462 (= 902b); VII, 21.

50 I, 2. In II, 669, the rule *sefeiqa de-rabbanan le-qulla* takes precedence over the stringent ruling of Maimonides in "the place of the Master."

51 II, 802; III, 499 (= 934): "All these provinces have the practice of ruling according to Alfasi."

52 I, 148; see Chap. 10.

53 I, 366; see Chap. 6.

54 I, 253. "Great loss" in conjunction with "the place of the Master" is a factor for leniency also in III, 527 (= 962), end, and VIII, 111. These are two cases that deal with the same issue.

55 III, 592 (= 1018). On this issue see: Katz, *Shabbes Goy*, 35–48; also, Ta-Shma, "Sailing," 168–88.

Radbaz first tells us that his own opinion agrees with that of Maimonides. He then adds that, in addition, it is "the place of the Master."

[115] In a similar vein, he writes in support of the right of a lessee to sublet, after having quoted Maimonides' ruling to that effect:

> The earlier and the later rabbinic authorities have already written in accordance with[56] the opinion of Maimonides, and we heed him because he spoke correctly (or: according to the law) (*ka-halakha*), and furthermore, because it is the place of the Master.[57]

(*d*) *The Weight Given to "The Place of the Master"*

If we read the previous passage literally, Maimonides is to be heeded primarily because Radbaz thinks that he ruled correctly, and secondarily because it is "the place of the Master." As a matter of fact, in the overwhelming number of instances in which "the place of the Master" is used together with another reason for the decision, the other reason takes precedence in the order of presentation, leaving the impression that "the place of the Master" is ancillary to other considerations. This impression is different from the one conveyed by Radbaz's rhetoric about "the place of the Master" as we have seen it earlier in this chapter, and as it is manifest, as we have seen, in the substance of some of his decisions. There are, as it turns out, a number of responsa in which Radbaz alludes to "the place of the Master" and nevertheless rules against Maimonides. The fact that he makes this allusion at all (in many other responsa he simply rules against Maimonides without referring to this principle) is indicative of a certain tension between fealty to Maimonides because "it is the place of the Master," and the attraction of other factors, a tension which leads to a conflicted stance.

The same responsum, which ultimately rejects Maimonides' ruling, can testify to the claim that "the place of the Master" had on Radbaz. In two responsa that apply the same law, Radbaz relies on a lenient school of opinion to overrule Maimonides in a case of special need. He does

56 Emending *be-sevarat* to: *ke-sevarat*.

57 I, 139. For similar examples in which "the place of the Master" and Radbaz's own opinion reinforce each other, see: I, 110; I, 415; I, 588; VIII, 93.

so while admitting that in more normal circumstances he would tend toward stringency because it was "the place of the Master."

[116] Sexual activity is forbidden with a woman who is in a state of menstrual impurity. A menstruant remains in a state of impurity until she undergoes the ritual of immersion after her menstruation had ceased. Maimonides had ruled that a marriage could not take effect if the bride was in a state of menstrual impurity because it could not be consummated.[58] Radbaz was asked about a situation in which the bride became a menstruant after the food for the wedding was already prepared. A delay in the wedding would have meant significant economic suffering, because, since there was no way to prevent spoilage, the food would have to be sold at a considerable monetary loss.[59] There is an implication in Radbaz's answer that the groom (or his father) would probably not be able to recoup the loss and prepare another wedding in a reasonable time.

Radbaz begins by referring to a controversy regarding whether a wedding can be conducted if it cannot be consummated immediately. Maimonides represents the stringent side of this controversy. The lenient side, which derived from the Ashkenazic halakhic tradition, applied an innovative interpretation to the relevant talmudic passage.[60] Radbaz, basing himself on an analogous situation discussed in the Talmud,[61] suggests that Maimonides would have conceded that the wedding may take place in such an extreme circumstance. He admits, however, that this suggestion is not at all certain, and concludes as follows:

---

58 *MT*, Women, Laws of Marriage, chap. 10, parags. 2 and 6.

59 I, 518.

60 See BT Ketubbot 56a: "Rabbi Ashi asked: If she entered the *ḫuppa* (marriage chamber) and became a menstruant—if you say that it is the love of the *ḫuppa* which acquires (the wife in marriage), is it (only) a *ḫuppa* which is fitting for intercourse ... or does it not matter? The question *ḫuppa* stands." The lack of resolution means that the question is resolved stringently, and the wife is not acquired in marriage. But Rabbenu Asher (*Pisqei ha-Rosh,* Ketubbot, chap. 5, no. 6) interprets the phrase "acquires (in marriage)" in a way that would allow the wedding to proceed even though it cannot be consummated. Rabbenu Asher's lenient position goes back to the Tosafist Rabbi Isaac: see the gloss to Rabbenu Asher, *ad loc.*; *Mordekhai*, Ketubbot *ad loc.*, no. 178.

61 BT Ketubbot 3b–4a, regarding the death of the groom's father after the food for the wedding was already prepared.

> Even if you choose to say that (Maimonides) differs even in a situation like the case at hand, it makes sense (*mistabber*) to decide the law according to the later authorities (i.e., Rabbenu Asher and those who follow him—SM), even in the place of the Master, because their reason makes sense (*de-mistabber ta'amaihu*), and such is the prevalent practice (*ve-ken nahagu*), and thus is it proper to render a decision when there is reason for it, as in the case at hand.
>
> But if he is wealthy, so that even if he sold what he had prepared he will be able to prepare again afterwards, it is not proper to rule leniently in the place of the Master.
>
> Therefore, it is proper for the one rendering the decision to examine carefully if there is a sufficient reason (for proceeding with the wedding) or not.

Note that according to this description of the state of affairs, the prevalent practice did not follow Maimonides, though Radbaz himself would have followed him, were it not for the catastrophic consequence of great monetary loss and an indefinite delay in the wedding. Again we see that "the place of the Master" may have represented an ideal, but not always the reality. Note also that Radbaz himself supports the argument of the lenient school ("their reason makes sense"), though he forgoes his own judgment in favor of Maimonides in "the place of the Master." But a situation of great need is sufficient grounds to rule against Maimonides even in his "place."

[117] In a parallel case, Radbaz was asked whether the nuptial benedictions, an indispensable part of the marriage ceremony, may be recited if the bride was "in the days of her whiteness."[62] This refers to a rabbinic extension of a menstruant's waiting period before sexual activity may be resumed to seven days of no bleeding after menstruation had stopped.[63] There is an implication in Radbaz's answer that a close relative was about to die, and a delay in the wedding would end up being protracted because of the anticipated period of mourning. Radbaz first suggests that perhaps Maimonides would allow her, under such dire and unusual circumstances, to immerse during "the days of her whiteness," since according to the law of the Torah itself, without its rabbinic expansion, she is permitted to do so. Thus, the marriage may theoretically be consummated according to the law of the Torah, though not in practice, since that would violate the law of the Rabbis.

---

62 VII, 62 (b).

63 The Talmud describes this as a stringency adopted by the women themselves; BT Nidda 66a.

But he does not base his ultimate decision on this line of argument. Instead he continues:

> I am inclined (*ve-qarov ani*) to rule permissively even without immersion if there is such a great apprehension as this, even though it is the place of the Master, since there are several great ones of the world who permit it, Rosh (Rabbenu Asher) and his son Rabbi Jacob (author of the *Turim* code) among them.

As he did in the previous case, Radbaz relies on an alternative legal tradition, one which represents a consensus of the "later authorities," to overrule Maimonides "in the place of the Master," but only "if there is such a great apprehension as this."

[118] A similar combination of a consensus of other authorities and accepted practice, which responds to a vital need, plays a role in overruling "the place of the Master" elsewhere. The issue is the licitness of selling on credit for a higher price, a practice that seems to run afoul of the prohibition of interest. Two responsa that refer to "the place of the Master" deal with this issue. In the second responsum cited below, Radbaz refers to other responsa that he wrote on this subject, and apparently the first one cited below is among them.

Maimonides had ruled:

> If one sold another moveable property, (with payment not due) until a certain time, for a hundred, and they were worth ninety in the marketplace for one who paid immediately with cash—this is forbidden. He need pay him only ninety, or return him the merchandise if it is still available.[64]

There was general agreement that selling on credit in this manner is illicit if there was a known fixed price, such as the price of produce in the market during season, which was firmly fixed by supply and demand, or a price determined by government regulation. But Maimonides' ruling includes also items for which the price is not fixed. This prohibition struck at the heart of a commercial economy. There was, however, a well-established alternative interpretation of the ambiguous talmudic passage upon which Maimonides' ruling is based, which allowed for sale on credit at a higher price, as long as the difference between paying now and paying later was not made explicit.[65] Radbaz points out that a long line of rabbinic authorities

---

64 *MT*, Civil Laws, Laws of Creditor and Debtor, chap. 8, parag. 1.

65 See BT Bava Metsi'a 65a–b; Rashi, *ibid.* 65a, s.v. *tarsha shari*; Tosafot, *ibid.* 65b, s.v. *ve-hilkheta ke-rav <u>h</u>ama.*

permitted sale on credit, and uses that to reinforce the legitimacy of long-established universal practice.[66] He confronts the issue of "the place of the Master" head on:

> Even though it is the place of the Master, all have adopted the practice (*kevar nahagu ha-'olam*) of selling their merchandise on credit for more than its (current) worth—and we have not seen anyone who protested against them! They relied in this matter upon all these great men, in order not to close the door in the face of those engaged in commerce.... And now, since the custom of the merchants is such, "custom overrules law"[67] in matters like this.[68]

In the other responsum he writes in a similar vein:

> Even though it is the place of the Master, and Maimonides is stringent, nevertheless, in order to provide livelihood for the sons of the covenant[69] we rely on the later authorities, who permitted it. And the practice of treating it permissively has become widespread.[70]

The law in practice was so well established in this case that Maimonides' ruling was a dead letter. It would appear that the litigant who cited it in the first responsum above sought advantage from what he thought was the letter of the law, hoping to evade the law as everyone knew it to be practiced. Radbaz would have none of it,[71] and in rejecting the plaintiff's claim Radbaz deals directly with the problem of "the place of the Master." However, this specific example cannot be used to show that Radbaz felt a need to make a special effort to contend with the issue. The question in the first responsum contains a specific reference to the relevant passage in Maimonides' code, so it is probable that it was the litigant who introduced the issue of "the place of the Master," and Radbaz is simply responding to it. (The phrase itself does not appear in the question, but we have already seen that the questions

---

66 R. Joseph Caro writes: "As for the law (in practice), the practice of being lenient has become widespread"; *Bedeq ha-Bayit* to *Beit Yosef, Yoreh De'a*, no. 173, s.v. *ve-kol zeh le-da'at rabbenu*.

67 This phrase, which is attested in Palestinian sources beginning with the Palestinian Talmud, Yevamot 12c (chap. 12, halakha 1), is cited particularly in the Ashkenazic rabbinic tradition.

68 III, 451 (= 892).

69 This phrase derives from Rabbenu Tam, who used it in justifying a legal fiction that would enable commercial lending among Jews. See Case [37] above, chapter 2, text at n. 13.

70 I, 493.

71 See Chapter 3, Section (*b*), pp. 111ff.

were edited and abridged by Radbaz.[72]) In the second responsum the question concerns an item with a fixed price (wheat from the king's storehouse) about which there is no legal controversy, and it is Radbaz who extends the discussion to a price which is not fixed, about which there is a controversy, and in that context introduces the theme of "the place of the Master." But this does not necessarily mean that Radbaz deliberately went out of his way to raise the issue. He refers there to responsa he had written earlier to similar questions, undoubtedly having in mind *inter alia* the first of our two, and the reference to "the place of the Master" was probably imported from there.

[119] The established legal practice in Egypt, supported by a consensus of rabbinic authorities arrayed against Maimonides, serves to outweigh "the place of the Master" in issues of less far-reaching import as well. Maimonides, citing the ruling of his teachers, ruled that a financial commitment for an unspecified sum ("I will feed you or clothe you for five years") is not binding, even though the commitment was made with all necessary legal formality.[73] This ruling was challenged by other authorities, and the author of *Maggid Mishneh*, the classic commentary on Maimonides' code, wrote, "As for the ruling of the author and his teachers—I do not know a proof for it." Radbaz was asked a question against this background:

> You asked me that I give you my opinion about Reuben, who has a brother whom he wants to marry to a (certain) woman. But they didn't want to give her to him unless he undertake a commitment, by means of legal formality (*qinyan*) and oath, to provide for his brother and his wife for so-and-so-many years.[74]

The questioner cited Maimonides, and wanted to know whether, in light of his position, Reuben's commitment was binding.

Radbaz, after having referred to the authorities who differ with Maimonides, concludes his responsum as follows:

> Even though it is the place of the Master, it seems to me (proper) to rule in accordance with all the later authorities. Furthermore, there is an oath, and he is well bound to fulfill his oath. Furthermore, the Master followed his teachers in this matter, and his teachers were in Spain. But in Egypt,

72 See Chapter 1, n. 79.

73 *MT*, Acquisition, Laws of Sales, chap. 11, parag. 16.

74 III, 583 (= 1011).

> everything goes according to legal formality (*qinyan*), and legal formality is conclusive.

There are three reasons here. The second, the oath, is specific to this case. The other two are the same that we have seen before: the consensus of the later authorities, and the current legal practice.

(*e*) *"The Place of the Master" and the Plea of* Qim Li

Unresolved controversy among legal authorities plays a special role in civil suits. The burden of proof is on the plaintiff, and part of that burden entails the plaintiff's proving that the side of the controversy favorable to himself is correct. If a controversy remains unresolved, the plaintiff cannot do that. A defendant's plea that he holds one side of a controversy to be correct, thus putting the plaintiff into the impossible position of proving that the other side is correct, is known as the plea of *qim li* (literally: "I hold the opinion"). *Qim li* is the subject of Chapter 9. I will deal with it here only in terms of its relation to "the place of the Master." What role does "the place of the Master" play in the definitive resolution of controversies, which would foreclose the plea of *qim li*? Radbaz's responsa yield contradictory evidence.

[120] On the one hand, Radbaz expressly states that the defendant cannot plead, "I hold like so-and-so," against the opinion of Maimonides:

> In any case, you should know that there are many preconditions, which are necessary for the use of this claim (*qim li*). First, the opposing opinion cannot be (the opinion of Maimonides) in the place of the Master....[75]

Similarly:

> In a place where they had the practice of ruling according to the opinion of Maimonides, like our place, or in accordance with Rabbenu Asher, as in your place, he (the defendant) cannot say, "I hold like so-and-so.[76]

[121] Two passages that have been cited earlier in this chapter also attest to Radbaz's explicit endorsement of the principle that Maimonides' opinion in "the place of the Master" forecloses other options as grounds for the defendant's plea.

---

75 II, 825.
76 IV, 116 (= 1187).

In one of them, Case [112], Radbaz, in accordance with the claim of *qim li*, expresses his general refusal to find for the plaintiff if the finding is based on one side of a controversy. There were two exceptions. One was a consensus among "those (legal authorities) according to whom it is our practice to rule." The other was:

> If it was the place of the Master (and Maimonides had ruled in a way favorable to the plaintiff)—in such a situation it is my practice to issue a verdict in accordance with him, even if it means exacting money.[77]

[122] The other passage has to do with whether the obligation to assume a debt is effected by means of a formal commitment alone, even though the creditor has not actually received a document to that effect.[78] Radbaz cites contrary positions on this, with Rabbenu Hananel, Alfasi and Maimonides ruling that he does not, and Ibn Migash, Nahmanides and Rashba ruling that he does. He then continues:

> You are well aware that we should rule in accordance with Rabbenu Hananel, Alfasi and Maimonides. Even though the others are later authorities, nevertheless, the words of Rabbenu Hananel are words of tradition (*divrei qabbala*), and it is the place of the Master, that is, Maimonides. For this reason I am wont to say that we exact money from him (the defendant),[79] and he (the defendant) cannot say, "I hold the opinion (*qim li*) of these, the later authorities." For since it is the place of the Master, it is as if they accepted him upon themselves.

In both of these passages, it is quite clear that in "the place of the Master," Maimonides' opinion provides the burden of proof necessary for the plaintiff, regardless of controversy. But elsewhere it is equally clear that the opposite is the case.

In a number of instances, Radbaz stresses "the place of the Master" when Maimonides' position would aid the defendant. He does so as a sort of "overkill" in emphasizing the strength of the defense. But in analyzing the very same situation with the roles of the plaintiff and the defendant reversed, so that Maimonides' position would now support

---

77 IV, 182 (= 1253).

78 I, 547. The end of the following passage was cited above in this chapter in the context of Case [109], text at n. 38.

79 The question was phrased generally, as an academic question. The wording here assumes a possible specific situation in which ruling like Maimonides *et al.*, that the oral obligation is not valid, works in favor of a plaintiff.

the plaintiff, Radbaz rules against him, treating controversy on a crucial legal issue as unresolved and the law as unprovable.

[123] In one such responsum the question reads as follows:

> You asked me to give you my opinion about Reuben, who was entrusted with a Torah scroll, and was negligent with it. Is he obligated to pay for it?[80]

The Talmud distinguishes different levels of responsibility for various types of bailees.[81] A gratuitous bailee, one who agrees to be entrusted with another's moveable property without any compensation, assumes the lowest level of responsibility. He is responsible only for loss due to negligence, but not for theft, as long as he guarded the object in a normally responsible manner. If the object is lost, he can escape making restitution for it if he takes an oath that he was not negligent. However, the requirement of an oath does not apply to property belonging to the Temple treasury.[82] It is assumed both by the questioner and by Radbaz that a Torah scroll has the status of Temple property for the purposes of this law.

The question Radbaz was asked does not talk about Reuben's protestation of innocence and the obligation of an oath. The assumption of the question is that he was negligent, probably by his own admission, or alternatively by the testimony of witnesses. Radbaz cites Maimonides, who is quite clear about the law in such a case. A gratuitous bailee who maintained that an item of Temple property in his possession was stolen without negligence on his part is free from the obligation of the oath imposed by the Torah,[83] but if it is certain that he was negligent he must make restitution.[84] However, he then cites a whole host of impressive authorities (Alfasi, Ibn Migash, Rabad, Nahmanides, Rashba, Tosafot) who disagree. They hold the opinion that the law as a whole does not apply to Temple property. The bailee is free from making restitution even if he admits to negligence.

---

80 I, 475.

81 Maimonides presents this material in *MT*, Civil Laws, Laws of Hiring, chap. 1, parags. 1 and 2.

82 Mishnah Bava Metsi'a 4:9; BT Bava Metsi'a 56a.

83 Nevertheless, the Sages imposed on oath upon him; *MT*, Civil Laws, Laws of Hiring, chap. 1, parag. 2. This case, however, deals with restitution.

84 *MT*, Civil Laws, Laws of Hiring, chap. 2, parag. 3. Radbaz deduces from Rashi's wording that he agrees with this position; Rashi to Bava Metsi'a 56a, s.v. *eino nishba'*.

Radbaz rules against Maimonides if the bailee has not yet paid, in other words, if he is still the defendant and does not bear the burden of proof. He does so explicitly in spite of the fact that it is "the place of the Master":

> Therefore, in the case at hand, even though Maimonides obligates him, and it is the place of the Master, still, since he is in possession (of the money for restitution), we do not exact it from him against (the opinion of) all these great authorities.

But this is just because the plaintiff cannot, in light of the contrary opinion of these authorities, sustain the burden of proof by reliance on Maimonides. If the plaintiff managed to seize the funds, however, matters would be reversed:

> My opinion is that if (the plaintiff) seized (the funds), it is not removed from his possession, because he can say to him (Reuben): "Bring proof that the law is not in accordance with those who obligate restitution, and collect." This is even more certainly so since it is the place of the Master.

[124] A similar pattern occurs in answer to a question of whether a witness who signed a document has the credibility to testify that there was an oral condition attached to it.[85] After all, his act of signing is viewed as testimony to the contents of the document as they stand, i.e., without any condition. Talmudic law does not recognize the right of a witness to change his testimony. The Talmud discusses this issue in terms of whether a condition is to be seen as a change in the original document or as an independent legal act.[86] Maimonides,[87] and Nahmanides after him, had ruled that a witness cannot impose a condition on a transaction in this manner. Hai Gaon, and Rabad and Rabbenu Nissim after him, had ruled that he can.[88] Here again Radbaz draws a distinction based on who is the defendant and who the plaintiff. After outlining the controversy between the two camps, he continues:

---

85 I, 433. In talmudic law, it is the witnesses and not the principals who sign documents.

86 BT Ketubbot 19b.

87 *MT*, Judges, Laws of Evidence, chap. 3, parag. 9.

88 Radbaz's source is the commentary of Rabbenu Nissim to Alfasi *ad loc.* This controversy assumes that the witness's signature can be independently confirmed. If the witness himself is the one who authenticates his own signature, then all would agree that he can add a condition, since the document itself is not valid anyway without his oral testimony. In the words of the Talmud, "The mouth which bound is the mouth which loosened."

> Therefore, if the condition favors the plaintiff,[89] it is clear to me that one cannot exact money against the view of Maimonides, for it is the place of the Master. But if the condition favors the defendant,[90] there is need for a great deal of deliberation. If it is possible for the judge to arbitrate, he should do it in a way that inclines toward the defendant, being lenient with him, since he (the plaintiff) would be exacting money from him. But if the litigants do not want arbitration at all, I see fit not to exact money from the one in whose possession it is, even though it is the place of the Master (and rejecting the condition, as Maimonides would have it, would favor the plaintiff—SM). First, because Rabbenu Hai is the father of all the children of the Exile, and his words are words of reliable tradition (*divrei qabbala*), and in his hand is the scepter of righteousness that derives from King David (peace be upon him).[91] And furthermore, Rabbenu Nissim, who is among the later authorities, agreed with him, as did Rabad.

Note that in this case, unlike in the preceding example, there is not an overwhelming consensus against Maimonides, though Radbaz tries to strengthen the opposition to him by stressing the prestige of Hai Gaon. Even without an overwhelming consensus, "the place of the Master" is not sufficient to resolve the controversy definitively in the plaintiff's favor.

[125] Another responsum exemplifies this point even more sharply. A ruling of Maimonides does not have sufficient strength in "the place of the Master" to resolve a controversy in favor of the plaintiff. The defendant may thus plead that the law agrees with the side that favors him, leaving the burden of proof to the plaintiff.

Radbaz's responsum concerns a man who wanted to marry a second wife, since his first wife did not bear him children. However, as was customary at the time, a clause in the marriage contract guaranteed the wife a veto on his right to do so. She refused to allow him to take a

---

89 *im ha-tenai hu le-hotsi mamon*, lit.: "if the condition is to exact money."

90 *le-ha'amid mamon*, lit.: "to have the money stand" (in the place where it is).

91 See Genesis Rabba, par. 99, to Gen. 49:10. "The scepter shall not depart from Judah" is associated there with Ps. 45:7: "A scepter of righteousness is your royal scepter." God granted David the "scepter of righteousness," which has been passed down to Hai Gaon.

rival unless he added a certain amount to her *ketubba*, the sum he was committed to pay her if he divorced her.[92]

The issue involves a disclaimer, issued to witnesses prior to a transaction, that the transaction that is about to take place is under duress. In this case, the husband acceded to his wife's demand, but not before notifying witnesses that he was under duress. He now wants to divorce her, and to disclaim his commitment.

The Talmud recognizes the legality of a prior disclaimer to a legal act about to be done under duress.[93] It therefore became customary, at the time of a transaction or other legal act, to invalidate any disclaimers that would have the effect of voiding it. This led to attempts to disclaim in advance such future invalidations, and hence to the cat chasing his tail *ad infinitum*. There were various suggestions of legal wording designed to withstand any attempt at a disclaimer and ensure the stability of a transaction. The rabbinic authorities were divided on this issue. Radbaz interprets Maimonides as taking the position that there is a way to assure the invalidation of all possible disclaimers.[94] He cites Tosafot and Rashba, whose positions also allow means to ensure the validity of a transaction in the face of future challenge.[95] The single opposing view he cites is that of Rabbenu Nissim, according to whom there is ultimately no way to vouchsafe a transaction in the wake of a prior disclaimer.[96] Nevertheless, if Rabbenu Nissim's position was in the defendant's interests, Radbaz would allow the defendant to plead that position, thus hamstringing the plaintiff's reliance on the majority

---

92 I, 404. Radbaz refers to IV, 54 (= 1126) for the detailed argumentation supporting his opinion.

93 BT Bava Batra 49a.

94 The argument is laid out in IV, 54 (= 1126). *MT*, Acquisition, Laws of Sales chap. 10, parag. 8, favors the validation of the disclaimer and the invalidation of the sale. But Radbaz interprets the passage in the light of *MT*, Women, Laws of Divorce, chap. 6, parag. 20. That paragraph discusses the possibility of a husband's disclaimer of a divorce he is about to issue. Maimonides recommends an effective method of eliminating the threat of such a disclaimer. Radbaz understands that Maimonides would credit the same method with regard to sales, even though in the Laws of Sales he doesn't say so.

95 Tosafot to Bava Batra 48a–b, s.v. *amar rava*, affirms the validity of the vendor's final words before the sale, which are an invalidation of all prior disclaimers. Rashba, *H̲iddushei ha-Rashba*, ad loc., suggests the disqualification of all witnesses who would testify to any disclaimer.

96 *H̲iddushei ha-Ran ʻal Massekhet Bava Batra* to Bava Batra 48b, p. 188, s.v. *i lav modaʻa*.

view, even though it includes the opinion of Maimonides. Radbaz puts it this way:

> It is proper for the judge to arbitrate (and thus avoid applying rabbinic law directly—SM). The reason is that (the defendant) would be able to plead, "I hold the opinion (*qim li*) of So-and-so." ... (I say this) even though in my opinion one cannot plead: "I hold the opinion of So-and-so," if "So-and-so" is a single authority against the majority. All the more so (is this true) in the case at hand, since it is the place of the Master. (But) it is nevertheless possible that the defendant will find other authorities who think as does Rabbenu Nissim, and will be able to plead, "I hold the opinion of these authorities." And then you will not be able to exact (the money) from him.

A single voice does not establish a legitimate controversy. But in the face of the mere possibility that others of like opinion may yet be located, Maimonides' ruling, even in "the place of the Master," carries no special weight.

Radbaz's view on the status of Maimonides' rulings thus remains ambiguous. Some of his utterances indicate explicitly that in "the place of the Master" they resolve outstanding legal controversies, while others indicate explicitly the opposite, that they do not.[97]

(*f*) *"The Place of the Master" and the Spanish Émigrés*

[126] Radbaz, in his reference to "the place of the Master," assumes throughout that the community of Spanish exilees in Egypt are bound by Maimonides' rulings by dint of their current residence in that country. Yet we find him justifying a practice at variance with Maimonidean law by explaining that it derives from the Spanish homeland. This appears to run counter to the logic of "the place of the Master," which assumes that the émigrés from Spain are now in the Master's place, and are bound by his rulings.

---

97 In Sections (*d*) and (*e*) I restricted myself to instances in which "the place of the Master" is mentioned explicitly. There are ample examples of Radbaz ruling against Maimonides without reference to that principle. In some cases he cites broad rabbinic consensus and general practice, e.g., IV, 260 (= 1331); III, 564 (= 994), end. In other cases he relies on his own evaluation of the law (*sevara*), e.g., I, 462; II, 612, end; VIII, 132. Elsewhere he refers to a number of reasons, e.g., IV, 205 (= 1276); IV, 186 (= 1257), ed. Warsaw, 52a, col. 1, middle.

At issue is the *ketubba*, the marriage contract, which expresses the obligations that a man undertakes toward his wife upon marriage. First, he undertakes a personal financial obligation. By the mid-first century BCE, the payment which had originally been due at the time of marriage had been converted into a debt which was payable to her at the termination of the marriage, either by means of the husband's death or by means of divorce. Second, the dowry that the wife brought into the marriage, traditionally in the form of goods, was to be returned to her. The husband undertakes to make good the original value of the dowry, paying from his own pocket (or from his estate) the loss and depreciation which had occurred over the years. Third, various stipulations were attached to the basic marriage contract, which already by the time of the Mishnah (early third century CE) had become mandatory. The one that will concern us here has to do with the wife's right to maintenance from her husband's estate after his death.

The Mishnah records a difference in custom in this regard between Jerusalem and the Galilee, on the one hand, and Judea, on the other.[98] According to the former custom, the wife was granted the option of deferring collection of the *ketubba* payments. If she did so, she had the right to live in her husband's home and be maintained by his estate until such time as she remarried (or, according to the Babylonian Talmud, began to actively seek remarriage). According to the latter custom, the heirs had the option of paying her the *ketubba* payments and thereby terminating her maintenance. The Babylonian Talmud records the continuation of this difference of custom in different regions of Babylonia.[99] Alfasi, however, ruled that the "default" custom, generally binding throughout the world, was the former, allowing the widow the option of continued maintenance at the heirs' expense.[100] Alfasi's ruling became accepted by subsequent rabbinic authorities.[101]

The widow's right to maintenance, however, was dependent on deferral of her collection of the *ketubba*. She ceded her right to maintenance when she put forward a claim for her *ketubba* payment. Maimonides, in a responsum, was asked about a widow who claimed

98 Mishnah Ketubbot 4:12; BT Ketubbot 52b.

99 BT Ketubbot 54a.

100 Alfasi on Ketubbot, end of chap. 4. Alfasi goes to some length to argue this position against the contrary view.

101 *MT*, Women, Laws of Marriage, chap. 18, parag. 1. Rabbenu Asher, *Pisqei ha-Rosh*, Ketubbot, chap. 4, no. 31. *Tur Even ha-'Ezer*, 93.

her dowry, including the loss and depreciation which had occurred over the years, but not the sum which the husband undertook to pay of his own.[102] It is that sum to which the term "*ketubba*" applies in its more limited sense. But the loss and depreciation of the dowry also had to be paid out of pocket, and in Maimonides' case it was a considerable sum, most likely exceeding the value of the *ketubba* in its limited sense.[103] The heirs maintained that the widow's claim for the full original value of the dowry was the equivalent of claiming the *ketubba*, and that she ceded her rights to maintenance. The widow maintained that the dowry was independent of the *ketubba* with regard to this issue. Maimonides ruled in favor of the widow: "The dowry is not included in the *ketubba*."

Radbaz quotes this responsum of Maimonides, in his own translation from its original Arabic.[104] He points out, though, that the practice in Egypt was not like that prescribed by Maimonides. In fact, the out-of-pocket payment for loss and depreciation of the dowry was treated as part of the *ketubba*, and a widow who put forward a claim for it ceded her right to maintenance. Radbaz offers two suggestions for the discrepancy between the law as stated by Maimonides in his responsum and the actual practice in Egypt. The first of these is that the law is in fact as Maimonides had stated it, but the actual practice is the result of a deliberate amendment of the original law:

> The reason for this practice is that the early authorities enacted it for the benefit of the orphans, in order to remove her from (her right to) maintenance by them. For if they would pay her the money for her dowry,[105] then sometimes her basic *ketubba* and its supplement[106] would be a small amount, and for its sake she would continue to live (at their expense) all her life, and would never claim them. And the orphans would lose out.

According to this suggestion, Maimonides' definition of the law is correct. Subsequently, though, an amendment to the law was adopted on a provisional basis to meet a perceived need. Radbaz admits that his

---

102 Maimonides, *Responsa*, no. 371.

103 See Goitein, *Mediterranean Society*, v. 3, 130 bottom, 139. In this case we are told that the husband had sold much of the dowry.

104 I, 92.

105 *nikhsei nedunyatah.* It is clear from Radbaz's later discussion that he is talking only about the out-of-pocket payment for loss and depreciation.

106 These were the constituents of the sum that the husband undertook to pay from his own funds.

intention in offering this interpretation was to reconcile practice with Maimonides' definition of the law. But he goes on to offer a different explanation for the state of affairs, which dispenses with such a reconciliation:

> You are well aware that there are those who differ with the Rabbi (i.e., Maimonides). They say that (the loss and depreciation of) her dowry is included within (the definition of) *ketubba*, because it is not extant (i.e., it must be paid out of pocket). Possibly this is what those who instituted the practice relied upon. For even though it is the place of the Master, they acted for the benefit of the orphans, and they did well in instituting this practice (*ve-yafeh nahagu*). I am inclined (*ve-qarov ani*) to say that this practice comes to us from Spain, where (in general) they acted in matters of marriage according to the opinions of Rabbenu Asher. For (Rabbenu Asher's son, the author of) the *Tur*, states: "If the woman brings in to him money or clothing, ... they are treated like the *ketubba*, and are paid with it—and this is what is called 'dowry'."[107]

Radbaz suggests that those who instituted the current practice simply ruled against Maimonides, and in accordance with others, who disagreed with him. Radbaz expresses his concurrence with their choice of the alternative view, apparently because he felt that it was more equitable, as he stated earlier. He further suggests a source for the influence of the alternative view, namely, the law as it was practiced in Spain. In any case, he fully supports the current practice, while admitting that it is in direct conflict with the principle of "the place of the Master."[108]

---

107 *Tur Even ha-'Ezer*, no. 66. *Beit Yosef ad loc.* makes no reference to Rabbenu Asher. Apparently the presence of this view in the *Tur* is sufficient evidence for Rabbenu Asher's opinion.

108 For another example see I, 33. The phrase "the place of Maimonides" occurs there in the question. Radbaz is asked to explain a common practice in the preparation of kosher meat, which is at variance with Maimonides' strict ruling (*MT*, Holiness, Laws of Forbidden Foods, chap. 6, parag. 10). Radbaz justifies the lenient practice, attributing it to an importation from the practice in the Spanish homeland, where the rabbis ruled accordingly. Nevertheless, he encourages adoption of Maimonides' ruling by the pious.

(g) *Conclusions*

The concept that the Jewish community in Egypt was bound by the rulings of Maimonides because it was "the place of the Master" appears to have originated in the *musta'rib* community, the indigenous Jewish population of Egypt. This concept is to be distinguished from the more general practice in various localities of ruling in accordance with Maimonides. In fact, on various specific issues it was the general practice in the Egyptian courts not to rule in accordance with Maimonides. The notion of Egypt being "the place of the Master" appears to have originated as an abstract concept, which then sought realization in specific rulings. This picture of the situation is exemplified by instances in which Radbaz overrules or modifies common court practice in order to rule like Maimonides because it is "the place of the Master." Radbaz expresses his acceptance of the principle of "the place of the Master" in theory, and frequently in practice. Most striking are a number of cases in which Radbaz forgoes his own conclusion in order to issue a practical ruling in accordance with Maimonides "in the place of the Master." More frequently, "the place of the Master" is supportive of a conclusion reached on other grounds.

In the latter cases, it is often the impression that "the place of the Master" is ancillary, and not one of the primary motivations for the decision. And in fact, in many instances in which Radbaz raises the issue of "the place of the Master," in spite of his rhetoric, he ends up ruling against Maimonides for a variety of reasons. This contrasts with the many responsa, not included in the purview of this chapter, in which Radbaz simply rules against Maimonides without reference to "the place of the Master." The need of Radbaz, in the former set of cases, to rationalize his rejection of Maimonides in "the place of the Master," is itself evidence of its hold on him in theory. On the other hand, the latter set of cases, in which "the place of the Master" never enters as a matter of consideration, indicates an ambiguous attitude on his part with regard to the role of "the place of the Master" in the process of arriving at legal decisions.

This ambiguity is borne out by an analysis of the power of Maimonides' rulings to conclusively determine the law. This was done through the prism of the principle of *qim li* ("I hold an opinion"), which gives a defendant in a civil suit the right to adopt the side of a legal controversy which would support him, leaving the plaintiff in the impossible position of having to prove that the other side of the controversy is the correct one. This plea is dependent on the concept that earlier controversies are never ultimately resolved on a theoretical level. The question examined here was whether Maimonides' ruling in "the place of the Master" is definitive, so that the defendant cannot stake his claim on a contrary ruling by means of a plea of *qim li*. Clear evidence can be found on both sides of this issue in Radbaz's responsa.

The principle of "the place of the Master," as indicated above, appears to have originated in the *musta'rib* community, in all probability long before the mass influx of Sephardic Jews in the wake of the Spanish Expulsion and its aftermath. Radbaz's many references to "the place of the Master" assume that the Sephardic Jews who immigrated to Egypt and its environs are bound by that principle, apparently because of their present domicile. This is not an obvious conclusion in an environment in which immigrants identified themselves in terms of their place of origin, bringing the customs and practices of their homeland with them, and in general refusing to assimilate into the indigenous Jewish culture. This perhaps explains the ambiguous attitude toward "the place of the Master" on the part of Radbaz, who in general had a strong affinity for Maimonides.[109]

---

109 Consider, for instance, that a significant part of Radbaz's oeuvre consists of commentaries to Maimonides' *Mishneh Torah*.

8. "Grant That One Should Not Add to It"

(*a*) *Introduction*

The Mishnah lists certain categories of creditors, who may not collect until they take an oath verifying their claim. In the course of this list we read, "And likewise orphans are not paid except with an oath: 'It is an oath that Father did not command us and did not tell us, nor have we found it among Father's documents, that this note is paid.'"[1] The Talmud understands this to refer to a case in which both the creditor and the debtor have died, and the heirs of the creditor are collecting from the heirs of the debtor. Any creditor collecting from heirs is required to take an oath that the debt has not been paid. Since the creditor's heirs cannot swear that it has not been paid, they take this oath instead. The Talmud continues, however, with the following dictum:

> Rav and Samuel both say: This applies only if the creditor predeceased the debtor. But if the debtor predeceased the creditor, then the creditor had already been obligated to take an oath (that it has not been paid) for the benefit of the debtor's children; and one does not bequeath an oath to one's children.[2]

That is to say, if the debtor dies first and then the creditor, the creditor's heirs have no recourse.

---

1 Mishnah Shevu'ot 7:7.

2 BT Shevu'ot 48a.

It is easy to understand the havoc that this ruling can wreak on commerce, and it is not surprising that there was objection to it. The Talmud records both instances of outright rejection and attempts to limit its range of application. In this spirit we read:

> Rabbi Naḫman happened to come to Sura. Rabbi Ḫisda and Rabbah son of Rabbi Huna came to him. They said to him, "Come, Sir, let us undo this (ruling) of Rav and Samuel." He said to them, "Have I taken pains to come all this distance just to undo this (ruling) of Rav and Samuel? Rather, grant that one should not add to it."[3]

That is, we will accept the rule in its original context, but we will construe it narrowly, and refrain from extending the principle to similar situations.[4] (Ultimately, the Talmud leaves it up to the judge whether to rule like Rav and Samuel, or like the opposing opinion of Rabbi Elazar, that in either case the heirs may take the oath prescribed in the Mishnah and collect the debt.)

The phrase, "Grant that one should not add to it" (*havu de-lo losif 'alah*) occurs in the Talmud only in the course of this discussion, but that is sufficient to make it available to post-talmudic authors for use in a variety of contexts. The earliest attributed use of this phrase is in reference to the legislative innovation of transferring a debt to a third party by means of an oral declaration in the presence of all three parties (*ma'amad sheloshtan*). The Talmud describes this as an innovation, "a law without a (legal) reason" (*hilkheta be-lo ta'ama*).[5] Rabbenu Tam had excluded its application to a non-Jew, and Rabbenu Asher cites as his rationale: "Since it is 'a law without a reason,' grant that one should not add to it."[6] Similarly, the phrase is occasionally applied to other instances of rationalizing a narrow construction of a legal anomaly, most commonly the rule accepting the testimony of a non-Jew "spoken

---

3 BT Shevu'ot 48b.

4 As Tosafot puts it: "Prepare yourselves not to add upon it, (not) to learn from it something which is similar to it"; Tosafot to Ketubbot 109a, s.v. *shenei devarim.*

5 BT Gittin 13b.

6 *Pisqei ha-Rosh* to Gittin, Chap. 1, parag. 17. Compare, however, Tosafot to Gittin 13b, s.v. *be-ma'amad sheloshtan qana*, where a different reason is attributed to Rabbenu Tam for his ruling. Rabbenu Asher, ibid., parag. 18, cites Naḫmanides as using this phrase in excluding such a transfer if the owner's agent acts on his behalf.

in innocence" regarding the death of a woman's husband.[7] In another context, it is used to convey the notion that rabbinic and communal enactments should be construed narrowly, in favor of the defendant.[8] Elsewhere it is found as a rhetorical flourish without any probative function, to reiterate that the law as it stands, or as it is understood by the writer, does not allow for extension to the case under consideration.[9]

The phrase, "Grant that one should not add to it," is used frequently in Radbaz's responsa, well out of proportion to its occurrence among his predecessors and contemporaries.[10] In the largest number of instances in which Radbaz uses it, it is in the last of the three ways just mentioned, that is, as a rhetorical flourish without any functional purpose. There is nothing worthy of special note in this usage. In the other two ways described above in which reference is made to it, namely, with regard to legal anomalies and to rabbinic or communal enactments, the phrase is indeed cited as a reason for the law. But its use in these cases is understandable and predictable. One can understand why a legal innovation which is anomalous (e.g., transfer by declaration in the presence of the three parties; accepting the testimony of a non-Jew in allowing a woman to remarry), which does not grow organically from conventional legal principles, should not be extended by analogy. In the case of an enactment, the defendant has the right to assume a narrow construction of the enactment, and the burden of proof to the contrary is, as always, on the plaintiff. But Radbaz utilizes "grant

---

7 E.g., R. Isaac bar Sheshet, *Responsa*, no. 377; R. Joseph ibn Lev, *Responsa*, II, 12, 13, 15. For an example of this principle with reference to another law see Rashba, *Responsa*, I, 39.

8 E.g., regarding the return of a deceased childless wife's dowry to her father: Rabbenu Asher, *Responsa*, *Kelal* 54, no. 1. Regarding the communal enactment that protected a leaseholder from losing his lease to a higher bidder (*h̲ezqat h̲atserot*): R. Samuel de Medina, *Responsa*, *H̲oshen Mishpat*, nos. 232, 253, 286.

9 E.g., Rabbenu Asher, *Responsa*, *Kelal* 84, no. 3.

10 The Bar Ilan Responsa Project lists 132 occurrences of this phrase and its close variants in Radbaz's responsa. (Included in the number are multiple occurrences in the same responsum, but there are not a great number of instances of this.) The next largest number of usages recorded there is in the responsa of his younger contemporary, R. Samuel de-Medina, which is 22. Even taking into account the large number of responsa in Radbaz's oeuvre, the difference is striking. R. David ha-Kohen's responsa are recorded as containing the phrase 13 times, which is a high occurrence given the small number of his responsa which have survived.

that one should not add to it" in other ways as well, which are attested but rarely in the responsa of his predecessors and contemporaries. In these instances this approach is either functional for the decision (or presented that way in the responsum), or else its use betrays a special emphasis. Its occurrence in these cases is dependent on Radbaz's deliberate decision to apply it, and this invites an exploration of the reasons why he chooses to do so.

The cases of "grant that one should not add to it" which are susceptible to such an analysis fall into two general categories. The first of these consists of instances in which Radbaz has some reservation regarding the law. Feeling himself constrained to accept the law, he minimizes its application. The second category consists of cases in which the interpretation of the dominant opinion is moderated by taking into account an opposing view.

(*b*) *Reservations Regarding the Law*

When Radbaz uses the phrase, "Grant that one should not add to it," because of reservations regarding the law, he is using it precisely as it was originally used in the Talmud. But it is documented in that original sense only rarely among Radbaz's predecessors. I have located only two such instances in pre-sixteenth-century responsa, and none in the responsa of his sixteenth-century contemporaries.[11] One of the two is a responsum of Rashba, who uses it in a ruling regarding a widow's claim to her right of maintenance at the expense of her late husband's estate.[12] That right was considered a stipulation of the *ketubba* (the financial settlement due her upon termination of the marriage). The Talmud reports the following in this connection:

> Rabin bar Hanina sat before Rabbi Hisda. He sat and said in the name of Rabbi Elazar: "If she cedes her *ketubba* to her husband, she has no claim to maintenance." He (Rabbi Hisda) said to him: "If you had not told me this in the name of a great man, I would have said to you: 'If a man returns evil for good, evil will not depart from his house.'"[13]

---

11 This is based on an analysis of the sources resulting from a search of the Bar Ilan Responsa Project's database for *havu de-lo losif/le-hosif.*

12 Rashba, *Responsa*, VI, 5.

13 BT Ketubbot 53a, citing Prov. 17:13.

Rabbi Elazar's law applies, however, only if the entire *ketubba* is ceded.[14]

In the case before Rashba, the woman had ceded her *ketubba* to her husband, but not her dowry. The question was whether the fact that the dowry was not ceded allows her to claim her right to maintenance; i.e., whether the woman's dowry is considered part of her *ketubba* for this purpose.[15] Rashba upholds the widow's right to maintenance, quoting the passage just cited from the Talmud:

> Grant that one should not add to it. For Rabbi Hisda said, "If Rabin bar Hanina had not said it in the name of a great man, I would have said: 'If a man returns evil for good'" etc.

In other words, the entire law is unfortunate, so one shouldn't extend it more than absolutely necessary.

The other instance is a responsum of Rabbenu Nissim. He had been asked by his disciple, R. Isaac bar Sheshet, who had assumed the rabbinical position in Saragossa, about the propriety of certain local practices which the latter considered objectionable.[16] One of them was a practice of announcing the sale of real estate in the synagogue during the Sabbath services, and expressly stating that anyone with a prior claim of ownership must report it to the communal officers within thirty days or forfeit his rights to it. R. Isaac bar Sheshet considered this public discussion of a commercial venture to be a violation of Sabbath restrictions, but the locals contended that R. Aaron ha-Levi, the great rabbinic authority who had been the rabbi there some generations earlier, had himself enacted this practice. Rabbenu Nissim sympathized with his disciple's objections, but was loath to overrule R. Aaron ha-Levi. Consequently, he interpreted R. Aaron ha-Levi's original enactment more narrowly. Since the express mention of the forfeiture of rights by the communal authorities could be understood as a legal act (which is prohibited on the Sabbath), Rabbenu Nissim understood that originally this was merely descriptive of what would happen if a prior claim was not reported, but was not part of the actual announcement as formulated by R. Aaron ha-Levi. True, the announcement itself was not to Rabbenu Nissim's liking, and he urged that it be made in the synagogue before the actual commencement of the Sabbath.

---

14 See BT Ketubbot 97b–98a.

15 For a fuller discussion of this issue, see Case [126], in Chapter 7.

16 The one under consideration here is R. Nissim, *Responsa*, no. 80; R. Isaac bar Sheshet, *Responsa*, no. 38. See EJ, v. 9, col. 32, s.v. Isaac ben Sheshet Perfet.

Nevertheless, in spite of his own feelings on the subject, he would not overrule R. Aaron ha-Levi outright. But:

> In any case, grant that one should not add to it. That is, the announcement should be made as he enacted it. The announcer should not conclude, "And if not, then he will lose all of his rights," for this is absolutely forbidden by (Sabbath) law, and it is improper to allow this at all. For this was not part of his enactment, but rather the matter occurred by mistake, without a doubt.

As in the original talmudic use of this term, there is a recognition that a precedent ruling is flawed. Rather than overruling it, it is restricted in its scope.

[127] Among Radbaz's responsa that employ the phrase, "Grant that one should not add to it," there are a few in which his reservations regarding the law are moral in nature, as in the example of Rashba's responsum discussed above.

One of these cases concerns the respect due to a rabbi because of his learning.[17] A rabbi has the right to sanction disrespect to his person by placing a minor ban, called a *niddui*, upon the offender.[18] This entailed certain acts which symbolically separate him from the community (e.g., he may not be counted in a prayer quorum), and certain acts which imply personal mourning (e.g., he may not cut his hair).[19] In the case presented to Radbaz, the disciple of a certain rabbi customarily functioned as the precentor (*sheliah̲ tsibbur*) on Rosh ha-Shana. When one year the rabbi assumed that role for himself, the disciple was insulted and left the synagogue. The rabbi interpreted his leaving as an insult to his person. A while later, when the disciple sought the position of precentor in another synagogue, the rabbi put him under a *niddui* for having insulted him, and publicized his action in the wider community, effectively preventing him from assuming the post. The questioners wanted to know whether the *niddui* is effective, and if so, then who exactly is bound by it. They also asked about the propriety of the rabbi's action.

Radbaz, while admitting that there might be some minimal insult involved, nevertheless takes exception to the rabbi's action:

> To be sure, there was a bit of insult to the rabbi in this, for he vexed him by not wanting to hear his prayer, and went out.

---

17 I, 378.

18 BT Mo'ed Qatan 16a.

19 *MT*, Knowledge, Laws of Learning Torah, chap. 7, parag. 4.

> What difference is there between vexing him with words and vexing him by leaving the synagogue? But in any case, it was not proper to put him under a *niddui*, because the insult was not so blatant. He could have said, "It was not for that reason that I left the synagogue."

Still, the rabbi was technically within his rights, and his action cannot be undone:

> Know that it is so (that the insult was not blatant), because he did not want to place him under *niddui* at the moment of the insult. That means that he was not culpable of being put under *niddui*. And when he sought to be a precentor in another congregation, he was not at that moment guilty of (an act warranting) *niddui*.... Nevertheless, I admit that once he put him under *niddui*, his *niddui* is effective after the fact, as long as he (the rabbi) says that he did so for the sake of his honor.

Radbaz clearly cannot fault the rabbi on technical grounds for the *niddui*, though his displeasure is evident. Ultimately, the *niddui* is effective. Though Radbaz does not relate to the issue explicitly, the implication of his decision is that the man cannot function as a precentor.[20] But Radbaz certainly does fault him for publicizing the *niddui*. That has no technical justification. Practically, such action may push the disciple's endurance to the point where he will lash back at the rabbi, thus inciting him to the sin of truly dishonoring a scholar of Torah. Radbaz refers to the verse, "Before a blind man do not place an obstacle,"[21] which the Talmud interprets figuratively as a prohibition of incitement to sin. The passage above continues as follows:

> But grant that one should not add to it, and publicize the matter in synagogues and marketplaces. Concerning this the rabbi certainly acted improperly. We have heard (about a rabbi's prerogative with regard to) *niddui*, but not (about any prerogative with regard to) publicizing. He should have been sensitive to his disciple's honor ... and placed him under *niddui* in private, without shaming him. He is destined to come before the bar of justice (in the future world). In my opinion he is in violation of (the stricture): "Before a blind man do not place an obstacle."... For not every man can withstand this kind of humiliation, even more so since in his (the disciple's) opinion, and in the opinion of some other enlightened people (*masqilim*), his action did not constitute dishonor which

---

20 Radbaz explains that only scholars who are greater than the rabbi who issued the *niddui* are not bound by it.

21 Lev. 19:14.

> warrants *niddui*. All the more so, since he (the rabbi) went overboard (in his actions).

Radbaz is scathing, though his strictures are unenforceable in a human court. While he recognizes the legality of the *niddui* at the same time that he condemns its propriety, he curtails any extension of its effects: "Grant that one should not add to it."

[128] The same pattern, in which Radbaz makes his peace with a law that yields an immoral result but restricts it to its minimum range of applicability, is evident also in the following instance.[22]

The responsum deals with competing claims on an estate, on the one hand by the creditors of the deceased, and on the other by his widow, who is claiming her *ketubba*. The respective claims of the widow and the creditors are supported by two conflicting legal principles. The one that works for the advantage of the widow emerges from the following discussion in the Talmud. The Mishnah states:

> One who dies, and leaves a wife and a creditor and heirs, and has a bailment or a loan (owed him) in the hands of others—Rabbi Tarfon says: They should be given to the weakest (party) among them. Rabbi Aqiva says: There is no compassion in judgment. They should rather be given to the heirs....[23]

The Talmud asks what is meant by "the weakest among them." Two views are given. The one that concerns us is the second:

> What is (meant by) "to the weakest"? ... Rabbi Yo<u>h</u>anan says: "For the *ketubba* of the wife, because of grace (*mi-shum <u>h</u>inna*)."[24]

Rashi explains the phrase, "because of grace," to mean that the intention is to encourage women to enter into marriage with peace of mind about their financial future: "So that men will find favor in the eyes of women, and (the women) will be willing to marry them and not worry about the loss of their *ketubba*." "Because of grace" is thus a principle which accords a marginal advantage to a woman in collecting her *ketubba* over other creditors who have competing claims.[25]

---

22 I, 78.

23 BT Ketubbot 84a.

24 *Ibid.*

25 Another similar application of this principle is the following. The Talmud discusses a passage in the Mishnah, which empowers the court to seize an absentee husband's property in order to pay his divorced wife her *ketubba*. One view would restrict the court's authority in this regard only to the payment of a *ketubba*, but not apply it to other creditors. The reason for this special treatment is "because of grace." BT Ketubbot 88a.

The principle that works to the advantage of the creditors emerges from a passage, which appears in the Talmud later in the same chapter. As background, it should be borne in mind that in talmudic law a wife has a lien on her husband's real property for the payment of the *ketubba*, and thus relies primarily on his real estate for its collection. Although creditors in general also hold such a lien, a lender's claim is primarily on the funds that had been loaned.

> Amemar said in the name of Rabbi Hamma: A man who has claims against himself for a wife's *ketubba* and (for debts owed to) a creditor, and has both lands and money—as regards the creditor, he is acquitted with money, and as regards the wife, she is acquitted with land: the one according to what is appropriate for him, and the other according to what is appropriate for her.[26] (Rashi: "He loaned money, and she relied on the lien upon the land and didn't give (him) anything.")
>
> And if there is only one (plot of) land, and it is fitting only for one—we give it to the creditor, we do not give it to the wife. What is the reason? More than a man wants to marry, a woman wants to be married.[27]

Thus, there is a presupposition that a woman's desire for marriage is such that she is willing to pay a price for it. The price in this case is her acceptance of a lower priority than other creditors with equal claims in the collection of her *ketubba* when funds are limited.[28]

In the query addressed by Radbaz, "Reuben" had died after formally confirming in writing a debt that he owed to "Simeon." However, upon his death, his wife seized possession of his property toward payment of her *ketubba*. The estate was insufficient for the satisfaction of both debts.

Radbaz begins by presenting the case against the widow, based on the presupposition that "more than a man wants to marry, a woman wants to be married."[29] But already at this stage, there is a hint that he is uncomfortable with the moral implications of this stance. There is, after all, a rule that creditors with equal claim divide limited funds.[30]

---

26 Current editions read: "him."

27 BT Ketubbot 86a.

28 Alfasi, in a lengthy and detailed argument, rejects a suggested narrow construction of this passage, and applies it broadly. Alfasi on Ketubbot, chapter 9, no. 341 (to Ketubbot 86a).

29 The questioner was apparently ignorant of the conflicting talmudic rationales for priority described above. He supplies his own, which are ignored by Radbaz.

30 *MT*, Civil Laws, Laws of Creditor and Debtor, chap. 20, parag. 4.

Why should this be different? The question, along with the answer that follows it, is not original with Radbaz. It is taken, more or less verbatim but without attribution, from Rabbenu Nissim's commentary to Alfasi.[31] The answer is based on the law that a creditor who seizes what is due him does not have to divide what he has seized with the other creditors. In our case, says Rabbenu Nissim, and Radbaz in his wake, the law views the creditors *as if* they have seized the assets. The law adopts this position because of the presupposition that "more than a man wants to marry, a woman wants to be married."

But this entire discussion is a parenthetical aside to Radbaz's purposes in the responsum.[32] Radbaz's decision to raise this issue, and his decision to use the following poignant language of Rabbenu Nissim, doubtless reflects his own predilections:

> You may say, since both of them are creditors, the law should be that they divide (the funds). Why do we rob the woman (*ammai gazlinan la-isha*)?

The fact that the answer rationalizes the law does not hide the discomfort that Radbaz feels with it (as does, apparently, Rabbenu Nissim as well), a discomfort evidenced by the choice of the word "rob." This sentiment reappears at the end of the responsum. Radbaz deals there with the special character of the case under consideration, in which the widow has seized the assets for payment of her *ketubba*. He shows that the consensus of authoritative opinion is that the woman may keep what she has seized. Nevertheless, he is concerned about one opinion to the effect that she may not keep it, that is, that in this situation too the creditors have precedence.[33] The passage reads as follows:

> There is one who wrote that we do remove the assets from her possession. It is proper, though, that we do not remove it from her possession.

Radbaz presents three arguments based on inferences from Maimonides' wording, which together do not bear the weight of a convincing proof. He then continues:

---

31 Rabbenu Nissim to Alfasi, *op. cit.*, s.v. *yoter mi-she-ha-ish*.

32 As long as the proper clause (*mittaltelei agav meqarqa'ei*) was written in the *ketubba*, as it was in this case, the problem of competing claims would not arise. The widow would have precedence, since the obligation to her was incurred earlier, at the time of the marriage.

33 Radbaz does not identify the source of this opinion, and I have not been able to identify it. Nevertheless, Radbaz takes it seriously and finds it necessary to counter it.

> And grant that one should not add to it. For properly speaking, the law should be (*min ha-din haya*) to divide (the assets) with the creditor. It is quite sufficient (*ve-dayyenu*) that we pass over her because "more than a man wants to marry, a woman wants to be married," and that we pay no heed to the rationale of "because of grace." But if she seized (the assets), we do not say this.

Thus, Radbaz's stance in this responsum parallels his stance in Case [127]. He accepts the legal implications of the presupposition that "more than a man wants to marry a woman wants to be married," even though he has moral objections to it. But he limits its range of applicability ("it is quite sufficient—*ve-dayyenu*") to the absolute minimum.

[129] The phrase, "it is quite sufficient (*ve-dayyenu*)," signifying a resigned acceptance of an established law alongside a moral objection to extending it beyond a narrow construction ("grant that one should not add to it"), occurs in another responsum.[34] Just as in the previous instance, in which Radbaz's conclusion is well within the consensus of legal opinion and does not need his emphasis on the moral aspect of the issue ("properly speaking," "we pass over her," "we rob the woman"), so here too his ruling simply reflects accepted practice, as he himself tells us, and the moral emphasis is redundant. It is apparent, therefore, that the moral emphasis is a testament to his personal point of view.

The issue concerns the law of the "rebellious wife," that is, a woman who refuses to live with her husband. This law has a complex history. For our purposes, it is sufficient to note Maimonides' ruling:

> A wife who has withheld sexual access from her husband is called "rebellious." She is asked why she rebelled. If she said: "He is detestable to me, and I cannot willingly submit to intercourse with him," he is compelled to divorce her immediately, for she is not like a captive woman, that she should submit to intercourse with one who is hateful to her. She should go out without any *ketubba* at all ... (except for what remains intact from her dowry). She takes nothing at all from her husband. Even the shoes on her feet and the kerchief on her head that he had bought her she removes and gives him. Likewise, any gift that he had given her she returns. For he did not give it to her on the understanding that she take it and leave.[35]

---

34 I, 205.

35 *MT*, Women, Laws of Marriage, chap. 14, parag. 8.

The consensus of subsequent rabbinic authority, however, rejected Maimonides' ruling, that the husband is compelled by the court to divorce his wife under these circumstances.

Maimonides' ruling draws on the distinction made by the Talmud between a wife who rebels pleading, "He is detestable to me," and one who does not make that plea.[36] The enigmatic wording of the Talmud is: "If she said, 'He is detestable to me,' we do not force her." Maimonides' apparent understanding of this is: We do not force her to remain married to him. On the other hand, since she initiated the divorce, she cedes whatever claims she may have had on his assets as a divorcee. The exception is her dowry. This consisted as a rule not of money but of goods. These goods represent her patrimony, and she takes them with her when she leaves.

According to the law of the Talmud, the *ketubba* obligations which a groom undertakes at the time of the marriage are payable only at the dissolution of the marriage, by the husband's death or by divorce. However, it was customary in Egypt (and in other Islamic lands) for a portion of the *ketubba* to be paid at the time of the wedding. These funds, referred to here and elsewhere by the biblical term *mohar* (brideprice), were then in the possession of the wife, and she was free to dispose of them at her discretion.

In the case presented to Radbaz, a woman had pleaded after her wedding[37] that her husband was detestable to her. She was warned several times by the court of the implications of being a rebellious wife. Since she continued to be in rebellion, and the accepted practice was to refrain from forcing the husband to divorce her (*contra* Maimonides), the court gave her husband permission to take another wife.[38] In the meantime the woman seized her dowry, as well as the *mohar* which had been given her. The husband insisted upon its return, since, in the

36 BT Ketubbot 63b.

37 *u-kenasah ve-shuv amera ma'is 'alai* (and he married her, and then she said, 'he is detestable to me'). Radbaz deals parenthetically with a situation of a wife who rebelled after they had been living together (see below), whereas the main brunt of his discussion deals with a situation in which she refused him from the beginning. It seems clear that the latter situation is descriptive of the case at hand, and her rebelliousness began immediately pursuant to the wedding.

38 Though theoretically the law permitted polygyny, a clause was customarily included in the marriage contract, which made this contingent on the wife's permission. Apparently what is meant here is that the court suspended that clause.

words of Maimonides, "He did not give it to her on the understanding that she take it and leave."

Radbaz begins his response as follows:

> Grant that one should not add to it—(would one have it) that we not force him to divorce (her), and (at the same time) force her to give him (back) the "*mohar* of her virginity"!?[39] Therefore, if he wants to retrieve what he gave her, let him divorce her. If he divorces her, we will obligate her to return the *mohar* that he gave....

Radbaz proceeds to describe the law in a case in which they had already been living together for some time. Then the husband can never retrieve the *mohar*, because he was already "compensated" for it. Radbaz continues:

> But in a case of a woman who from the very first moment said, "He is detestable to me," and he did not have intercourse with her at all—in a case like this I rule that she return to him that which she took in the capacity of *mohar*.
>
> All this, however, applies when he chooses to divorce her. But if does not choose to divorce her, we do not do both things to her: to "anchor" her (i.e., to withhold a divorce from her so that she cannot remarry), and (to insist) that she return her *mohar* to him. It is sufficient (*ve-dayyenu*) that we apply the law of the rebellious wife to her (i.e., deprive her of her *ketubba* when he divorces her), as the commentators wrote, and not force him to divorce her, as the later authorities wrote (i.e., *contra* Maimonides).

Radbaz, immediately following this, concludes:

> We have never seen in our days one who would compel her to return the *mohar* of her virginity. And this is obvious to me.

From the point of view of a practical ruling, this says it all. The need to anchor legal practice in codified law could have been satisfied by the formal distinction between the situation before the divorce and after the divorce. But that is not sufficient for Radbaz. "Grant that one should not add to it," he tells us, because it would be morally wrong to do so.

[130] We have been considering cases in which Radbaz makes his peace with a law to which he has some objection, but restricts its application by a narrow interpretation. In the cases considered so far, the objection has been moral. Following is an instance in which the objection is based on *sevara*, that is, his personal understanding of what the law should properly be.

---

39 Exodus 22:16. NJPS: "The brideprice for virgins."

The case concerns a man who died, leaving a widow and four minor daughters.[40] The eldest, at least, was not the daughter of the surviving widow. Before his death he had arranged for his eldest daughter to be married at a certain date, though she would still be a minor at that time. The man's estate was considerable, and upon his death the court appointed a guardian to manage the estate and the affairs of the deceased's minor daughters.[41] The guardian concluded that it was in the interest of the engaged daughter, who had neither father nor mother, to be married as soon as possible, though she was only ten years old. Though normally assets would not be placed under the control of a minor, the guardian nevertheless sought that she be allowed to collect her share of the inheritance immediately, so that she would have a dowry.[42]

The Talmud recognized the right of a father to give his daughter in marriage while she is still a minor, though it sought to prohibit the exercise of that right:

> A man is forbidden to betroth his daughter when she is a minor, until she grows up and says, "I want so-and-so."[43]
>
> One may not make an agreement regarding a minor to give her in marriage while she is still a minor, but one may make an agreement regarding a minor to give her in marriage after she is grown.[44]

The medieval authorities later made their peace with child marriages in spite of these talmudic rulings, recognizing it as a fact of life.[45] Radbaz, however, in the wake of the original talmudic position, disapproves of the court allowing the marriage of the girl while she is a minor, even though her father had arranged for it. It is proper for the court, he says, to insist that they wait until she reaches her majority. As for the financial penalty assumed by the father if the marriage is delayed on his behalf, it is not applicable, since it is the court that is delaying the

40 VI, 2338 and VI, 2339.

41 It would seem from this that the widow was not the mother of the other daughters either, but the responsum is silent on this point.

42 The father had stipulated a specific dowry, and in VI, 2338, Radbaz rules that the stipulation lapsed with his death. VI, 2339 deals with the issue of the inheritance of the estate by a minor, the subject of the current discussion.

43 BT Kiddushin 41a.

44 BT Ketubbot 57b.

45 See, for instance, Tosafot on the passage from Kiddushin 41a, s.v. *asur le-adam*.

marriage, not the father. Radbaz admits that ultimately the court should do what is best for the girl:

> If the fiancée does not want to wait until she grows up, and the court sees that he is proper for her, and (are afraid that) if he escapes their hold they will not find another like him, and that it is (accordingly) in the best interests of the orphan, then they have the right to allow her to marry at the time that the father agreed upon (though she would still be a minor—SM).

Nevertheless, this is as far as Radbaz is willing to go. The statement continues:

> But not any earlier. Even if the guardian wants to give her in marriage before the time that the father set, he is not heeded.

Radbaz's reluctance to allow the girl to be treated as if she were an adult carries through also to his attitude regarding the settling of the estate. He is opposed to entrusting assets to a minor. It is on this point that he is faced with a contrary ruling by Maimonides:

> If the testator said, "Let the share of the minor be given to the minor, and let him do with it as he pleases," he has the right to do so.[46]

Maimonides does not derive this from an explicit talmudic ruling, though his classic commentator, the author of *Maggid Mishneh*, cites the passages from which the ruling can be deduced. Radbaz, of course, accepts Maimonides' ruling. But he construes it narrowly:

> As for the dowry, if the father ordered, at the time of death, that she be given her dowry even though she was still a minor, he has the right to do so.... (He refers to the passage of Maimonides just cited.) But if the father did not order it, assets are not given to a minor. It was necessary to teach us this new point of law,[47] that he has the right to order that they should give the share of the minor to the minor. And grant that one should not add to it.

Radbaz's deduction from the wording of Maimonides, that *only* the father has the right to have the assets given to a minor, *but not the court*, is not completely compelling. After all, Maimonides was not addressing the prerogatives of the court. Furthermore, Radbaz himself is fond of the phrase, "The court is the father of orphans," which he cites later in this very responsum. One can easily, if so inclined,

---

46 *MT*, Civil Laws, Laws of Inheritance, chap. 10, parag. 6.

47 *ve-hutsrekhu le-hadesh lanu. vehutsrekhu*, literally: "they found it necessary." It is not clear to me who "they" is, since it refers to Maimonides. Without the final letter it would read, "He found it necessary," and perhaps it should be so emended.

interpret Maimonides as not excluding the court from acting *in locus parentis* in this regard. But Radbaz's guiding principle is that "assets are not given to a minor." So he makes his peace with Maimonides' ruling, but restricts it to its narrowest construction. "Grant that one should not add to it."

(*c*) *Harmonizing Opposing Views*

[131] Radbaz's use of the phrase, "Grant that one should not add to it," often occurs in the context of a controversy among rabbinic authorities. It is usually used in reference to an interpretation of one side of the controversy, which would bring it into consonance with the other side in its application to the case at hand. This process can be demonstrated by the following example. It is of particular interest, because Radbaz explicitly formulates an interpretive approach that seeks to harmonize conflicting opinions.

The question emanates from Rhodes.[48] "Reuben" had bought a quantity of wax from "Simeon." Before he had a chance to examine it, he immediately had it shipped to the island of Chios, a seaport which served as a commercial center for Rhodes.[49] He hurried to do so without examining the purchase, because a ship was leaving for Chios at that very time. It was delivered to a colleague of his, who stored it until Reuben's brother arrived in Chios and sold it to a merchant. The consignment was then opened and examined, and it was discovered to be adulterated with dirt and flour. Further examination, conducted before witnesses, showed that the shipment contained only about three-quarters of the wax it was said to contain. The circumstances appeared to indicate that the captain of the ship did not have other wax aboard with which he could have switched it. The questioner asks whether the evidence is sufficient to find Simeon guilty of cheating Reuben and to charge him with reimbursing Reuben for the difference, or whether Simeon has the option of taking an oath, that it was not he who cheated Reuben. It may, after all, have been the one who stored the wax in Chios, or perhaps even the captain, in spite of the circumstantial evidence to the contrary.

Radbaz dismisses the suggestion that the evidence supports the conviction of Simeon. But he shows that the questioner's other option,

---

48 III, 492 (= 928).

49 Goldman, *Life and Times*, 182.

namely, that Simeon be compelled to take an oath if he wishes to clear himself, is also open to question. The type of oath that this would be is a type called a *heset* oath. A *heset* oath is imposed on a defendant when a plaintiff claims, without proof, that he owes him money. This is an oath mandated by the Rabbis, and is distinguished from oaths that are mandated by the law of the Torah. The Talmud puts it this way:

> Said Rabbi Nahman: He is made to take a *heset* oath. Why? There is a presumption that one does not put forth a claim unless one (really) has a claim against him.[50]

This presumption assumes that the plaintiff states a claim of which he is certain: "I know for a fact that you owe me money." Such a claim is called in the Talmud "a claim of certainty." It is contrasted to "a claim of 'perhaps,'" for example, "I have reason to suspect that you owe me money." Accordingly, Maimonides rules:

> One may impose a *heset* oath only for a claim of certainty. But for a matter that is in doubt, he (the defendant) is acquitted (of having to take an oath).
>
> How so? "I think that I have in your possession a *maneh* (i.e., a hundred dinars—SM)," or if he said, "The *maneh* which I loaned you—it seems to me that you have not paid it," ... and the defendant says, "You have nothing at all in my possession," then he is acquitted even of a *heset* oath.[51]

The problem in this case, therefore, is that Reuben's claim against Simeon is a claim of "perhaps." As plausible as it may be, he cannot know for sure that it is Simeon who cheated him.

Radbaz argues that Simeon is indeed obligated to take an oath if he wishes to avoid having to pay. In order to do so, he has to overcome the obvious problem, that a claim of "perhaps" does not necessitate an oath. To this end he presents a string of arguments, most of which cite an exception to this rule, and then show that the case at hand falls under the category of the exception. For instance, he cites an opinion that a claim of "perhaps" which is plausible and not of unusual occurrence is sufficient to necessitate an oath.[52] One of these arguments is relevant to our issue.

---

50 BT Shevu'ot 40b.

51 *MT*, Civil Laws, Laws of Pleading, chap. 1, parag. 7. See *Maggid Mishneh*, who cites the talmudic passage cited above as the source of the restriction of a *heset* oath to claims of certainty.

52 Radbaz cites this as the opinion of Rabbi Barukh. His source is *Mordekhai* to Shevu'ot, no. 772. Much of Radbaz's treatment derives from that passage of the *Mordekhai*.

The passage of Maimonides just cited presents examples of claims based on "a matter that is in doubt." The quotation above contained an ellipsis in this list of examples. A fuller quotation of the passage reads:

> How so? "I think that I have in your possession a *maneh*," or if he said, "The *maneh* which I loaned you—it seems to me that you have not paid it"; "Father told me that he has a *maneh* in your possession," or, "He testified to me before his death[53] in front of witnesses that he has a *maneh* in your possession"; ... and the defendant says, "You have nothing at all in my possession"—then he is acquitted even of a *heset* oath.

In other words, according to Maimonides, even the father's testimony before witnesses, to the effect that the defendant owed him money, is not to be construed as a claim of certainty on the part of his son.

Radbaz offers the following interpretation of Maimonides. The reason why the father's testimony does not constitute a "claim of certainty" for the son is because it is hearsay knowledge. The son does not of his own accord know that the money was owed. Had he in fact claimed that he had first-hand knowledge of the debt owed to his father, then, says Radbaz, Maimonides would agree that it would constitute a "claim of certainty." Furthermore, the reason why the claim in the first set of examples, "The *maneh* which I loaned you—it seems to me that you have not paid it," is insufficient to compel the defendant to take an oath, is because the plaintiff should have known whether or not it was paid. His failure to do so is negligence on his part, and he cannot come now and demand an oath of the defendant. That is not so, argues Radbaz, if the defendant's uncertainty does not stem from negligence on his part. In the case of Maimonides' second set of examples, if the son had claimed, "I know first-hand that you owed him the money, but I am not sure whether or not you paid him," the son's lack of knowledge of his father's affairs is not a matter of negligence. In such a case, asserts Radbaz, Maimonides would agree that the defendant would have to take an oath to defend himself.

It is this position, which Radbaz attributes to Maimonides, which is the core of his argument. Reuben paid Simeon for a certain quantity of wax. This is a claim of certainty. It is analogous to: "I know first-hand that you owed my father money." Reuben's claim of "perhaps" is: "I believe that it is you who adulterated the wax," which is the equivalent of: "I believe that you didn't give me what I paid for." This is analogous to: "But I don't know whether or not you paid my father." Accordingly, Simeon must take an oath.

---

53 *tsiva li*, which usually implies a testimony in contemplation of death.

But Radbaz does not leave the matter there. He reinforces this interpretation of Maimonides by means of a "grant that one should not add to it" argument. Maimonides' critical glossator, Rabad, had taken issue with him, insisting that the plaintiff's report of his father's testimony is indeed considered a claim of certainty. Radbaz, after citing Maimonides' ruling, that the plaintiff's claim: "The *maneh* which I loaned you—it seems to me that you have not paid it," is a claim of "perhaps" and does not necessitate a denial by oath, then continues:

> This applies because he should have known whether he paid him or not. That is why he (the defendant) is not made to take an oath. But if he claimed, "I know that you owe my father a *maneh*, but I don't know if you paid him," it seems to me that the Master (i.e., Maimonides) would admit that he is made to take an oath.... (He argues by inference from Maimonides' wording that this is the case.)[54]
>
> Furthermore, Rabad differs with him on the essence of the law, and grant that one should not add to it.
>
> And so ruled *Mordekhai* explicitly,[55] that if he claimed, "I know that you owe my father a *maneh*, but I don't know if you paid him," that he is made to take an oath.
>
> And so, we should not introduce a controversy (*ein lanu le-haddesh mahaloqet*) between the authorities in a matter that is not explicit.

The opinion cited in the *Mordekhai* is merely corroborative, and Radbaz is not basing his claim primarily on it. This is clear from its late, almost offhand, introduction, and from its minor role in the structure of the argument. It is also a conclusion consonant with the relative weight given by Radbaz to the *Mordekhai* throughout his responsa. The "authorities" he refers to in the last sentence are Maimonides and Rabad. Radbaz takes the position that although we rule in accordance with Maimonides, our understanding of Maimonides should be moderated by interpreting him in a way, which lessens the gap between his position and that of his disputant. He tells us that this approach to interpretation is based on a general hermeneutic principle: "We should not introduce a controversy between the authorities in a matter that is not explicit." This concept is encapsulated in a variant of

---

54 Maimonides' example, "Father told me," implies that the son did not know this first hand. Had Maimonides meant to include even first-hand knowledge on the part of the son, he would have worded it that way explicitly, and a situation of hearsay knowledge would have then been implied *a fortiori*.

55 *Mordekhai* to Shevu'ot, no. 772.

the usual phrase, "Grant that one should not add to it," which appears a number of times when Radbaz uses it in the context of a controversy: "Grant that one should not add to the controversy (*havu de-lo losif 'al ha-mahaloqet*)."

[132] This notion, that in the case of a controversy among authorities, the accepted opinion is to be interpreted in such a way as to lessen the difference between the disputants, and that the application of this interpretive principle is referred to by the aphorism, "Grant that one should not add to it," is not original with Radbaz. In one example of it, which is independent of Radbaz, it is employed by a contemporary of his, as cited by Radbaz himself. This lengthy and important responsum presents Radbaz's position regarding the status of members of the Karaite sect who chose to rejoin the mainstream Rabbanite majority.[56] The issue was a matter of contention among the rabbinic authorities of the sixteenth century. The sticking point was the unacceptability of Karaite divorces from the perspective of rabbinic law. That implied that Karaite wives who were divorced and remarried were considered to be living in a state of adultery, and their children and children's children were illegitimate, and forbidden to intermarry with Rabbanite Jews. Thus, the entire community was suspect. Radbaz's ultimate conclusion is that the original marriages within the Karaite community are invalid from the point of view of rabbinic law, so that subsequent remarriages are not adulterous. Thus, his lenient conclusion is built on the foundation of a fundamentally stringent stance with regard to the Karaites.[57] Radbaz's responsum is in the form

---

56 II, 796. The responsum was censored out of the Sudilkov edition, which served as the basis of the Warsaw edition. It was belatedly discovered by the Warsaw editors, and printed at the end of Part II, with its own pagination. See Lifschitz, "The Responsa of Radbaz," 37, n. 40.

57 A similar approach is utilized by Radbaz in Radbaz, Marx. The responsum deals with the indigenous Jews of Cochin, who, it was alleged, originated as slaves of Jewish owners. Once manumitted, such a slave would be a Jew. But they were never legally manumitted, and cannot be so now, since their legal owners cannot be identified. Thus they are not able to convert now, and, as slaves, can never be permitted to intermarry with Jews. Radbaz argues that technically they never had the halakhic status of slaves, but simply of non-Jews, and could now convert. He bases this decision on a stringent ruling, that the change of status from non-Jew to slave of a Jew is dependent, even *ex post facto*, on the fulfillment of certain technicalities. They can therefore convert now, and marry within the Jewish fold: "And

of a point by point rejoinder to the responsum of a contemporary, R. Samuel ha-Levi.[58] R. Samuel ha-Levi had assumed an exceedingly liberal attitude toward the Karaites, which is summed up by Radbaz's student, R. Jacob Castro, in reference to the disputant in our responsum: "Rabbi Samuel ha-Levi, who wanted to allow intermarrying with Karaites while they were still Karaites."[59]

A significant part of this dispute was related to the fact that the Karaites rejected the Rabbanite calendar. As a result, they did not observe the festivals on the days that the Rabbanites considered to be the true dates for them, so that from the Rabbanite perspective, they were guilty of desecrating the festivals. A passage in the *Sifra* (a work which is part of the corpus of talmudic literature) draws an analogy between desecration of the Sabbath and desecration of the festivals.[60] The Talmud sees the public desecration of the Sabbath as a patent rejection of fundamental Jewish belief, and therefore as tantamount to idolatry.[61] Thus, the Karaites had the status of idolators. R. Samuel ha-Levi, however, argued that the identification of public Sabbath desecration with idolatry and with the total rejection of fundamental Jewish belief was not a unanimous opinion. He showed that this issue was in dispute between two *tanna'im* (that is, early talmudic Rabbis). He admitted that the late talmudic Rabbi, Rabbi Ashi, adopted the view that violation of the Sabbath was indeed the equivalent of idolatry, but R. Samuel ha-Levi then proceeded to neutralize the weight of Rabbi Ashi's position in the context of the present discussion:

---

even though there are some authorities have the opinion that (the technicalities in question) do not prevent (the change of status from non-Jew to slave), those who are stringent, who say that they do prevent (this change of status), are worth relying upon in a situation of emergency, in order to permit this large congregation to enter the congregation of Israel, and to remove from them hate and division" (ibid., 300).

58 R. Samuel ha-Levi is not mentioned by name in our responsum, but Radbaz does mention him by name when he refers to the responsum under discussion in I, 73. See also the reference to him in the next note. He is apparently to be identified with R. Samuel ha-Levi ibn Haqan (also: ibn Hakim) of Egypt. For various references to him in 16th century responsa see the index in Conforti, *Qore ha-Dorot.*

59 *Oholei Ya'aqov*, no. 33.

60 *Sifra*, ed. Weiss, parasha 9, parag. 7, to Lev. 23: 3, where reference to the Sabbath is inserted in a context dealing with the festivals.

61 BT 'Eruvin 69b. The identification of public Sabbath violation with a rejection of belief in God's creation of the world is spelled out by Rashi in the parallel pericope in BT Hullin 5a, s.v. *ella lav hakhi ka-amar.*

> In any case, it is a dispute among *tanna'im*. And grant that one should not add to it, that one who desecrates the festivals should also be (considered) a rejecter of the entire Torah (*mumar le-kol ha-tora kullah*).[62]

That is to say, Rabbi Ashi's view is the accepted law. But given that there is an alternative opinion, Rabbi Ashi's ruling is to be interpreted narrowly, as extending only to desecration of the Sabbath itself, which he mentions specifically, but not to desecration of the festivals. This is exactly the same way in which Radbaz had used "grant that one should not add to it" in the previous example. It is clear, though, that R. Samuel ha-Levi's use of it is not derivative of Radbaz, but independent of it.

Radbaz's response to this is instructive. Referring to the juridical rule that the law follows the later authorities,[63] he responds:

> Since Rabbi Ashi, who is the late authority, concludes this, it is therefore not applicable to say, "Grant that one should not add to it."

He does not challenge the general legitimacy of the principle that the difference between conflicting opinions should be lessened by interpretation as much as possible. He just rejects its application to the present situation. Rabbi Ashi's ruling, according to Radbaz, is absolute, and overrides the residual legitimacy of opposing views that may otherwise affect it.

Incidentally, it should be noted that in this case the dispute which is the subject of "grant that one should not add to it" is talmudic, not a dispute between post-talmudic authorities. Radbaz does not question its applicability on those grounds. In fact, on rare occasion, the application of "grant that one should not add to it" to talmudic disputes in the manner described is attested in Radbaz's responsa.[64]

R. Samuel ha-Levi is an example of a contemporary of Radbaz who, like him but independently of him, uses the phrase, "Grant that one

---

62 II, 796, ed. Warsaw folio 1d, bottom. Radbaz's rejoinder is that Rabbi Ashi's view is determinative, and forestalls the application of "grant that one should not add to it."

63 See Chapter 10.

64 Thus I, 34; IV, 217 (= 1288). Perhaps also I, 549, but I am inclined to interpret that as simply a rhetorical expression with no functional role. (It is not possible to ascribe the lack of the clause in the deed to a scribal oversight (*ta'ut sofer*), simply because it was an oral transaction, and without a deed there is no scribe. This is not a compromise between the two opinions regarding whether or not the omission of the clause is to be considered an oversight.)

should not add to it," in the context of a legal dispute, to modify the interpretation of the dominant opinion. There is also a parallel to Radbaz's formulation of the hermeneutic principle that underlies that use, by another (perhaps older) contemporary, R. David ha-Kohen of Corfu (d. 1530). Radbaz's formulation read:

> We should not introduce a controversy between the authorities in a matter that is not explicit.

R. David ha-Kohen, in a lengthy responsum, dealt with the law of levirate marriage, the law that governs the case of a widow whose husband has died without children.[65] The law requires her to marry her deceased husband's brother, the levir, or alternatively, to be released by him by means of a ceremony called a *halitsa*. Without a *halitsa*, she would not be free to remarry. Were the levir to marry her, he would inherit his deceased brother's estate, to the exclusion of his surviving brothers, the other heirs. The Talmud leaves unresolved whether it is more meritorious in our times to perform the religious obligation (*mitsva*) of levirate marriage, or the religious obligation of *halitsa* (i.e., to release her), since in our times people no longer "intend it (levirate marriage) for the purpose of fulfilling a religious obligation (*le-shem mitsva*)."[66] Later rabbis differed over this issue, the fault line generally being between the Ashkenazic authorities, who ruled that "the religious obligation of *halitsa*" was preferable, and the Sephardic authorities, who ruled that "the religious obligation of levirate marriage" was preferable.[67] R. David ha-Kohen was from the Romaniot community (that is, the indigenous Balkan Jewish community), and had studied under Ashkenazic tutelage in Italy. Writing from the perspective of the school that favors *halitsa*, he analyzed the attitude of the law toward a levir who nevertheless chose levirate marriage over *halitsa*.

The Talmud commentator Rashi, though he was a member of the school that preferred *halitsa* to levirate marriage, nevertheless held the opinion that if both parties so desired, levirate marriage was permitted. However, if the wife had clear grounds for objection (*amera devarim nikkarim*, literally: "stated recognizable things"), and insisted on *halitsa*, then the recalcitrant husband may be tricked into releasing her with false promise of payment. Failing that, he may be physically compelled to comply. The Tosafot school, followed by subsequent influential authorities as documented by R. David ha-Kohen, held that

---

65 Radakh, *Responsa*, *Bayit* 2.

66 BT Yevamot 39b.

67 See Katz, "Levirate Marriage."

actual levirate marriage is not an option, and even if they both desired it, attempts are made to induce the levir to release her.[68]

R. David ha-Kohen endeavored to deduce Rashi's position in a case in which the widow does not produce "clear grounds," but simply objects to the marriage. He argued as follows. "All the great authorities," aside from Rashi, who represent the school that *halitsa* takes precedence, clearly hold the opinion that if she demands *halitsa*, even without stating objective grounds, then the recalcitrant levir is induced (at least without physical compulsion—there is disagreement on this point) to release her. Rashi, it is true, allowed levirate marriage to take place if they both desired it, "even if it is not known to us that their intention is for the purpose of fulfilling a religious obligation." But:

> Grant that one should not add to it. For only in this case (of their both being in agreement—SM) did he differ with them, but not if she demands a *halitsa*. For after all, he too is of the opinion, as are they, that the religious obligation of *halitsa* takes precedence. *For we must equalize their opinions regarding whatever it is that they do not differ on explicitly.* (Emphasis mine—SM)[69]

Apparently, the principle that the difference between opposing views should be narrowed through interpretation was in the air, as was the reference to the application of this principle by means of the aphorism, "Grant that one should not add to it." Indeed, the use of "grant that one should not add to it" in this way can be traced further back. However, its occurrence is very rare. Aside from Radbaz, I have not located any example from any author in the sixteenth century except for the two cited above, and only three prior to the sixteenth century,[70] one by R. Isaac bar Sheshet (14th and early 15th centuries), and the other two by R. Israel Isserlein (15th century).[71] It was

---

68 Rashi and Tosafot, BT Yevamot 39b, both s.v. *amar rav ein kofin*.

69 Radakh, *Responsa*, *Bayit* 2, *Heder* 4.

70 Based on a study of the results of a search of the database of the Bar Ilan Responsa Project.

71 R. Isaac bar Sheshet, *Responsa*, no. 302. Isserlein, *Terumat ha-Deshen*, no. 12, and Isserlein, *Pesaqim u-Ketavim*, no. 168. (In *Terumat ha-Deshen* no. 12, the word *qasheh,* in the phrase *qasheh listor divreihem* in the current editions, is abbreviated in the first edition: *q'*, and should apparently be completed: *qal*. *Pesaqim u-Ketavim* 168 appears to require the emendation of *de-lo talei be-pelugta de-ravevata* to *de-talei be-pelugta de-ravevata*.) There is a superficial resemblance to this use of "grant that one should not add to it" by Rabbenu Nissim, *Responsa*, no. 22, p. 92, and by Tsemah b.

apparently Radbaz who first used this approach on a more widespread basis.

[133] The use of "grant that one should not add to it," to mediate between conflicting opinions, bears a resemblance to Radbaz's use of the "middle way." The following is an instance in which the two are virtually identical.

According to the Book of Deuteronomy, all debts are cancelled on the sabbatical year.[72] As explained in Case [87], the Talmud tells us that Hillel the Elder, upon observing that people were loath to lend money for fear of the debt's cancellation, established a legal fiction, called a *prosbul*, which allowed for the collection of debts after the sabbatical year.[73] The *prosbul* took the form of a document, which the lender had to have secured in advance of the sabbatical year. Radbaz is asked for his opinion regarding one who claims, "I had a *prosbul*, but I lost it."[74] The questioner acknowledges that "most of the authorities" decide that the lender's word is accepted on this, and he is not made to take an oath to substantiate his claim. The question is whether the borrower can insist on the pronouncement of "a *h̲erem* on anyone who may be lying." A *h̲erem* is a ban, and it was believed to have not only social consequences but divine consequences as well. This type of *h̲erem* was known as an "unspecified *h̲erem*" (*h̲erem setam*). It had no social consequences, of course, but the guilty party knew that he was in violation, and would be accountable in the eyes of God.

Radbaz begins with the obvious:

> At first sight, it would seem that we pronounce a *h̲erem*. For, since we do not subject him to an oath, what have we lost? If he is pleading the truth, the *h̲erem* would not afflict him, and if he is pleading a falsehood, let him fend for himself!

He informs us that Maimonides, in an Arabic responsum, had indeed ruled this way in an analogous situation, and for the same reason,[75] and though the present situation is not identical, the same law should apply here, too. He then adds:

Solomon Duran, *Yakhin u-Boaz*, I, 133, p. 383. But in both cases, these do not seem to be true examples of this usage.

72 Deuteronomy 15:1–2. "At the end of seven years," which is identified with the "sabbatical year" of Leviticus 25:4.

73 BT Gittin 36a.

74 I, 94.

75 I have not located this responsum in ed. Blau of Maimonides' responsa.

> And grant that one should not add to the controversy, for there is one (or perhaps understand: there are those[76]—SM) who ruled that he is put to an oath.

This is identical to a "middle way" argument. The middle way between the view that he is free of an oath, and the view that he is subjected to an oath, is the view that he is free of an oath but subjected to an unspecified *ḥerem*. A minority (and hence rejected) opinion is cited, in order to frame the accepted opinion as the median stance.

Parenthetically, it can be noted that this example of "grant that one should not add to it," though it supports Radbaz's ruling on the law in theory, is at odds with his ruling in practice. Radbaz is concerned with the implications of relieving the plaintiff of an oath, yet binding him by an "unspecified *ḥerem*," for he fears that he would not take it seriously. Since a plaintiff who lacked a *prosbul* in hand might be ignorant of his rights under the law, it was the practice of the court to suggest to him: "Perhaps you had a *prosbul*, and it was lost?" Radbaz fears that this procedure might lead the plaintiff to think that a defense, handed to him so easily by the court itself, could surely be adopted with impunity. He would thus be guilty of incurring the *ḥerem*. Radbaz therefore rules that in practice the "unspecified *ḥerem*" be waived, though if the defendant takes the initiative and utters on his own, "May anyone who is lying be under *ḥerem*," then *ex post facto* it would be binding.

(*d*) *Conclusions*

The phrase, "Grant that one should not add to it," conveys the meaning that a specific law should be construed narrowly. Although the phrase originated in the Talmud, and was used occasionally in earlier rabbinic literature, Radbaz's widespread use of it implies its association with his specific literary style. In a large percent of the cases, Radbaz uses it as a rhetorical flourish, reflecting the conclusion he had reached on substantive grounds, that the law does not apply to the case at hand. However, there are a number of instances in which the phrase, "Grant that one should not add to it," plays a functional role in Radbaz's responsa. In these cases, the narrow construction flows from a deliberate decision on the part of Radbaz to choose that path of interpretation. An examination of those instances leads to the conclusion that they fall into two categories.

---

76 *de-ikka man de-pasaq*

One group consists of laws to which Radbaz had an objection. He did not feel at liberty to ignore the law, but limited its application by interpreting it narrowly: "Grant that one should not add to it." In most of these cases, the objection was of a moral nature. In one instance, the objection stemmed from Radbaz's own sense that the codified law was wrong, because it was at odds with a more general principle of the law that Radbaz upheld. Radbaz's juridical stance in these cases is indicative of his general broad approach to the law, in which the law is subservient to the requirements of justice, equity and rationality. This is an approach that has been demonstrated in Part One of this study.

The second group of cases in which a narrow interpretation is deliberately and explicitly applied are those in which Radbaz, faced with controversy among the authorities, attempts to harmonize, or at least to narrow the gap, between the accepted opinion and the one which has been rejected. Underlying this approach is a conception of the law that allows for the legitimacy of conflicting opinions, so that the rejected view can still play a role in the way the operative law is applied. This conception has already been noted in the rhetoric underlying Radbaz's "middle way."

9. Qim Li

Chapter 7, "The Place of the Master," dealt with a principle of adjudication which Radbaz faced as a "given" in Egypt, and traced the way and the extent to which that principle was assimilated by him. "*Qim li*," the subject of the present chapter, is an example of another such principle of adjudication which Radbaz faced as a "given." It was touched upon in Chapter 7 because of its relationship to "the place of the Master." In this chapter I will explore its manifestation in Radbaz's responsa more systematically.

I have dealt with the subject of *qim li* in a work on the methodology of R. Joseph ibn Lev of Constantinople, a contemporary of Radbaz.[1] My remarks on the subject there can serve to introduce it here, and I will cite them in the following two paragraphs.

> The issue has its genesis in the well-known principle that the burden of proof is on the plaintiff. A successful suit of a plaintiff in a civil case is expressed in the Talmud in terms of "extracting money" from the defendant, and his unsuccessful suit is expressed as "establishing it" in the defendant's ownership. It is axiomatic that the proof the plaintiff must bring to "extract money" must produce certainty in the mind of the court: "We do not extract money on the basis of uncertainty."

---

1 Morell, *Precedent and Judicial Discretion*.

> Among Ibn Lev's contemporaries in Turkey, we find the widespread use of a legal argument known as *qim li*.[2] The literal meaning of the term is, "I hold (the opinion)," and is an abbreviation of: "I hold the opinion of rabbi So-and-so, whose view would support my case." *Qim li* is thus an argument put forward by (or, more accurately, in the name of) a defendant in a civil suit, who enjoys the advantage of the fact that the burden of proof is on his antagonist. It rests on the assumption that contemporary halakhic authorities are inherently the inferiors of their predecessors, and are therefore not competent to render an ultimate resolution to a controversy that has been left unresolved by earlier generations.[3] True, there are rules for deciding the law in cases of controversy, and on a practical level that determination is generally binding. But on a theoretical level, such a determination does not constitute an absolute certainty that the law is indeed so. Since "we do not extract money on the basis of uncertainty," and since the plaintiff is incapable of proving with certainty that the law is not as the defendant holds, he cannot "extract money" from him, and loses his case. The claim of *qim li* thus strives to override the conventional rules for deciding the law in cases of controversy. In their reluctance to find for a plaintiff on the basis of an uncertain law, the proponents of *qim li* were similar to the jurists of previous periods. They differed from them, however, in automatically extending the concept of "uncertainty" to include every legal controversy."[4]

The legal mentality which underlies this approach to jurisprudence stems from a deep sense of inadequacy in relation to the great rabbinic authorities of the past, an attitude known as *yir'at hora'a* (literally, the fear of making halakhic decisions). This was an attitude that typified, more than any other generation, the Ashkenazic rabbis of the fifteenth century. Indeed, it has been shown that the origins of the *qim li* argument, in its classical form as outlined above, first appeared in the

2 On *qim li*, see Ben-Menahem,"Origins of Kim Li"; "Jurisprudential Analysis"; "Doubt, Choice and Conviction."

3 Although *qim li* is in theory an argument put forward by the defendant, it was generally, if not universally, assumed by the judge, thus evolving into a jurisprudential rule. See Ben-Menahem, "Doubt, Choice and Conviction," 17, specifically the third of his "three possible reactions."

4 Morell, *Precedent and Judicial Discretion*, 119f, slightly modified. Ben-Menahem points out, as I did in my chapter in *Precedent and Judicial Discretion*, that it is the judge who in fact decides when to utilize *qim li*, so that actually not "every legal controversy" is subject to it. See "Doubt, Choice and Conviction," 17.

Terumat ha-Deshen of R. Israel Isserlein (Austria, 15th century). Earlier occurrences are found only in instances in which the respondent had a real doubt about the law.[5]

In the 16th century, the *qim li* argument, so foreign to earlier Sephardic legal traditions, nevertheless infiltrated the judicial methodology of the Sephardic rabbis in the Ottoman diaspora.[6] It was not necessarily accompanied, however, by the mentality of *yir'at hora'a* which gave it birth.[7] Radbaz, as can be seen by everything we have learned about him so far, was certainly far removed from this way of thinking. Nevertheless, the *qim li* argument had become part of the legal discourse of his period.

[134] Radbaz does not reject the use of *qim li* outright, but at the same time he does not allow it to really affect his decisions. I have identified only one apparent exception, to be discussed below, in which he allows *qim li* to affect his preferred decision in actual practice.[8] In all other cases in which *qim li* is considered positively, he at most integrates it into his argument as an auxiliary support for a position that he adopts on other grounds.[9]

Thus, for instance, in a case dealing with the liability of an active partner, who manages a business with funds provided entirely by a silent partner. The basic law in the Talmud is formulated as follows:

---

5 Ben-Menahem, "Doubt, Choice and Conviction," Section ii (18–31); on Isserlein specifically, 20–23.

6 The main channel of influence seems to be the responsa of R. Joseph Colon, a French rabbi resident in Northern Italy (d. 1480). R. Samuel de Medina tells us that *qim li* "was hardly disseminated until the responsa of Colon were disseminated." *Responsa*, *Hoshen Mishpat*, no. 61.

7 See Morell, *Precedent and Judicial Discretion*, 120f. and accompanying notes.

8 Discussed below, Case [139]. See also I, 433, where, citing *qim li*, he is hesitant to rule with Maimonides against the defendant in opposition to Hai Gaon, whose special authority he lauds in extraordinary terms; quoted above, Case [124]. But it is not so clear there that Radbaz's own inclination, on the substance of the matter, would be to favor Maimonides' ruling over that of Hai Gaon.

9 In addition to the responsa discussed below, examples include: I, 177; II, 627; III, 551 (= 981); IV, 204 (= 1275); VI, 2340 (duplicated in VII, 62, the first so numbered). In VI, 2298, he allows *qim li* in accordance with Alfasi and Maimonides, even outside of "the place of the Master," against the hypothetical possibility that many authorities are discovered to have disagreed with them.

"Half (of the assets that are entrusted to the active partner) is a loan, and half is a bailment."[10] What this means is that half of both the profit and the risk belongs to the active partner (the "loan" half), and the other half (the "bailment" half) belongs to the silent partner. With regard to the "bailment" half, there is agreement that the active partner would nevertheless be liable for negligence. There is a controversy, though, between Maimonides and Rabad, as to whether the active partner would be liable for the "bailment" half in case of theft and loss, when these are not a result of gross negligence.[11] Maimonides rules that he is not liable, and Rabad rules that he is. An early commentator on Maimonides' code, the author of *Migdal 'Oz*, raises a series of difficulties with Rabad's position. He suggests that the latter's comment is not authentic, and that Rabad never meant to differ with Maimonides on this point. Rather, he says, it is most likely a gloss by a beginning student that entered the text: "Certainly, one of the beginners wrote it." Radbaz, after citing *Migdal 'Oz* with approval, continues as follows:

> Even if you say that he does differ with him (i.e., Rabad with Maimonides), we have nothing (that we rely on) other than the words of Maimonides, for such is the practice in the entire country. Even if those who differed with him were many, they (i.e., the Jews of this land) have already accepted him (as the sole authority) governing them. Certainly when it comes to monetary matters, we would not exact money contrary to his opinion. Furthermore, he (i.e., the active partner) can say, "I hold an opinion (*qim li*) like So-and-so."[12]

Radbaz has raised a series of arguments in support of the active partner. First, Rabad's comment has been shown to be of questionable authenticity. Second, even if one were to admit its authenticity, we would in any case rule in accordance with Maimonides, because his authority has been accepted in this land. Third, even if a case might be made for occasionally ruling against Maimonides, that may be so in other areas of Jewish law; but in a civil suit, where the plaintiff bears the burden of proof, surely he cannot prove that the law supports his position, against the opinion of Maimonides. Finally, even if this were not Maimonides, but some other authority whose opinion supported the defendant, the defendant can put forth a plea of *qim li*: "I hold like So-

10 BT Bava Metsi'a 104b.

11 *MT*, Acquisition, Laws of Agents and Partners, chap. 6, parag. 2, and Rabad ad loc.

12 II, 638.

and-so," leaving it to the plaintiff to prove that the law is otherwise. Clearly, the *qim li* argument here is auxiliary to an already proven case.

[135] In a particularly interesting example, we find Radbaz using *qim li* in support of a ruling that he would normally reject, but which, in the context of the responsum, contributes to the conclusion he reaches for other reasons entirely.[13]

The question has to do with a widow's rights to her *ketubba*, the sum which her husband or his estate is contractually bound to pay her at the time of the termination of the marriage. There is a lien on all the husband's property toward payment of this debt, so that if insufficient assets were left in the estate, the widow could collect her debt from real property that he had sold during the course of the marriage.[14] A widow has the right to live off the estate and to delay the collection of her *ketubba* until such time as she makes plans to remarry.[15] In any case, it appears that in this case the widow did not seek the payment of her *ketubba* immediately. The question is as follows:

> You asked for my opinion regarding Reuben, who sold a house to Simeon, and (subsequently) died. Simeon went and sold the house to a non-Jew.[16] When the woman came to collect her *ketubba*, there were not (sufficient) assets. She had the legal right to seize the house (from the purchaser), except that Simeon had sold it to a non-Jew. Is Simeon obligated to redeem the house from the non-Jew, allowing the woman to seize it in payment of her *ketubba* at Simeon's expense, or not?

Radbaz begins by reviewing the law regarding the liability of one who causes potential loss to the holder of a lien by injuring his ability to seize the property. The Talmud discusses this matter. It refers to the situation as "one who damages his neighbor's lien." There is a controversy regarding the issue, which is based on the example of one who had mortgaged his slave as surety for a debt, and then freed him.[17] Maimonides had ruled that the slave's owner is liable, the view attributed by the Talmud to R. Simeon ben Gamliel.[18] Rabad

13 I, 134.

14 *MT*, Women, Laws of Marriage, chap. 16, parag. 10.

15 Ibid., chap. 18, parag. 1. Case [126] above.

16 The sequence seems to imply that he sold it after Reuben's death, but the implication may have been unintentional. The responsum does not take note of that point, only of the fact that he sold it before the woman sought payment.

17 BT Gittin 41a.

18 *MT*, Torts, Laws of Wounding and Damaging, chap. 7, parag. 11.

commented that "the Master," by whom Rabad usually means Alfasi, had not ruled that way. The classic commentary on Maimonides' code, *Maggid Mishneh*, questions whether Rabad really meant Alfasi when he wrote "the Master" in this case, since the ruling attributed by Rabad to "the Master" is not found in Alfasi's compendium, and in fact some editions of the compendium actually state that the law is in accordance with R. Simeon ben Gamliel![19] Radbaz, however, suggests that Rabad might have been referring to a responsum by Alfasi that has been lost.[20] Thus, says Radbaz,

> In any case, it is a controversy among the authorities, and he (Simeon, the defendant) can say: "I hold an opinion (*qim li*) in accordance with Alfasi according to the testimony of Rabad," and she cannot exact it from him.

At this point, one might think that Radbaz is actually reaching a conclusion on the basis of *qim li*. Furthermore, this appears to be an astounding example of the power of the *qim li* argument. First of all, Rabad's entire comment is questionable, given the evidence from Alfasi's compendium. Radbaz goes out of his way to suggest, without any evidence, that Rabad based himself on an unknown responsum! Second, Radbaz would normally rule in accordance with Maimonides, not with Rabad, except when there were strong reasons to do so. It would seem that Radbaz is allowing *qim li* to lead him to a conclusion he would otherwise reject!

But as we read further, it turns out that this is far from the case. Radbaz continues:

> But if you study it carefully, you will find that in the case at hand, everyone would agree that he is not liable. For this is not an example of "one who damages his neighbor's lien."

That is, even ruling like Maimonides, that "one who damages his neighbor's lien" is liable, Simeon would still not be liable.

The case is not so easy to make. Radbaz first draws a distinction between "damaging" a lien which is in one's own possession, as is the case with Simeon, who owned the house which constituted the lien, and "damaging" a lien which is in someone else's possession. He then faces the obvious objection, that the classic case in the Talmud consists of one who freed his own slave, who was also in his possession. Radbaz suggests an original distinction, between an act done in malice, as indicated by the lack of benefit for the tortfeasor, as is the case with the

---

19 Thus in the current printed editions of Alfasi, ed. Romm, Gittin, chap. 4, no. 471.

20 See a similar suggestion by Radbaz in I, 433.

manumission of the slave, and an act done for benefit and personal need, as is the case with Simeon, who sold a house which was in his possession before it became subject to litigation, for financial need.[21] He proceeds with another argument for his conclusion that Simeon is not liable, based on the notion that he was not at fault for selling the house.

One could ask why Radbaz is so insistent that Simeon is not at fault. After all, there was a lien on the house, which he knew about, and he knew that selling it to a non-Jew removed it from recovery by the holder of the lien, in this case the wife. I suggest that this type of lien is different from others because of its universality. Everyone who buys a house buys one that is under a lien to the vendor's wife in case she is eventually widowed or divorced. To argue in favor of the widow would mean that no purchaser of real property could ever own it outright, as long as the vendor's marriage remained intact. Perhaps it is to assure the integrity of commerce in real estate that Radbaz goes out of his way to argue in favor of Simeon. In any case, it becomes clear that the *qim li* argument, though it goes against what must have been his opinion on the issue of "one who damages his neighbor's lien," works in favor of his ultimate conclusion in the case at hand.

[136] There is another example of Radbaz's employment of *qim li* this way, that is, to overrule his own position on a specific point of law, but in support of his broader goal. In this instance *qim li* is extended beyond its natural frame of reference, which is limited to civil suits.

The subject in question is the law governing oaths, specifically, an oath to do something or not to do something. The Talmud provides a mechanism for release from ill-considered oaths by a rabbinic court, but there are certain restrictions on its use. Two of these restrictions concern us here. One applies to an oath undertaken in the context of insuring the integrity of a financial commitment. Release from such an oath results in a harm to the interests of the other party, and therefore one may not be unilaterally released from it. In fact, in post-talmudic times such oaths were standard practice in business contracts, and an integral part of the enforcement procedure. The other restriction is similar, but without the financial implications. It applies to an oath undertaken at the personal request of another party, for the latter's

21 It is not clear whether Radbaz is assuming that there must have been such a need, or whether he is privy to details that he does not describe in the formulation of the question. For the latter possibility, see Chapter 1, n. 79.

benefit. Such an oath can be released only in the presence of the involved party, which implies the latter's consent.[22] There was a controversy, though, among the authorities, on the status of such an oath if the restriction was violated, and the oath released in spite of it. Some ruled that the release was invalid, and the oath remained binding. Others ruled that the restriction on release only applied *a priori*, but *ex post facto* the release remained in force, and the oath was no longer binding.[23]

This is the question that Radbaz was asked:

> You asked about "Simeon," whose wife died, and whose mother-in-law wanted to put a certain garment (of hers) on top of the shrouds. Simeon saved the garment from her by taking an oath that he will never sell it in this land, nor will he give it to another wife whom he may marry. Simeon subsequently married another wife, and gave her the garment. When people said to him, "How did you violate your oath?" he answered, "I have already requested a release and it was granted to me." You asked whether Simeon is culpable for having violated his oath.[24]

Radbaz feels strongly that Simeon is to be commended for preventing the waste of an article of value. Though he does not cite it, his position is undoubtedly informed by the prohibition of wasting useful things, a prohibition generalized from Deuteronomy 20:19, which forbids the cutting down of fruitbearing trees during a siege.[25] This is a prohibition known as, "Thou shalt not destroy." Radbaz begins:

> Answer. Simeon did well to save the garment from his mother-in-law, so that he not add more worms to the dead.

This is not a case, he says, of an oath undertaken to ensure the integrity of a financial commitment. Such a restriction, says Radbaz, does indeed apply *ex post facto*, and remains in force even if one is technically "released" from it; "for if you do not rule this way, no business

---

22 BT Nedarim 65a. The Talmud talks about a *neder* (usually translated "vow"), which is technically different from a *shevu'a* (usually translated "oath"). But Radbaz's responsum involves a *shevu'a*, and Radbaz applies the same rules to it. I therefore use the term "oath" throughout this discussion.

23 The controversy is discussed in the commentary of Rabbenu Nissim to Nedarim ad loc., s.v. *tanya ha-mudar hana'a me-havero*.

24 VI, 2255.

25 *MT*, Judges, Laws of Kings and Wars, chap. 6, parag. 10.

arrangement would be enforceable by means of an oath."[26] In this case, however, the oath was undertaken only to placate the mother-in-law. However, this brings Radbaz to the second restriction. After all, Simeon certainly did undertake the oath at the request of his mother-in-law and for her psychological benefit. But on this issue, says Radbaz:

> The commentators were divided. There are those who ruled that if they (the members of the court) released him, he is not (in fact) released. And there are those who ruled that if they released him, he is released *ex post facto*. Even though my opinion is that that if they released him he is not released, Simeon can still plead, "I hold an opinion (*qim li*) like those who say that if they released him he is released."

And Radbaz concludes:

> Therefore, I have covered all aspects of the matter, and I do not see that Simeon is culpable at all.

As in the previous example, Radbaz utilizes *qim li* against the legal ruling that he himself upholds. Radbaz himself rules that a release from an oath, which is improper because the oath was undertaken for the benefit of another party, is not only improper but invalid. However, he allows Simeon to use *qim li* to plead the opposite position, because he supports the broader goal of "thou shalt not destroy."

Qim li has its theoretical underpinnings in the necessity of the plaintiff to bear the burden of proof, coupled with the unwillingness of rabbinic decisors to take a stand *de jure* when faced with an unresolved controversy among earlier authorities. Under this set of conditions, the defendant bases his claim on the rejected opinion—rejected, that is, only *de facto*. The preceding case fits the *qim li* pattern only by analogy. Simeon is defending his honor, rather than his financial assets, against public approbation. This is an extension of the use of *qim li*, and bears witness to its rhetorical, rather than its functional application.[27]

[137] Another particularly blatant example of the rhetorical extension of *qim li* beyond its theoretical limits, which are as a defense against a plaintiff in a civil suit, occurs in a responsum that has been discussed above in another connection.[28] The issue involves the prohibition of interest. The biblical prohibition of interest was defined

26 For this type of rationale in deciding law, see Chapter 4, "Considerations of Public Policy."

27 It may be, though, that public approbation entailed some concrete form of sanction. In that case it would not be entirely rhetorical.

28 IV, 278 (= 1349). Case [59].

very narrowly by the Talmud. But a much wider range of commercial activity, permitted by the law of the Torah, was considered to be prohibited by the authority of the Rabbis. Radbaz was asked about a situation in which an attempt was made to evade the rabbinic prohibition by the having the debtor taking an oath, valid according to the law of the Torah, to pay such interest. Thus he would be bound by the law of the Torah to fulfill his vow. Does this biblical obligation in fact supersede a prohibition that is, after all, prohibited only by the Rabbis, but permissible by the law of the Torah? Radbaz cites a difference of opinion in this regard. Rashba's opinion was that the oath takes precedence, even if it requires the performance of a positive act that the Rabbis prohibited. Ritba, on the other hand, ruled that the rabbinic prohibition takes precedence, even though the biblically binding oath was violated. For reasons of public policy, Radbaz feels strongly that the vow should be violated and the rabbinic prohibition maintained. In support of this position, Radbaz presents the following argument:

> Even according to the opinion of Rashba, who holds the view that an oath is valid in nullifying rabbinic prohibitions even when (the oath) involves active performance (of a rabbinically prohibited act), he can say, "I hold an opinion (*qim li*) like Ritba...."[29]

In the usual formulation, "He can say: 'I hold an opinion like So-and-so,'" "he" refers to the defendant. Here, the borrower is not being cast as a defendant; the question revolves around the permissibility of the act of paying interest itself. In fact, Radbaz extends his discussion to include vows to perform any rabbinically prohibited act, even of a purely ritual nature. For instance, he brings as an example, *inter alia*, an oath to drink non-Jewish wine that is prohibited only by the authority of the Rabbis (*setam yeinam*). In this context, the entire use of *qim li*, understood literally, makes little sense. Radbaz uses *qim li* here as a stereotyped expression for its rhetorical effect, without regard for the logic of the argument.

[138] In another responsum in which *qim li* appears to play a critical role in the decision, it is a decision that clearly reflects Radbaz's preferences. He discusses the issue of whether a contract with a private teacher, engaged to teach Torah to one's son, can be terminated merely

29 The passage continues: "for he is a later authority, and saw the words of Rashba." This rationale for resolving a controversy is the subject of Chap. 10.

by mutual oral consent, or whether such termination requires legal formality.[30] The basic rule regarding a laborer is that he may quit work whenever he wants:

> A laborer may change his mind (about working) even in the middle of the day.... For it says, "For it is to me that the Israelites are slaves (*'avadim*—KJ; NJPS *et al.*: servants)" (Lev. 25:55)—and not the slaves of slaves![31]

It would seem that a teacher fits into this category. And if he has the right to quit unilaterally at any point, there is no question that he can quit with mutual oral consent.

However, Radbaz cites a responsum by R. Meir of Rothenburg (Germany, 13th century) which deals directly with this issue.[32] R. Meir, assumedly with the interests of maximizing the learning and knowledge of Torah, did not view a teacher of Torah in the same category as a standard laborer. He cannot, according to R. Meir, quit unilaterally, nor is mutual oral consent, without legal formality, sufficient to terminate his contract. R. Meir cites two reasons for this. The first of these is very weak. On the basis of a forced reading of a passage in the Talmud, R. Meir draws an analogy between a laborer and a Hebrew slave, who needs a formal manumission to be free of his master.[33] The second reason is that the teacher's employer, the student's father, may indeed be able to forgo, without any formality, an obligation which the teacher had to him, but here there is also an obligation to the son, who, being a minor, is not legally capable of forgoing an obligation. In insisting on the special obligation of a teacher of Torah to persist in his labor, R. Meir follows in the footsteps of earlier Ashkenazic opinion. R. Meir's student, who reports this responsum, tells us that it was in accordance with[34] Rabbenu Joel and his son Rabiah, eminent authorities two and

---

30 I, 333. The question that was asked is broader, namely, whether in general a contractual obligation can be terminated this way. Radbaz breaks it down into different situations.

31 BT Bava Metsi'a 10a.

32 Incorporated among a series of R. Meir's responsa in Rashba, *Responsa*, I, 873. The question concerns an oral termination of contract by mutual consent, after which the employer changed his mind.

33 See BT Bava Metsi'a 12b. The Mishnah states that a Hebrew slave is entitled to keep his own findings. The Talmud asks why he should be more privileged than a laborer who is hired for general, undefined tasks, whose findings revert to his employer.

34 The text in Rashba, *Responsa*, I, 873, reads: *u-teshuva zo heshiv lifnei rabbenu yoel ve-rabbenu avi ha-'ezri.* The translation assumes the emendation of *lifnei* to *lefi*, see ed. Mekhon Yerushalayim, n. 10. Rabiah

three generations earlier. These authorities, R. Meir's student tells us, held that a teacher is in the category of a laborer who is hired to work with perishables that require immediate attention. Such a laborer is not similar to an ordinary laborer. Unlike the latter, he is not permitted to quit at will.[35]

Radbaz dismisses the first argument out of hand. He points out that one cannot maintain an analogy between a Hebrew slave and a laborer under contract, because the former requires formal manumission for a change in his legal status, whereas the latter obviously does not. Radbaz suggests that this argument is merely rhetorical, and that R. Meir himself did not base himself on it, but relied for his conclusion on the second argument, that the student, as a minor, cannot forgo an obligation due him. That too is not to Radbaz's liking: "With regard to this (second) reason, too, one can raise objections."[36] Nevertheless, Radbaz asserts that he would be unwilling to rule against R. Meir's precedent.[37]

However, Radbaz points out, this entire line of approach is a matter of controversy:

> All this, though, is according to those who hold the opinion that a teacher is not similar to a(n ordinary) laborer. But according to those who hold the opinion that he is similar to a laborer, he can quit even without any forgoing (of obligation by the employer).

Radbaz is harking back here to the opinion of Rabbenu Joel and his son Rabiah.[38] It was their opinion that a teacher is in a different category than an ordinary laborer, and it is this fundamental position which informs R. Meir's responsum. Radbaz infers that their opinion stands in contrast to another, namely, that a teacher is no different from any ordinary laborer. And accordingly, since a teacher is in possession of his own person, he can advance the same defense as one who is in possession of property:

> He can say, "I hold (*qim li*) like the other great authorities," and we do not compel him (to continue working).

---

died when R. Meir was young, though he did learn from him personally. But his father, Rabbenu Joel, could not have been alive.

35 *MT*, Civil Laws, Laws of Hiring, chap. 9, parag. 10.

36 *ve-gam ha-rav ha-nizkar nir'eh she-lo samakh ella 'al ha-ta'am ha-sheni ve-gam ba-ta'am ha-zeh yesh le-gamgem*

37 *ella she-kevar hora zaqen*

38 This is obviously the case, though he does not cite this addendum to R. Meir's responsa.

Radbaz asserts that he would in fact honor R. Meir's precedent ruling and abide by it, even though he himself does not agree with it. He would rule against the teacher's privilege to break his contract. He would do so in spite of the fact that he is not convinced by R. Meir's reasoning. However, in the case at hand, he utilizes *qim li* to arrive at a ruling that is more to his liking, allowing the teacher the right to leave.

[139] I have seen only one instance in which Radbaz modifies his true position on the basis of *qim li*.[39] It is a responsum discussed above in Chapter 7, Case [125]. The question regarded a man who wanted to marry a second wife, and needed his wife's permission. She would agree only after he consented to increase her *ketubba* payments. He did so after making a disclaimer before witnesses that he was doing so under compulsion, and now, after the second marriage, was challenging his agreement. Without repeating the details here, suffice it to say that the single view that would uphold the husband's position was that of Rabbenu Nissim, against Rashba and others. Radbaz's own opinion is that "it is upon Rashba that one should rely," and the condition is binding.[40] Yet, he allows that a defendant may plead, "I hold an opinion (*qim li*) like Rabbenu Nissim." As a result, Radbaz urges arbitration as a first step, and only if the defendant does not budge, does Radbaz admit that, ultimately, he may plead *qim li*. This is a particularly powerful example, because Rabbenu Nissim's is a lone opinion. Radbaz takes note of this. In urging arbitration, he says:

> (I say this) even though in my opinion one cannot plead: "I hold an opinion like So-and-so," if "So-and-so" is a single authority against the majority.... (But) it is nevertheless possible that the defendant will find other authorities who think as does Rabbenu Nissim, and will be able to plead, "I hold the opinion of these authorities." And then you will not be able to exact (money) from him.

So it is the fear of a (merely possible!) plea of *qim li* which induces Radbaz to urge the judges to negotiate a settlement.

Nevertheless, this does not mean that Radbaz himself endorsed the use of *qim li*. *Qim li* had infiltrated the judicial methodology of the courts, whether it was to Radbaz's liking or not. He therefore offers a suggestion, rather than an order, to judges, designed to avoid the

---

39 I, 404. See also IV, 54 (= 1126) 36, to which Radbaz refers for the detailed argumentation supporting his opinion.

40 IV, 54 (= 1126), ed. Warsaw, 7d.

possibility of a plea of *qim li*: "It is proper (*ra'ui*) for the judge to negotiate a compromise."

In fact, Radbaz himself was uneasy about the use of *qim li*. In a number of responsa, Radbaz narrows the range of controversies to which *qim li* can be applied. One cannot plead, "I hold an opinion like So-and-so," when So-and-so's opinion controverts the opinion of "those authorities according to whom it is our custom to rule";[41] or when it conflicts with Maimonides in "the place of the Master,"[42] or with *Maggid Mishneh*'s interpretation of Maimonides (even though Radbaz himself has doubts about its correctness);[43] or when it is customary in a given locality to rule in accordance with a certain authority, and So-and-so's opinion is different;[44] or when ruling like So-and-so would violate the rule that the law is like the later authorities.[45]

[140] These reservations are expressed in a concentrated fashion in a responsum which bears directly on the issue of *qim li*.[46] Radbaz was asked whether the same individual may, in one case, plead, "I hold like Rabbi X," and then, in another case, when it is to his advantage to do so, plead, "I hold like Rabbi Y," who differs with Rabbi X. Radbaz

---

41 I, 405.

42 I, 281. I, 547: "It is the place of the Master, and for this reason I am wont to say that we "extract" it from him (i.e., the defendant), and he (the defendant) cannot say, 'I hold an opinion (*qim li*) like these later authorities'. For since it is the place of the Master, it is as if they accepted him (Maimonides) upon themselves." The latter sentence occurs virtually verbatim in I, 281.

43 I, 355. After stating his own hesitations, and suggesting a possible explanation for *Maggid Mishneh*'s interpretation, Radbaz writes: "In any case, since the author of *Maggid Mishneh*, who was expert in the words of Maimonides, says that the opinion of Maimonides was (such and such), we heed him," and disallow a plea of *qim li* based on another interpretation (Radbaz's own!) of Maimonides.

44 IV, 116 (= 1187). Cited by Ben-Menahem, "Doubt, Choice and Conviction," 30.

45 I, 148. This is coupled with the argument that the opposing opinion is against Maimonides in "the place of the Master." See also I, 539, where he rejects *qim li* against Alfasi, because "Alfasi saw all the responsa of the Geonim, this one included, and differed with it." On the subject of ruling like the later authorities, see Chapter 10.

46 II, 825. Cited by Ben-Menahem, "Doubt, Choice and Conviction," 16 and 22.

refers to a responsum of R. Israel Isserlein, who had ruled that one can adopt contrary positions at different times for the purpose of *qim li*.[47] He then presents a list of limitations which, he says, apply in general to the use of *qim li*:

> In any case, you should know that many conditions apply to this plea. First, it cannot be used if the opposing view represents (the law which is operative in) "the place of the Master." Nor (can it be used) if it is not the practice to rule like him (i.e., like the authority upon whom the defendant purports to rely). Moreover, (it can be used) only if it is a controversy of one on one. Moreover, only if it is a controversy among equals. Moreover, only if both of them are well known, so that their compositions are found and their words are disseminated throughout most of the Jewish world.

And Radbaz concludes by explaining the reason for these limitations, a reason that goes to the heart of his objection to *qim li*:

> For if you do not say this, then no ruling would ever be rendered definitively.[48] For all things contain differences and controversies. Everyone would say, "I hold an opinion like So-and-so," and it would not be possible to exact (the money) from him. And robbery and ill-gotten gain will flourish.[49]

So much for *qim li* in general. But in regard to the specific question of adopting contrary positions at different times, Radbaz breaks openly with Isserlein:

> Even between equals (in stature)—such as the case in which Ra'avan and Rabiah differed... (i.e., the issue discussed by Isserlein)—in a case such as this I do not agree with the ruling of Rabbi Israel (Isserlein). For if it were so, the words of the rabbis would be a joke! We would become a byword among fools! A while ago he said, "I hold like Ra'avan," and we decided the law according to him (Ra'avan), and now he says, "I hold like Rabiah," and we decide the law according to him (Rabiah)! Even the litigant himself would say that this is biased! ... Imagine what would be if two people made claims against him together. Could he say to the one, "I hold like Ra'avan," and to the other, "I hold like Rabiah"? Therefore, it only makes sense to say that his pleas must always be in accordance with the one or the other.

---

47 *Terumat ha-Deshen,* Part 1, 310.

48 *lo yippaseq din me-'olam*

49 Much of the same arguments against *qim li*, in a similarly concentrated fashion, occur also in Radbaz's responsum published by A. Scheiber, "An Unknown Responsum."

Note that Radbaz, for all his reservations, has not denied the legitimacy of the plea of *qim li* altogether. But in the lines which follow he makes it clear that he accepts it only as a *fait accompli*, one which he disagrees with in principle, and which he seeks to contain, but cannot uproot:

> The law (that one may plead *qim li*) is itself a great novelty.[50] For if a judge had supported reasons to rule in accordance with the differing opinion (from the one that the defendant is adopting), or if his intellect is inclined toward one of the views, why can the litigant say, "I hold like the opposing view"? Since it is a novelty, you have nothing but the novelty itself—but he should not be able to turn about howsoever he chooses.
>
> Furthermore, I say that if the judge is a recognized expert (*mumheh le-rabbim*), and it is his opinion to rule like one of the contesting authorities, then the litigant cannot say, "I hold like the opposing authority." Rather, they exact (the money) from him against his will.... Since he is a recognized expert, he relies only on what he sees proper under the present circumstances."

The Talmud recognizes a category of judge who is "a recognized expert," and grants him special prerogatives. Such a judge may judge alone, and is not bound by the rule that there be a court of three. He cannot be rejected as a judge by one of the litigants, as can other judges. He is not liable to suit for damages by a litigant if he made a mistake in judgment.[51] The term "recognized expert" had been defined by Sherira Gaon as follows:

> One who was ... expert in Mishnah and Gemara, and expert also in rational thinking (*shiqqul ha-da'at*), and who has studied the laws several years, and who has been put to the test many times with no error being seen in what he did—such a one is a recognized expert.[52]

For Radbaz, the category of "a judge who is a recognized expert" was not merely a theoretical possibility, a rhetorical echoing of talmudic phraseology. He refers to such judges on occasion as part of the prevailing judicial landscape. He contrasts them to arbitrators appointed by the litigants, and puts them in the same category as

---

50 See n. 5 above.

51 BT Sanhedrin 5a, 23a, and 33a respectively.

52 Taubes, *Otsar ha-Geonim Sanhedrin*, 26 (to Sanhedrin 5a).

official judges appointed by the community.[53] He thus disallows the plea of *qim li* altogether for cases adjudicated before such judges.

[141] Radbaz is thus ambivalent about the use of *qim li.* This ambivalence is brought into bold relief in the following responsum.

"Reuben" had opened an access onto his neighbor's flat roof.[54] He was sued, and it was ruled that he must seal up the access. However, he failed to do so. The law recognizes a period of three years during which the owner can object to such illicit encroachment on one's property. After that period, if no objection is registered, an easement is created. In the case at hand, no objection was registered during the three years.

That would have been the end of the story, were it not for the fact that Reuben, by having access to his neighbor's roof, could see into his private quarters.[55] Such visual trespass is known as "sight damage" (*hezeq re'iya*), and is an actionable offense. Radbaz shows that there is a controversy concerning whether one can establish an easement if it involves sight damage. Maimonides "and some authorities" rule that one can, and Alfasi "and most of the later authorities" rule that one cannot. In light of this, Radbaz concludes:

> Therefore, if the case occurred in a place where they had the practice of ruling in accordance with Maimonides, he is not forced (to close his access to the roof). Furthermore, since he is the defendant, he can say, "I hold an opinion (*qim li*) like Maimonides." And if it is (in) a place where they had the practice of ruling like the other authorities, or a place in which there is no fixed practice, one should rule like Alfasi, for so did the later authorities decide, and one should rule according to them.

The phrase, "or a place in which there is no fixed practice," indicates how Radbaz would rule in a neutral situation, one in which he was not bound by a custom of ruling like Maimonides or like another

53 "You should know, that all that was said applies only to judges who were chosen by the litigants. But if he (the judge) was a recognized expert, or if the community appointed him to judge them, then he judges them against their will;" II, 789, end. "Regarding what the widow argued, that the judge acted alone and that he was a relative, in this matter I do not accept her words for several reasons. First, because .... And furthermore, since he was a recognized expert, he was able to judge...; III, 565 (= 995), toward the end.

54 I, 370.

55 Radbaz does not know if that in fact was the case. He discusses what the law is if the situation turns out to be that way.

specified authority. He would, in such a case, rule against Maimonides. In doing so he would ignore the defendant's plea of *qim li*. But Radbaz had just recognized the cogency of that plea. He used it as additional support for ruling like Maimonides in a place where it was customary to do so as a matter of rule. So here we have it. Radbaz uses *qim li* where it supports his conclusion, and ignores it where it does not.

Conclusions

The plea of *qim li* allows the defendant to adopt a legal opinion which would be rejected by the normal channels of arriving at a decision, an thereby shift the burden of proof to the plaintiff, leaving him with the impossible task of proving that the normally unaccepted opinion is in fact not correct. The right of a defendant to plead *qim li* thus frustrates a decision that would normally result, but which favors the plaintiff. This approach had its origins in fifteenth-century Germany and Austria, and derived from a deep sense of inadequacy, which did not permit the resolution *de jure* of controversies among earlier authorities. By the time of Radbaz, the use of *qim li* had passed to the post-Expulsion Sephardic rabbis of the Ottoman Empire, and was well entrenched in a broad spectrum of judicial practice.

Radbaz is fundamentally opposed to the use of *qim li*, and to the legal philosophy that it represents. Nevertheless, it was part of the judicial landscape that faced him. Radbaz uses *qim li* in support of conclusions he would reach in any case, and rejects it where it would oppose the decision he considers proper. On occasion he relies on *qim li* to escape from the conclusions of a specific legal decision which he believes to be correct, but which he is anxious to avoid in the case at hand because of broader concerns which are operative in that situation.

The result is that *qim li*, as used by Radbaz, is generally a rhetorical device. Its rhetorical nature is borne out by its extension to situations beyond the area of civil law, where the burden of proof, which lies at the heart of *qim li*, is not an issue. Where *qim li* would have operational effect, that is, where it would force a decision contrary to Radbaz's sense of what the law is, the *qim li* plea is totally rejected. The one exception that we encountered is testimony not to Radbaz's submission to *qim li*, but to its prevalence, and the inevitability of its application in local courts. With his customary sensitivity to practicalities, in that responsum Radbaz sought to protect the plaintiff by urging the local court to arbitrate, and avoid the possibility of a *qim li* defense.

10. "The Law is in Accordance with the Later Authorities"

On a number of occasions, we have seen Radbaz refer, or at least allude, to a principle that "the law is in accordance with the later authorities."[1] This is the rule known by its Aramaic term, *hilkheta ke-batra'ei*. It is one of the rules that have evolved for arriving at decisions in cases of controversy among the authorities.

Hilkheta ke-batra'ei, which appears at first glance to run counter to the veneration accorded the sages of yore, has been the subject of a number of studies in recent years. The agenda was established by I. Ta-Shma.[2] Ta-Shma showed that in its original form, which dates to the ninth century,[3] the rule referred only to disputed rulings within the Talmud itself. According to Ta-Shma, the first recorded application of *hilkheta ke-batra'ei* to disputes among post-talmudic authorities is found in the works of the sons of Rabbenu Asher, in the first half of the fourteenth century.[4] Ta-Shma attributed this development to a fundamental cultural change, in which human knowledge came to be conceived as cumulative. This notion was expressed by means of the parable of a dwarf who sits on the shoulders of a giant, and can therefore see further than the giant. The parable thus presented a model

---

1 P. 289, at n. 37; 225, at n. 52; 230, at n. 70; 231, bot.; 233; 236; 289.

2 Ta-Shma, "*Hilkheta Kebatrai.*"

3 In *Seder Tanna'im ve-Amora'im*, see Ta-Shma, "*Hilkheta Kebatrai*," 63.

4 Ta-Shma, "*Hilkheta Kebatrai*," 59.

for maintaining the traditional veneration of earlier sages, while making room for innovations that contradicted their teachings. The parable of the dwarf on the shoulders of a giant makes its appearance in Christian scholastic circles in the twelfth century, and appears first in Jewish writings in the responsa of R. Isaiah di Trani, in the first half of the thirteenth century.[5] An important implication of this justification of innovation is that it only applies if the dwarf is actually sitting on the giant's shoulders, that is, if the later scholar is aware of the works of the earlier one.

Ta-Shma stressed the Christian environment in which this parable appeared, and with it, he asserted, the concept of knowledge as cumulative. This conception was absent, according to Ta-Shma, in the Islamic milieu. Thus, he says, "This state of affairs left its mark on the Sephardic methodology for arriving at legal decisions until the time of R. Joseph Caro."[6] The phrase, "until the time of R. Joseph Caro," is meant to include that time as well.[7] Ta-Shma demonstrates the Sephardic opposition to applying *hilkheta ke-batra'ei* to post-talmudic authorities by citing a slightly older contemporary of Caro, R. Moses Alashqar (1466–1542). Alashqar insisted on the original sense of the rule, that it referred only to disputes among the Sages of the Talmud. He was derisive in his attack on the conception that rabbis of recent generations should take precedence over the great sages of the past.[8]

In the wake of Ta-Shma's article, a number of studies appeared which took issue with some of its points.[9] The conception of knowledge as cumulative, the consequent empowerment of later scholars to challenge their predecessors, and reference to *hilkheta ke-batra'ei* in this regard, can be traced back to Abraham Maimonides (13th century).[10] The rule of *hilkheta ke-batra'ei* was shown to thrive in the Ashkenazic milieu without reference to the parable of the dwarf, and perhaps even independently of the concept of cumulative

---

5 Ta-Shma, "*Hilkheta Kebatrai*," 70 ff.

6 Ta-Shma, "*Hilkheta Kebatrai*," 75 (translation mine).

7 This is the clear implication of Ta-Shma's reference to Isserles' criticism of Caro's failure to employ the rule of *hilkheta ke-batra'ei.*

8 Alashqar, *Responsa*, no. 54, cited by Ta-Shma, "*Hilkheta Kebatrai*," 59.

9 Raffeld, "The Halakha Follows the Later Sages"; Raffeld, "'Ashkenaz' in the East"; I. J. Yuval, "*Rishonim* and *Aharonim*"; Wosner, "*Hilkheta ke-Batra'ei*".

10 Abraham Maimonides, *Sefer ha-Maspiq le-'Ovdei ha-Shem*, ed. N Dana, 176–78. Cited by Raffeld, "*Hilkheta ke-Batra'ei*," 1992, 120, n. 2; Wosner, "*Hilkheta ke-Batra'ei*", 158–59.

knowledge.[11] Alashqar, who so vehemently opposed the extension of *hilkheta ke-batra'ei* to post-talmudic scholars, was shown to represent a small minority of sixteenth-century Sephardic rabbinic opinion on this issue.[12] The majority of 16th-century Sephardic rabbis did not question the application of *hilkheta ke-batra'ei* to controversies among their predecessors. In the course of this discussion, Radbaz's position on *hilkheta ke-batra'ei* has been referenced as well.[13]

Radbaz is not oblivious to, nor does he ignore, the application of *hilkheta ke-batra'ei* to post-talmudic authorities. He stands with one foot in each camp, and (if the metaphor may be extended) he hops back and forth between them as it suits his purpose.

[142] The following case can serve as an introduction.[14] A man had died, leaving only two daughters, who thus inherited him. One had been betrothed (or perhaps just engaged to be married).[15] The court in Jerusalem, to where they had moved from Egypt before his death, arranged for the marriage. According to talmudic law, a husband inherits his wife.[16] In this case, however, a clause was incorporated in the marriage contract, according to which the inheritance from her father would revert to her father's heirs rather than be inherited by the husband.[17] Subsequently the unmarried daughter died, and was inherited by her married sister. The latter then died herself. There are a number of aspects to this case (which is more complex than indicated by my summary here), but the one that concerns us is the identification of the father's rightful heir. That heir was a somewhat distant relative, and the testimony that supported his relationship to the deceased did not include an attestation that he was the closest relative. The question was whether the inheritance should be confirmed in his possession, or

---

11 Wosner, 158ff.

12 Raffeld, 1995; Wosner.

13 Raffeld, 1995, 122–24; Wosner, 157, n. 12.

14 III, 564 (= 994). Cited by Raffeld, 1995, 123.

15 The responsum states that he married his daughter, but it is clear from the sequel that the actual marriage took place after his death. I therefore understand the phrase, "he married one of them" (*ve-hisi a*<u>*h*</u>*at meihen*), to mean either that he betrothed her, or that he arranged for her engagement.

16 *MT*, Laws of Marriage, chap. 22, parag. 1.

17 This was common practice in one form or another with dowries of wives who died childless. The legal instrument was generally a communal enactment. In this case it was a matter of assets inherited by the wife rather than dowry, so it required a special clause.

whether it should be held pending the possible appearance of a closer relative.

Radbaz presents two diametrically opposed precedent opinions on this issue. One is a responsum by R. Isaac bar Sheshet (d. 1408), who ruled that an heir's claim could not be established without proof, or without a presumption based on common knowledge, that he is the closest relative.[18] Radbaz is adamant in his rejection of this view, presenting a number of proofs to the contrary, and pointing out that R. Isaac bar Sheshet "did not bring any proof at all, but (arrived at this position) only on the basis of *sevara* (i.e., his own reasoning)." He would, says Radbaz, have ruled against Bar Sheshet on these grounds alone. He was fortunate, however, to discover a contrary ruling, supportive of his own position, in a responsum by Rabbenu Asher (d. 1327).[19] After referring to the great prestige of Rabbenu Asher, Radbaz raises the issue of *hilkheta ke-batra'ei*:

> Do not err concerning those who say that the law is according to the later authorities (*hilkheta ke-batra'ei*), and that R. Isaac bar Sheshet was much later than Rabbenu Asher.... First, for they did not say that except concerning the *amora'im* (the rabbis of the Talmud). And even according to those who say that we say this even concerning the post-talmudic authorities, when is that so? When the later one cited the words of the earlier one, and responded to them, and buttressed his proofs with the text of the Talmud. Since the words of the earlier one did not seem to him to be correct, one can (then) rely on him (the later one). But if he did not cite the words of the earlier one, it means that he did not see them. Under these conditions, all would agree that the law is according to he earlier one. For if he (the later one) would have seen his words, he would have retracted his position.

All the elements of Radbaz's attitude toward *hilkheta ke-batra'ei* are exposed here. Both understandings of *hilkheta ke-batra'ei* are entertained, the original one (argued so poignantly by his Sephardic contemporary, R. Moses Alashqar), and the innovative, broader understanding, which had long been adopted by the rabbis of Christian Europe. Though he appears to betray a preference for the former, he does not reject the latter out of hand, as did Alashqar, but takes it into account. He thus leaves it open as a possible option in other situations. In referring to *hilkheta ke-batra'ei*, he consistently stresses the rationale that the later authority was aware of the position of the earlier one.

18 R. Isaac bar Sheshet, *Responsa*, nos. 46 and 47.
19 *Kelal* 86, no. 9.

Furthermore, his initial rejection of *hilkheta ke-batra'ei* is consonant with his opinion on the specific case at hand, which he presents as independent of Rabbenu Asher's precedent: "Even if there were no one upon whom to rely, I would actively apply the law[20] (i.e., *contra* Bar Sheshet—SM), taking (the inheritance) from the husband and giving it to the heir." In other responsa, Radbaz does not hesitate to adopt the application of *hilkheta ke-batra'ei* to post-talmudic authorities. But whether he accepts it or rejects it, what he does is generally in support of the position that he adopts on other grounds.[21]

[143] In clarifying the opinion that *hilkheta ke-batra'ei* applies to post-talmudic authorities as well, an opinion with which he purports not to identify, Radbaz mentions the requirement that the later authorities be aware of what the earlier authorities said. Elsewhere, Radbaz adopts the broadened conception of *hilkheta ke-batra'ei*, and gives due emphasis to the later authorities' knowledge of their predecessors' rulings and the reasons for them. That is, after all, the theoretical basis for the reliance on the later authorities, as indicated by the parable of the dwarf on the shoulders of the giant.

In a responsum dealing with a scenario we have seen before, the plaintiff is suing for return of funds he had paid, which, he now claims, constituted illicit interest, while the defendant claims that the transaction was licit.[22] The question was whether the defendant must take an oath to substantiate his claim. This was a matter of dispute between Rashba, who ruled that an oath was required, and Rabbenu Asher, who ruled that it was not. Radbaz argues that the objections to an oath that Rashba parries do not include the one that Rabbenu Asher had raised. That is sufficient reason, he says, to reject Rashba's opinion:

---

20 *hayyiti 'oseh ma'aseh be-yadayim*

21 In addition to the responsa cited in this chapter, and those from other chapters listed in n. 1 above, see the following responsa. (a) *Hilkheta ke-batra'ei* is quoted with approval, and linked to the awareness of later authorities regarding what the earlier ones said: I, 148, I, 281; I, 26 (the putative reasoning behind the ruling of anonymous others). (b) *Hilkheta ke-batra'ei* is quoted with approval without that link: IV, 282 (= 1353), VI, 2316. (c) Mention is made that the later authority knew what the earlier ones had said, but the formulation *hilkheta ke-batra'ei* does not appear: I, 540, IV, 278 (= 1349). The examples of Radbaz's rejection of *hilkheta ke-batra'ei* are cited below.

22 IV, 297 (= 1369). See Cases [28], [29], [39].

> If Rashba had mentioned Rabbenu Asher's reason and rejected it, there would have been grounds (*maqom*, perhaps translate: a possibility) for relying on him. But since he (apparently) was not aware of it, we presume (in the defendant's favor, since the burden of proof is on the plaintiff—SM), that if he had been aware of it, he would have perhaps accepted it and retracted (his opinion).

These two authorities were contemporaries, so that *hilkheta ke-batra'ei* would presumably not apply to them.[23] But Radbaz then adds:

> Similarly, we say in general, that whenever there is a controversy between earlier and later authorities, if the later authorities saw the words of the earlier authorities and their reasons, and rejected them, we hold that the law is in accordance with the later authorities (*hilkheta ke-batra'ei*). But if the later authorities did not see their reasons, the law is in accordance with the earlier authorities, for if they had seen their reasons perhaps they would have agreed with them. This rule is a tradition in our possession.

There is no mention here of any question about the range of application of the rule that the law is in accordance with the later authorities. The earlier conception, that it does not apply at all to post-talmudic authorities, a conception forcefully argued by Alashqar, and which Radbaz himself had favored in the responsum of Case [142], disappears here entirely, and the later conception is simply taken for granted.[24] But it is peripheral to the case at hand, in which the parties to the dispute are contemporaries.

[144] I began this discussion with Case [142], a responsum in which Radbaz appeared to adopt as his own the earlier view, that *hilkheta ke-batra'ei* applies only to the *amora'im*, the rabbis of the Talmud. At the same time, in strengthening his case, he argued it on the basis of the opposing view as well, thus opening the door to the broader conception of *hilkheta ke-batra'ei*. We then saw that elsewhere Radbaz himself seems to take for granted the application of *hilkheta ke-batra'ei* to post-talmudic authorities.

---

23 But see Case [147] below.

24 Admittedly, it is only that conception of *hilkheta ke-batra'ei* which can serve as a parallel to the point he is making, that is, the necessity of knowing the opposing position. Nevertheless, there could have been some acknowledgment of the other understanding. For instance, instead of "we say in general (*amrinan be-'alma*)," he could have written, "there are those who say."

In one responsum, Radbaz defends his right to rule stringently on a question concerning the propriety of ritual immersion in the Nile.[25] There had been a long tradition of permitting the practice, which Radbaz believes is forbidden, and he presents an impassioned defense of the right of innovation:

> If you do not say this, you have not allowed an opportunity for any of the later scholars to offer any new interpretation or deduction (*she-yithadesh shum hiddush ve-lo shum diqduq*), either in reasoning or in textual tradition (*lo sevara ve-lo gemara*). For we would say to him, "If what you say is true, the early scholars would have mentioned it!" But this is not so, because there is no perfect knowledge, except to Him to whom perfection belongs.

Radbaz then cites for support the passage of the 13th-century Abraham Maimonides, alluded to above.[26] Abraham Maimonides produced a justification for innovation, which is closely parallel to the parable of the dwarf and the giant, though he apparently was not aware of that parable. More importantly for our purposes, he explicitly tied the right of innovation to the principle of *hilkheta ke-batra'ei*. It is clear that Radbaz, in this responsum, has totally identified himself with the broader conception of *hilkheta ke-batra'ei*.[27]

[145] In fact, Radbaz's acknowledgment of the older understanding, that *hilkheta ke-batra'ei* does not apply at all to post-talmudic authorities, is exceptional. In most cases in which he rejects its

---

25 VIII, 141. This is a follow-up to the original responsum, VIII, 139.

26 See n. 10. Radbaz produces his own translation of the passage from the Arabic.

27 As Ta-Shma pointed out, *hilkheta ke-batra'ei*, at least in its classic form, is a rule which directs a rabbinical judge how to rule. It does not empower him by allowing him to assume himself the mantle of the "later authority." Ta-Shma asserts that in more recent times the rule did become extended in that direction, a point that has been a matter of discussion. Wosner has this to say: "There are, however, a few places, in which the author of the responsum justifies the fact that he differs with early authorities on the strength of this rule. But in these cases too, the claim was not made explicitly that the rule itself bestows authority. Rather, from the rule it can be inferred that the power of the late authorities are greater sometimes than the early authorities" (Wosner, 152, n. 5; translation mine). In this connection Wosner alludes *inter alia* to this passage of Abraham Maimonides.

application, he does not do so on those grounds. He simply gives preference to other considerations. The following is an example.[28]

If a woman is divorced or widowed, she collects her *ketubba*, the financial obligation that her husband had assumed at the time of her marriage. Under talmudic law, the *ketubba* is collected from her husband's real property. There is a lien on the property, so that she can reclaim it from a subsequent purchaser. A purchaser who wishes to safeguard himself against this, therefore, must obtain the wife's forfeiture of her rights to it. However, there is a fear that the wife may be intimidated by her husband to agree to such a forfeiture. Thus, we read in the Mishnah:

> If he purchased it from the husband, and then purchased it from the wife, the sale is invalid. If he purchased it from the wife, and then purchased it from the husband, the sale is valid.[29]

The Talmud grants the wife the right to repudiate her consent to the sale, with the plea: "What I did was (merely) to please my husband."[30] Radbaz is asked whether she can repudiate her consent to the sale of her dowry. The questioner points out that there appears to be a controversy between Maimonides and Rabbenu Asher in this regard. Maimonides had ruled that she could present such a plea about the dowry.[31] Rabbenu Asher, in a responsum, without making reference to Maimonides, had ruled that she could not.[32] The questioner wanted to know whether this is truly a controversy, and if so, how does one rule.

Radbaz responds:

> There is no doubt that Maimonides differs (with Rabbenu Asher), and it is upon him (Maimonides) that one should rely. Even though Rabbenu Asher is a late authority, and we hold that the law is in accordance with the later authorities (*hilkheta ke-batra'ei*), in any case Maimonides is the Master of the place, and all these provinces have already accepted his ruling.[33]

---

28 II, 604.

29 Mishnah Gittin 5:6. BT Gittin 55b.

30 BT Bava Batra 49b.

31 *MT*, Laws of Marriage, chap. 22, parag. 18.

32 *Kelal* 38, no. 7.

33 He continues: "Furthermore, Rabbenu Asher did not cite Maimonides' words and reject them with reasoned arguments." But this appears to be a supplementary argument, not meant to bear real weight. Radbaz could not seriously suggest that Rabbenu Asher was unaware of Maimonides' ruling, and granting that, he could as well have taken the position that Rabbenu

Radbaz takes it for granted that "the law is according to the later authorities" in controversies among post-talmudic authorities as well. He parries that rule by reliance on a competing rule, that the law is decided in accordance with Maimonides.

[146] But in another controversy between Maimonides and Rabbenu Asher, Case [116] above, Radbaz attaches the reverse relative value to these two principles, "the place of the Master" and *hilkheta ke-batra'ei.*[34] In that responsum, Radbaz was faced with a situation in which a bride became a menstruant at the time of the wedding. Maimonides had ruled that in such a situation the wedding must be postponed, and Rabbenu Asher had ruled that it might proceed. Postponement would have entailed significant, perhaps unrecoverable, financial loss, and the marriage itself might have been in question. For those reasons, Radbaz rules like Rabbenu Asher. Taking the very opposite approach to the one he adopted in the previous case, he rejects Maimonides in "the place of the Master," in favor of *hilkheta ke-batra'ei*. Radbaz's attitude toward *hilkheta ke-batra'ei* appears to be dependant on his position in the case at hand.

[147] The previous case was a situation in which *hilkheta ke-batra'ei* was utilized, while the reasons underlying the decision clearly lay elsewhere. Thus it is indicative of the role of *hilkheta ke-batra'ei* as a rhetorical device. The rhetorical nature of *hilkheta ke-batra'ei* is especially apparent when it is inappropriately applied to disputants who are contemporaries. Such is the case in the following responsum.[35]

At the time of a marriage, it was routine for the groom to commit himself to refrain from marrying a rival without his wife's permission.[36] The common reason for wanting to take a second wife was the failure of the first wife to produce children. Procreation is considered a religious obligation incumbent upon the husband, though not upon the wife. As the Rabbis understood the law of the Torah, the obligation of procreation is specifically defined as the fathering of two viable children, one of each sex. If, by the end of ten years, the wife had not borne children, then he must divorce her and marry someone

---

Asher, in this very terse responsum, must have had valid reasons in mind for rejecting it.

34 I, 518.

35 I, 126.

36 See Cases [43] and [55].

else, unless he were to take a second wife. If a child was born and later died, the counting of ten years begins again from the beginning.[37]

Radbaz was asked as follows:

> You asked me about one who swore to his wife that he would not marry (another) alongside her; however, if ten years[38] went by and she did not give birth, he would be free of his oath. She gave birth to a viable child during the time, but it died. Ten years went by subsequent to the death of the child, and she did not give birth. Is he free (of his oath) or not?

The question is about a child that died. That was considered an open and shut case by Radbaz; once ten years have passed since the clock was reset, the husband is free of his oath. But Radbaz raises the question of the status of the husband's oath if the child were still alive.

There was a controversy over whether the section of the law about the obligation of the husband to divorce and remarry after ten years of childlessness was governed by the same rule that defined the basic law of procreation. Radbaz cites two authorities in this regard. Rabbenu Asher had ruled that even though she had borne him one living son, as long as the husband's obligation to procreate, defined as the siring of one son and one daughter, was not satisfied in ten years, he had to marry another.[39] Rashba had ruled that for the purpose of obviating the requirement to divorce his wife and remarry, one viable child was sufficient.[40] After explaining this controversy, Radbaz sums it up as follows:

> If she gave birth and they died, and ten years elapsed, according to everyone he is permitted to marry another (even

---

37 *MT*, Laws of Marriage, chap. 15, parags. 1–5, 7, 12.

38 Thus the wording of the question, in accordance with the period of time cited in the Mishnah, Yevamot 6:6. But from Radbaz's answer, it appears that the time specified in the oath was eight years. This appears to be another case where details are omitted in the phrasing of the question, and appear only later in the course of the responsum. See Chapter 1, n. 79.

39 "This appears to be the opinion of the *Tur*, and the conclusion of Rabbenu Asher. But Rashba wrote...." For Rashba, see below. But I have not been able to locate either the source in the *Tur* alluded to here, where the subject in general is discussed (*Even ha-'Ezer* 154), or in the responsa of Rabbenu Asher, or in his *Pesaqim* in Yevamot ad loc. Caro, in *Beit Yosef*, who cites Rashba's responsum in *Even ha-'Ezer* 154, does not mention Rabbenu Asher. See *Nimmuqei Yosef* to Alfasi on Yevamot at our Mishnah, referred to by Radbaz here, who also refers to these two views, but identifies only Rashba as the proponent of one.

40 Rashba, *Responsa*, III, 339–40.

> without her permission, notwithstanding his oath—SM). But if she gave birth to one, and he is alive, this depends on a controversy. And even though a close reading of the Mishnah (yields a meaning) in accordance with Rashba—for we learn in the Mishnah: "(If he married a woman and stayed with her ten years) and she didn't give birth,"[41] and after all, she did give birth—nevertheless, it makes sense to me (*mistabbera li*) to rule in accordance with Rabbenu Asher.
>
> First, because he is a later authority (*batra'a hu*).
>
> And furthermore, because it makes sense that since he stipulated with her, he did so for the purpose of fulfilling the religious obligation, and he has not yet fulfilled it with (only) one.
>
> And furthermore, because (otherwise) he would be sitting idle, and (in reference to God's creation of the earth we read:) "He did not create it (the earth—SM) a waste, but formed it for habitation."[42]

Radbaz presents three reasons for ruling in accordance with Rabbenu Asher. The third is that the husband has not fulfilled his obligation of procreation, so how can the law permit him to remain married to a woman who is presumed unable to allow him to do so? The second is that the husband's oath must be interpreted in the light of its context. The first is *hilkheta ke-batra'ei*, that the law is in accordance with the later authorities. The use of *hilkheta ke-batra'ei* here makes no sense on the face of it. Rashba and Rabbenu Asher were contemporaries.[43] It is obvious that the second and third reasons are the ones that motivated Radbaz to rule as he did.

Conclusions

In the former case, in which Rabbenu Asher can hardly be described chronologically as a "later authority" in relation to Rashba, it is clear that *hilkheta ke-batra'ei* is used purely as a rhetorical device.

This is consistent with Radbaz's approach to *hilkheta ke-batra'ei* throughout. With one noted exception, Case [142], Radbaz takes for granted the application of the rule *hilkheta ke-batra'ei* to post-talmudic

41 Mishnah Yevamot 6:6, BT Yevamot 64a.

42 Isaiah 45:18. Ironically, in the Talmud, BT Yevamot 62a, this verse is used as a prooftext for the rejected view that one child is sufficient to satisfy the biblical requirement of procreation.

43 See Case [143], and n. 23 there.

authorities, even when he rejects its application to the case at hand. In one instance, Case [144], in the course of a spirited appeal for the right of innovation in the interpretation of law, he fully identifies, through his citation of Abraham Maimonides, with both the principle of *hilkheta ke-batra'ei* and the logic underlying it. Nevertheless, we never find that *hilkheta ke-batra'ei* governs his decision. It is either accepted in support of an otherwise determined outcome, or rejected in a way which (with one exception) leaves the concept of *hilkheta ke-batra'ei* intact.

Conclusions from Part Two

Part Two is a study of Radbaz's utilization of five phrases. Four of the five are formulated in a way that presents them as "rules for decision-making" (*kelalei pesiqa*), that is, rules which limit the judge's judicial discretion in the case of earlier controversy, and mandate a specific decision. One of the five, "Grant that one should not add to it," is a plea for a narrow construction of a specific law, and thus also purports to guide the decision-making process.[1] Radbaz's insistence on judicial independence was the theme of Part I. It behooved me, therefore, to investigate the way Radbaz handles limits on that independence within the judicial process itself.

In three of the five instances, Radbaz faced a rule which confronted him as a "given." *Qim li*, that is, the right of a defendant to adopt an opinion that would support his case, and shift the burden of proof to the contrary onto the plaintiff, had already infiltrated the judicial process.[2] So had *hilkheta ke-batra'ei*, the rule that the law is bound to follow the later authorities. The third, the notion that in Egypt the law follows Maimonides because it is "the place of the Master," was already

1 This is a description of those instances of this terminology that were of interest in this study. Elsewhere, the phrase is merely a comment by Radbaz describing his conclusion.

2 Ben-Menahem asserts that *qim li* is not a juridical rule which directs the judge how to decide, but a defense put forward by the defendant; "Origins of Kim Li," p 89. Nevertheless, on a practical level it is treated as a juridical rule.

entrenched among the indigenous Jews of that country by the time Radbaz and his Sephardic contemporaries arrived there.

The use of *qim li* presents a clear example of Radbaz's exploitation of a rule, ostensibly meant to limit the area of judicial discretion, for the purpose of actually broadening it. Radbaz is opposed in principle to the premise on which *qim li* is based, namely, that a controversy among earlier authorities is theoretically unresolvable *de jure.*[3] He rejects the use of *qim li* when it works in opposition to what he believes is the correct ruling. However, he does not reject *qim li* outright, and does not hesitate to cite *qim li* whenever it serves to strengthen his case. It cannot be said that in these instances Radbaz gives real weight to the plea of *qim li.* However, exploiting its wide acceptance, he uses it as a rhetorical device, which he knows will resonate among a significant segment of his audience. Radbaz's exploitation of *qim li* to support his desired goal is especially striking in cases in which it works against a specific legal ruling which Radbaz accepts, but in favor of the broader goal which he seeks in the case at hand.[4] Its use as a rhetorical device is glaringly apparent when he extends it beyond its theoretical borders, namely, a defendant's plea in a civil suit, and applies it to situations in which there is no defendant, including purely ritual matters, where it has no theoretical basis at all.[5]

Radbaz's attitude toward *hilkheta ke-batra'ei* is fundamentally different from his attitude toward *qim li*, because he enthusiastically supports the premise underlying the rule that the law follows the later authorities. That premise, as Radbaz explains by unmistakable implication, is that knowledge is cumulative, and that later authorities have the right to innovate.[6] In spite of this difference in attitude between *hilkheta ke-batra'ei* and *qim li*, Radbaz's stance toward the utilization of both is identical. He uses it where it helps his cause, and marginalizes it where it does not. In one notable case he gives the impression of personally rejecting *hilkheta ke-batra'ei*, though he quickly presents the alternative position of those who accept it, and shows that even according to the latter premise it would not apply in the case at hand.[7] As is the case with *qim li*, *hilkheta ke-batra'ei* never

3 Case [141].
4 Case [136].
5 Cases [137], [138].
6 Case [145].
7 Case [143].

determines his position.[8] Its practical application is rhetorical, never truly functional.

The third instance of a rule which confronted Radbaz was the tradition of the indigenous Jewish population of Egypt, that Egypt was "the place of the Master," and that therefore the law should be decided there in accordance with Maimonides' rulings. Radbaz expresses support for the rule of "the place of the Master," and, unlike *hilkheta ke-batra'ei*, there are instances where it determines his decision. But in many other instances he neutralizes it, and in many other cases, not analyzed in this study, he simply rules against Maimonides, without making any reference to "the place of the Master."

In each of these three cases, *qim li*, *hilkheta ke-batra'ei*, and "the place of the Master," the rule in question is the practical embodiment of a principle. In the case of *qim li*, it is the principle of the qualitative decrease in capacity from an earlier period to the present one. Radbaz does not subscribe to this principle. This is borne out by his use of *qim li*, which is purely utilitarian, and never serves as a platform for an articulation of the ideology behind it. The same is not true for *hilkheta ke-batra'ei*. Here the underlying principle, insofar as Radbaz understands it and articulates it, is the right of later generations to innovate, and Radbaz expresses his support for this point of view.[9] So too concerning "the place of the Master," a rule which encapsulates the reverence of the *musta'rib* Jews for Maimonides, and their conception of him as their teacher, to whom they owe allegiance.[10] Nevertheless, Radbaz's support for these principles does not carry through in his application of the rules that reflect them to his actual decisions. *Hilkheta ke-batra'ei* does not, on its own, determine Radbaz's ruling. "The place of the Master" does on occasion, but not consistently. The principle is one thing, and its practical application is another.

This dichotomy between the two aspects of a rule, one as the representation of a principle, the other as a means of practical legal decision, is more apparent, and the tension between them more acute, in Radbaz's concept of the "middle way." That is because unlike *qim li*, *hilkheta ke-batra'ei* and "the place of the Master," the concept of the

8 The one apparent exception with regard to *qim li*, Case [140], is in fact a purely pragmatic response to the prevalence of *qim li* in the local courts.

9 Case [145]. It is possible, though, that other principles underlie the use of *hilkheta ke-batra'ei* in its earlier Ashkenazic setting; see Chapter 10, text at n. 11.

10 Case [106].

"middle way," as a rule in determining legal decisions, appears to be the creation of Radbaz himself. Radbaz goes to great lengths to establish his chosen position as the "middle way," on occasion dredging up a marginal opinion, or even one which is highly suspect, as one extreme in a set of three, so that his desired ruling can be cast as the "middle way."[11] Yet, it cannot be convincingly demonstrated that Radbaz ever really bases his decision on the "middle way." It is always introduced as supplementary to a conclusion that is reached on other grounds. Its use is thus rhetorical only, a conclusion which would also explain his occasional dubious use of the rule.

The rhetoric of the "middle way" rests upon two concepts. One is the legitimacy of conflicting opinions, which implies that there is no substantive reason to prefer one to the other. The second is that, other things being equal, there is inherent merit in the choice of a median path. The first of these concepts also underlies a number of instances of the phrase, "Grant that one should not add to it," where it introduces an attempt to narrow the gap between two conflicting opinions, by bringing one of them closer to the other through a narrow interpretation.[12] But this concept runs counter to Radbaz's approach to arriving at decisions throughout his responsa. He routinely analyzes conflicting opinions in terms of their substantive merits, and expresses preferences for some authorities over others. Thus, as in the case of *hilkheta ke-batra'ei*, Radbaz uses the rule of the "middle way" to affirm a principle, in this instance the theoretical legitimacy of conflicting opinions, but evades or ignores the implications of the principle on a practical level. With regard to *qim li* he also separates the principle from its practical application, but in a different way. On the practical level, he utilizes *qim li*, though only where it suits his purpose. On the other hand, he expressly negates the principle that underlies it.

In two cases, the term "middle way" refers to Radbaz's original formulation of a compromise position between two sides of a controversy, in other words, one that agrees with neither.[13] This conception of the "middle way" is fundamentally different from the way it is generally used by Radbaz, where it refers to a choice among the opinions of others, implying a dependence on those opinions. In these two instances, the "middle way" is an expression of Radbaz's right to forge a position of his own, independent of the opinions of

---

11 Cases [93] to [97].

12 Chapter 8, Section (*c*), p. 249ff.

13 Chapter 6, Section (*f*), p. 191ff.

others. That same expression of independence is manifest in Radbaz's use of the phrase, "Grant that one should not add to it," an expression, which implies that one, should apply a narrow construction of the law under question. Frequently, Radbaz uses this phrase merely to refer to the conclusion he had reached on other grounds. But elsewhere the phrase plays a functional role, indicating a deliberate initiative on the part of Radbaz in applying a narrow interpretation to the law under consideration, curtailing the range of application of the law under consideration. In a number of cases, Radbaz chose to do so because of moral qualms regarding the law.[14] In one instance, his hesitation stemmed from his view of the role of law as protecting the interests of the weak, which he felt would be compromised in the case at hand by a broad interpretation of the law.[15]

This attitude brings us back to Part One of our study, where Radbaz's judicial independence was the central concern.

---

14 Cases [128] – [130].

15 Case [131], regarding entrusting funds to the direct control of a minor.

Biographies

Below are the names of the rabbinic authorities cited in this study, with essential biographical information, and reference to their listings in the *Encyclopaedia Judaica* (EJ). The names are listed in the form in which they appear in the book. Occasionally, listings are the titles of works. Dates are generally based on EJ, though the frequent indications of approximate dating are omitted. An asterisk indicates that a name is included in this list.

Aaron ha-Levi

Aaron b. Joseph ha-Levi (acronym: Ra'ah), 1235–1300. R. Aaron ha-Levi was a native of Barcelona, where he lived most of his life, though he was the rabbi of Saragossa for some years. He was the author of novellae on the Talmud and other works of *halakha*, many of which have not survived. He was one of the two major teachers of *Ritba, the other being *Adret. EJ 2: 14.

Alashqar

Moses Alashqar, 1466–1542. Alashqar left Spain with the Expulsion in 1492. He lived in Tunis and in Greece, before settling in Egypt. He eventually settled in Jerusalem. EJ 2: 511.

Alfasi

Isaac Alfasi (acronym: Rif), 1013–1103. Born in Qal'at Hammad, in Algeria, Alfasi lived most of his life in Fez. In 1088, at the age of 75, he fled North Africa after being denounced to the government, and settled in Spain, where he subsequently headed the rabbinic academy in Lucena. Alfasi produced a code organized in the form of an abridgement of the Talmud (commonly known as *Hilkhot ha-Rif*), which became widely accepted in Spain as authoritative, and had immense influence on subsequent legal authorities. EJ 2: 600.

Asher

Asher b. Yehiel (Rabbenu Asher), 1250–1327. Rabbenu Asher was the prime student of R. Meir of Rothenburg, the leading rabbinic authority in Germany in the second part of the 13th century, and inherited the latter's position. In 1303, fearing that he would be held for ransom as was his mentor, R. *Meir of Rothenburg, he left Germany for Spain, and became the rabbi of Toledo. Rabbenu Asher had immense influence on the development of Jewish law in Spain. His two most influential works were his responsa and his legal compendium, *Pisqei ha-Rosh*. EJ 3: 706.

Avqat Rokhel

See: Caro, Joseph

Caro, Joseph

Joseph Caro, 1488–1575. Caro was born in Toledo. After the Expulsion from Portugal in 1497 he lived in Istanbul and the Balkans for about 40 years. In 1536 he settled in Safed. Caro was a leading rabbinic authority, his major fame resting on his encyclopedic *magnum opus*, *Beit Yosef*. His later well-known code, *Shulhan 'Arukh*, was intended as an abridgment of the former work. Two volumes of responsa of Caro have been published: *Responsa Beit Yosef*, and *Avqat Rokhel*. The latter also contains responsa by those of Caro's contemporaries who responded to the same questions. EJ 5: 194.

Colon, Joseph

Joseph Colon, 1420–1480. Colon (acronym: Mahariq) was born in France, but lived his adult life in Northern Italy. Colon is the author of an influential volume of responsa. He was a repository of French and earlier German rabbinic learning, and his responsa are cited by the post-Expulsion Sephardic rabbis. EJ 5: 747.

David ha-Kohen

David ben Hayyim, rabbi of Corfu, off the Adriatic coast of Greece, d. 1530. He was from the Romaniot (indigenous Balkan) community. His rabbinic training was undertaken in Northern Italy. EJ 5: 1350.

Eliezer ben Nathan

Eliezer ben Nathan of Mainz, 1090–1170, was a leading German rabbinic authority. He was the author of a compendium of early Ashkenazic halakhic traditions, called *Even ha-'Ezer* (or alternatively: *Sefer Ra'avan*). EJ 6: 626.

Elijah Mizrahi

Elijah Mizrahi, 1450–1526, Constantinople. Mizrahi, who, after 1498, was the chief rabbinical authority in Constantinople, and perhaps recognized officially as such, was from the Romaniot (indigenous Balkan Jewish) community. His decisions were influential throughout the Ottoman lands. EJ 12: 182.

Hagahot Maimoniot

A commentary on Maimonides' code, *Mishneh Torah*, by Meir ha-Kohen, a student of R. *Meir of Rothenburg. A collection of R. Meir of Rothenburg's responsa, relevant to the subject matter of the various books of the *Mishneh Torah*, and placed at the end of each book, is addended to the work. In standard editions it is referred to as *Teshuvot Maimoniot.*

Hai Gaon

Hai ben Sherira, 939–1038, was the Gaon (Head of the Academy) of Pumbedita from 998, an office in which he succeeded his father, *Sherira Gaon, during the latter's lifetime. Hai Gaon, whose death conventionally marks the close of the Geonic period, is acknowledged as one of the greatest Geonim. EJ 7: 1130.

Isaac bar Sheshet

Isaac bar Sheshet Perfet (acronym: Rivash), 1326–1408. Rivash, a student of R. *Nissim Gerondi, left Spain, where he had been a rabbi in Valencia, during the anti-Jewish riots of 1391, and settled in Algiers. He is the author of an influential volume of responsa. EJ 9: 32.

Isaac of Dampierre

R. Isaac (acronym: Ri; Ri the Elder), d. 1185. Ri, following in the footsteps of his uncle, Rabbenu *Tam, was the central force in the creation of the multigenerational commentary to the Talmud called **Tosafot*. EJ 9: 31.

Isaiah di Trani

Isaiah b. Mali di Trani, 1200–1260, an important Italian halakhist. R. Isaiah was a pupil of R. Simha of Speier. He is cited a great deal in the Italian work **Shibbolei ha-Leqet*, and also in **Or Zarua'*. EJ 9: 73.

Isserlein, Israel

Israel Isserlein, 1390–1460, Wiener-Nuestadt, Austria. Isserlein was the most influential rabbi in Germany in the 15th century. He is generally referred to as the author of *Terumat ha-Deshen*, a book of responsa in which the questions are believed to have been literary creations of the author. A collection of responsa to questions which were asked of him are included in the volume *Pesaqim u-Ketavim* [*Decisions and Writings*], which is published as "Part 2" of the *Terumat ha-Deshen*. EJ 9: 1080.

'Ittur

A compendium of civil and ritual law by Isaac ben Abba Mari of Marseilles, 12th century. EJ 9: 12.

Jacob b. Asher

Jacob b. Asher, 1270–1340. The son of *Asher b. Yehiel, Jacob migrated with his father from Germany to Spain in 1303. He is the author of the expansive four-part code of Jewish law, *Arba'a Turim* [*Four Columns*], one of the major works of halakhic codification. EJ 9: 1214.

Joseph Caro

See: Caro

Joseph Colon

See: Colon

Joseph Habiba

Spain, first half of the 15th century. Author of *Nimmuqei Yosef*, an extended commentary on *Alfasi's *Hilkhot ha-Rif*. EJ 7: 1026.

Joseph ibn Lev

Joseph b. David ibn Lev, 1505–1580. Ibn Lev spent the earlier part of his career in Salonica. In or about 1550 he moved to Constantinople, where he subsequently headed the *yeshiva* endowed by Dona Gracia Mendes in that city. EJ 11: 64.

Joseph ibn Migash

Joseph ibn Migash, 1077–1141, Spain. Ibn Migash was a student of *Alfasi's, and succeeded him as the head of the *yeshiva* in Lucena. One of Ibn Migash's students was Maimonides' father. EJ 8: 1188.

Joseph ibn Tsiyah

Joseph b. Abraham ibn Tsiyah, a Kabbalist and rabbinic authority, was from the *must'arab* (indigenous, Arabic speaking) community. He lived in Jerusalem as early as 1518, and subsequently moved to Damascus, apparently before 1560. See A. David, *To Come to the Land*, p. 155.

Judah al-Bargeloni

Judah b. Barzillai al-Bargeloni, Barcelona, late 11th–early 12th century. R. Judah al-Bargeloni was an author of several extensive codes of law, which strongly influenced subsequent Sephardic halakhists, though most of his work has been lost. EJ 10: 341.

Kesef Mishneh

A commentary on Maimonides' code, *Mishneh Torah*, by Joseph *Caro.

Levi b. Habib

Levi b. Habib (acronym: Ralbah), 1483–1545. Originally from Spain, Ralbah lived in Salonica, and then moved to Jerusalem, where he was the leading rabbinical authority. EJ 11: 98.

Maggid Mishneh

The classic commentary on Maimonides' code, *Mishneh Torah*, by Vidal Yom Tov of Tolosa, second half of the 14th century. The work seeks to identify the talmudic sources of Maimonides' rulings. EJ 16: 119.

Maimonides

Moses b. Maimon (acronym: Rambam), 1138–1204. Maimonides was very likely the most influential figure in the post-talmudic history of philosophy and Rabbinic law. After fleeing his native Cordoba with his family in 1148, and wandering about for some years, Maimonides lived for a while in Fez, then traveled to Palestine, and ultimately to Cairo. Maimonides' most significant legal work was his comprehensive and highly original code, *Mishneh Torah*, which had a revolutionary effect on the subsequent history of Rabbinic law and codification. EJ 11: 754.

Meir ha-Levi Abulafia

Meir ha-Levi Abulafia (Ramah), Toledo, 1170–1244. Abulafia was the scion of an aristocratic Sephardic family. He was a renowned talmudic scholar, who authored novellae to many tractates of the Talmud. Only two of these have survived, but he is cited by many later writers. Abulafia was a representative of the traditional school of talmudic interpretation in Spain, a tradition which was soon to be eclipsed under the impact of the writings of *Nahmanides. He is known also as an early opponent of Maimonides' interpretation of the doctrine of resurrection. EJ 2: 189.

Meir Katzenellenbogen

"Maharam of Padua," 1473–1565, originally from Prague, was the Ashkenazic Rabbi of Padua. Maharam of Padua was a leading rabbinic authority. EJ 10: 829.

Meir of Rothenburg

Meir bar Barukh (acronym: Maharam Rothenburg), 1215–1293. Maharam was the chief halakhic authority and rabbinic communal leader in Germany in the 13th century. He is considered the last of the Tosafists (see: *Tosafot), and his passing marks the end of an era. About a thousand responsa of his are in print, in addition to halakhic works in other genres. Maharam's most eminent student was *Asher b. Yehiel, but many other students of his also authored works, which perpetuated his influence (among them see below: *Mordekhai*). Maharam had a profound effect on subsequent Ashkenazic legal traditions. Maharam was taken prisoner and held for ransom, which he refused to allow, and remained imprisoned for seven years until his death, and for some years thereafter until his body was finally ransomed. EJ 11: 1247

Mordekhai

A work by Mordekhai b. Hillel (d. 1298), a student of R. *Meir of Rothenburg. It is a copious compilation of earlier Ashkenazic legal teachings, arranged according to *Alfasi's *Hilkhot ha-Rif.* EJ 12: 311.

Moses Alashqar

See: Alashqar

Nahmanides

Moses b. Nahman (acronym: Ramban), 1194–1270. Nahmanides was born and lived in Gerona. Nahmanides was the leading rabbinic authority in Spain, and produced significant and influential works in a number of different genres. Nahmanides was heir to the scholastic traditions of the French Tosafists (see: *Tosafot), with whom he also studied, as well as to traditional Sephardic scholarship, and blended the two different traditions in his talmudic novellae. His methodology was perpetuated by his student, *Rashba, and had a profound influence on subsequent talmudic learning in Spain. In 1263, Nahmanides was compelled to represent the Jewish faith in a debate with the Dominicans. In the wake of that event, he was forced to leave Catalonia in 1265, at an advanced age. He settled in Jerusalem, where he was instrumental in rebuilding the moribund Jewish community. EJ 12: 774.

Nimmuqei Yosef.

See: Joseph Habiba.

Nissim b. Jacob

Nissim b. Jacob ibn Shahin of Qairouan, 990–1062, a leading North African rabbinical authority and a representative of the Geonic academies in North Africa. EJ 12: 1183.

Nissim (Rabbenu Nissim)

Nissim b. Reuben Gerondi (Rabbenu Nissim), 1310–1375, was the main rabbinic authority in Spain in the 14th century. He is the author of an expansive commentary to *Alfasi's code, of novellae to a number of tractates of the Talmud, and to a basic commentary to the tractate Nedarim. In addition, some of his responsa and his sermons have been preserved. EJ 12: 1185.

Or Zarua'

A compilation of religious and civil law by Isaac b. Moses of Vienna, 1180–1250. EJ 9: 25.

Perets

Perets b. Elijah of Corbeil, d. 1295. R. Perets was one of the most prominent French rabbis of his time. He had spent some time in Germany, and had studied with R. Meir of Rothenburg. R. Perets wrote glosses to the *Sefer Mitsvot Qatan* of Isaac of Corbeil, one of his teachers. Notes and comments of his on the customs of R. Meir were subsequently published by one of his students as glosses to the *Sefer Tashbets* of Samson b. Tsadoq, another student of R. Meir. EJ 13: 283.

Ra'avan

See: Eli'ezer b. Nathan.

Rabad

Acronym of R. Abraham b. David of Posquières, 1125–1198. Rabad was perhaps the greatest Provencal rabbi of his time, whose influence continued to resonate throughout subsequent generations. Rabad's contributions to halakhic literature encompassed various genres, including novellae to the Talmud, codes on specific areas of law, and critical glosses to the works of others. Among the latter are his extensive glosses to Maimonides' code, *Mishneh Torah*. EJ 2: 136.

Rabiah

Acronym of R. Eli'ezer ben Joel ha-Levi of Bonn, 1140–1225. His work, a collection of responsa and legal rulings, is an important source of older Ashkenazic legal traditions. EJ 6: 625.

Rashba

Acronym of R. Solomon ben Abraham Adret, 1235–1310. Rashba headed the *yeshiva* in Barcelona. Rashba was a student of *Na<u>h</u>manides. He was the most eminent rabbinic authority in Spain, and his influence extended well beyond the confines of that country. He is the author of about 1000 responsa, and novellae to much of the Talmud. EJ 2: 305.

Rashbam

See: Samuel b. Meir.

Rashi

Acronym of R. Solomon b. Isaac, 1040–1105. The acronym derives from "Rabbi Shelomo Yitshaqi," or, as suggested by A. Grossman, from what his students called him in his lifetime, "Rabbi Shelomo *Yi<u>h</u>yeh* (May he live!)." Rashi was from Troyes, in the Champagne region of France. He studied in the

Rhine Valley academies of Mainz and Worms. He then returned to Troyes, and established it as a major center of learning, drawing students from great distances. Rashi's outstanding literary contribution is in the genre of commentary. He produced commentaries on nearly all the books of the Bible, and on most of the Babylonian Talmud. His commentary on the Pentateuch became integral to the study of the text itself, and his commentary to the Talmud remains indispensable for any approach to the talmudic text. EJ 13: 1558.

Ritba

Acronym of R. Yom Tov ben Abraham Isbili, 1250–1330, Spain. Ritba's major work is his novellae to the Talmud, in which he continues the interpretive tradition begun two generations before him by Nahmanides, and continued by Rashba, who was one of his two teachers. Ritba was the leading authority in Spain after the death of his teachers. EJ 16: 846.

Samuel b. Meir.

Samuel b. Meir (Rashbam), 1080/85–1174, Northern France. Rashbam was a grandson of *Rashi, with whom he studied and collaborated, and an older brother of Rabbenu *Tam. Rashbam was one of the earliest Tosafists (see: *Tosafot), and a highly original Bible commentator. He is also the author of the standard commentary on parts of the Babylonian Talmud which were not completed by Rashi, most significantly, most of the tractate Bava Qamma. EJ 14: 809.

Samuel de Medina

Samuel de Medina, 1506–1589, Salonica. De Medina was one of the most important rabbinic authorities of his generation, the author of over a thousand published responsa. EJ 11: 1212.

Samuel ha-Sardi

Samuel b. Isaac ha-Sardi, 1185/90–1255/6, Barcelona. Ha-Sardi was the author of a compendium of civil law, *Sefer ha-Terumot*. He was a student of *Nahmanides', and his work preserves many of Nahmanides' responsa to questions which he had asked him. Ha-Sardi's book was a basic source for the relevant section of the *Arba'a Turim* of *Jacob b. Asher. EJ 14: 875.

Sherira Gaon

Sherira, 906–1006, was the Gaon (Head of the Academy) of Pumbedita from 968, until succeeded by his son, *Hai, in his latter years. EJ 14: 1381.

Shibbolei ha-Leqet

A compendium of religious law by R. Zedekiah b. Abraham Anav, 13th century, Italy. EJ 2: 939.

Simha b. Samuel

Rabbenu Simha. Speyer, Germany, second half of 12th and early 13th century. EJ 14: 1569.

Tam

Rabbenu Jacob Tam, 1100–1171, France. Rabbenu Tam, a grandson of *Rashi, was the moving spirit in the development of the scholastic interpretive method which produced the *Tosafot. He was a highly influential legal authority, whose preeminence was recognized well beyond the borders of his region, and who had a lasting effect on subsequent rabbinic law. EJ 15: 779.

Teshuvot Maimoniot

See: *Hagahot Maimoniot*.

Tosafot

The *Tosafot* (literally, "supplements," i.e., supplements to Rashi's commentary), are a collective, multi-generational commentary on the Talmud, which addressed specific difficulties in Rashi's interpretation of the text, or difficulties stemming from the implications of the present passage and those of another elsewhere in the Talmud. In many cases, in resolving these difficulties the Tosafot revised the traditional understanding of the Talmud, and the resulting law that derived from it, thus having a profound effect on the development of rabbinic law. EJ 15: 1278.

Trani, Moses b. Joseph

Moses b. Joseph Trani (self-adopted acronym: Mabit), 1500–1580. Trani was the rabbi of an important congregation in Safed and one of his generation's great halakhic authorities, in which capacity he produced many responsa. He differed with Joseph *Caro on a number of halakhic issues which resulted in public disputes. EJ 15: 1315.

Tsiyah, Joseph ibn

See: Joseph ibn Tsiyah.

Tur, *Turim*:

See: Jacob b. Asher.

Yeruham

Rabbenu Yeruham b. Meshullam, first half of 14th century. Rabbenu Yeruham was originally from France, but with the expulsion of Jews from France in 1306, he migrated to Spain, where he became a student of Rabbenu Asher's for a while. Rabbenu Yeruham is the author of two halakhic compendia, *Sefer Mesharim* and *Sefer Adam ve-Hava*, which were later published together.

Zerahia ha-Levi

R. Zerahia, 12th century, lived in Provence, to which he moved at an early age from Gerona, Spain. R. Zerahia, who was very much influenced by the French rabbinic tradition, was outspoken in his criticism of *Alfasi, as well as of his Provencal contemporary, *Rabad. EJ 7: 509.

Works Cited: Primary Sources

Abraham b. David of Posquières (Rabad). *Hasagot ha-Rabad* [Glosses of Rabad (to Maimonides' Mishneh Torah)]. Printed with *Mishneh Torah.*

——— *Perush ha-Rabad 'al Massekhet 'Avoda Zara* [*Commentary on the Treatise of Abodah Zarah by R. Abraham ben David of Posqières*]. Edited by A. Sofer. New York, 1960.

Abraham Maimonides. *Sefer ha-Maspiq le-'Ovdei ha-Shem*. Edited by N. Dana. Bar Ilan: Ramat Gan, 1989.

Adret, Solomon b. Abraham. *Hiddushei ha-Rashba.* Mossad Harav Kook: Jerusalem, 1983–.

——— *Hiddushei ha-Rashba 'al Massekhet Bava Metsi'a.* Torah u-Tevuna: Jerusalem, 1931. Reprint. Orah: Jerusalem, 1961.

——— *She'elot u-Teshuvot ha-Rashba* [Responsa]. Mekhon Yerushalayim: Jerusalem, 1997. 7 Parts, plus *Responsa of Rashba Attributed to Nahmanides* (= Attributed Responsa).

Alashqar, Moses. *She'elot u-Teshuvot Maharam Alashqar* [Responsa]. Jerusalem, 1959.

Alfasi, Isaac. *Hilkhot ha-Rif.* Printed with BT.

Asher b. Yehiel. Pisqei ha-Rosh. Printed with BT.

——— *She'elot u-Teshuvot* [Responsa]. Mekhon Yerushalayim: Jerusalem, 1994.

Beit Yosef. See: Caro.

Betsal'el Ashkenazi. *Shitta Mequbbetset.* Tractates Ketubbot and Bava Metsi'a. Warsaw, 1904. Reprint. Israel, n.d.

BT. Babylonian Talmud. Romm: Vilna, 1898. Reprint. Shulsinger: New York, 1944, and frequently thereafter.

Caro, Joseph. *Avqat Rokhel.* Leipzig, 1859. Reprint. n.p., n.d.

——— *Beit Yosef.* Printed with Jacob b. Asher, *Arba'a Turim.*

——— *Kesef Mishneh.* Printed with Maimonides, *Mishneh Torah.*

——— *She'elot u-Teshuvot Beit Yosef* [Responsa Beit Yosef]. Jerusalem, 1960.

Colon, Joseph. *She'elot u-Teshuvot Mahariq* [Responsa]. Jerusalem, 1988.

Conforti, David. *Qoreh ha-Dorot.* Edited by D. Cassel. Berlin, 1846. Reprint. Jerusalem, 1969.

Duran, Tsemah b. Solomon. *Yakhin u-Boaz.* Jerusalem, 1992.

Eliezer b. Joel ha-Levi. *Sefer Rabiah.* Edited by V. (A.) Aptowitzer. 2d. ed. Harry Fischel Institute: Jerusalem, 1964.

Eliezer b. Nathan. *Even ha-'Ezer, Hu Sefer Ra'avan.* Parts 1–2. Simleul-Silzanei, 1926. Reprint. Jerusalem, 1975.

Hagahot Maimoniot. Glosses to Maimonides' *Mishneh Torah*, by R. Meir ha-Kohen, pupil of R. Meir of Rothenburg. Printed with *Mishneh Torah.*

Hiddushei ha-Ramban. See: Nahmanides.

Hiddushei ha-Ritba. See: Yom Tov Isbili.

Isaac b. Moses of Vienna. *Or Zarua'.* Parts 1–2. Zhitomer, 1862. Reprint. Brooklyn, n.d.

Isserlein, Israel. *Terumat ha-Deshen.* Warsaw, 1882. Reprint. Tel Aviv, n.d.

——— *Pesaqim u-Ketavim.* Printed as Part II of *Terumat ha-Deshen.*

'Ittur, Sefer ha-. Edited by Meir Yonah. Part 1. Warsaw, 1883. Part 2. Vilna, 1874. Reprint. Parts 1–2. New York, 1955.

Jacob b. Asher. *Arba'a Turim.* Warsaw, 1861. Reprinted frequently.

Joseph Haviva. *Nimmuqei Yosef.* Commentary to Alfasi's *Hilkhot ha-Rif.* Printed with BT.

Joseph ibn Lev. *She'elot u-Teshuvot Mahari ben Lev* [Responsa]. Vol. 1. Jerusalem, 1959. Vol. 2. Jerusalem, 1960. Vols. 3 and 4. Amsterdam, 1726. Reprint Parts 1–4. Jerusalem, n.d.

Jacob Tam. *Sefer ha-Yashar le-Rabbenu Tam, Heleq ha-Hiddushim.* Edited by S. Schlesinger. Jerusalem, 1959.

Kesef Mishneh. See: Caro.

Kol Bo. Lemberg, 1860. Reprint. Tel Aviv, n.d.

Levi b. Habib. *She'elot u-Teshuvot ha-Ralbah* [Responsa]. Lemberg, 1865 Reprint. Brooklyn, 1962).

Lewin, B. M. *Otsar ha-Geonim.* Haifa, 1928–Jerusalem, 1943.

Maggid Mishneh. Printed with Maimonides, Mishneh Torah.

Maimonides, Moses. *Mishneh Torah* (MT). S. Frankel ed. Jerusalem, 1975– .

——— *Mishneh Torah.* Edited by J. Qafih. n.p., 1984–96.

——— *Teshuvot ha-Rambam* [Responsa]. Edited by J. Blau. *Meqitsei Nirdamim*: Jerusalem. Vols. 1–3, 1958–61. Vol. 4, 1986.

Meir of Rothenburg. *She'elot u-Teshuvot Maharam be-R. Barukh* (Prague ed.) [Responsa Prague]. Edited by M. A. Bloch. Budapest, 1895. Reprint. Tel Aviv, 1969, as *Teshuvot Maharam me-Rothenburg*, vol. 4.

——— *Teshuvot Maimoniot.* Printed with Maimonides' Mishneh Torah.

——— *Teshuvot Pesaqim u-Minhagim* [*Responsa, Rulings and Customs*]. Edited by I. Z. Kahana. Vol. 2. Mossad ha-Rav Kook: Jerusalem, 1960.

Migdal 'Oz. Printed with Maimonides, *Mishneh Torah.*

Mordekhai b. Hillel. *Mordekhai.* Printed with BT.

——— "Sefer ha-Mordekhai to tractate Kiddushin." *Mehqarim u-Meqorot – Ma'asaf le-Mada'ei ha-Yahadut* [*Texts and Studies, Analecta Judaica*]. Vol. 2. Edited by H. Z. Dimitrovsky. Jerusalem, 1990. Part 1. Edited by Joel Roth.

Moses Trani. *She'elot u-Teshuvot Mabit* [Responsa]. Lvov, 1861. Reprint. Brooklyn, 1961.

MT. *Mishneh Torah.* See: Maimonides, Moses.

Nahmanides, Moses. *Hiddushei ha-Ramban 'al Talmud Bavli.* Benei Beraq, 1959.

Nimmuqei Yosef. See: Joseph Haviva.

Nissim b. Reuben Gerondi. Commentary on Alfasi's *Hilkhot ha-Rif.* Printed with BT.

——— Commentary to BT Nedarim. Printed with BT.

——— *Hiddushei ha-Ran 'al Bava Metsi'a.* Edited by Y. G. Grossberg. Harry Fischel: Jerusalem, 1994.

——— *Hiddushei ha-Ran 'al Sanhedrin.* Benei Beraq, 1981.

——— *Hiddushei ha-Ran 'al Massekhet Bava Batra.* Edited by A. Sofer. Jerusalem, 1963.

——— *She'elot u-Teshuvot ha-Ran* [Responsa]. Edited by L. Feldman. Jerusalem, 1984.

Or Zarua. See: Isaac b. Moses of Vienna.

Pisqei ha-Rosh. See: Asher b. Yehiel.

PT. Palestinian Talmud. Venice, 1524. Reprint. n.p., n.d.

Ra'avan. See: Eliezer b. Nathan.

Rabad. See: Abraham b. David of Posquieres.

Rabiah. See: Eliezer b. Joel ha-Levi.

Radbaz. Marx, Alexander. "Contribution a l'histoire des Juifs de Cochin." Revue d'es Études Juives 89 (1930): 293–304.

——— Scheiber, Abraham. "An Unknown Responsum of David Ibn Abi Zimra." *Essays on the Occasion of the Seventieth Anniversary of the Dropsie University*. Eds. A. Katsh and L. Nemoy. Philadelphia, 1979.

——— Zimmels, H. Z. "Eight Responsa of Radbaz from Manuscript" (Hebrew). *Sefer ha-Yovel le-Profesor Shemuel Krauss le-Melot Lo Shiv'im Shana* [Jubilee Volume for Professor Samuel Krauss, on his Seventieth Year]. Jerusalem, 1937: 179–87.

Rashba. See: Adret, Solomon b. Abraham.

Rashbam. See: Samuel b. Meir.

Rashi. Commentary on BT. Printed with BT.

——— *Teshuvot Rashi* [Responsa Rashi]. Edited by I. Elfenbein. New York, 1943.

Ritba. See: Yom Tov Isbili.

Samson b. Tsadoq. *Sefer Tashbets*. Lewin-Epstein: Jerusalem, 1962.

Samuel b. Meir (Rashbam). Commentary to BT Bava Batra. Printed with BT.

Shibbolei ha-Leqet. See: Zedekiah b. Abraham ha-Rofe'.

Shitta Mequbbetset. See: Betsal'el Ashkenazi.

Sifra. Edited by I. H.Weiss. Vienna, 1862. Reprint. New York, 1947.

Sirkes, Joel. *Bayit Hadash* (*BaH*). Printed with Jacob b. Asher, *Arba'a Turim*.

——— *She'elot u-Teshuvot ha-Bah (ha-Yeshanot)*. Ostraha, 1834. Reprint. New York, 1966.

Tam. See: Jacob Tam.

Taubes, Hayyim Tsevi. *Otsar ha-Geonim Sanhedrin*. Mossad Harav Kook: Jerusalem, 1966.

Tosafot. Commentary to BT.

Tsemah b. Solomon Duran. See: Duran, Tsemah b. Solomon.

Tur. See: Jacob b. Asher. *Arba'a Turim*.

Yeruham b. Meshullam. *Sefer Toledot Adam ve-Hava*. Venice, 1553 Reprint. Israel, n.d.

Yom Tov Isbili (Ritba). *Hiddushei ha-Ritba*. Mossad Harav Kook: Jerusalem, 1975–93.

Zedekiah b. Abraham ha-Rofe'. *Shibbolei ha-Leqet ha-Shalem*. Edited by S. Buber. Vilna 1886. Reprint. Menorah: New York, 1959.

Zerahia ha-Levi. *Ha-Ma'or ha-Gadol*. Printed with Alfasi's *Hilkhot ha-Rif*.

Works Cited: Secondary Sources

Ashtor, Eliyahu (Strauss). *Toldot ha-Yehudim be-Mitsrayim ve-Suriya Tahat Shilton ha-Mamlukim* [The History of the Jews in Egypt and Syria under the Mamluks]. Jerusalem, 1951. Vol. 2: 458–70.

Assaf, Simha. "Slavery and the Slave Trade among the Jews during the Middle Ages" (Hebrew). *Tsiyon* 4 (1939): 91–125. Reprint. *Be-Oholei Yaaqov.* Jerusalem, 1943: 223–56.

——— *Meqorot u-Mehqarim be-Toldot Yisra'el* [Sources and Studies in Jewish History]. Jerusalem, 1946.

Bashan, Eliezer. *Sheviyya u-Pedut* [*Captivity and Ransom in Mediterranean Jewish Society*]. Bar Ilan: Ramat Gan, 1980.

Bazak, Ya'aqov. "Maritime Insurance Agreements (Cambium) in the Responsa Literature of the 16th Century" (Hebrew). *Sinai* 75 (1974): 43–60.

Ben-Menahem, Hanina. "Doubt, Choice and Conviction: a Comparison of the *Kim Li* Doctrine with the Catholic Doctrine of Probabilism" (Hebrew). *Studies in Jewish Law in Honor of Professor Aaron Kirschenbaum: Dine Israel* 20–21 (2001): 13–41.

——— "The Historical and Jurisprudential Origins of the Kim-Li Argument" (Hebrew). *Dine Israel* 3 (1972): 89–96.

——— "Towards a Jurisprudential Analysis of the Kim-li Argument" (Hebrew). *Shenaton ha-Mishpat ha-Ivri: Annual of the Institute for Research in Jewish Law* 6–7 (1979–80): 45–60.

Bentov, Hayyim. "Autobiographical and Historical Notes of R. Joseph mi-Trani" (Hebrew). *Shalem* 1 (1974): 195–228.

Cohen, Amnon. *Jewish Life under Islam: Jerusalem in the Sixteenth Century*. Cambridge, MA, and London, 1984.

Conforti, David. *Qoreh ha-Dorot*. Edited by D. Cassel. Berlin, 1846. Reprint. Jerusalem, 1969.

David, Abraham. *To Come to the Land: Immigration and Settlement in 16th Century Eretz-Israel*. Alabama: Tuscaloosa and London, 1999.

——— "The Economic Position of the Jews in the 16th Century in the Light of the Responsa of Radbaz" (Hebrew). *Mi-Qedem umi-Yam* 1 (1981): 85–100.

——— "The Termination of the Office of *Nagid* in Egypt and Biographical Data concerning the Life of Abraham Castro" (Hebrew). *Tarbits* 41 (1971–72): 325–37.

——— "More on the Business Dealings of Radbaz" (Hebrew). *Pe'amim* 32 (1987): 131–34.

Dimitrovsky. "A Controversy which Took Place between R. Joseph Caro and the R. Moses Trani" (Hebrew). *Sefunot* 6 (1962): 71-123.

Elon, Menahem. *Ha-Mishpat ha-'Ivri*. Magnes: Jerusalem, 1973. Translation: Auerbach and Sykes. *Jewish Law: History, Sources, Principles*. Philadelphia & Jerusalem, 1994.

Freimann, Avraham H. *Seder Qiddushin ve-Nissuin Aharei Hatimat ha-Talmud* [The Marriage Ceremony after the Talmud]. Mossad Harav Kook: Jerusalem, 1945. Reprint. Jerusalem, 1964.

Gilat, Yitzhak D. "Thirteen Years Old: Age of Commandments?" (Hebrew). *Peraqim be-Hishtalshelut ha-Halakha* [*Studies in the Development of the Halakha*]. Bar Ilan: Ramat Gan, 1992: 19–31.

Goitein, S. D. *A Mediterranean Society*. Vol. 3. University of California Press: Berkeley, Los Angeles, London, 1978.

Goldman, Israel. *The Life and Times of Rabbi David Ibn Abi Zimra*. JTSA: New York, 1970.

Goodblatt, Morris S. *Jewish Life in Turkey in the XVIth Century, As Reflected in the legal Writings of Samuel De Medina*. JTSA: New York, 1952.

Hacker, Joseph. "The Payment of *Djizya* by Scholars in Palestine in the Sixteenth Century" (Hebrew). *Shalem* 4 (1984): 63–117.

Hartman, David. "Maimonides' Epistle on Martyrdom" (Hebrew). *Mehqerei Yerushalayim be-Mahshevet Yisra'el* 2 (1983): 362–403.

Havlin, Shelomo Zalman. *R. Abraham ha-Levi, Author of Responsa Ginnat Veradim, and his Contemporaries* (Hebrew). Ph.D. Dissertation, Hebrew University. 1983.

Helener, Melina. "The Theory of Reincarnation in R. David ibn Zimra's Kabbalistic Works" (Hebrew). *Pe'amim* 43 (1990): 27–50.

Kahana, Yitshaq Ze'ev *Sefer ha-'Agunot*. Mossad Harav Kook: Jerusalem, 1954.

——— "The Controversy Surrounding Establishing Legal Decision according to Maimonides" (Hebrew). *Mehqarim be-Sifrut ha-Teshuvot* [*Studies in the Responsa Literature*]. Mossad Harav Kook: Jerusalem, 1973.

Katz, Jacob. "Even though He Sinned, He Is Still a Jew" (Hebrew). *Tarbits* 27 (1958): 203–17. Reprint. *Halakhah and Kabbalah* (Magnes: Jerusalem, 1984): 255–69.

——— "Levirate Marriage and *Halitsa* in the Post-Talmudic Period" (Hebrew). *Tarbits* 51 (1984): 59–106. Reprint. *Halakhah and Kabbalah*. Magnes: Jerusalem, 1984: 127–74

——— *The "*Shabbes Goy*": A Study in Halakhic Flexibility*. JPS: Philadelphia & New York, 1989.

Kirschenbaum, Aaron. *Equity in Jewish Law—Halakhic Perspectives in Law: Formalism and Flexibility in Jewish Civil Law.* Ktav: Hoboken, NJ, 1991.

——— *Self-Incrimination in Jewish Law.* New York, 1970.

Landau, Jacob, ed. *Toldot Yehudei Mitsrayim ba-Tequfa ha-'Othmanit, 1517–1914* [*The Jews in Ottoman Egypt*]. Jerusalem, 1988.

Lewin, B. M. *Otzar ha-Gaonim.* Haifa, 1928 – Jerusalem, 1943.

Lieberman, Saul. *Tosefta ki-Fshutah, Bava Qamma–Bava Metsi'a.* Jerusalem, 1988.

Lifschitz, Jacob ha-Levi. "The Responsa of Radbaz" (Hebrew). *Qovets Torani Zekhor le-Avraham.* Edited by A. Berger. Holon, 1992: 30–79.

Morell, Samuel. *Precedent and Judicial Discretion: The Case of Joseph ibn Lev.* Scholars press: Atlanta, 1991.

——— "Profile of a Jurist: Joseph Ibn Lev's Rulings Regarding *'Agunot.*" *Jewish Law Annual* 9 (1991): 171–204.

Pagis, Dan. *Shirat ha-Hol ve-Torat ha-Shir le-Mosheh ibn Ezra u-Benei Doro* [*Secular Poetry and Poetic Theory: Moses ibn Ezra and his Contemporaries*]. Bialik Institute: Jerusalem, 1970.

Passamaneck, Stephen M. *Insurance in Rabbinic Law.* Edinburgh, 1974.

Raffeld, Avraham Meir. "The Halakha Follows the Later Sages" (Hebrew). *Sidra* 8 (1992): 119–39.

——— "'Ashkenaz' in the East: '*Hilkhata K'Bathrai*' in the Era of Rabbi Joseph Caro" (Hebrew). *Sidra* 11 (1995): 113–30.

Sagi, Avi. "A Philosophical Analysis of *S'vara.*" *S'vara* 2, no. 1 (1991): 3–7.

——— "*S'vara* and the Concept of Torah." *S'vara* 2, no. 2 (1991): 5–7.

Scheiber, Alexander. "An Unknown Responsum of David Ibn Abi Zimra." *Essays on the Occasion of the Seventieth Anniversary of Dropsie College.* Edited by Abraham Katsh and Leon Nemoy. Philadelphia, 1979: 397–403.

Shilo, Shmuel. *Dina de-Malkhuta Dina* [*The Law of the State is Law*]. Jerusalem, 1974.

Shochetman, Eliav. "The Obligation to State the Reasons for Legal Decisions in Jewish Law" (Hebrew). *Shenaton ha-Mishpat ha-Ivri: Annual of the Institute for Research in Jewish Law* 6–7 (1979-80): 319–97.

Slae, Menahem. *Ha-Bittuah ba-Halakha* [*Insurance in the Halakha*]. Tel Aviv, 1980.

Soloveitchik, Haym. "Guidelines for Halakhic Ruling" (Hebrew). *Mehqerei Yerushalayim be-Mahshevet Yisra'el* 3 (1984): 683–87.

——— "Maimonides' *'Iggeret Ha-Shemad*: Law and Rhetoric." *Rabbi Joseph H. Lookstein Memorial Volume*. Edited by Leo Landman. KTAV: New York, 1980: 281–319.

——— *Pawnbroking*

Halakha, Kalkala ve-Dimui 'Atsmi [*Pawnbroking: a Study in the Inter-Relationship Between Halakhah, Economic Activity and Communal Self-Image*]. Magnes: Jerusalem, 1985.

Strauss. See: Ashtor.

Ta-Shma, Israel. "The Exemption of *Talmidei Hakhamim* from Taxes" (Hebrew). *'Iyyunim be-Sifrut Hazal, be-Miqra uve-Toldot Yisra'el, Muqdash leProfessor Ezra Melammed* [*Studies in Rabbinic Literature, in Bible and in Jewish History: Dedicated to Prof. Ezra Melamed*]. Bar Ilan: Ramat Gan, 1982: 312–22. Reprint. *Halakha, Minhag u-Metsi'ut be-Ashkenaz, 1000–1350* [*Ritual, Custom and Reality in Franco-Germany*]. Jerusalem, 1996: 228–40.

——— "'*Hilkhata Kebatrai'* – Historical Aspects of a Legal Rule" (Hebrew). *Shenaton ha-Mishpat ha-Ivri: Annual of the Institute for Research in Jewish Law* 6–7 (1979–80): 405–23. Reprint. *Halakha, Minhag u-Metsi'ut be-Ashkenaz, 1000–1350* [*Ritual, Custom and Reality in Franco-Germany*]. Jerusalem, 1996: 58–78

——— "Sailing on Rivers on the Sabbath" (Hebrew). *Maimonidean Studies* 1 (1990): 23–42. Reprint. *Halakha, Minhag u-Metsi'ut be-Ashkenaz, 1000–1350* [*Ritual, Custom and Reality in Franco-Germany*]. Jerusalem, 1996: 168–88

Taubes, Hayyim Tsevi. *Otsar ha-Ge'onim le-Massekhet Sanhedrin*. Mossad Harav Kook: Jerusalem, 1966.

Tykocinsky, Hayyim. *Taqqanot ha-Geonim* [*The Gaonic Ordinances*]. Edited and translated from German to Hebrew by Meir Havazelet. Sura & Yeshiva University: Tel-Aviv and Jerusalem, 1959.

Wosner, Shai Akiva. "*Hilcheta ke-Batray* – A New Perspective" (Hebrew). *Shenaton ha-Mishpat ha-Ivri: Annual of the Institute for Research in Jewish Law* 20 (1995–97): 151–67.

Yuval, Israel J. "*Rishonim* and *Aharonim, Antiqui et Moderni*" (Hebrew). *Tsiyon* 57 (1992): 369–94.

Zimmels, H. J. *Rabbi David ibn abi Simra* (German). Breslau, 1932.

List of Cases

Index of Responsa

Index of Legal Issues

General Index

Studies in Judaism
Titles in the Series

S. Daniel Breslauer

Creating a Judaism Without Religion. A Postmodern Jewish Possibility. Lanham, November 2001. University Press of America. Academic Studies in Ancient Judaism series.

Jacob Neusner

Dual Discourse, Single Judaism. Lanham, February 2001. University Press of America. Academic Studies in Ancient Judaism series.

The Emergence of Judaism. Jewish Religion in Response to the Critical Issues of the First Six Centuries. Lanham, April 2000. University Press of America. Academic Studies in Ancient Judaism series.

The Halakhah and the Aggadah. Lanham. February 2001. University Press of America. Academic Studies in Ancient Judaism series.

The Hermeneutics of Rabbinic Category Formations. Lanham, February 2001. University Press of America. Academic Studies in Ancient Judaism series.

Rivka Ulmer

Pesiqta Rabbati. A Synoptic Edition of Pesiqta Rabbati Based upon all Extant Manuscripts and the Editio Princeps, Lanham. January 2002. University Press of America. Academic Studies in Ancient Judaism series. Volume III

Edited by Jacob Neusner and James F. Strange

Religious Texts and Material Contexts. Lanham. August 2001. University Press of America. Academic Studies in Ancient Judaism series.

Leslie S. Wilson

The Serpent Symbol in the Ancient Near East. Nahash and Asherah: Death, Life, and Healing. Lanham. December 2001, University Press of America. Academic Studies in Ancient Judaism series.

Jacob Neusner

Talmud Torah. Ways to God's Presence through Learning: An Exercise in Practical Theology. Lanham, January 2002. University Press of America. Academic Studies in Ancient Judaism series.

Jacob Neusner

The Aggadic Role in Halakhic Discourses. Lanham. February 2001. University Press of America. Academic Studies in Ancient Judaism series. Volume I

The Aggadic Role in Halakhic Discourses. Lanham. February 2001. University Press of America. Academic Studies in Ancient Judaism series. Volume II

The Aggadic Role in Halakhic Discourses. Lanham. February 2001. University Press of America. Academic Studies in Ancient Judaism series. Volume III

A Theological Commentary to the Midrash. Lanham. April 2001. University Press of America. Academic Studies in Ancient Judaism series. Volume I. *Pesiqta deRab Kahana.*

A Theological Commentary to the Midrash. Lanham. March 2001. University Press of America. Academic Studies in Ancient Judaism series. - Volume II. *Genesis Raba.*

A Theological Commentary to the Midrash. Lanham. April 2001. University Press of America. Academic Studies in Ancient Judaism series. Volume III. *Song of Songs Rabbah*

A Theological Commentary to the Midrash. Lanham. April 2001. University Press of America. Academic Studies in Ancient Judaism series. Volume IV. *Leviticus Rabbah*

A Theological Commentary to the Midrash. Lanham. June 2001. University Press of America. Academic Studies in Ancient Judaism series. Volume V *Lamentations Rabbati*

A Theological Commentary to the Midrash. June 2001. University Press of America. Academic Studies in Ancient Judaism series.Volume VI. *Ruth Rabbah and Esther Rabbah I*

A Theological Commentary to the Midrash. June 2001. University Press of America. Academic Studies in Ancient Judaism series.Volume VII. *Sifra*

A Theological Commentary to the Midrash. July 2001. University Press of America. Academic Studies in Ancient Judaism series.Volume VIII. *Sifré to Numbers and Sifré to Deuteronomy*

A Theological Commentary to the Midrash. August 2001. University Press of America. Academic Studies in Ancient Judaism series.Volume IX. *Mekhilta Attributed to Rabbi Ishmael*

The Unity of Rabbinic Discourse. January 2001. University Press of America. Academic Studies in Ancient Judaism series. Volume I: *Aggadah in the Halakhah*

The Unity of Rabbinic Discourse. February 2001. University Press of America. Academic Studies in Ancient Judaism series. Volume II: *Halakhah in the Aggadah*

The Unity of Rabbinic Discourse. February 2001. University Press of America. Academic Studies in Ancient Judaism series. Volume III: *Halakhah and Aggadah in Concert*

TITLES

Texts without Boundaries. Protocols of Non-Documentary Writing in the Rabbinic Canon, Lanham, 2002: University Press of America. Academic Studies in Ancient Judaism series. Volume Two. *Sifra*

Texts without Boundaries. Protocols of Non-Documentary Writing in the Rabbinic Canon, Lanham, 2003: University Press of America. Academic Studies in Ancient Judaism series. Volume Three. *Sifré to Numbers.*

Texts without Boundaries. Protocols of Non-Documentary Writing in the Rabbinic Canon, Lanham, 2003: University Press of America. Academic Studies in Ancient Judaism series. Volume Four. *Sifré to Deuteronomy.*

Texts without Boundaries. Protocols of Non-Documentary Writing in the Rabbinic Canon, Lanham, 2004: University Press of America. Academic Studies in Ancient Judaism series. Volume Five. *Genesis Rabbah.*

Texts without Boundaries. Protocols of Non-Documentary Writing in the Rabbinic Canon, Lanham, 2004: University Press of America. Academic Studies in Ancient Judaism series. Volume Six. *Leviticus Rabbah.*

Texts without Boundaries. Protocols of Non-Documentary Writing in the Rabbinic Canon, Lanham, 2004: University Press of America. Academic Studies in Ancient Judaism series. Volume Seven. *Pesiqta deRab Kahana.*

Texts without Boundaries. Protocols of Non-Documentary Writing in the Rabbinic Canon, Lanham, 2004: University Press of America. Academic Studies in Ancient Judaism series. Volume Eight. *Esther Rabbah and Ruth Rabbah.*

Texts without Boundaries. Protocols of Non-Documentary Writing in the Rabbinic Canon, Lanham, 2004: University Press of America. Academic Studies in Ancient Judaism series. Volume Nine. *Song of Songs Rabbah.*

Texts without Boundaries. Protocols of Non-Documentary Writing in the Rabbinic Canon, Lanham, 2004: University Press of America. Academic Studies in Ancient Judaism series. Volume Ten. *Lamentations Rabbah.*

Texts without Boundaries. Protocols of Non-Documentary Writing in the Rabbinic Canon, Lanham, 2004: University Press of America. Academic Studies in Ancient Judaism series. Volume Eleven. *Mekhilta Attributed to Rabbi Ishmael.*

Texts without Boundaries. Protocols of Non-Documentary Writing in the Rabbinic Canon, Lanham, 2004: University Press of America. Academic Studies in Ancient Judaism series. Volume Twelve. *Abot deRabbi Natan.*